Physical map of China

U.S.S.R.

Amur R.

Sungari R.

MONGOLIA

Liao Ho

Hai Ho

Hwang Ho

Hwai Ho

Kan

Yangtze Kiang

Yalu

KOREA

Sea of Japan

Yellow Sea

East China Sea

TAIWAN

South China Sea

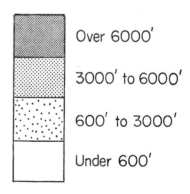

▓	Over 6000'
▒	3000' to 6000'
░	600' to 3000'
☐	Under 600'

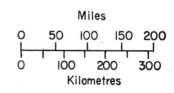

Miles

0   50   100   150   200

0   100   200   300

Kilometres

AN ECONOMIC GEOGRAPHY

OF

CHINA

AN ECONOMIC GEOGRAPHY
OF
CHINA

T. R. TREGEAR, B.Sc. (Econ.), Ph.D.

LONDON
BUTTERWORTHS

ENGLAND: BUTTERWORTH & CO. (PUBLISHERS) LTD.
LONDON: 88 Kingsway, W.C.2

AUSTRALIA: BUTTERWORTH & CO. (AUSTRALIA) LTD.
SYDNEY: 20 Loftus Street
MELBOURNE: 343 Little Collins Street
BRISBANE: 240 Queen Street

CANADA: BUTTERWORTH & CO. (CANADA) LTD.
TORONTO: 14 Curity Avenue, 374

NEW ZEALAND: BUTTERWORTH & CO. (NEW ZEALAND) LTD.
WELLINGTON: 49/51 Ballance Street
AUCKLAND: 35 High Street

SOUTH AFRICA: BUTTERWORTH & CO. (SOUTH AFRICA) LTD.
DURBAN: 33/35 Beach Grove

Suggested U.D.C. No.: 911·3:33(510)

Suggested additional U.D.C. No.: 911·3:6(510)

SBN   408   18140   O

Printed in Great Britain by R. J. Acford Ltd., Chichester, Sussex

CONTENTS

CONTENTS

GLOSSARY

Chinese Term	Explanation
ch'ang	long
ch'eng	city, city wall
chou (chow)	island
feng	wind
feng shui	the spirit of wind and water much used in geomancy
hai	sea
hei	black
ho	river—Hwang-ho
hsi or si	west
hsia	lower, below
hsiao	small
hsien	a district, a county
hu	lake
hung	red
hwang	yellow
kang (hong)	port
kiang	river—Yangtze Kiang
king	capital
k'ou	mouth—Hankow (mouth of the Han)
ling	hill or mountain
men	door or gate—San Men
nan	south
pei or peh	north
sha	sand
shan	mountain
shang	upper, above, on
shui	water, often used for smaller rivers
ta	large
t'ien	field
t'ien	heaven
ts'un	village
tung	east

INTRODUCTION

In this book it is the author's intention to give a description and analysis of the country and the economy of the people from a geographical standpoint, having particular reference to the development and changes that have taken place since 1949. But, because we are dealing with a country deeply immersed in a communist revolution, the purpose of which is nothing less than the conversion of a quarter of the earth's population to a radical change of outlook and way of life, we shall often have to modify our conventional western geographical approach.

In China today politics impinge at every point. There is constant emphasis in every field, on the farm, in the factory, in the school, in the office, and in general, political i.e., ideological correctness as the *sine qua non* of success. It is held that correct thought will determine correct action in all fields, political, economic, social, military, recreational, cultural, even geographical. While thought cannot materially affect basic geographical phenomena such as relief, climate, mineral resources, it can and does vitally affect man's use of his environment. This is a fact that communists in general—and Chinese communists in particular—have seized on, and it is the reason why, in season and out of season, they seek to mould men's minds with all means in their power.

The Chinese Communist Party (C.C.P.) has set itself to build a modern socialist state and to do this it must create a socialistically-minded people. Unless this fact is understood and held constantly in mind, most of what has happened in the last two decades makes no sense. It is a colossal undertaking for it is nothing less than an attempt to convert some 700 million people (80% of whom are of conservative peasant stock and nearly all of whom have a long Confucian heritage) from an individualistic and clannish outlook to a national and international outlook in which the greatest good is held to be 'the good of the people'. The years ahead alone will prove the success or failure of this endeavour. Many reports seem to show that some initial headway has been made, witness the enthusiasm and willingness of farmers to share their agricultural experience and of technicians and workers to share knowledge of successful experiments in industry. It remains to be seen how far this spirit can be extended and how long it can be maintained.

The subject of China is charged with emotions—and consequently with much inaccurate information—for all[1]. Accounts of developments in China during the last 20 years, whether emanating from China itself or from the West, have often been written with so much bias and sometimes with deliberate intent to mislead, that the formation of correct conclusions becomes elusive. It is very difficult to prevent preconceived ideas and moral judgments from intruding into what is intended to be a scientific study. For instance, when dealing with communes, a real effort will be needed to exclude a mass of erroneous data, particularly in regard to the family, that has gathered round the subject. When matters of personal freedom and standards of living arise, it is difficult not to project western standards on to a situation to which they are not really relevant. The more enlightening comparisons, political and economic, are those between pre-1949 and post-1949 China rather than between China and the West.

There has been a tendency, at least until recently, for many writers in the West to belittle Chinese achievements since the revolution of 1949. There are many reasons for this, not least being that fear is felt of the growth and spread of communism, leading to a desire to play down any success that has been made. Another reason stems from western ignorance of the Chinese mind and way of approach to many questions. A further reason arises from the mistakes that the Chinese themselves have made. For example, the fantastically exaggerated claims of production which accompanied the 'Great Leap Forward' in 1958 and 1959 have led Westerners to look askance at and undervalue subsequent reports of advancement, which often are of real substance. In the release of energy which so often is the accompaniment of revolution, the Chinese are doing things in unusual and often in seemingly inefficient and unintelligent ways. Enthusiasm, confidence and sometimes fanaticism attend much of their efforts and these are bolstered and fostered by slogans, which to western ears sound childish and naive but which flow easily in Chinese. Slogans in China have the sanction of usage of 2,000 years and more. Any success or achievement is invariably and monotonously attributed to the wisdom and writings of Chairman Mao Tse-tung and, until recently, to the leadership of the C.C.P. Again, this sounds naive, but its educative and indoctrinizational effect should not be under-rated.

This book is supplementary to my *A Geography of China*, and is largely an amplification of the third section of that book. Consequently, it gives only cursory treatment to physical and climatic factors, which are fully dealt with in the earlier book. It also forms, in some measure, a companion to Cole and German's *A Geography of the U.S.S.R.*[2], but it cannot be written in the same way for the simple reason that equivalent material is not available. Statistical material in all fields, except Customs before the revolution of 1949, is very patchy; some is excellent for small areas but, on the whole, figures lie in the realm of estimates and even guesses rather than statistics. After 1949 the State Statistical Bureau was formed and the slow, laborious process of building a reliable, objective statistical service progressed. Fairly dependable figures for population were forthcoming in 1954 after the first real census. Production began to be presented in amounts instead of percentage increases. Then, in the year of the Great Leap Forward 1958–9, the work of the Bureau was shattered. In the enthusiasm and fanaticism which attended that unwise burst of energy, returns of production were exaggerated or falsified and eventually had to be repudiated[3]. Since then very few firm figures of production have been published. Progress has been reported once more in terms of percentages, of rise or fall on the previous year's achievements, and these are of little value unless they can be traced back to a firm basic figure. Thus the picture has to be drawn in more general lines than that for Russia. Nevertheless, by constant day-to-day study of Chinese newspapers, magazines and reports, and the careful assessing and sorting of real achievement from mere propaganda, a fairly accurate picture can be drawn. It is only fair to mention a reciprocal Chinese scepticism in the acceptance of western statistics. Chen Chao-hsing, commenting on the use of United States economic statistics, writes: 'We must pay attention to their deceptive character. This means that in our quotation of bourgeois statistics, we should undertake the task of "removing the false and retaining the true". To do this we have to trace the sources, understand their methods of compilation, if we are to find out where their mistakes lie and to what degree their mistakes have been carried'[4].

Although what is happening in China today is revolutionary and in so many ways—politically, economically and socially—a drastic break with the past, there is, none the less, a real consciousness of past greatness and a pride in her history and literary heritage and this in spite of their bitter condemnation of feudalism and the oppression of former rulers. Great interest is taken and much work done in archaeology, and her expanding museums have been crowded with everyday folk. It is reported, however, that most museums have been closed since the onset of the Cultural Revolution. Chinese museums today are focused almost entirely on things Chinese, revealing a parochialism and preoccupation with their own affairs reminiscent of their former sense of self-sufficiency. More care is being taken to preserve historic monuments than has been the case for many years.

When the C.C.P. came into power in 1949, it was full of confidence and had little regard for geographical determinism. It was held that man is master of his environment, and all problems, great and small, if tackled with enthusiasm and determination, can be resolved. The greater the number of people, the more hands for production; the age-old enemies of flood, drought and famine can be laid low in a few years by water conservancy, afforestation and the like, if attacked with sufficient energy. Such were the sentiments and the assurance of those first years, but it was fairly soon realized that geographical factors were not so easily amenable to man's will. Although confidence has been retained, a soberer approach has gradually gained ground. One small evidence of a growing recognition of the importance of geography has been the formation of the Geographical Society of China, which held its first conference in October, 1964 in Lanchow at which 90 papers were read. Technical Institutes and Institutes for Research in all fields have sprung up all over the country. These are not so sharply differentiated as they are in the West.

Throughout the text, maps have been included to assist the reader in identifying places. Place names in China have been subject to rapid and confusing change, a confusion which is further increased by the use of various romanization systems in different atlases. As far as possible the *Times Atlas* (1958 edition) nomenclature has been used.

Some of the economic maps have a verisimilitude which may be misleading. The dot maps have not the statistical exactness with which they are usually associated. Nevertheless, they do give a fairly accurate picture of relative distributions.

No attempt at consistency in the use of one system of measurements has been made. Miles, kilometres, kilograms, pounds, *tan*, *chin*, acres, hectares and *mow* are used indiscriminately. In dealing with China it is necessary to become conversant with all of them. It is hoped that the Conversion Tables will help the reader.

My warm thanks are due to my daughter, Mary Tregear, for the pen drawings in this book.

REFERENCES

[1] GREENE, F. *A Curtain of Ignorance*, Cape, London, 1965
[2] COLE, J. P. and GERMAN, F. C. *A Geography of the U.S.S.R.*, Butterworths, London, 1961
[3] PERKINS, DWIGHT H. *Market Control and Planning in Communist China*, Harvard University Press, Cambridge, Mass., 1966, pp. 215–225
[4] CHEN CHAO-HSING. 'The Use of United States Economic Statistics,' *Ching-chi Yen-chiu (Economic Research)*, No. 5, 15 May, 1964

WEIGHTS AND MEASURES AND CONVERSION TABLES

A DECREE was made in 1929 attempting to bring China's multifarious weights and measures into a nation-wide metric system, but it was never really applied. A KMT survey in 1936 revealed that there were still 53 different lengths of '*chih*' ranging from 0·2 to 1·25 m, 32 different measures of *sheng* ranging from 0·5 to 8·0 l and 36 different weights of *chin* varying from 0·3 to 2·5 kg. In March, 1959 the People's Government proclaimed a unified metric system which has been much more successfully implemented[1]:

1 *chih*	one-third metre
1 *chin*	one-half kilogram or 1·1023 pounds
1 *mow*	one-fifteenth hectare, i.e. 0·066 hectare or 0·1647 acre
1 *picul*	100 *chin* or 110 pounds or 0·984 hundredweight
1 *sheng*	1 litre
1 *tan*	100 *chin* (formerly regarded as one man's load)
1 acre	0·405 hectare
1 hectare	2·471 acres
1 kilogram	2·205 pounds
1 kilometre	0·621 miles
1 sq. kilometre	0·386 sq. miles
1 pound	0·454 kilograms
1 sq. mile	2·589 sq. kilometres
1 *tael* (Haikwan)	583·3 grains silver

EXCHANGE RATES

There is a fixed exchange rate between China and eleven socialist countries, but a different selling and buying rate with the rest of the world[2].

Canada 100 dollars—229·40 yuan (selling rate), 227·20 (buying rate)

France 100 francs—50·10 yuan (selling rate), 47·70 (buying rate)

U.K. £1—6·92 yuan (selling rate), 6·859 (buying rate)

U.S.S.R. 100 roubles—129·00 yuan

---

[1] C.R. June, 1965

[2] Hughes, T. J. and Luard, D. E. T. The Economic Development of Communist China, 1949–1958. O.U.P., London, 1959, p. 44

1

THE ECONOMIC GROWTH OF CHINA

'The agrarian problem, of primary importance in any agricultural society, has always been China's major problem. Its solution determined the well-being of the peasant masses and of the ruling minority, the fate of governments and, in the last analysis, the rise and fall of dynasties.'

E. Balazs. *Chinese Civilization and Bureaucracy*, p. 113

THE EARLY DEVELOPMENT OF AGRICULTURE

THERE are established evidences of human or sub-human occupation of China from very early times. Traces of very primitive Palaeolithic Man were found in a cave at Chou Kou Tien, south of Peking, between 1921 and 1926, and further similar finds have been made recently at Lantian, south of the Wei Ho near Sian (Sinanthropus Pekinensis and Sinanthropus Lantianensis respectively). No further trace of human presence has yet been found between this and evidence of Old Stone Age Man at Chou Tong K'ou, a few miles east of Yinchwan (Ningsia). Remains of settlements, estimated to be about 50,000 years old, were found in alluvial Pleistocene deposits, which are covered by loess laid down in the bitter, dry Wurm glacial period[1]. This suggests that the adverse conditions of that period brought an end to human habitation in that area for there is no further trace of man until fairly late Neolithic times (4,000–3,000 B.C.) when we find settlements widely and thinly spread over the loess and alluvial areas of the north.

The first evidences of this Neolithic culture were found by Andersson in 1922 at Yang Shao Tsun, near Loyang. He discovered artifacts of a people characterized by their fine painted pottery of flowing design, by their great burial urns and by their polished stone tools, including hoes, adzes and axes. They are thus known as the Yang Shao or Painted Pottery People. Further discoveries, in 1929 and subsequently, were made of a different culture, which made a very hard, fine, highly polished, wheel-made pottery. The artifacts of this Black Pottery, as it is called, lie above those of the Yang Shao, signifying later origin.

It is these two primitive cultures which have particular interest for us because it is from them that the earliest beginnings of agriculture in this region spring. The early Neolithic people were hunters and gatherers; they were scattered and their use of the environment undifferentiated. During the later Neolithic period there is evidence that specialization into primitive agriculture and pastoralism had begun to take place, notably in the loess.

A change from a predominantly hunting economy to one of primitive agriculture involves a change from a migratory way of life to one of settlement and this can only be achieved when the natural environment is especially favourable, since the more primitive the culture, the firmer is the control by the physical environment. The loess of north China provided just those conditions which made the change possible. It forms a light, friable soil, much more easily worked than most alluvial soils, and thus was well suited to the crude stone

1

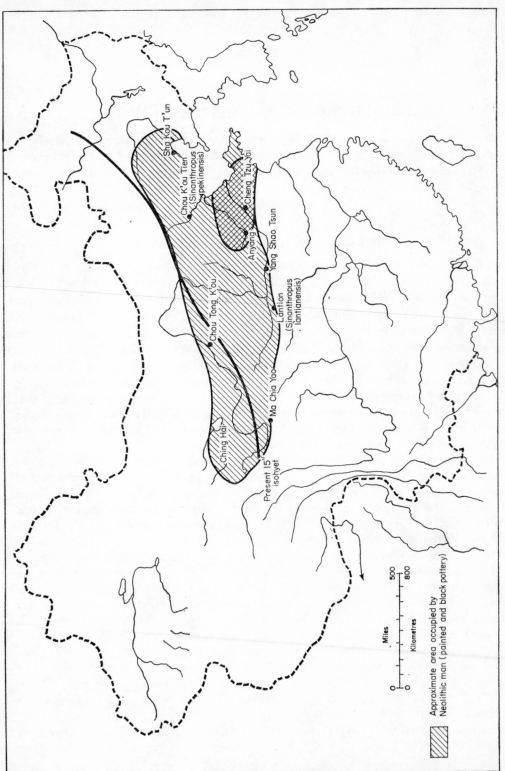

Map 1. *The birth of China*

Miles
Kilometres
0   500
0   800

Approximate area occupied by
Neolithic man (painted and black pottery)

Shg Kou T'un

Chou K'ou Tien
(Sinanthropus
pekinensis)

Cheng Tzu Yai

Yang Shao Tsun

Anyang

Lantien
(Sinanthropus
lantianensis)

Chou Tong K'ou

Ma Chia Yao

Ching Hai

Present 15"
isohyet

and wood implements available to Neolithic Man. Although there must have been considerable areas of forest and woodland to support the hunting which he continued alongside his primitive agriculture, the main vegetation of the area was grassland. There was, therefore, little clearing to be done as compared with the densely wooded lands farther south. Evidence goes to show that 5,000 years ago rainfall in this region was heavier than it is today and that the water table was higher. Nevertheless it was, even then, an area of precarious and variable rainfall, a factor which forced man to be forward-looking if he were to survive as a tiller of the soil—and forethought is an essential trait in any advancing civilization. The greatest danger to be faced was that of drought, which was met by the construction of wells and simple irrigation systems, made possible only by the workable nature of the soil in face of the crude tools available. Another danger, that of flood from torrential downpours, was much less on the loess plateau river valleys than lower down on the alluvial plain. A further characteristic of the loess is its peculiar vertical cleavage, which lends itself easily to the construction of cave dwelling in the sides of the steep valleys. The resulting dwellings are cool in summer and warm and dry in winter and still form, even today, the typical housing of most villages in the region.

All these factors combined to encourage the development of primitive agriculture in the more favourable parts of the loess and from this centre the culture spread. However, the farther north and north-west one presses, the drier and more extreme the climate becomes and the tendency here was towards a development of a pastoral economy and a continuance of a nomadic way of life. Thus a differentiation between a nomadic pastoralism and a settled agricultural economy grew up, which has persisted throughout the centuries to the present day[2]. There has been periodic pressure by the land-hungry peasants to push their fields northward and there have been raids and invasions by the nomads into the opulent green fields of the south, but the natural frontier between these two ways of life has constantly re-asserted itself. That frontier is marked roughly by the 15 in isohyet. Long experience has proved that north of this line rainfall is too sparse and too variable to admit of reliable agriculture. However, modern scientific knowledge and new farming techniques are now challenging the frontier afresh; farmlands and fodder crops are pushing out into the steppelands.

There is a remarkable coincidence between the 15 in isohyet and the line of the Great Wall, which was constructed originally by Ch'in Shih Hwang (221–206 B.C.). This he did by connecting up already existing inter-state walls in the east and extending it westward along the great northern bend of the Hwang-ho to include the Ordos within its bounds. But within 100 years this section had been rebuilt to exclude the desert, for the Great Wall had a double purpose. Its primary function was to act as a barrier against the encroaching nomad, but it was also intended as a restraint on the agriculturalist within its bounds from pushing too far north and so becoming infected by the frontier spirit and estranged from the settled Chinese way of life.

Within the confines of this settled agricultural economy a fusion of the Yang Shao and Painted Pottery peoples probably took place and from that fusion Chinese civilization emerged. By the middle of the second millenium B.C. the Wei valley and part of the North China Plain were occupied by quite highly organized tribes under the leadership of the Shang (Yin) kings, living in planned, walled cities[3] and forming the first authentic Chinese dynasty. The governing classes, at least, lived in well-constructed houses[3]. Evidence of excavated tombs clearly shows that this was a society based on slavery, but, together with inscriptions on oracle bones, it also shows an advanced agrarian society.

With the decline of the Shang dynasty and rise of the Chou (1030–221 B.C.) this slave-based society gradually gave place to a feudal age to which Chinese reformers, through the centuries, have looked back as the 'golden age'. Land was held on the well-field, '*ching-t'ien*' (ching = well; t'ien = field). Ideally the estate was divided into nine fields, as in the *ching* character, the central field belonging to the lord and the other eight to the serfs or peasants, who were bound to the soil and who were responsible for the cultivation of the lord's land. Each field was 100 *mow* in extent, an area considered sufficient for the needs of the ideal family of five and thus regarded as an equitable and equal distribution of land.

The Chou dynasty was overthrown by Ch'in Shih Hwang Ti (221–207 B.C.)[4], who broke the power of the feudal lords and brought together many feudal states under unified, central rule for the first time. This constitutes one of the most significant periods in China's long history. Among the many changes wrought by Ch'in Shih Hwang Ti, and developed during the long Han dynasty, was the freeing of the peasant from his bondage to the soil. This brought with it a certain loss of security; serfdom, in one form or another, reappeared right up to the twentieth century. Another change was the creation of a mobile labour force, non-existent under the '*ching-t'ien*' system. It was the presence of this force which enabled Ch'in Shih Hwang Ti to carry out the building of the Great Wall, and later emperors, the great canal and irrigation schemes[1].

Inevitably, with the break up of the '*ching t'ien*' system, there came a redistribution of the land, the development of large estates and a land-owning class, from which has stemmed the cause of the ever-recurring peasant revolts through the centuries.

'During the course of Chinese history, the free peasant was frequently reduced to servitude as a result of the formation of large estates and whenever this threatened to occur, voices were raised warning the government against the fatal consequences of the latifundia and demanding a return to the *ching t'ien* system'[5].

Laws attempting to restrict the size of land holdings were periodically passed but were never really effective. Officials, i.e. nobles and scholar-administrators, who were exempt from taxes and corvee, were allowed by law estates varying between 5,000 and 1,000 *mow* according to rank, but, since it was they who administered the law, the restriction was seldom kept. The peasant, time and time again, through natural disaster, taxation, debt, forced labour, slipped into tenancy and then back into serfdom. Then, when conditions became intolerable, bloody revolt ensued, often leading to the fall of a dynasty. The land reform carried out since 1949 by the People's Government, with which we shall attempt to deal fully later, is one of a succession of attempts to deal with this agrarian problem. For example, in the Later Wei (386–534) laws were passed for the equal distribution of land, each individual receiving some arable land to be worked until the age of 60, when it was handed back to the state. These strivings towards the equalization of land were short-lived.

The pattern and structure of Chinese society remained unchanged from Han times right down to the twentieth century. The great peasant mass, living on a subsistence economy, holding their small plots of land either in ownership or on precarious tenancy, formed the broad base. There was a comparatively small class of merchants, artisans and handi-craftsmen. Above all these was a very small but all-powerful oligarchy of land-owning scholar-officials, which, through its control of education—the only channel of admission

4

to its ranks—and by its extolling of the Confucian virtues of respect, submission, humility and filial piety, governed practically all walks of public and private life.

Southward Movement

Growth of population in the region of established Chinese culture in the valleys of the Ch'ing, Wei, Fen and Lower Hwang-ho made expansion necessary. While the north and north-west presented a natural climatic barrier and a hostile human nomad barrier to the extension of Chinese agriculture in that direction, the south offered no such opposition. The imperceptible Hwang-ho–Hwai-ho watershed between Loyang and Kaifang made movement into the Hwai-ho and Yangtze basins easy. It did, however, bring the northern Chinese into contact with a different culture. Here was a heavily forested country, with a heavier rainfall than in the north. Although sparsely populated, it was far from unoccupied. There were some 800 folk groups, loosely knit into tribes, the chief being the Miao, Pai Man and Yao, known collectively as the T'ai People. To the south-west were other tribes, notably the Lolo, the Fan and the Ch'iang[6]. Ssu Ma Chien, the great Han historian, described the Yangtze basin into which the Chinese were penetrating in these words: 'A large territory, sparsely populated, where people eat rice and drink fish soup; where land is tilled with fire and hoed with water; where people collect fruits and shellfish food; where people enjoy self-sufficiency without commerce. The place is fertile and suffers no famine and hunger. Hence the people are lazy and poor and do not bother to accumulate wealth. Hence, in the south of the Yangtze and the Hwai, there are neither hungry nor frozen people, nor a family which owns a thousand gold'[7]. Most of the T'ai people were rice growers, practising a primitive 'cut and burn' (ladang) cultivation, while tribes such as the Miao, Lolo and Fan were hill rovers, relying almost entirely on hunting. These tribes were either conquered and absorbed or driven south-west into the mountains. Only in the last decade or so has their integration been undertaken seriously.

During the long Earlier and Later Han dynasties (202 B.C. to A.D. 220) all the land to the south, included in what is known as China Proper, was conquered, with the exception of the south-east coastlands, but was not really settled by the Chinese and sinicized until the T'ang dynasty (A.D. 618–906). People of south China, at least until very recently, have called themselves T'ang Jen (Men of T'ang); those of the north were known as Han Jen (Men of Han), although the latter term is now used generally for all true Chinese.

Thus the Han Jen, moving south, found themselves in a very different physical environment from that of the loess of Shansi or the north China Plain. North China and south China are clearly demarked, except in the east, by the Chinling Shan, which form at once a geological, physical and climatic divide. To the north lie the dry wheat and millet farmers and to the south the wet rice farmers—a division which still holds, although now less decisively under the impact of modern farming techniques.

The Plight of the Peasant

Although the peasant figured high in the social scale and although he formed the base of the country's well-being, this did not prevent his being exploited. For the most part he was very poor and lived near the level of subsistence. When conditions became intolerable, whether through natural calamity or bad government, he rebelled. He was organized in secret societies, which, at times, were powerful, and peasant revolt has resulted not infrequently throughout the centuries in the fall of dynasties. Consequently wise government has taken care to see that his lot was not too oppressive. Provincial granaries were kept stocked to insure against drought and famine; river dykes were kept repaired against flood, and, as we have seen, some attempt was made to protect him against oppressive landlordism.

Early in the nineteenth century the Ch'ing (Manchu) dynasty was showing signs of decay and demoralization; the state of the peasantry was deteriorating rapidly and unrest was widespread. In 1850 the T'ai Ping rebellion broke out under the leadership of Hung Hsiu-ch'uan, the son of a Hakka farmer. This rebellion, which lasted 14 years, was a strange mixture of peasant revolt and religious crusade. Its early promise of great social reform degenerated later into a terrorist regime, attended by great devastation and loss of life, until it was finally quelled, largely by foreign forces under General Gordon in 1864.

From this time on, the plight of agriculture and the farmer grew steadily worse. Famine, in one part or another, as a result of natural calamity or political disorder, was endemic, highlighted by such catastrophes as the famines of 1878–79 and 1920–21 and the floods of 1931, each of which was attended by the loss of millions of lives. In spite of this, population has risen rapidly in the last 100 years, resulting in the further fragmentation of the already pitifully small peasant holdings and a great land hunger. Conditions of tenure varied throughout the land. In the north, with its larger farms (8–9 acres) about two-thirds of the farmers were occupying owners, while in the south more than half were tenants, although some owned part of the land. Rents, whether of the share or crop variety, were very heavy, usually amounting to about 50% of the crop. Absentee landlordism, with all its attendant disabilities, increased very rapidly during the first half of the twentieth century.

Although the farmer was so industrious and so meticulous in the care of his fields, he worked within a very narrow compass of technique and knowledge. He reaped and sowed according to his agricultural calendar; his tools were few and primitive; his seed selection, if any, poor; his fertilization of the fields by night soil, careful but inadequate; his loss from pests and plant disease enormous. The result was a low output per acre.

While the peasant was, to a large extent, self-sufficing, such surplus or cash crop that he produced found only a very confined and restricted market and he was largely at the mercy of the merchant. Communications were poor and transport, mainly by coolie pole, wheelbarrow or mule cart, very expensive—40 times as costly as by rail even though the coolie received a mere pittance for his toil[8].

Agriculturalists the world over are at a disadvantage, *vis-à-vis* the industrialists, in that most of their products are slow to mature and therefore their turnover is slow. Their need for credit is thus urgent. Co-operation and co-operative banks would seem to be the obvious remedy, but until 1949, little use was made of these means by the peasant. It is estimated that in 1932 in the whole of China there were 1,500 societies with 100,000 members. Instead, the peasant had recourse to the traditional means, the money lender, who might be his own landlord, the pawn shop, the bank or the merchant. Two per cent per month was a recognized rate of interest, but often it was four times as high.

The peasant was tightly bound by rural custom, which demanded of him that he mark the three great events of life, birth, marriage and death, with appropriate ceremony. This always involved him in heavy expenses and almost invariably landed him in the hands of the money lender from whose clutches he might never escape except by forfeiting his lands.

6

(See Appendix.)* In order to secure ready cash he often sold his main crop of rice, wheat or millet as soon as it was reaped, i.e. he sold on a buyer's market when prices were low, only to find that he had to buy grain for his family's use in the spring when prices were high.

These were the normal hazards of peasant life, but they were greatly aggravated by political events during the first half of the twentieth century, which were years of continual political unrest. As the nineteenth century closed, Japan defeated China in 1894; then followed the disorder of the Boxer Riots. The Manchu dynasty fell in 1911 and the Republic of China was proclaimed, only to be followed by 15 years of disunity under contending war-lords, who despoiled all and sundry. The revolution of 1927, which promised relief to the peasant, turned out to be the prelude to 22 years of civil war or war with Japan, which are described in some detail below (Rise to Communism). These years brought havoc and distress to most Chinese, but it was the peasant who felt the full brunt. Spoiled alike by war-lord, bandit, landlord, government troops and the Japanese, his plight was desperate.

Tawney[8], writing in 1932, struck a warning and prophetic note: 'Much that the press ascribes to communist machinations seems, indeed, to the western observer to have as much, or as little, connection with theoretical communism as the Peasants' Revolt of 1381 in England or the *Jacquerie* in France. What is called the communist question is in reality, in most parts of the country, either a land question or a question of banditry provoked by lack of employment . . . The revolution of 1911 was a bourgeois affair. The revolution of the peasants has still to come. If their rulers continue to exploit them, or to permit them to be exploited, as remorselessly as hitherto, it is likely to be unpleasant. It will not, perhaps, be undeserved.'

THE EARLY DEVELOPMENT OF INDUSTRY

'The world owes far more to the relatively silent craftsmen of ancient and mediaeval China than to the Alexandrian mechanics, articulate theoreticians though they were.' Needham[9].

Archaeology testifies to the advanced state of Chinese craftsmanship in very early times and history contains a long record of the inventiveness and ingenuity of the Chinese people. A glance at the bronze castings of ceremonial vessels of the Shang (Yin) and Chou dynasties reveals at once the great skill of those early workmen. The metal was precious and used almost exclusively for ceremonial purposes.

Iron was introduced in 6 B.C. and by 3 B.C. wrought iron was being produced. The already existing bronze casting skills were applied to iron, which largely replaced the bronze. Iron ore being in much readier supply, its use was much wider spread. Weapons, notably swords and axes, agricultural implements (ploughshares, hoes and adzes), cast iron evaporation pans for the production of salt and the like were made. Iron was also used in the casting of large statues and animal figures. A still extant 13 storey pagoda in Hupeh was built entirely of cast iron in A.D. 1061. The use of iron chains for suspension bridges was general, as early as the Sung dynasty (A.D. 960–1279). Production was carried out in small units and foundries, and from a very early date was kept under the control or the scholar-administrator bureaucracy, which, in this and all other industry, deliberately restricted

* D. Y. Lin's figures for Hong Kong.

its commercialization throughout the centuries. Needham[9] writes: 'About 120 B.C. all iron production was carried on in forty-nine government factories, scattered throughout the empire.'

Chinese inventiveness was by no means confined to metallurgy but extended over a very wide field. Engineers of the Earlier Han dynasty (202 B.C. to A.D. 9) were already exploiting the great underground natural brine resources of Szechwan and quite early were sinking wells to a depth of 1,000 to 2,000 ft by means of bamboo shafts and steel bits[9]. Chinese bridge-building skill is epitomized by the beautiful segmental stone arch bridge, which was built by Li Ch'un in the Sui dynasty (A.D. 581–618) at Chao-Hsien, Hopei over the Tzeya-ho and which still stands[3]. In other fields are Chinese early knowledge of magnetism; they had some knowledge of polarity even in Han times. The invention of gunpowder occurred in T'ang times (A.D. 618–906); happily the Chinese did not exploit it for warlike purposes. Movable block-type printing was in use in China centuries before Europe. These are but a few of the many innovations and serve to show how advanced scientifically the Chinese were in the early centuries. They will also serve to curb a Westerner's too-easily assumed superiority in the scientific world and to check too-great surprise at the ingenuity and inventiveness in the technical sphere, which has been evinced in so many walks of life in China of the last decade.

In view of all this knowledge and invention over so many centuries in China, while the West remained in relative ignorance, it is legitimate to ask why it was that China did not develop into an industrial nation at an early age and why it did not undergo an industrial and technical revolution such as that experienced by Europe at the great break-through of the Renaissance and after. There are many factors contributing to the answer to that question but, undoubtedly, the basic one is to be found in the stable and static, self-recruiting scholar-civil servant administration, which controlled life, directly or indirectly, throughout the country for 20 centuries and which was able to absorb and bend to its own purposes each succeeding innovation. On the subject of iron, Professor Needham[9] writes: 'Like the legendary ostrich, China could digest cast-iron and remain unperturbed thereby: Europe's indigestion amounted to a metamorphosis'.

This bureaucracy assisted in and, indeed, to a large extent, initiated invention but, whenever development moved in the direction of private commercialization, it was taken over by the administration and, insofar as it was exploited at all, this was done as a state monopoly. For example, the production and distribution of salt, from early times, was a state monopoly, the control of which was in the hands of the scholar-officials who farmed it out to the merchant classes. Officials were prohibited from taking part directly in business and commerce, although this was indulged in secretly. It must be remembered that the merchant class, although wealthy, was scorned by the gentry. It stood low in the social scale, which descended from scholar-administrator, through peasant and craftsman, to merchant and soldier, and the governing class was always alive to prevent the merchant from becoming powerful. Both peasant and merchant looked up to the scholar-administrator and it was the ambition of all to enter its ranks. The only real gate of entry was through scholastic success in civil-service examination, but possession of land and rank did help in the rise. Thus capital tended to go to the purchase of land rather than into industrial enterprise.

Throughout the centuries, industrial production continued at the cottage industry-workshop-handicraft stage, using some form of apprenticeship for recruiting labour and operating, on the whole, on quite small capital. The merchant's sphere was largely that of middleman in the local district, centred on the walled city of the *hsien* or county. There he made his profit, often considerable, by buying cheap from the peasant, who had access to only a very restricted market, and selling dear in the centre.

This was the situation in which the Chinese reformers of the later half of the nineteenth century tried to act, in following the Japanese Meiji example of national industrialization, but before describing their activities we must look very briefly at the events which began to shake China out of its old complacency and stability.

Although signs of imperial decadence and decay were evident in the eighteenth century, it was the impact of the West on China in the nineteenth century that hastened the process and which eventually led to the revolutionary changes of the twentieth century. On the whole, any direct contact with Europe in early times was made by Chinese initiative by such travellers as Chang Ch'ien (138–126 B.C.). In the seventh century A.D. Syrian monks introduced Nestorian Christianity to China. Notable western travellers, such as William Rubruch, Friar John and Marco Polo, followed in the thirteenth and fourteenth centuries and Jesuit missionaries in the seventeenth and eighteenth centuries enjoyed a measure of popularity with the Chinese Court and intelligentsia on account of their scientific learning but, in total, this contact amounted to very little indeed. China, over the centuries, remained self-contained, self-sufficient and self-satisfied. In so far as it was known, it inspired the envy and admiration of the outside world for its stability, wealth and learning, especially by the West.

With the awakening of the West in the seventeenth and eighteenth centuries, expressed in part by its feverish exploration of the world for trade and markets, this vision of China naturally attracted first the Portuguese and then the Spanish, British and Dutch traders. But China, feeling no need for the goods of barbarians, showed no enthusiasm and confined trade through a government foreign trade monopoly to one port, Canton. Exports from China far exceeded imports, with a result that western traders had to meet the balance in cash (silver). To overcome this they sought a commodity desired by the Chinese and this they found in opium from India. The opium habit and demand for the drug grew very rapidly, resulting in a great increase in its importation and a consequent reversal of the flow of silver. The attempted suppression by the Chinese government of the opium trade, both for this reason and for the demoralization which the drug habit was causing, resulted in clashes between traders and officials in Canton and was the direct cause of war in 1840 between China and Great Britain[2].

China's defeat in that war marks the beginning of a century of constant, persistent imposition of western political, economic, religious and educational ideas, disrupting the old stability and hastening the downfall of the decadent and discredited Ch'ing dynasty. With each succeeding war and defeat more and more Chinese ports, known as Treaty Ports, were thrown open to foreign trade, concessions, i.e. areas of land under foreign jurisdiction, were leased to foreign powers and extra-territorial status granted. Christian missions extended their work beyond the evangelical into the medical and educational fields. The West, in which Japan must be included, with its superior military and economic power, imposed its will on China at every turn.

It was in this turmoil that the Chinese reformers in high circles sought, in the later half of the nineteenth century, to introduce into China some adaptation to modern industrial and commercial conditions similar to that which had occurred in Meiji Japan and to secure

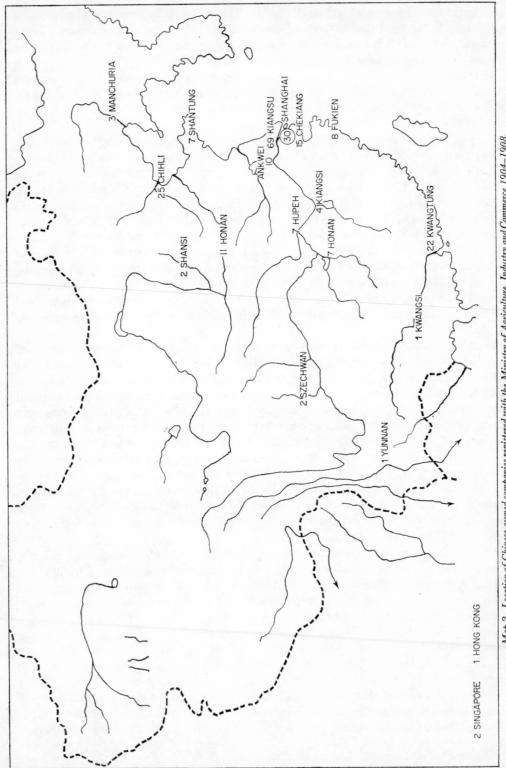

Map 2. *Location of Chinese-owned companies registered with the Ministry of Agriculture, Industry and Commerce 1904–1908.*
(Compiled from A. Feuerwerker, China's Early Industrialization)

for China the economic benefits enjoyed almost exclusively by foreigners at that time. Their efforts met with opposition from many sides, not least being the conservative Court itself.

The first attempts at modern industry were in the military field. The ease with which the British had defeated the Chinese forces in the two wars of 1840 and 1856 emphasized the need for China to modernize her armaments. Small arsenals and shipyards were established in Kiangsi and Anhwei by Governor-General Li Hung-chang (1823–1901) and, in spite of Court opposition, 120 students were sent to U.S.A. and Europe to study western engineering, technology and science. But it was quickly realized by a few that there were many more things involved than the mere production of arms if China was to meet the challenge. Modern communications (rail, telegraph and steamship) had to be established and these entailed the production of coal and iron on a much larger scale than hitherto.

Working under the protection of Li Hung-chang, Governor-General of Chihli and Chang Chih-tung, Governor-General of Hu-Kwang (Hupeh and Hunan), it was Sheng Hsuan-huai (1844–1916) who spearheaded the late nineteenth century attempts at the promotion of modern industry. He came of a long-established official family in Hupeh. Although his methods were by no means always above suspicion, he was responsible for the initiation and management of most of the outstanding enterprises of the time. The earlier enterprises were entirely government owned and supervised (arsenals, railways) or joint official-merchant concerns (*kwan-tu, shang-pan*, meaning government supervised, merchant managed), which drew their capital from official funds, plus contributions from official-administrators and merchants. True joint-stock companies were not permitted until the end of the century. Some idea of the rate of progress in the development of these joint official-merchant concerns can be gathered from the following list: China Merchant Steam Navigation Company (C.M.S.N.C.) 1872; K'ai-p'ing Coal Mines, 1877; Shanghai Cotton Cloth Mill, 1878; Imperial Telegraph Administration, 1881; Mo-ho Gold Mines, 1887; Hanyang Iron Works, 1896; Imperial Bank of China, 1896; P'ing-hsiang Coal Mines, 1898[10]; Some of these were later converted into joint-stock companies, notably the C.M.S.N.C. and also the Hanyang Iron Works, Tayeh Iron Mines and P'ing-hsiang Coal Mines, which became the Hanyehping Coal and Iron Co. Ltd. in 1908. Official supervisors and often the merchants themselves were ignorant of modern practice and thus there was incompetence in planning and in poor regulations. Enterprises were subject to official exactions and levies and there was much graft and malpractice. The Government attempted to relieve its embarrassed finances, which were strained by the additional burdens of indemnity following the Sino-Japanese War (1894) and the Boxer Rebellion (1902) by levies on industry. One such was the institution of *Likin*, a transit tax, imposed in the first instance on goods passing through the Grand Canal, and later on goods in transit in all provinces. It further became a a production tax at source and a sales tax at destination, proving a great millstone about the neck of all enterprise. On this subject Feuerwerker[10] quotes Cheng Kuan-ying, who, in these words, bemoans the lack of competent and honest men who will devote themselves to commerce:

'The officials do not protect the merchants, on the contrary they do them harm by regarding the merchants' wealth in the same way as Ch'in looked at Ch'u's prosperity. Although

11

they fill their private purses, the sources of general wealth (*li-yuan*) are blocked up. This is the evil from above.

As for the merchants, there are many who are ignorant and few with knowledge; many that are false and few that are truthful . . . Therefore shares are collected (to start companies), but there are losses of capital; joint-stock enterprises are inaugurated, but they fail. This is the evil attributable to those below.'

This failure on the part of the Ch'ing government to comprehend or to co-operate in the efforts at industrialization contrasts strongly with the attitude of the Japanese Meiji government, which worked in close co-operation with industrial managers and contributed considerably in capital investment in industry.

Likin was all the more hated in that the goods of foreign merchants were exempt under treaty and were shipped throughout China under 'transit pass', enabling Westerners to move all goods, even local Chinese produce, at a much lower cost than the Chinese themselves. It enabled foreign merchants and companies to compete on very unequal terms with the Chinese merchants dealing in cotton, timber, vegetable oil, tobacco, opium, etc. and drove large numbers of them either into bankruptcy or into dealing in foreign imported goods under foreign direction. This was not the least of the grievances which fanned the fire of a growing nationalism and anti-imperialism at the turn of the century and which flared eventually into revolution, overthrowing the Manchu dynasty in 1911[11].

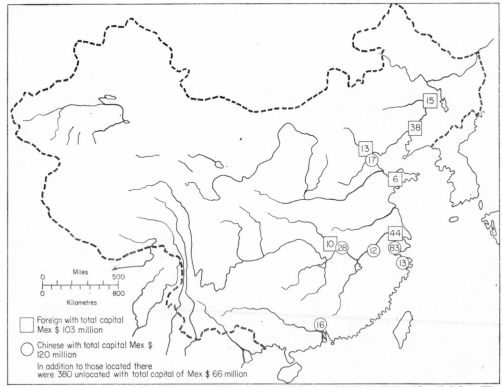

Map 3. Distribution of Chinese and foreign-owned firms inaugurated between 1895 and 1913. (Compiled from 'The Economic Development of China and Japan'. Ed. C. D. Cowan, Edgar Allen 1964 and A. Feuerwerker, 'China's Nineteenth Century Industrialization: The Case of Hanyehping Coal and Iron Co. Ltd.')

12

A noticeable change, occurring in the later part of the nineteenth century, was the movement of governmental power away from the centre at Peking into the hands of powerful governor-generals, such as Li Hung-chang in Chihli and Chang Chih-tung in Hupeh. The latter was the initiator of the Hanyang Iron Works (1896) and No. 1 Cotton Mill, Wuchang.

Joint-stock companies began to make some progress in the first decade of the twentieth century after foreigners had gained the right to engage in manufacturing in China as a result of the Treaty of Shimoseski in 1895 at the close of the Sino-Japanese War. The Ministry of Agriculture, Industry and Commerce reported that between 1904 and 1908 there were 227 registered joint-stock companies. However, of these only 54 had a capital of over Taels 100,000 and only five of over Taels 2,000,000. (1 tael = 583·3 grains silver.) Commenting on the industrial situation, Feuerwerker[10] says: 'It has been estimated that in 1912 there were 20,749 "factories" in China, a term left undefined but one whose scope becomes quite clear when we note that only 363 of this huge total employed mechanical power, while the remaining 20,386 were operated with human or animal power only.'

Cheng Chu-yuan estimates that in 1933 only 250 units could be registered as modern factories and even so commanded comparatively little capital. Only about 28% of the total industrial production was carried out by private modern factories. The remainder was produced in workshops and by handicraft workers.

Foreign investment rose from 789·9 million dollars in 1902 to 3,242·5 million in 1931 and 3,671·4 million in 1936 and controlled 39% coal, 82·5% pig iron, 48·2% shipbuilding, 29·1% cotton yarn and 61·5% cotton cloth production[10].

Foreign industrial development was confined to the Treaty Ports and thus distributed along the littoral and the middle and lower Yangtze. Much of Chinese industry was initiated by compradors, who having gained their experience in the employment of foreigners, later set up business on their own account. Their geographical distribution tended to follow closely that of the foreigners (see Map 3).

THE RISE OF NATIONALISM

The instrusion of Westerners into China in the second half of the nineteenth century, the vice-like grip over industry and the privileged position which foreigners enjoyed, was a constant and growing offence to all Chinese. It needs very little imagination to realize the deep resentment felt at the existence of concessions, pockets of foreign territory, often right in the heart of the country, such as Hankow, Kiukiang and Nanking, in which foreign rule held sway and into which Chinese were allowed only on sufferance and not by right. This resentment was further deepened by extra-territorial rights by which foreign nationals in China lived under their own laws and were tried by their own courts even though plaintiff or defendant were Chinese. This right was, to some extent, extended to Chinese converts to Christianity and was one of the reasons why Christian missions were regarded as an integral part of the imperialist invasion and why, subsequently, under Communism the Chinese Christian Church was regarded with suspicion. Hostility to Christianity was particularly strong amongst the scholar-gentry class, with its deep-rooted Confucian ancestral tradition and strict code of conduct and personal behaviour. 'To eat Christianity', i.e. to embrace the Christian religion in these circles involved disownment. The 'barbaric' manners of Westerners were a further cause of Chinese dislike and disdain. Their arrogance,

13

superiority, loudness and forthrightness of speech, lacking Chinese finesse and innuendo, were an offence, as were, also, their table manners, which even involved the use of a knife at table!

This was a fertile emotional field, always ready at hand, when the effete, corrupt Court of the failing Manchu (Ch'ing) dynasty wished to divert the attention of the oppressed peasantry from its own short-comings, as it did in the days of the Boxer riots. But it was also a ready tool at the hand of the group of reformers and nationalists, who began to try to create a national consciousness out of a deep-rooted and universal clannishness.

Growing hatred of the alien dynasty, which, as it became progressively more decadent and corrupt in the nineteenth century, became also more oppressive, was evinced in the Taiping Rebellion (1851–1864), largely a peasant uprising, which came very near to success. The Manchu Court was saved only by the intervention and help of the foreign powers, who feared the probable chaos and loss of trade that would follow the fall of the tottering dynasty. Working underground, largely through secret societies, a national leader emerged in the person of Sun Yat Sen. He was born in 1866, soon after the end of the Taiping Rebellion. At 13 years of age he went to Honolulu to live with his brother, who kept a general store. While there he attended the English Mission School until he returned to his native Kwang-tung. He was converted to Christianity and spent the years 1887 to 1892 studying at the College of Medicine, Hong Kong, from which he graduated with a doctor's degree. However, he turned his attention from doctoring to politics and devoted the rest of his life to the task of overthrowing the Manchu dynasty and to the establishment of a democratic republic. He was proscribed and spent many years in exile in Japan and England, whence he planned several abortive revolutionary attempts. At first he was rejected by scholars 'because he was not of the literati; nor did he hold a degree under the old civil service examinations', but later they recognized his leadership. He also received much support from Overseas Chinese, especially those in North America and Malaya. Success came rather suddenly and unexpectedly in 1911, when a revolutonist's bomb was unintentionally exploded in the Russian Concession in Hankow and so sparked off an uprising which quickly spread throughout the whole country and toppled the Manchus. The Chinese Republic was declared with Sun Yat Sen as its first president.

However, hope and elation were quickly followed by disillusionment. Sun Yat Sen was ousted and forced again into exile by Yuan Shih-kai, the powerful military commander, who had ambition to found a new dynasty and become the next emperor. His death in 1916 marked the beginning of the disastrous and chaotic period of 'war-lordism', which continued unabated until 1927. Military governors in the various provinces or groups of provinces seized power and fought each other to extend their control; the central government's writ ceased to run. Powerful war-lords, such as Wu Pei-fu (central China), Chang Tso-lin (north China and Manchuria) and Feng Yu-hsiang (the 'Christian' general of the north-west) emerged and under them hundreds of smaller tyrants operated. The miserable years that followed were marked by continuous civil war, widespread banditry, extortion by the armies, corruption and oppression. To raise funds for their wars, the war-lords taxed the countryside unmercifully and, as usual, the peasantry were the main sufferers. Able-bodied men in the fields were conscripted into the armies or pressed into forced labour gangs; heavy taxes were collected years in advance; farmers were forced to grow opium, a great revenue raiser, to the detriment of food crops, and the armies lived like locusts off the countryside wherever they happened to be.

14

Realizing that if he was to halt this tyranny and build a unified, strong, democratic China, he must create a mass party with popular support and must back it with its own army, Sun Yat Sen returned to Canton and proceeded to form the Kuomintang (K.M.T.)—the Nationalist Party. He looked to the West for help, but the Great Powers, either because they were too exhausted by the struggles of World War I or because they looked with suspicion on an emerging radical China, turned a deaf ear to his appeals. Frustrated and disillusioned, it was then that Sun Yat Sen repudiated western democaracy and turned to young, revolutionary Soviet Russia.

Believing that his newly-formed K.M.T. and the Communists could co-operate and that that the latter would submit to his leadership, he set about a big reorganization of his party. The army, assisted by Russian advisers, was built up under the young General Chiang Kai-shek, who was to lead the victorious Northern Expedition in 1926 and over-throw the power of the war-lords. But Sun Yat Sen was a sick man and in 1925 he died with his mission unfulfilled. As a man of action he had not been a conspicuous success, but he had been the honest and disinterested inspirer and mouthpiece of the emerging patriotism and nationalism, which eventually was to unite China. In his opening chapters of his 'San Min Chu Ih', which had great influence at the time, he exhorts the people to get rid of their old overriding loyalties to clan and family and to think and act in terms of a nation.

We have seen the desperate state of the peasantry at this time, clearly ripe for drastic reform or revolution. It was this rural situation which, in 1926, made the progress of the army of the united K.M.T. and Communists from Canton into the Yangtze valley so easy and triumphant. The well-disciplined army, which was preceded by widespread propa-ganda promising agrarian redress and reform, was received by the peasantry with open arms. Wu Pei-fu's forces disintegrated and the whole of the Yangzte valley quickly fell to Chiang Kai-shek in late 1926. Scarcely had the victorious army reached Nanking than a rift between K.M.T., based in Nanking and the Communists in Wuhan, arose. It quickly grew into open conflict and civil war, which was not to be resolved finally until 1949.

THE RISE OF COMMUNISM

Phase I (1921–1927)

During and after the 1911 Revolution various socialist groups came into existence and out of these the Chinese Communist Party (C.C.P.) emerged. In the spring of 1921, a group of twelve met in Shanghai under the leadership of Ch'en Tu-hsiu and Li Ta-chao and form-ally inaugurated the Party. Mao Tse-tung was present. It became a member of the Third International and naturally was under Russian tutelage. In October, 1921 a first Provincial branch was formed in Hunan under Mao Tse-tung's leadership.

At the Third Conference of the C.C.P., under the directive of the Comintern, they took the momentous decision to co-operate with the K.M.T. and in 1924 the First National Congress of the K.M.T., under Sun Yat Sen's leadership, inaugurated the K.M.T.–C.C.P. with the avowed object of ridding China of its pestilential war-lords and its imperial over-lords, and of establishing a national government. As we have seen, the building of an army was undertaken under the young general Chiang Kai-shek and his Russian advisers. A Peasants Department was established in Canton. This was an institute for training cadres to go out into the countryside and to spread revolutionary propaganda amongst the peasants. It was markedly communist in emphasis—Mao Tse-tung was one of its lecturers—

and its trainees did their work with enthusiasm. Already there were many shades of opinion and doctrine in the K.M.T. and C.C.P., leading to the formation of cliques. It was activities, such as those of the Peasants Department, that tended to accentuate them.

In November, 1924, whilst Sun Yat Sen was in Peking taking part in a National Convention, Chen Chiung-ming, military governor in East Kwangtung, revolted against Sun Yat Sen and the K.M.T. This resulted in two 'Eastern Expeditions' and the final defeat of Chen; it also marked the remarkable rise to power of the newly-formed peasants unions, under P'eng P'ai, who, in a matter of months had succeeded in securing a membership, mainly agrarian, of 210,000 in 22 *hsien*. These unions, centred in Hai-feng, took over control of the countryside and established soviets. This accession to power was accompanied by excesses and the ruthless liquidation of the landlords and 'rascals'; rents were drastically reduced or abolished entirely; directives from the K.M.T. in Canton urging moderation were disregarded.

Communist thinking in these early days was tied very closely to Russian orthodox ideology and looked to the factory worker in the city as the spearhead of revolution. How little faith was placed in the peasantry is shown by Chen Tu-hsiu's statement in 1923: 'In such a country as China, over half the farmers are petit bourgeois landed farmers, who adhere firmly to private property consciousness. How can they accept Communism'[12]. Even in the heart of the country in east Kwangtung where the soviets were actually being established, mainly by the initiative of the peasants and where industry was confined entirely to small factories and workshops engaged in weaving, food processing, paper making and the like, we find this same adherence to orthodox ideology that the leadership resides in the urban proletariate. The Draft Resolution of the First Peasant Congress of Kwangtung soviet stated: 'Our struggle must be concentrated in the city because the political centre is located in the city, therefore, the working class must strive to lead the peasants to participation in this struggle'[13].

However, the main interest and effort of K.M.T. and C.C.P. between 1924 and 1926 was concentrated on preparations for the Northern Expedition, which was started in the summer of 1926 and attended with such success. By autumn the whole of the Yangtze valley below the Gorges was in the hands of the combined forces, with Chiang Kai-shek established in Nanking, and the C.C.P. and their Russian advisers, led by Borodin, in Wuhan. As the combined forces swept northward many rural districts, especially in Hunan, encouraged by Mao Tse-tung, copied the Hai-feng example and established soviets. The difference in objective of the K.M.T. and C.C.P. became more and more marked and rifts began to be obvious. However, Russia was anxious to hold the alliance together and the Comintern issued a directive late in 1926 ordering that there should be no split with the K.M.T., that peasant demands should be boldly met and that the time was not yet ripe for the establishment of soviets. The first two of these directives were incompatible and mutually exclusive for the orthodox and right wing members of the K.M.T. were firmly opposed to any far-reaching land reform. The inevitable rupture came, although the left wing of the K.M.T. and the C.C.P. held together for some time. From this time (1927) on, the C.C.P. has been virtually independent of Moscow in making its major policy decisions, although, until 1960, it continued to regard the U.S.S.R. as the Father of Communism.

16

Phase II (1927–1936)

The split between the K.M.T. and C.C.P. marks the beginning of a bloody and bitter civil war. Chiang Kai-shek made the extermination of the Communists his major objective, which he pursued unrelentingly until the outbreak of the Sino-Japanese War in 1937. The C.C.P. was weak and divided in leadership and policy. Chen Tu-hsiu held to the Russian line of revolution through the worker in the city. Mao Tse-tung disagreed with him violently, regarding him as half-hearted and far too moderate. Mao placed his reliance on the peasant masses, a faith he has maintained unswervingly right through to the present day. His Report of 'an Investigation into the Peasant Movement in Hunan, March, 1927', presented to and rejected by the Party, clearly revealed the direction in which his mind was moving. It strongly urged the full development of a peasant movement.

Communist efforts at revolution and uprisings in cities were all failures and were suppressed most violently. However, between 1928 and 1934, in the mountainous countryside of Hunan and Kiangsi very considerable areas came under Communist control and were governed by peasant soviets[14]. Here in the mountain fastness of Ching Kan Shan, under the leadership of Mao Tse-tung, Chu Teh, Lin Piao, Chou En-lai, P'eng Teh-huai and other well-known names today, a military force was built up and the early strict puritanical disciplines, which later characterized the P.L.A. (People's Liberation Army) and the C.C.P., were learnt, as were also the military tactics, which were practised with success here against the K.M.T. and later against the Japanese. 'When the enemy advances, we retire; when he halts, we harass; when he retires or weakens, we attack'.

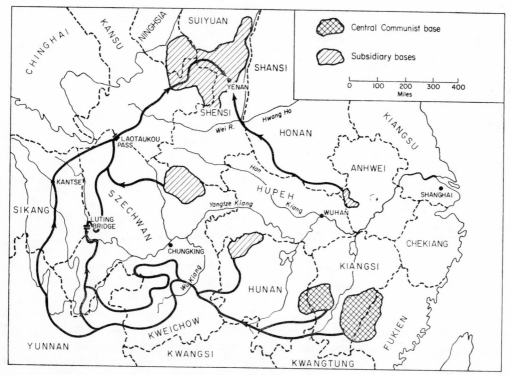

Map 4. Lines of the Long March

17

Chiang Kai-shek, in all, carried out five big campaigns against this central China large enclave of communism, all of which were accompanied by terrible loss of life, destruction of livelihood and consequent famine. It was only in the last, the fifth campaign, with German military staff assistance, that the Red Army was dislodged and then mainly because it failed to adhere to its well-tried guerilla tactics of retreat and harassment and instead engaged in a war of confrontation.

Although defeated, the Red Army of about 90,000 men was able to extricate itself and then, in October, 1934, began the now famous 'Long March', a retreat of thousands of miles, which carried them west through Kweichow and Szechwan into the high mountains and deep valleys of the eastern edge of the Tibetan plateau and so north, and then east again into the dry, loess lands of Shensi. It was during this march that Mao Tse-tung's leadership was finally established and it was out of its bitter hardships that the hard core was forged which, in 1949, was to form the new central government and which has undergone remarkably little change. Another far-reaching effect of the 'Long March' was the amount of indoctrination and education in communism that this retreating army was able to carry out in the districts through which it passed and sojourned[15]. The strict discipline of the Red Army, so much in contrast to that of the K.M.T. or remote war-lords' troops, and its immediate application of land reform in favour of the poor peasant, ensured considerable rural support when it came into power later. The eight rules the Red Army was taught to obey were:

(1) Replace all doors (used as beds) when leaving a house.
(2) Return and roll up the straw matting on which you sleep.
(3) Be courteous and polite to the people and help them when you can.
(4) Return all borrowed articles.
(5) Replace all damaged articles.
(6) Be honest in all transactions with the peasants.
(7) Pay for all articles purchased.
(8) Be sanitary and especially establish latrines a safe distance from people's houses[14].

Of the 90,000 who set out on this retreat, a mere 30,000 reached Yenan, Shensi, which was to be the base of Communist activity for the next 10 years or so. Here they were less vulnerable to Chiang's continuing attacks than they had been in Central China.

Phase III (1936–1945)

This was a period of recovery, reconstruction and expansion in spite of the fact that the Communist armies were locked in continuous war with Japan during this period. Some idea of that expansion can be gleaned from the fact that, in 1937, the C.C.P., from its drought-stricken loess base in Shensi, controlled a population of about one-and-a-half million. In 1945 the Party numbered 1·2 million members alone, had an army of 900,000 and controlled 19 Communist-organized bases or soviets with a population of over 90 million[16].

One of the results of the revolution of 1927 was the surrender of concessions and some extra-territorial rights by western nations, but Japan took the opportunity of China's continued civil strife and weakness, first to annex Manchuria (Manchukuo) in 1930 in the face of League of Nations' condemnation and then progressively to make further inroads into China's sovereignty to the growing chagrin of all patriotically-minded Chinese. In

18

December, 1935 strikes occurred in Peking and throughout the country demanding a cessation of civil war between the K.M.T. and C.C.P. and calling for national unity to meet Japanese aggression. This agitation was largely at the instigation of the Communists and was strenuously opposed by Chiang-Kai-shek, who was bent on the extermination of communism as a *sine qua non* of unity. Dissident troops under Chang Hsueh-liang, who had been ousted from the north-east and who were clamouring for action against Japan, kidnapped Chiang in December, 1936 while he was in Sian organizing a sixth campaign against the Communists. For a while he was in danger of his life; curiously it was Chou En-lai who was mainly instrumental in Chiang's release, after he had agreed to the formation of a united front against Japan[14]. Barely 6 months later (7th July, 1937) the 'incident' of Marco Polo Bridge in Peking sparked off the Sino-Japanese War.

Chiang Kai-shek was the recognized Commander-in-Chief but he continued to look in two directions; the war was pursued with far greater vigour and determination by the C.C.P. than by the K.M.T. Mainly by guerilla tactics, the C.C.P. penetrated the areas occupied by the Japanese and in this way kept in touch with the peasantry and stimulated them to greater resistance. In this way the C.C.P. came to be regarded by the masses as the patriotic and national party. In the regions which were under Communist control, moderate policies were pursued with a view to uniting the landless, the peasants and the landlords to form a united resistance front. Mao Tse-tung declared 'For a people being deprived of its national freedom, the revolutionary task is not immediate socialism, but the struggle for independence. We cannot even discuss Communism if we are robbed of a country in which to practice it.'[14] This fight for freedom gave Chinese Communism the very strong flavour of patriotic nationalism, which it still retains in a very high degree.

It was during these 8 years of warfare against Japan that much of Chinese Communist thought was hammered out. It is not the purpose of this book to discuss the development of Communist thought in any detail, but it is absolutely essential to an understanding of China today in any field, not least the economic and geographic, that the salient points should be appreciated. The planning and the activities of the whole nation are consciously geared to and directed by that thought and ideology. Everyone in the country is caught up in Communist ideology, which permeates every walk of life, from the highest powered research worker to the humblest peasant. That ideology is presented as stemming from the thought of Chairman Mao. Practically every article, report and statement, no matter in what subject, is prefaced with such words as 'Guided by the thought of Mao Tse-tung and the leadership of the C.C.P. . . .'. It is necessary, therefore, to pause and examine the main aspects of Mao's thought[16].

Mao Tse-tung was born in 1893 in Shao Shan, Hunan of lowly stock. His father was a poor peasant, who, by hard work and parsimony, rose to the ranks of the rich peasant. He was hard, grasping and avaricious and was hated by his children. Mao ran away from home and spent many years as an impecunious student. His life has been one of hardship, adventure and peril. One of his earliest interests was in physical fitness, an 'advanced' subject in those days and his first published article, in *New Youth*, 1917, was on this topic. It is interesting to note that he has retained his physical fitness through the years. Payne[17], writing of him in 1946, says: 'Then Mao came into the room. He came so quietly that we were hardly aware of his presence . . . Today he looked like a surprisingly young student . . . He was fifty-three and he looked twenty.'

19

Through reading, study and contact with 'advanced' associates at the Normal College, Changsha, and under Li Ta-chao in the Peking University Library where he worked for a while, he progressed through the liberalism of J. S. Mill, Adam Smith and Bentham to arrive in the Communist fold at a time when it was dangerous to be known even as a liberal. His brothers, his sister and his wife, who were akin to him in thought, were all killed or executed.

Mao is a strict Marxist-Leninist, holding firmly to dialectical materialism and repudiating all shades of the metaphysical approach and of determinism, as being static and lifeless. Dynamic development, he contends, is found in dialectical materialism and this he expounds in his *On Contradiction*, delivered first as a lecture in 1937 in Yenan to combat doctrinairism, which already was a serious problem within the Party, and later revised as an essay. This is probably Mao's main contribution to Communist thought. In it he maintains that within everything there are contending forces, which constitute the very essence of life. 'There is nothing that does not contain contradiction; without contradiction there would be no world' and again 'Contradiction is universal, absolute, existing in all processes of the development of things and running through all processes from beginning to end.'[18] Thus struggle is the stuff of life: every thing, every idea, every movement, every problem, contains within itself opposites, which strive together until resolution leads on to a unity in which new opposites are present and in which the process is repeated on a higher plane. Speaking to the Red Army in 1937 and urging them to greater efforts, he said 'It is a good thing, not a bad thing, to be opposed by an enemy.' The presence of the enemy reveals clearly the contradictions, shows clearly what is to be done and stimulates to action and to struggle. This thesis is universal and is applied not only to military enemies but to each and every activity. The peasant must look for and understand the contradictions, the contending claims as between the crops in his fields, water supply and the one thousand and one things that come within his purview. The worker in the factory must meet his problems in the same spirit. The planner must adjust continually the contending claims of the productive and distributive forces to the right use of transport and communication and so on throughout society. This stress or emphasis on struggle accords well with the characteristic trait of the Chinese peasant's perseverance, born of centuries of contending with hostile natural forces and calamities.

For all his strict adherence to the Marxist-Leninist line, Mao has had a deep distrust of dogma and bookishness from early years. This comes out clearly in both essays, *On Contradiction* and *On Practice*. In the former he says, 'Our doctrinaires are lazy; they refuse to make any painstaking study of specific things, but regard general truths as something emerging out of the void, and turn them into purely abstract and utterly incomprehensible formulae, thereby completely denying, as well as reversing, the normal sequence in which man comes to know truth.'[18] Each and every particular contradiction must be examined and treated on its merits and its own particular solution found. He asserts that man's knowledge depends mainly on his activity in material production[19] and knowledge grows in the normal sequence by practice, i.e. actual experience (induction) leading to thought (deduction) on the experience gained, which, in its turn, leads to further action or corrected practice based on that thought[19]. He is conscious of the need to create confidence and initiative in the great mass of people and exhorts them to have courage and not be afraid of making mistakes. To the man who says 'I am not sure I can handle it' he says, 'In many instances, failures have to be repeated many times before errors in knowledge can be corrected and correspondence with the laws of the objective process achieved.'[19] This advice has been acted on very widely and has released a great deal of ingenuity and inventiveness in agriculture and industry. It has also brought its heavy crop of mistakes, witness the Great Leap Forward itself in 1958.

Although Mao is presented as theoretician, he is probably even more a practitioner and innovator. He has been fearless and resolute in applying his theories. His refusal to be bound by dogma has nowhere been more clearly demonstrated than in his reliance on the peasant masses as the basis of the Chinese revolution, as we have already seen. It is this faith in the peasantry, which, more than anything else, distinguishes Chinese Communism from Russian, which has been based firmly from its inception on the industrial proletariat. 'Mao Tse-tung has stood out as one of the very few national leaders in twentieth century China who has shown sustained concern with the hardships, brutality and grinding want which characterized the lot of the poorer peasants.'[16] He also recognized 'that a major source of potential political energy rested in the Chinese peasants; and that the leader able to exploit and mobilize that energy source was destined to triumph in China in the long run.' Mao insists that there must never be an alienation of the masses, as there was in Russia and which he suggests was Stalin's great mistake, i.e. that he went against history[20]. In assessing the respective contributions of peasant and worker to the revolution in China, he attributes 70 per cent to the peasantry: 'The people are the sea: the government is the fish.'

It is interesting to note another difference between Russian and Chinese revolutionary experience. Russia, from the start, was faced with the problem of the integration of the army. The C.C.P. grew very largely out of its army, which was a missionary force carrying the doctrine wherever it went. China's problem was and still is the integration of its intellectuals, through whom runs a marked element of anarchism, of 'tze chi kai kao', meaning self-reform and personal purification and of deep distrust of government and thus runs counter to the massive and complex organization of Communism.

Finally, Mao and his colleagues have evinced a steadfast faith in the ultimate victory of their cause. They have maintained that all jobs are conquerable, however great the obstacles may appear to be. 'All reactionaries are paper tigers. In appearance the reactionaries are formidable, but in reality they are not so powerful. From a long-term point of view, it is the people who are powerful.' Chinese Communism is infused with a sense of world mission to spread its gospel and it sees itself as the liberator of all oppressed peoples.

Phase IV (1945–1949)

On the defeat of Japan in 1945, the Japanese army was ordered to surrender to the Chinese C-in-C, Chiang Kai-shek, whose troops were mainly in the west, and in order to take this surrender there had to be a rapid transport of Chinese troops eastward. This was accomplished largely with the aid of the U.S. Air Force. Chinese Communist forces occupied a considerable area of north China. Soviet forces had moved into the North-East (Manchuria) and stripped that industrial region of most of its Japanese-made plant.

With the elimination of an external enemy, the old enmity between the K.M.T. and C.C.P., which had scarcely been hidden during the war years, once more came clearly to the surface. Attempts at forming a coalition government on a democratic basis were made

21

in October, 1945 and January, 1946, but, to the dismay and disappointment of the mass of the people, ended in failure and were followed by a renewal of bloody civil war.

The K.M.T. (Nationalist) army was, at first, very strong, far outnumbering the P.L.A. (People's Liberation Army) and far better equipped, receiving from the U.S. larger quantities of surplus war stores. But corruption and indiscipline, which were already present, grew rapidly and defeat in the field in many places was followed by demoralization. The P.L.A., on the other hand, although outnumbered, was disciplined and schooled to a conscious purpose; morale was high. It pursued the same tactics as it had used against the Japanese, i.e. holding the countryside and leaving the towns to the enemy. The K.M.T., attacking Yenan and the north-west, 'found themselves in a position not dissimilar to that of the Japanese during their war with China', while the P.L.A. 'succeeded in keeping their own units intact and mobile for eventual concentration and use at points of their own choosing.'[21] These evasive and harassing tactics led to great dissatisfaction and exhaustion in K.M.T. ranks, resulting in large-scale surrender of men and equipment. The growing demoralization of the army is shown in the U.S. report: 'the exhaustion of the Nationalists, their growing indignation over the disparity between officers' enrichment and soldiers' low pay and their lack of interest in fighting far from home among an unfriendly populace, whereas the Communists are in the position of fighting for native soil'.[21]

While the civil war was being pursued with great intensity, the state of the country was deteriorating rapidly. Production steadily decreased to reach its lowest point in 1949. Nationalist rule became more and more repressive; a police state, albeit an inefficient one, came into being, with its usual accompaniment of spying, executions, assassinations, which bore especially severely on workers' associations, trade unions and on the student and academic world. Conscription and forced labour of the peasantry were particularly resented, especially when the farmers were required to dig great tank traps and trenches across their paddy fields, thus playing havoc with the irrigation systems. The falling production, which huge relief supplies from U.N.N.R.A. did little to alleviate, and the great military expenditure led inevitably to two periods of galloping inflation. During the Sino-Japanese War there had already been serious inflation. The volume of banknotes in 1945 was 465 times greater than that in 1937[10a], but what followed was disastrous. The last 'currency reform' occurred in September, 1948, when all Mexican silver dollars, the only viable currency, were called in by the K.M.T. on threat of death. At that time the price index stood at 5,482 as compared with 100 in 1937. For each Mexican dollar two paper Gold Yuan were issued; by May, 1949 the equivalent exchange had fallen to 2 million and more. This inflation, probably more than any other factor, led to the utter collapse of the K.M.T. in 1949.

'Liberation', the name given to the 1949 Revolution, came with a suddenness unforeseen either by victor or vanquished. By November, 1948 the whole of the North-East (Manchuria) was in C.C.P. hands; Peking and Tientsin fell in January, 1949; the P.L.A. crossed the Yangtze in April and the entire country was in its hands by the end of the year. Chiang Kai-shek and the remnants of his army retired to Taiwan, having left behind them a trail of desolation and destroyed communications.

The suddenness of this collapse presented the C.C.P. with great administrative problems. Although the mass of people was apprehensive of what the future might hold, it was thoroughly disillusioned by the incompetence and venality of the K.M.T. A wave of patriotism swept the country and this, together with the exemplary behaviour of the P.L.A. wherever it penetrated, gave reassurance generally and paved the way for immediate changes.

Map 5. Administrative districts 1949–1954

North China Control Area
Hopei, Shansi, Chahai, Pingyuan, Suiyuan—Municipalities=Peking, Tientsin.
North-East Administrative
Liaotung, Liashsi, Jehol, Kirin, Sungkiang, Heilungkiang—M= Mukden, Fushun, Penhsi, Pt A-Dairen, Anshan.
East China Administrative
Shantung, Chekiang, Fukien, N. & S. Kiangsu, Wanpei (Anhwei), Wannan—M=Shanghai, Nanking.
Central South Administrative
Hupei, Honan, Hunan, Kiangsi, Kwangtung, Kwangsi—M=Hankow, Canton.
North-West Administrative
Shensi, Kansu, Ninghsia, Chinghai, Sinkiang—M=Sian.
South-West Administrative
Yunnan, Kweichow, Sikang—M=Chungking.
Szechwan

The country was divided into six administrative areas (see Map 5) under central control from Peking. From these the country was governed until 1954, when they were abolished and the present provincial divisions and autonomous regions substituted (see Map 5). Considerable difficulty was encountered in early years in recruiting adequate personnel for the civil service.

To the surprise of most people, the chaotic monetary situation was brought to a state of reasonable stability and the budget balanced within a year. This was achieved by a number of measures. A unified, efficient tax collection, free from bribery and corruption, was initiated and its proceeds found their way into the national treasury. With land reform and the abolition of heavy rents, the grain tax yielded a heavy return without bearing oppressively on the peasantry. In so far as communications allowed, grain and goods were shuttled from surplus to deficiency areas. This helped to stop hoarding and speculation, which had been rife and also to steady prices. It is reported that in that year (1950) 1,030,000 ton of grain were sent from the North-East to east China; 110,000 ton from the south-west to Hankow and 339,000 ton from south to east and north[22]. Vast stores of valuable goods in K.M.T. warehouses were confiscated and sold, thus enabling the Government to cut expenditure. In this way the monetary situation was stabilized. Interest rates, which at the height of inflation in early 1949, were sometimes as high as 100% per day, fell from around 50% p.a. in February, 1950 to 3 to 5% in May, 1950. Prices were tied to a grain-cotton index and have remained remarkably steady ever since. The wholesale price index of 1952 was 100, that of 1958, 92·7[23].

First steps towards socialization were taken immediately. In agriculture, land reform and distribution of 'land to the tiller' were put in hand. In industry, the first steps towards public ownership of productive and distributive forces were taken. These are given full treatment later.

Perhaps the most remarkable immediate changes were in the social sphere. Backed by an intense patriotic fervour, Communist puritanism made its appearance almost overnight. Gambling, thieving and prostitution disappeared. Beggars were brought into productive employment or returned to their villages for rehabilitation. Women were given equal status with men and the marriage laws radically revised. Public hygiene, street cleanliness and care of public property became the responsibility and the care of all.

This was the setting in which the Communist programme of building a modern industrial, socialist state began to take shape.

REFERENCES

[1] ANDERSSON, J. G. *Children of the Yellow Earth*, Routledge & Kegan Paul, London, 1934, p. 142
[2] TREGEAR, T. R. *A Geography of China*, University of London Press, London, 1965, pp. 45–53, 96–100, 199–206
[3] CREEL, G. H. *The Birth of China*, Waverly, Baltimore, 1937
[4] COTTRELL, L. *The Tiger of China*, Evans, London, 1962; Pan Books, London, 1964
[5] BALAZS, E. *Chinese Civilization and Bureaucracy*, Yale University Press, New Haven, Conn., 1964
[6] EBERHARD, W. *A History of China*, Routledge & Kegan Paul, London, 1952
[7] SSU MA CHIENG. *Biographies of Merchants and Industrialists*, Chuan 102, p. 12
[8] TAWNEY, R. H. *Land and Labour in China*, Allen, London, 1932, pp. 87, 74
[9] NEEDHAM, J. 'Science and China's Influence in the World', *The Legacy of China*, R. Dawson (Ed.), Oxford University Press, London, 1964, pp. 238, 293, 290–1, 293
[10] FEURWERKER, A. *China's Early Industrialization: Sheng Hsuan-huai and Mandarin Enterprise*, Harvard East Asian Studies, 1958, pp. 9, 33, 5
[10a] CHENG CHU-YUAN. *Communist China's Economy* 1949–1962, Seton Hall University Press, 1963
[11] HAN SU-YIN. *The Crippled Tree*, Cape, London, 1965
[12] SHINKICHI ETO. 'Hai-lu-feng—the first Chinese Soviet Government', *China Quart.*, No. 8 (1961) 177
[13] SHINKICHI ETO. 'Hai-lu-feng—the first Chinese Soviet Government', *China Quart.*, No. 9 (1961) 155
[14] SNOW, EDGAR. *Red Star over China*, Random House, New York, 1938, pp. 164–188, 176, 431–471, 455
[15] TSAI SHUN-LI. 'The Long March', *China Reconstructs*, XIV, No. 10
[16] BOORMAN, H. L. 'Mao Tse-tung: the Lacquered Image', *China Quart.* No. 16 (1963) 33, 50
[17] PAYNE, R. *Portrait of a Revolutionary: Mao Tse-tung*, Abelard-Schumann, New York, 1961, p. 222
[18] MAO TSE-TUNG. *On Contradiction*, Foreign Language Press, Peking, 1960, pp. 2–4
[19] MAO TSE-TUNG. *On Practice*, Foreign Language Press, Peking, 1964, pp. 1–4
[20] WITTFOGEL, KARL A. and SCHWARTZ, BENJAMIN. 'The Legend of Maoism', *China Quart.*, Nos. 1 and 2 (1960)
[21] *United States' Relations with China*, U.S. State Dept., Washington, 1949, pp. 314, 316
[22] YANG PEI-HSIN. 'How China Conquered Inflation', *People's China*, June 16, 1950
[23] *Far East Trade*, 20, No. 4, April 1965

2

GEOGRAPHICAL BACKGROUND

IT is not the author's intention to embark on a long and detailed analysis of the physical geography of China. This has already been done by a number of writers. We need look at only those physical phenomena that exercise control or influence on the country's economic resources and on man's use of them, and to hold them constantly in mind as a background to the detailed picture of development which follows in later chapters.

GEOLOGY

In the geological field there are certain factors, which, although remote, have very considerable bearing on the country's economic wealth. The whole country is underlain by a floor of ancient rock from which rise three archaean massifs, known as Tibetia in the west, Gobia in the north and Cathaysia in the south-east, each of which is now a complex of crystalline rocks and metamorphic formations. Between them in the Primary Era lay the great Cathaysian geosyncline. None of these massifs has been completely submerged since these early times. Tibetia has remained most stable; Gobia was covered in part by Tertiary seas; Cathaysia has been subject to violent faulting and folding, and much of it was deeply submerged in late Palaeozoic times[1].

In permo-Carboniferous times a line of Hercynian folding cut right across this Cathaysian geosyncline on an east-west axis. This has remained a significant feature down to the present day and constitutes a physical, economic and ethnological divide. This axis was renewed by further folding in Jurassic (Yen Shan) times and exists today as the Nan Shan–Chin Ling line. The fact that the area north of this divide has not been deeply submerged since Ordovician times has economic significance. During permo-Carboniferous times the geosyncline to the north of the axis formed an extensive continental shelf on which the vast coal measures of Shensi, Shansi, Hopei and Honan were laid down. At this time the geosyncline to the south of the axis was deeply submerged. It was not until the Mesozoic that conditions conducive to coal formation were present. The main coal measures of the south were laid down in the Rhaetic epoch, i.e. the transitional period between the Triassic and Jurassic, when the Himalayan and Chinese Tethys covered the area[2].

During long periods of quiescence in late Triassic, Jurassic and especially Middle and Upper Cretaceous times, thick beds of clays, sandstones and limestones were laid down in the Red Basin of Szechwan and in the lower Yangtze and also in north-west Shansi, north Shensi and Kansu. It is in these formations that the main oil wealth of China has been found[2].

An era of violent volcanic activity followed these periods of quiescence, particularly in south-east China and along the western borders of Szechwan abutting the Tibetan massif, extending northward through Tsinghai and the Kunlun and southward into Indo-China. This volcanic activity resulted in extensive intrusions of granite, granodiorite and porphyry, which are largely responsible for the wealth of non-ferrous minerals, wolfram, tin, antimony, lead, zinc and copper, particularly in south-west China.

Subsequent Tertiary folding of the Alpine Revolution affected China only in west Yunnan, in Sikang and the Himalayan borders of Tibet. Its main economic effect has been to erect a most formidable physical barrier to human movement and to isolate China from Burma and India by means of the deep longitudinal valleys which run from north to south in this region.

Expert geological opinion is divided as to the extent which the Ice Age affected China. There are evidences of considerable ice action in Shansi and in Central China in Kiangsi. However, by far the most significant economic and social effect left by the Ice Age is the widespread deposition of deep beds of loess over north-west China. This fine, air-borne soil lies, in places, to a depth of 250 ft and more. Given adequate water supply, it is very fertile.

TOPOGRAPHY

Greater China, in its western parts, consists of a series of descending plateaux, from the ancient massif of Tibet with peaks rising from 25,000 to 28,000 ft from a floor with a general level of over 12,000 ft successively downward to the north and north-east through Tsinghai, Tarim Basin, Dzungaria and Inner Mongolia.

The Tibet Plateau is, for the most part, an inhospitable alpine plateau, consisting of a series of mountain ranges having a marked east-west trend, between which lie wide, windswept, unoccupied valleys. Only in the lower, more hospitable south-east corner of Tibet is there chance of immediate development.

Moving in a north-easterly direction from Tibet, one steps down to an average level of between 7,000 and 10,000 ft in the Tsaidam of Tsinghai, which is bounded on the south by the Kunlun Mountains and on the north by the Astin Tagh and Nan Shan. Much of the region is covered by salt marsh and salt lakes. Nevertheless, it has considerable potentialities for agricultural and industrial development.

Still farther north-east beyond the Nan Shan lies the plateau of Inner Mongolia, which has an average level of between 3,000 and 6,000 ft. Inner Mongolia forms the southern part of the great Mongolian basin, which has the Gobi Desert at its heart and semi-desert and steppeland at its periphery.

Immediately to the north of Tibet and lying between the Kunlun and the T'ien Shan is the Sinkiang Uighur Autonomous Region. The Kunlun constitute a formidable mountain wall, descending in a matter of 30 to 40 miles from snow-capped ranges of 18,000 to 20,000 ft to a mere 3,000 to 5,000 ft, which is the general level of the basin. Along the northern borders of the basin, the Tarim flows from west to east, losing itself eventually in the sands of the Taklamakan, one of the world's most forbidding deserts. The oases surrounding this desert are watered by streams descending from the ice fields of the Kunlun and T'ien Shan and have been the foci of the Turko population over many centuries, and are the centres of very marked development today.

Yet another basin, Dzungaria, somewhat lower than the Tarim Basin, lies to the north between the T'ien Shan and the Altai. This consists mainly of semi-desert and steppe and is the scene of China's recently discovered and most promising oilfield.

Although these huge plateau regions differ radically from each other, they have one common factor. They are all areas of inland drainage, being cut off by high surrounding ranges from the influence of inflowing moisture-laden winds. Consequently they are studded, to a greater or less degree, with salt lakes and salt deposits, making them potentially valuable mineral resource areas but complicating future agricultural development.

South-east of Tibet is the highly dissected plateau of Yunnan and Kweichow. The western edge of this plateau was very heavily folded in the Alpine era and is characterized by very deep, steep-sided valleys, running longitudinally north and south. As we have seen, these form a very marked frontier barrier, which has prevented communication between China and India. Drainage of this plateau, unlike the rest, is entirely seaward. It was into this highland that many of China's indigenous southern tribes retreated in the face of the Han Jen southward expansion in the early centuries of the Christian era.

East of these plateaux lie the great river basins of China. In the far North-East—the name given today to Manchuria—are the wide plains of Heilungkiang and Kirin, drained by the Sungari river, which, flowing northward, empties into the Amur on the Sino-Russian Siberian border; while further south the Liao-ho drains Liaoning and finds its outlet in Liaotung Wan, an arm of Po Hai. China's greatest industrial development is taking place in the north-east; it is also the region of large-scale farming and mechanization.

In 'China Proper', i.e. the 18 provinces of old Imperial China, the three great rivers, Hwang-ho, Yangtze Kiang and Si Kiang, flow down from the western plateaux and follow a general easterly direction to the sea.

The Hwang-ho rises in Baya Kara Shan in southern Tsinghai, cuts through this mountainous area to emerge on lower ground at the Liukia Gorge where one of China's new hydro-electric dams has been built. Thence it starts on its great north bend through the Ordos Desert, turns south at Hokowchen to cut its way through deep, soft loess until it is joined by its big right-bank tributary, the Wei-ho. Turning again east, it cuts through the Tungkwan Gorge where the famous multi-purpose San Men Dam has been constructed. Here it spills out on to the Cathaysian geosyncline over which it has built and is still building the great alluvial North China Plain, one of China's most densely populated areas. As more and more detritus is deposited each year during the summer floods, so the geosyncline sinks, keeping time with the deposition. Hwang-ho silt and sands to a depth of over 2,800 ft have been measured and still the base has not been reached. This bids to be a line of tectonic revolution at some future date.

The river has changed its course innumerable times and has successively found its outlet to the sea north and south of the Shantung peninsula. In 1851 it shifted from a course south of Shantung via the Hwai-ho to its present northern outlet into the Po Hai. In 1937, however, the Kuomingtang breached the banks and diverted the waters south again in an attempt to halt the Japanese advance, flooding a vast area and causing great loss of life. The breach was repaired in 1947[1].

The Hwang-ho, Yangtze, Mekong and Salween all have their sources in the highlands of East Tibet and Tsinghai, but whereas the Hwang-ho takes and maintains a general easterly course, the other three swing southward, following the north-south trend of the alpine folding. Until the middle of Pliocene times the Yangtze continued this direction in company with the Mekong and Salween. Then, as a result of the capture by rivers of Szechwan, it swung east through the Red Basin and, after cutting its way through the gorges between Wanhsien and Ichang, emerged into the two great alluvial, lake-studded basins of Central China (Hupeh and Hunan) and the delta region of Anhwei, Kiangsu and Chekiang. Both basins are of the Yangtze's own making. These three basins, the Red, the Central and the Delta form China's largest, richest, most productive and most populated area[1].

The Si Kiang (West river), smallest of China's great river basins, rises in the Yunnan-Kweichow plateau and flows in an easterly direction to enter the sea in the Pearl river estuary, where it is joined by the Peh Kiang (North river) and Tung Kiang (East river). The river, which drains Kwangtung and Kwangsi Chuang Autonomous Region, lies very largely within the tropics and is consequently the chief double-cropping rice region of the country. This is the land of the Cantonese—the T'ang Jen[1].

Mention must be made of the deeply dissected peneplain of the south-east, which covers a large part of Chekiang and Fukien provinces. In ancient times this was the land of the Min-Yueh, who for long resisted the Han expansion southward. It has also been the home of large numbers of Hakka (Guest) people when they were driven south. It is a mountainous region of short, fast-flowing rivers down to a rugged, indented coast, the home of China's main seafaring people.

CLIMATE

The People's Republic of China has an area of 3,657,765 square miles. It covers 36° latitude, stretching from Hainan (18°N) in the tropics to Dzhalinda (54°N) in north Heilungkiang, and 60° longitude from Fuyuan (134°E) to the borders of west Sinkiang (74°E).

Its vast size can best be demonstrated by comparison with North America and Europe. Superimposed on North America, east Kirin would coincide with Nova Scotia and Sinkiang with California, north Heilungkiang with Hudson Bay and Hainan with Jamaica. Superimposed on Europe it would cover the whole of the Mediterranean from end to end; Heilungkiang would coincide with the heart of Russia in Europe and Hainan would lie in the vicinity of Khartoum.

Once this immensity is realized, one appreciates that it is inaccurate to speak of 'the Climate of China'. Like North America, China has a variety of climates, covering the whole gamut of temperate zone types, with the exception of Temperate Maritime and Mediterranean, which are absent because China has no western seaboard. The big range of latitude, longitude and altitude account for much of these differences from the tropical climate of Hainan and Kwangtung to the continental climate of the North-East, the temperate desert of Sinkiang and Inner Mongolia and the high desert of Tibet.

Yet, in spite of this great variety, one common causal factor can be traced throughout, giving to all a certain family likeness. China forms a considerable part of the eastern side of the great Euro-Asian land and it is this continentality, which imparts the common factor. The deep high pressure system, which forms rapidly in winter over the heart of the continent as a result of rapid cooling of the land, gives rise to cold, dry, out-flowing winds. As summer approaches and the land mass heats up, this high pressure gives way to a widespread low pressure with resulting moisture-laden inflowing winds. Thus, this alternation of pressure sets up a seasonal monsoon rhythm, which is reflected in greater or less degree throughout the whole country[1].

All regions without exception show a summer maximum of precipitation, however small. The difference in amount is very great, varying from 85 in p.a. in Hongkong to 4 in p.a. in Kashgar. The heaviest rainfall is over the uplands of the south-east provinces; it decreases as winds penetrate the land mass in a north and north-westerly direction. Here again the tectonic axis of the Tsinling–Funiu Shan comes into evidence. It marks roughly the 25 in isohyet and, in consequence, the divide between the main rice and wheat producing regions.

Two other rainfall factors are of considerable economic importance. The farther inland toward the north-west one proceeds, the greater is the percentage of the annual rainfall during the summer months. When to this fact is added the second, that in this same north-west region the percentage variability of annual precipitation is much greater than in the wetter south-east, the reason for drought and famine disaster here becomes apparent. Unreliability of rainfall increases in inverse ratio to the amount that falls.

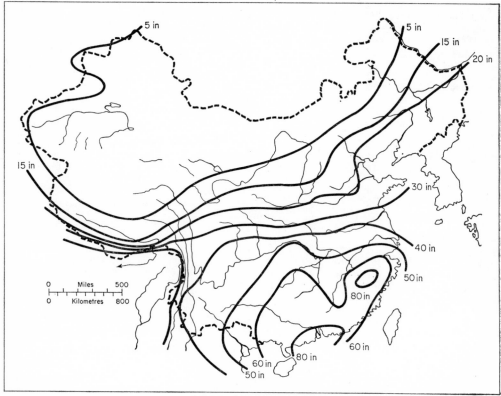

Map 6. Annual mean rainfall

All regions in China have hot summers. Few places, unless of great altitude, have a mean monthly average temperature of less than 70°F. Annual range of temperature increases markedly with continentality. Thus, the farther inland one goes, the greater the extremes. Hong Kong, with a January minimum of 60°F and July maximum of 82°F, has a range of 20° as compared with Harbin with —2·0° in January and 72°F in July, and Lukchun, in the Turfan depression, with 14°F in January and 90°F in July.

Although China is not harassed by the terrors of tornados as is the United States, its south-east shores suffer considerable damage from typhoons, which originate in equatorial Pacific Ocean somewhere north of New Guinea and proceed westward over the Philippines to Indo-China, China and Japan. They are most prevalent between July and November. Many of them turn north and north-east as they approach Taiwan, but a number strike Kwangtung and Fukien each year, bringing disaster to crops and shipping. Happily they quickly lose their typhoonic force if they continue an inland track. Nevertheless inland regions suffer some damage from 'pao feng', fierce winds, which spring up suddenly in summer.

29

Table 2.1.   *Mean Monthly Temperature* (°F) *and Rainfall* (inches)

Agricultural Region	Jan.	Feb.	Mar.	Apl.	May	Jun.	Jly.	Aug.	Sept.	Oct.	Nov.	Dec.	Total (in)
Pastoral													
Urumchi	5	8	19	48	62	68	73	70	60	40	24	12	
(2,969 ft)	0·2	0·1	0·2	0·4	0·5	0·6	0·2	0·3	0·4	0·6	0·2	0·2	3·9
Kashgar	22	32	47	64	67	76	82	78	67	54	39	28	
(4,003 ft)	0·2	0·2	0·2	0·6	0·8	1·0	0·2	0·2	0·0	0·6	0·0	0·0	4·0
Luchun (−56 ft)	14	27	46	66	76	85	90	86	74	55	33	18	
Spring Wheat													
Saratsi	5	15	32	47	64	69	73	70	57	44	24	5	
(3,078 ft)	0·1	0·2	0·3	0·3	0·9	1·8	3·9	2·9	2·0	0·6	0·1	0·1	13·5
Lanchow	20	24	39	53	61	70	73	71	62	49	37	25	
(5,105 ft)	0·2	0·2	0·2	0·6	1·2	1·1	4·0	5·9	2·6	0·6	0·0	0·1	16·7
Winter Wheat, Millet													
Sian	33	39	50	63	75	82	86	82	72	63	44	35	
(1,095 ft)	0·4	0·3	0·6	1·7	2·0	2·8	3·3	5·0	1·6	1·6	0·2	0·4	20·0
Taiyuan	17	26	39	54	65	73	77	73	63	51	36	22	
(2,592 ft)	0·3	0·0	0·4	0·3	0·6	1·7	4·9	3·4	1·6	0·6	0·0	0·1	13·8
Winter Wheat, Kaoliang													
Peking	23	29	41	57	68	76	79	76	68	54	38	27	
(131 ft)	0·1	0·2	0·2	0·6	1·4	3·0	9·4	6·3	2·6	0·6	0·3	0·1	24·9
Tsinan	30	35	47	61	71	80	82	80	72	61	47	34	
(154 ft)	0·4	0·3	0·4	0·8	1·4	2·8	7·7	7·1	2·2	0·7	0·6	0·4	24·8
Corn, Kaoliang													
Harbin	−2	5	24	42	56	66	72	69	58	40	21	3	
(525 ft)	0·2	0·2	0·4	0·9	1·7	4·1	5·8	4·2	2·2	1·2	0·4	0·2	21·5
Shenyang	9	14	28	46	60	70	76	74	62	48	29	14	
(144 ft)	0·2	0·2	0·8	1·1	2·2	3·4	6·3	6·1	3·3	1·6	1·1	0·2	26·4
Wheat, Rice													
Shanghai	39	39	46	56	65	73	80	80	73	63	52	42	
(33 ft)	2·0	2·3	3·4	3·7	3·6	7·4	5·9	5·7	4·7	3·1	2·0	1·3	45·2
Hankow	40	43	50	62	71	80	85	85	77	67	55	45	
(118 ft)	1·8	1·9	3·8	6·0	6·5	9·6	7·1	3·8	2·8	3·2	1·9	1·1	49·6
Szechwan Rice													
Chengtu	44	46	55	63	70	76	78	78	71	64	56	46	
(1,560 ft)	0·2	0·4	0·6	1·7	2·8	4·1	5·7	9·7	4·1	1·8	0·4	0·1	31·6
Chungking	47	50	58	67	74	79	82	84	76	67	59	50	
(755 ft)	0·6	0·8	1·4	4·0	5·5	7·1	5·6	5·1	5·8	4·6	2·0	0·9	43·5
Yangtze Rice, Tea													
Changsha	43	46	51	63	71	79	86	86	77	66	55	43	
(295 ft)	1·8	3·8	5·8	6·1	7·8	8·8	4·8	5·2	3·4	3·6	3·1	1·8	56·0
Hangchow	40	42	48	59	68	76	83	82	74	65	53	43	
(44 ft)	2·8	3·6	4·6	5·2	5·4	8·9	5·3	5·7	6·4	3·2	2·8	2·3	58·3
Plateau Rice													
Kweiyang	37	42	53	63	71	72	76	77	68	57	53	47	
(4,560 ft)	1·0	1·1	0·9	2·9	7·0	8·1	9·0	4·1	5·4	4·2	2·0	0·6	46·3
Kunming	48	51	60	66	70	72	70	70	66	63	56	49	
(5,940 ft)	0·5	0·5	0·6	0·7	3·8	6·1	9·4	8·2	5·4	3·6	1·7	0·6	41·1
Double Cropping Rice													
Canton	56	57	63	71	80	81	83	83	80	75	67	60	
(49 ft)	0·9	1·9	4·2	6·8	10·6	10·6	8·1	8·5	6·5	3·4	1·2	0·9	63·6
Foochow	53	52	56	64	72	80	84	84	76	67	59	50	
(66 ft)	1·8	3·8	4·5	4·8	5·9	8·2	6·3	7·2	8·4	2·0	1·6	1·9	56·5

SOILS AND NATURAL VEGETATION

All soils are derived originally from parent rock, which is broken down by either mechanical (sun, frost, wind, etc.) or chemical action. The nature of the soil will thus depend, in the first instance, upon the character of the parent rock, but in the long run, climate, augmented by biological agents, including man, is the more important formative factor. This being so, and bearing in mind the great diversity of climates in China, it is not surprising to find a similar diversity of soils and also that soil zonality corresponds closely with climatic regions. The natural vegetational cover, in its turn, is determined by climate and soil cover.

Soils are usually classified into two major categories, pedocals and pedalfers. Pedocals are those soils which are rich in lime. They are found in regions of low precipitation and consequently are unleached. Pedalfers, on the other hand, are acid soils from which lime has been leached, leaving a considerable alumina and iron residue. Pedalfers are found in regions of high precipitation.

Once again the Nan Shan–Tsin Ling line asserts itself as a divide. With the exception of saline and calcareous coastal strips in Chekiang and Kiangsu and the neutral purple and brown forest soils of Szechwan, where a balance between the two is maintained, all China south of the Tsin Ling has pedalfer soils. All regions north of this line, with the exception of Shantung, where precipitation is greater than other northern areas and soils are leached to some extent, have unleached pedocal soils.

Subdivision of these two main categories is very complicated. Ma Yung-Chih has divided the country into 14 major divisions and then subdivided these into a further 54[3, 4]. However, it is sufficient for our purposes to note broader subdivisions, first of pedocals and then of pedalfers, having reference to their economic implications.

Pedocals

(1) The alluvial plain of north China has been built up, as we have seen, by the silt deposited by the annual summer flooding of the Hwang-ho and Hwai-ho. To this is added the fine dust brought from the loess region farther west by the winter dust storms each year. The resultant soil is yellow or yellow-grey in colour and is light in texture; thus it is easy to work. It is naturally fertile, but has been occupied for 40 centuries by peasant farmers, who have worked, cropped and fed it until it is impossible to distinguish between what is nature's and what is man's handiwork. This is also true of plant growth. Man has cut, cleared and planted to such an extent that vegetation is almost entirely of his determining. On the highlands, less under this dominance, the natural vegetation is deciduous broad-leaved forest.

(2) Farther west is the great loess plateau of Shansi, Shensi and Kansu. Loess is a fine aeolian dust, transported from the dry interior and deposited on the hills of these provinces to depths of over 250 ft, obliterating much of their outlines. In places the dust is as fine as talcum powder. The soil formed from it is yellow and chestnut, designated siero-korichnevyi by Ma, and is very fertile, given adequate moisture. Stone Age deposits go to show that this region was then covered by primaeval forest. Either through man's action or climatic change, it is now treeless[5]. Loess is very prone to erosion; terracing of the hill-sides is essential, a development which is going on very extensively in this region today.

(3) Stretching from the north-east in the Upper Liao and Upper Sungari basins and through eastern and central Inner Mongolia is a long belt of chernozem, chestnut and brown soils. These are the great steppelands of China, which lie north of the 15 in isohyet. Light soils have been developed under the natural grass cover. In the last 10 years there has been considerable extension of agriculture, under irrigation, in these grasslands. Unless care is exercised, this could easily become a 'dust bowl'.

(4) Podzolic and brown soils occur on the mountain lands of the Ta Hingan and Siao Hingan in Heilungkiang, and along the Sino-Korean-Soviet border. These are regions of coniferous forest and mixed coniferous and deciduous broad-leaved forest. They provide one of the main sources of timber today.

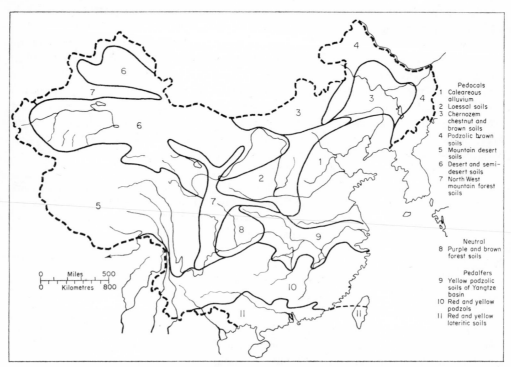

Map 7. Soil-vegetation regions of China

(5) Lying west of both the loess and steppelands are the wide desert and semi-desert lands. Tibet is covered entirely by mountain steppe and mountain desert soils, which have a high salt content and, except in the south-eastern part of the plateau, which is lower and wetter and has Alpine meadow soils, has a very sparse halophytic vegetational cover.

(6) West Inner Mongolia and Sinkiang, although lower than Tibet, are equally land-locked and dry. Their soils are characterized by low humus content and little chemical activity. They have a high lime content and are salinized to varying degrees. Natural vegetation consists of drought-resisting grasses and halophytic shrubs.

(7) The mountains of west and north-west China border much of the steppe, desert and semi-desert and have marked vertical changes of soil, ranging from chernozem, through chestnut soils and forest soils to mountain meadow soils at great heights. The vegetational zones are likewise distinct.

Neutral Soils

(8) Over much of Szechwan and on the mountains of east Shansi and Shantung there are purple and brown forest soils. These are regions in which leaching is moderate and a

32

balance is maintained between acidity and alkalinity. As the soil description indicates, the associated vegetation is mixed coniferous and deciduous forest.

Pedalfers

South of the Tsin ling ranges rainfall is heavier and temperatures are higher; therefore chemical processes in soil formation are intenser and leaching is greater than in the areas to the north. Soils increase in acidity as one goes southward.

(9) The lower Yangtze basin, including much of the basin of the left bank tributary, Han river and right bank tributaries, Siang and Kan, is overlain with thick deposits of alluvium, which result in yellow podzolic soils. Like the Hwang-ho basin, deposition is still going on, but because of heavier rainfall and consequent leaching, Yangtze basin soils are rather more acid. Formerly this was a region of dense mixed deciduous and evergreen broad-leaved forest. It is now even more densely populated than the North China Plain and all forest has been cleared, except on the remoter mountain sides, and all land intensively cultivated.

(10) Red and yellow podzolic soils cover the vast hill-lands lying between the Yangtze and Si Kiang alluviums and extend westward over the Yunnan-Kweichow plateau. These soils increase in acidity southward. The associated natural vegetation is evergreen broad-leaved forest.

(11) South Kwangtung, South Kwangsi, Hainan and Taiwan lie within the tropics and have highly acid yellow and red soils, with marked lateritic tendencies. Leaching is excessive and constant feeding of the soil is essential. Monsoon rain forest is the natural cover, which has been extensively cleared, especially over the alluvial plain of the Si Kiang.

REFERENCES

[1] TREGEAR, T. R. *A Geography of China*, University of London Press, London, 1965, pp. 1–8, 206–226, 230–254, 254–260, 13–33
[2] LEE, J. S. *Geology of China*, Murby, London 1939, pp. 155–161, 183–184
[3] MA YUNG-CHIH. 'General Principles of Geographical Distribution of Chinese Soils', *Rep. 6th Int. Congr. Soil Sci.* 1956
[4] HU HSIOH-YU, CHEN CHANG-TU and WANG HSIEN-PU. 'Vegetation of China with Special Reference to the Main Soil Types', *Rep. 6th Int. Congr. Soil Sci.*, 1956
[5] ANDERSSON, J. G. *Children of the Yellow Earth*, Routledge & Kegan Paul, London, 1934, p. 169

3

CONTEMPORARY AGRICULTURAL DEVELOPMENT

'If, in a period of roughly three five-year plans, we cannot fundamentally solve the problem of agricultural co-operation, if we cannot jump from small-scale farming with animal-drawn farm implements to large-scale farming with machinery—which includes state-sponsored land reclamation carried out on a large scale by settlers using machinery (the plan being to bring under cultivation 400–500 million *mow* of virgin land in the course of three five-year plans)—we shall fail to resolve the contradiction between ever-increasing demand for marketable grain and industrial raw materials and the present generally poor yield of staple crops. In that case our socialist industrialization will run into formidable difficulties: we shall not be able to complete socialist industrialization.'

Mao Tse-tung. *The Question of Agricultural Co-operation*, Peking, 1956

ORGANIZATION

WE have recorded (pp. 8–9) the warning given by R. H. Tawney in 1932 as he reviewed the miserable and parlous state to which the peasantry had been reduced during the decades of unrest in the twentieth century. Land reform, the return of 'the land to the tiller', had been one of the main planks of Sun Yat Sen's platform as he built up his Nationalist Party, the Kuomintang (K.M.T.) in the early twenties. This and the redress of the peasants' grievances figured prominently in the propaganda which preceded the victorious march of the K.M.T. and Communist armies of the Northern Expedition in 1926 and it was this promise and expectation which did much to gain the support of the land-hungry peasantry in the overthrow of the war-lords. Failure in succeeding years to implement this promise of land reform was one of the deep causes of the eventual collapse of the K.M.T.

Land Reform

The C.C.P., after their expulsion from central China and after their Long March, found a comparatively secure centre in the north-west in Yenan, Shensi. From this centre they ruled a wide area of loess land in which they experimented and developed theory and practice in the change from private land ownership and individual cultivation to co-operation and socialization. After three years of bitter civil war the Communists swept southward in 1949 and within 12 months were masters of the whole country. The invading armies were preceded by propaganda almost identical with that used in the Northern Expedition of 1926 and again the peasantry clutched at the chance of escape from their poverty and oppression. This time they were not disappointed. The C.C.P. set about land reform, but the process was not completed until the end of 1952 or beginning of 1953.

Land reform, the dispossession of the landlord class and the redistribution of land among the tillers, must be regarded as a deliberate and integral first step in a progression towards communal ownership of the land. The C.C.P. made no secret that this was their intention, although, in the early stages, it is doubtful if this was appreciated by any but a very small minority of the peasantry. On the political side of the C.C.P. intention was, at one and the same time, to create a lively sense of class consciousness and hatred in the peasantry, a hatred which at times and places ran beyond the power of the central government to control, and also to secure the loyalty and support of the poorer peasantry, which formed, by far, the greater proportion and on which the Communists have throughout placed their main reliance. The overthrow of the landlord class from which, throughout the centuries, the scholar-administrators have been drawn, has been and still is a very present objective in the communist revolution—and with some reason. Chinese history abounds with examples of peasant revolts against intolerable conditions, resulting in the overthrow of an oppressive government or dynasty only to find the old scholar-administrator, because of his monopoly in government know-how, quickly back in the saddle.

For purposes of land redistribution the rural population was divided into six classes: landlords, rich peasants, middle peasants, lower middle peasants, poor peasants and labourers or landless. In China there were few, if any, landlords owning large estates comparable with those of the big Russian land-owners. Most Chinese estates did not exceed 100 acres. Nevertheless, landlords were stripped of all land that they were renting out. Rich and middle peasants had to surrender any land which they were not farming directly themselves. The central authorities ruled that, in certain circumstances, land which was worked by hired labour might be retained, but more often than not, rich peasants were dispossessed of this surplus at village meetings. The confiscated land was then redistributed to the middle and poor peasants and the landless on a *per capita* family basis and title deeds issued. This distribution, which was completed earlier in the northern regions than the south, was carried through with a great deal of bitterness and vindictiveness and not a little loss of life. Public denunciation meetings fanned class hatred to a pitch difficult to control at times.

Mutual Aid Teams

At this time the C.C.P. was trying to do two things which were mutually contradictory. While land reform, the distribution of 'land to the tillers' was absolutely obligatory if the loyalty of the peasantry was to be secured, it was, by its very nature, inimical to the second essential which was the immediate, rapid increase of food. The immediate effect of land reform was to increase fragmentation of holdings, which already were minute. Moreover, the new land-owners, although enthusiastic and proud of their property, were, on the whole, less experienced and less competent cultivators. In consequence there was a decline rather than an increase in agricultural production.

To meet this situation the C.C.P. drew on the experience they had gained in the liberated regions of the north-west[2]. Mutual Aid Teams were quickly instituted. Three to six households came together to work on common tasks on each other's lands during the busy seasons —the simplest form of co-operation. This was no real innovation as it had been practised in an attenuated form in China throughout the centuries. The mutual advantages were obvious and, since it in no way challenged the newly acquired title to ownership, it quickly received fairly universal acquiescence and practice. Between 1949 and 1952 the functions of the Mutual Aid Teams were expanded. Teams were extended to include a larger number of households and were formed for the whole year; some tools and animals were owned jointly. Any reclaimed land became common property and was cultivated by the whole team. Thus the embryo of socialization was introduced, but so small a degree of co-operation was quite inadequate to achieve the necessary increase in food production and was only the first small step towards the full collective ownership of land and means of production.

Elementary Producers' Co-operatives

In 1953 experiments were made in the formation of what came to be known as elementary or semi-socialist producers' co-operatives in which members contributed their land, animals and tools for joint cultivation by the whole. Because this involved some encroachment of the newly acquired rights of ownership, the C.C.P. Central Committee was very conscious of possible opposition and therefore moved very cautiously. To soften the transition, it laid down certain requisites and directives to cadres involved. Entry by the peasant was to be voluntary and to be undertaken only when the whole scheme was fully understood. Each co-operative was to be economically independent; profit and loss its own concern[3]. The mutual benefits of co-operation were emphasized; the rich and middle peasants were assured that at least there would be no fall in income and the poor peasant could look to a rise. Withdrawal from the co-operative was optional, although, as might be expected, this was a difficult and socially unpopular step. Nevertheless, at a later stage, in some regions where returns to rich and middle peasants fell below their former receipts, there were wholesale withdrawals for a time.

Although there was no universal standard or blue print laid down for these early co-operatives, they were expected to conform to a general pattern[4]. Central Committee directives required that they should be democratically based on annually elected management committees. Theoretically this placed management in the hands of the members, but in fact, in the vast number of instances leadership and control fell into the hands of Party-appointed cadres and keen Party members.

Remuneration to co-operative members was calculated partly on the amount of capital in the form of land, animals and tools contributed, and partly on the amount and quality of labour performed for which 'work points' were awarded. Work was organized on the basis of 'production terms' of 7 to 10 households. The intention was that there should be a gradual change in the proportion of return from land and from labour, starting from 60% from land and 40% from labour, moving to 50% each, then to 30% and 70% respectively, until eventually no rent at all should be paid. It was pointed out that, if production increased sufficiently, the return to, say, a middle peasant from labour alone could be greater than his original receipts from both land and labour. All members kept their own small holdings for private cultivation[5].

Urged on by periodic speeches by Mao Tse-tung, these elementary producers' co-operatives increased more rapidly than had been anticipated, nearly doubling their numbers between April and August, 1954, from 58,000 to 100,000 and having 1,700,000 members. At this time the size of co-operatives varied between 20 and 50 households. By May, 1956 it is estimated that 110 million families, comprising 91% of the rural population were organized into a million or so elementary producers' co-operatives. By the end of the year this figure had risen to nearly 2 million[6]. Doubtless, the ease and rapidity of growth was fostered by obvious advantages to the members. The larger fields made ploughing easier and the use of better techniques possible. Also, the under-employed farm labour in the off-seasons was put to better use in such small works as local road building and irrigation works with clear advantage to the whole village. From the point of view of the central government, the bigger units made control and direction of agricultural output more feasible.

Advanced Producers' Co-operatives

Although these semi-socialist co-operatives had achieved considerable increase in agricultural production, politics and economics demanded further advances. Politics required a further move towards the ultimate objective of communism. Economics required still more rapid production since it was almost entirely on the surplus—the savings—of agriculture that the capital needed for vast industrial development depended. Thus it was that early in 1956 elementary producers' co-operatives began to be converted into advanced or socialist producers' co-operatives, which were, in effect, collective farms. Individual title to land, which had been upheld till now, was forfeited, together with ownership of draught animals and farm implements. The individual farmer received some compensation for his capital contribution, but his income henceforth was based entirely on the labour he contributed. Private ownership of small holdings and the family holding of hog and chicken alone were permitted. The size of these new units was considerably larger than the elementary co-operatives, embracing between 100 and 200 families, who were organized into Production Brigades and Production Teams. It should be noted that the transition from one form to the other was uneven throughout the country. As might be expected, it was quicker and more complete in the north and north-east and slower in the south-west among the minority groups.

The loss of ownership rights brought considerable initial unrest and opposition to the formation of advanced co-operatives, but this melted surprisingly quickly and their inauguration was very rapid. It is estimated that by the end of June, 1956, 75 million rural households (62·5%) out of a total of 120 millions were members of advanced co-operatives and that by the end of the year over 105 million households had joined. More serious and deep-seated criticism emerged later in 1957 due largely to the growth of bureaucracy consequent on the increased size of units. Officious and often ignorant direction from cadres led to much discontent among the peasants and to some fall in production. Government decisions to reduce the size of co-operatives and so ensure the placing of greater responsibility and power in the hands of the actual cultivator were taken but, before they could be implemented, a greater change in a diametrically opposite direction took place.

The Commune

The precise manner by which communes came into existence is still somewhat obscure, but what is certain is that some 25 to 30 advanced co-operatives in Honan in April, 1958 amalgamated to form one single unit, the first commune. This took place at the beginning of the period of fanatical enthusiasm and energy, which came to be known as 'The Great Leap Forward' and marked a spate of such amalgamations. After Mao Tse-tung had visited the Honan commune and given it his approval, the movement swept the country. Before the year was out 99% of the rural population was organized into these large units, reducing the 700,000 or so advanced co-operatives to 26,500 communes, averaging 4,750 households apiece.

They are by no means uniform either in size, management or function, although they all conform to a general pattern. Northern farms in the past generally have been larger than those in the south and therefore one would expect the same to be true of northern communes. On the whole this is so, but there are notable exceptions. For example, the Fwah Tung People's Commune, 45 miles from Canton, has a population of 51,050, covers 150 square miles and has 365 production teams, each having about 80 families[7], while the Yangtan People's Commune in south Shansi numbers only 11,000 persons, has only 61 production teams and covers only 150 km[8].

The communes have taken over all the local government functions previously performed by the 'hsiang' and much more besides, but they still remain integral parts of the 'hsien' or county. They have become responsible for the organization of all the activities of the people within their compass—for agriculture, rural industry, water conservancy, afforestation, communications, education, civil defence, health and public hygiene, cultural and recreational activities.

Such an all-embracing local authority has required a vast re-organization. It is remarkable that, considering the inexperience of the majority of administrators—the emphasis placed on class struggle and giving authority to the poor and lower-middle peasantry as far as possible—the transition has taken place without utter chaos and catastrophe.

The structure of the commune is clear and straightforward. At the head is the commune, under which are the production brigades and the production teams. Once every 2 years commune members elect delegates to a Commune Delegates Conference. Election and representation is indirect, from production team through production brigade. An endeavour is made in a well-run commune to see that the various facets of its life are properly represented. The Delegates Conference is responsible for the general policy and direction of the commune and usually meets about twice a year. From its members it elects its administrative and executive body, the Commune Management Committee, which invariably will include the local C.C.P. secretary and the Communist Youth League secretary. Sub-committees are then appointed to take care of the various aspects of the commune's activities, production, finance, trade, education, health, militia, etc.

Apart from its general co-ordinating functions, the commune is required 'to organize its activities with high militancy and improve its productive efficiency and labour discipline'. The Commune Management Committee periodically receives from the State Planning Organization the production targets proposed for the commune for the year. These proposals are sent down to the production brigades for discussion, amendment and approval and the brigades, in their turn, refer them to their respective production teams. The success or failure of commune production is closely bound up with these discussions and decisions and a great deal depends on the quality of brigade and team leadership, which is most onerous. It has been found by experience that the full consent of production teams must be secured if fulfillment is to be assured. In the early stages, ignorant and officious direction from above, without sufficient regard for local conditions, led to much discontent and a campaign for the relegation of local decisions to 'the tillers', i.e. the production teams, who will best know the local conditions. The following newspaper article voiced this complaint at the time:

'What are the characteristics of a particular plot? What is the quality of the soil? What are the crops suited to the land? How should sowing be arranged? Over these questions, only those team members and cadres who are most familiar with local conditions have the right to speak. Under no circumstances may other people, regardless of the concrete circumstances, require production teams to plant crops that are not suited to the concrete conditions, though such people may have good intentions. If they do so, even high-yield crops will frequently be turned into low yield ones.'

'If such powers of production administration are not delegated to the production teams, if their rights are not respected, if they are not allowed to make their own decisions, and if everything is managed from the production brigade level, it will be impossible to arrange production according to the land, the seasons, crops and manpower. It will do great harm to agricultural production.'[9]

We have indicated above that the inception of the commune was one manifestation of the Great Leap Forward, that fanatical upsurge of enthusiasm, which had as its objective the attainment of 'communism in our time', a call to all to implement at once the ideal of 'from each according to his ability, to each according to his need'. All things, with the exception of intimate personal belongings, were to be held in common. Private plots held by individual members of co-operatives became commune property; all houses and house sites, tree holdings and livestock came under public ownership. Food at communal halls and kitchens was to be free to all regardless of work performed. Collective living, under the slogan 'Five-together' (working, eating, living, studying and drilling together) was the order of the day.

It required no great length of time to demonstrate clearly that the peasantry was in no way ready for so great an innovation. There was great resentment at the loss of private plots and a marked fall in production followed. Therefore, they were restored quite soon to private ownership with the proviso that they should not exceed 5% of the commune's holding of agricultural land.

Communal feeding, which apparently never attained great proportions, also quickly reverted to the normal family pattern and the system of payment according to work done, i.e. work points, which had been in force under the advanced co-operatives was restored. However, the more complex the organization becomes, the more complicated the assessing of services rendered and of work points becomes. Undoubtedly it is one of the general topics of discussion in all communes.

All, except a few salaried members of the Commune Management Committee, who are working full-time on administration, are paid by work points. The problem of equating the value of the thousand and one jobs, from agricultural and forestry work, through the numerous workshops to transport and educational services is most exacting, especially when one remembers the lack of workers with any degree of experience in accountancy in virtually all districts. The situation in Yangtan is fairly typical:

'The young accountant was busy with his abacus totting up the work points earned by (production) team members last month. We were introduced and learnt that he had had a full primary school education, and had been elected accountant in 1964 when he was 17. He did this work part time and also worked in the fields.'[10]

Jan Myrdal[2] discusses intimately these difficulties and problems.

The basic accounting unit in a commune may be either the production brigades or the individual production teams. Whichever it is, it is responsible for gain and loss and is the owner of the means of production—land, draught animals, tools, etc.—within its jurisdiction, and its management committee is responsible for the working out and implementing the production plans and targets agreed upon, and for the distribution of income. The

39

following table shows the income of the Second Team of the Paching Brigade in 1964 and gives a general idea of its distribution[10].

Expenditure	Amount in yuan	Percentage of expenditure
Production expenses	13,124	38·6
Agricultural tax	2,207	6·5
Reserve fund	1,697	5·0
Welfare fund	330	1·0
Reserve grain	1,488	4·4
Distributed to members	15,104	44·5
Total	33,950	100·0

The production expenses included seed, fertilizer, insecticide and the hiring of tractors, etc. 38·6% is a higher figure than is general (25–30%) and was accounted for by heavy rain and hail storms, necessitating the replanting and fertilizing of the crop. The reserve fund is, in fact, used mainly for capital expenditure on buying new tools, buying livestock, afforestation and land improvement. The Welfare Fund (1% is below what is generally allocated for this purpose) is used in cases of accident, sickness and old age and is intended mainly for those who have no-one in family to depend on. All old people in China are supposed to enjoy security under the 'Five Guarantees'—enough to eat, adequate housing, clothing, day-to-day necessities and a decent burial. The reserve grain, required of all communes against natural disaster, is eventually distributed to members. The 44·5% for distribution to members is below the norm of about 50% on account of bad weather. This is not a high percentage, but it is considerably higher than the poorer peasant could expect from his labours before 1949 when his rent usually took half his produce and he was liable to un-predictable taxation, to say nothing of his endemic indebtedness at exhorbitant rates of interest. His present income is fairly assured and, in most instances, is enough for him to save a little privately, enabling him, in due course, to buy such things as a bicycle, sewing machine and radio. In addition he works his recovered private plot assiduously—too assiduously for the approval of the more communistically minded. The following report from the Peng-pu Commune, near Shanghai gives some idea of the rise in income during the first decade of communist rule:[11]

	yuan
1949 (before Land Reform)	115
1952 (after Land Reform)	130
1954 (elementary co-op.)	169
1956 (advanced co-op.)	190
1958 (early commune)	332

There is considerable discrepancy of income between brigade and brigade, production team and production team owing to differences in natural conditions of soil, water availability, etc. and also to differences in skill in management. A good deal of prominence has been given to efforts to redress this imbalance. A slogan much used in industry and agriculture is 'Compare with, learn from, catch up with and overtake the advanced and help the less advanced'. To this end communes are directed to group their brigades into three categories and exhort the better-off to contribute a higher percentage of their income to the communal reserve fund than the poorer. In this connection Richard Hughes has produced the following table[12]:

Brigade	State taxes %	Cost of Prod. and management %	Communal reserve fund %	Communal welfare fund %	Consumption fund %
Better Production	7	21	21	3	48
Ordinary Production	7	21	18	3	51
Inferior Production	7	21	15	3	54

He points out that, although the percentage allotted to the Consumption Fund of the Better Production Brigades is less than the others, the actual income they receive is higher because of their higher production.

The advantages accruing to this larger unit, the commune, are not difficult to see. Soon after their establishment, a United Nations report (March, 1959) stated that 'the people's communes appear to possess marked advantages from the point of view of technical organization of production'. Specialization and division of labour are possible to a degree denied to the largest of advanced co-operatives. The many departments of agriculture contained within the commune—arable, animal husbandry, market gardening, orchards, afforestation—can be developed and given specialized attention. It has made possible quite simple and obvious techniques, which formerly could not be practised.

'The peasants of Yinhsi (Fukien) had always known that yields could be increased by rotating paddy rice with dry-land crops such as sweet potatoes, peanuts and beans; but when plots were owned by individual peasants, cultivation of a wet crop next to a dry one led to disagreements between neighbours . . . Yinhsi brigade now practises a four-year rotation:

    1st year—early rice, late rice, then barley
    2nd year—beans, then sweet potatoes and peas
    3rd year—early rice, late rice, wheat
    4th year—peanuts, late rice, legumes (to be ploughed in).'[13]

As a result of improved techniques, big increases in production are claimed, as reflected in the Yangtan report[7]:

Crop (average yield (per mow)	Period of individual farming 1951 (catties)	Period of Advanced Co-op. 1955 (catties)	Per cent increase	Under the People's Commune 1965 (catties)	Per cent increase c.f. 1956
Wheat	104·2	168·9	62·1	303	79·4
Cotton	30·2	45·3	50·0	71	56·7

The local industries and handicrafts can be rationalized and speeded up to serve agricultural needs. Labour, so often unemployed or under-employed between peaks of agricultural activity, can be mobilized and productively employed. This factor, more than any other, has enabled the communes to carry out much greater water conservancy works of irrigation and drainage than could be contemplated by the smaller units, although, as will be seen below, this ability to mobilize was carried to impossible lengths in the early stages. This co-ordination of effort, made possible by the bigger unit, has already done much to give greater security to the community in times of natural disaster, the meeting of the threat of flood by dyke raising and strengthening, the care of and replanting of crops

41

in time of drought. The failure of harvests during the years 1959 to 1961 would have resulted in disastrous famine and the loss of millions of lives, as in 1928, had it not been for the co-operation made possible by the communes. As it was, the people escaped with hardship and malnutrition only.

Further virtues of the larger unit are the improvement in communications and the increased opportunities for the mechanization of agriculture which it offers, but one must beware of exaggerating the achievements in these spheres if the Yangtan Commune can be taken as at all typical.

'We have 10 production brigades, but when we started, four of them could not be reached by lorry. Six brigades moved their goods mostly by shoulder pole. The commune repaired the old roads, built new ones, and put all the field paths in order. We laid 38 kilometres of motor road to link up the brigades. We arranged the fields so that 80% of all the commune's land can be worked with tractors.

'There are 42 engines, steam, gasoline and diesel in the commune. Every brigade has a fleet of small carts running on two cycle wheels, 640 of them all told, versatile little things that carry manure, fuel, water, cotton and what not; 68 pneumatic-tyred carts pulled by horses, mules or oxen. The Yangtan Brigade has three lorries. The back-breaking work of carrying heavy loads on men's backs has ended.'[8]

Better credit facilities and marketing have resulted. Also, there has been greater capital accumulation—a very welcome fact from the central authority's point of view. With increase in production there has been increased individual saving and a willingness to plough back profits into the team's or brigade's holding.

The advent of the commune has enabled big changes to be made in the social field. Amongst these are the public health and hygiene services, which have been greatly expanded; serious attack has been possible on such diseases as malaria, hookworm, and schistosomiasis, which have been so debilitating and a constant cause of low production[14].

It has already been indicated above that, in spite of, and to some measure, because of—the extravagant enthusiasm which accompanied the launching of the rural people's communes that were supposed to be like 'a fine horse, which having shaken off its bridle, is galloping courageously directly towards the highway of Communism'[15], their early history is full of problems and shortcomings. Egged on by local party cadres, in their initial enthusiasm, commune management committees, brigades and teams vied with each other in setting production targets, which became impossibly high. Rather than admit failure or inadequacy, returns were falsified, resulting quickly in confusion and a breakdown in the State Statistical Bureau, which was just attaining a professional basis and status. This upsurge was not confined to agriculture. The Great Leap Forward called for immediate and immense increases in industrial production, particularly in iron and steel. In 1958–9 there was an outburst of rural iron production in hundreds of thousands of tiny mud-brick blast furnaces in backyards, which drew much-needed agricultural workers away from their fields just when they were most needed to reap a bumper harvest. In the ensuing confusion the central government was slow to recognize the imminent agricultural crisis and to diagnose its true causes. 'The leadership was also unable to ascertain fully the true causes of the crisis. To accomplish this latter objective they would have had to require detailed seasonal and area breakdowns in data so that they could separate out the effects of poor organization from the effects of the bad weather that affected most of China between 1959 and 1961.'[6]

Disillusionment accompanied these bad harvests. There had been wide discontent with the loss of private plots and a discernible fall in production followed. Their restoration to private ownership was essential, but higher authority was reluctant to do so as it was a retreat in the march towards Communism. An attempt was made to hedge their return with restrictions. Not more than 5% of the cultivated land of the commune may be held in private plots and some attempt was made to limit the time and fertilizer that individuals might expend upon them. Free markets in towns at which co-operative members were able to sell their surplus produce had been discontinued on the formation of communes. During the acute shortages between 1959 and 1962 these markets were reopened but, with the better harvests of succeeding years, they have largely faded out since 'commune members found it uneconomic to peddle their produce in towns, as had been done during the period of shortage. Consequently they sold their surplus to producers and consumers' co-operatives where the price was at par with the Government-operated markets.'[16]

During the first years of the communes there was a great deal of regimentation of labour. Millions of men and women were organized on a military basis, formed into battalions, brigades and companies, assembled at bugle call and marched with banners flying to whatever the assigned task. Many of the tasks were enormous and, in most instances, were tackled with great patriotic zeal. The report of the famous Hua Mu-lan women's battalion reads like an emulation of the legendary Yu, who, whilst quelling the floods, never once entered his home although he frequently passed his door[17].

'They were just like men, acting as if fighting a battle. They ate and slept right in the field. After the establishment of the battalion not a single member left her post for 10 days and nights. Continually, during this period of combat labour, they passed the doors of their homes without entering or requesting permission to visit the premises even briefly.'

'In Shantung province 15 million men, women and children, deployed together from neighbouring communes, were organized into divisions and regiments to deep-plough 80 million *mow* of land. In Liaotung province, to rush through the deep-ploughing of 45 million *mow*, 4·2 million persons were mobilized for the same "combat labour manoeuvres". To transport iron ore and coke in Shantung, before deep-ploughing, 100,000 civilian workers were organized, queuing up in untiring lines, day and night; many slept only 3 hours a night during the emergency.'[12]

This initial outburst of energy was too exhausting. It could not be maintained, even by so tough a people as the Chinese, and had to give way to a more reasonable approach and more reasonable hours of work. After 6 or 7 years of experiment and adjustment the communes have settled to an accepted general pattern. They have proved their worth as organizations for carrying out the necessary larger works, such as water conservation, irrigation and drainage, and have surrendered much of their original bureaucratic powers to the production brigades and production teams. It is to be hoped that they will be permitted to work out their salvation during the coming decades, undisturbed by further upsurges.

State Farms

In 1949 China was in urgent need of greater food production. Any development from traditional individual peasant farming to large socialized units was bound to take time. Therefore the Government embarked immediately on what, for China, was an entirely new departure—state farming. Once started, the growth of state farms has been very

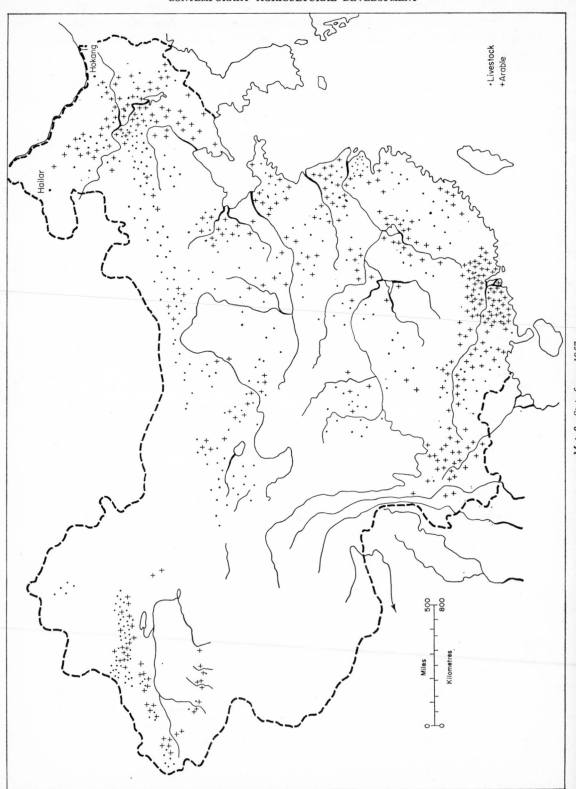

• Livestock
+ Arable

Hokang
Hailar

Miles
Kilometres
500
800

Map 8. State farms, 1957

rapid. In 1952 there were 52 relatively large state farms, covering more than 3·3 million *mow*, (550,000 acres). By 1957 this figure had grown to 710 with an acreage of more than 15 million *mow*. Half a million workers and 10,000 tractors (in terms of 15 h.p. units) were employed, giving a yield of 1,190 *chin* of grain. It is recorded[18] that in 1960 the Ministry of State Farms and Land Reclamation had under its control 2,490 state farms, employing 2·8 million workers and staff members, cultivating more than 78 million *mow* (13 million acres), using 28,000 tractors and producing over 5,000 million *chin* of grain. Since then there have been no comprehensive figures published, but continued reports of new state farms and their achievements indicate that this expansion has continued, probably with increasing intensity, e.g. 36 state farms were opened in 1966 in the north-east bringing 1,112,000 acres of virgin black soil under the plough. Mao Tse-tung has consistently put his faith in this development and has urged the people 'fundamentally solve the problem of agricultural co-operation (that is) . . . jump from small-scale farming with animal-drawn farm implements to large-scale farming with machinery—which includes state-sponsored land reclamation carried out on a large scale by settlers using machinery.'[19]

The objectives of state farms are clearly stated. They are to be the means of greatly increasing production; they are to stand as examples to co-operatives, and later to communes, and to provide them with help wherever possible; they are to be the main agents in the reclamation of the wastelands, especially in border and coastal areas, and they are to be the main means of large-scale resettlement of the people.

On the production side, the task of the state farms is 'to provide the state with marketable grain, cotton, meat and other types of farm and animal products'. Most of the state farms have the virtue that they come into production rapidly and are able to produce considerable quantities of grain in the same or following year in which they are set up. Their recorded performance to date, however, is not very spectacular, and in 1960 yields were judged, on the whole, to be rather disappointing. Sinkiang state farms reported the following yields in 1960:

300 *chin* wheat per *mow* on 100,000 *mow*
960 *chin* maize per *mow* on 600 *mow*

which is low when compared with most eastern commune yields, but this is not a fair comparison since state farming is extensive and commune farming very much more intensive.

By far the greater part of the present production of agricultural machinery goes to these big farms, which, with their huge fields are better able to use the machines than the communes. It is on the state farms that the knowledge and skills in their economical use is learnt. It is the intention that this acquired knowledge shall be disseminated as quickly and as widely as possible. One advantage of China's socialized economy is that there is generally a greater willingness to share knowledge of newly-learnt techniques than there is in a competitive society.

'The majority of China's state farms have been set up on wasteland or uninhabitable land subject to drought or waterlogging, on difficult alkaline or acid soils and in areas regularly hit by sand and wind storms.'[20] These are found mainly in the north-east, north-west, far west and along the coast. It should cause no surprise that the state farms are sited in these marginal, inhospitable regions when it is remembered that all good, easily-worked land has long since been densely occupied.

Many of the earliest state farms were established by soldiers of the P.L.A. (People's Liberation Army) in the first years of the new regime, notably in Sinkiang and the northeast. On or before demobilization they set about land reclamation and settled on it. By 1960 180 mechanized state farms, occupying 11·6 million *mow* had been established in Sinkiang on the north and south slopes of the Tienshan. Many millions of peasants in China Proper, displaced by water conservancy works and the like, together with youngsters just leaving school, have been resettled—not always successfully—on these frontier farms.

Thirty State-owned Overseas Chinese Farms have been set up in Kwangtung, Kwangsi, Yunnan, Kweichow and Fukien to accommodate and settle more than 60,000 Chinese who have returned from overseas. These returnees are seldom agriculturalists and are mainly former workers, small producers and small business men, who require training before they become productive farmers[21].

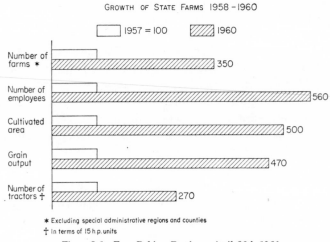

GROWTH OF STATE FARMS 1958-1960

1957 = 100   1960

Number of farms *	350
Number of employees	560
Cultivated area	500
Grain output	470
Number of tractors †	270

* Excluding special administrative regions and counties
† In terms of 15 h.p. units

Figure 3.1. From Peking Review, *April 28th 1961*

The many state farms, which are situated in regions having long and rigorous winters, as in Heilungkiang, Tsaidam and Sinkiang, are faced with the problem of adequate productive employment during the long non-growing period. In spite of the hardships of the inner Asian winter, the 'slack' period has been occupied with capital construction—drainage, irrigation, land reclamation, the building of pumping stations, together with repair work in the farm's workshops. The slogan in this connection has been 'self-reliance', i.e. avoidance of the use of state capital in these works[22].

Experimental Farms and Demonstration Farms

A number of farms and agricultural institutes have been established specifically for experimenting in all aspects of agriculture, from methods of planting and harvesting to farm management. It is reported that at the end of 1964 there were 10 big, consolidated experimental centres and hundreds of smaller ones in the country[23].

Supplementary to these experimental farms are the demonstration farms, which have multiplied enormously in recent years. In 1965 it is stated that there were more than 10,000 run mainly by the communes themselves. These demonstration farms have two main functions. They test the results of the experimental farms on sample plots in local conditions and then, as their name indicates, they demonstrate their results and findings to the brigades and teams throughout the countryside in very much the same way as the T.V.A. popularized their scientific findings among the Tennessee peasantry. This education is their most important work. Over the centuries the Chinese farmer has earned for himself a high reputation. Nevertheless, in spite of all his meticulous care and devotion to the soil, he is conservative and has been the slave to his agricultural calendar, which he has followed religiously[24]. Professor Ts'ai Hsu of Peking Agricultural University, writing on this subject, says: 'The North China peasants hold that wheat becomes pregnant during the solar term of "summer begins" and draws ears during the solar period of "grain fills". Therefore they do not pay much attention to over-wintering wheat at the time of resumption of growth (February and March) when the wheat ears begin to grow. But, if the soil is dressed and hoed at the time, the ears grow bigger. If this dressing and hoeing is done only at the jointing stage, only bigger grain results.'[25] He maintains that the dissemination of ideas such as this are the main job of the demonstration farm and the sample plot, which must be very well run. When properly demonstrated, innovations and changes are accepted by the peasants with acclaim.

Agricultural Planning

We have sketched the chaotic state of the country in 1949 when the C.C.P. came into power and the immediate steps that were taken to bring some law and order into being. The succeeding 3 years until 1952 were engaged in the work of rehabilitation and preparation for planned development. The general scheme of things was set out in a series of Five-year Plans of which there have been three to date: 1953–57; 1958–62 and 1966–70. Although the State Planning Commission, formed in 1952, must have formulated full, detailed blue prints of their plans, these have never been published in any comprehensive form. They have appeared as a series of yearly targets set for various sections of agriculture and industry and have therefore been subject to the handicaps of such target planning, viz. lack of co-ordination and the constant danger of bottlenecks resulting in imbalance.

The First Five-year Plan stated clearly three main planning aims. First and foremost was the transformation of China from an agricultural to an industrial nation; second was the change from a capitalist to a socialist society; and third was the change from an individual peasant economy to one based on co-operation. We have followed the progress of this last change from 1953 to 1957 and also its continuance during the Second Five-year Plan (1958–62) to the establishment of the commune.

At the Second National People's Congress of the Chinese People's Republic in April, 1960, the National Agricultural Development Program (1956–1967) was approved. This program has come to be known as the Twelve-year Plan and it attempts to give some direction over this period. Clearly it was formulated during the First Five-year Plan since it speaks only of co-operatives and not of communes, although these had already been in existence for 2 years at the time of its publication. Its preamble states its purpose:

'This is a program of endeavour to increase productive capacity in agriculture rapidly, in order to reinforce socialist industrialization in our country and to raise the standard of living of the peasants, as well as all people, during the period from the First Five-year Plan to the third.'[26]

The program is in 40 sections and covers the whole gamut of agricultural development from co-operative organization to moral welfare and the conversion of landlords and rich peasants. The section headings are:

1. Consolidation of the System of Agricultural Co-operatives.
2. Active Increase of the Output of Food Crops and Other Agricultural Crops.
3. Development of Livestock.
4. Promoting Implementation of Measures for Output Increase and Adoption of Advanced Experiences: Two Fundamental Conditions for Increasing Agricultural Output.
5. Building Water Conservation Works to Develop Irrigation and Prevent the Scourge of Flood and Drought.
6. Vigorous Increase of Rural Manure and Chemical Fertilizers.
7. Improvement of Old-style Farm Tools and Popularization of New-style Farm Tools.
8. Actively Multiply and Popularize Recommended Strains and Varieties of Crops Suitable to Local Conditions.
9. Expansion of Multiple Crops Acreage.
10. Increasing Cultivation of High-yielding Crops.
11. Actively Improve Farming Techniques, with Suitable Measures Adopted to Meet Local Needs.
12. Improvement of Soil.
13. Promote Water and Soil Conservation.
14. Protect and Multiply Draft Animals.
15. Prevention and Treatment of Plant Diseases and Insect Pests.
16. Reclamation of Wasteland and Expansion of Acreage Cultivation.
17. Economic Development of Mountainous Areas.
18. Development of Forestry, and Afforestation, Wherever Possible, of all Wasteland and Mountains.
19. Expand Output of Marine and Fresh-water Fishing and Increase Cultured Aquatic Products.
20. Perfect the Management of State-owned Farms.
21. Improve Research in Agricultural Sciences and Technical Guidance.
22. Strengthen Meteorological and Hydrological Services.
23. Industrious and Frugal Management of Co-operatives and Households.
24. Raise the Rate of Manpower Utilization and the Rate of Labour Productivity, and Develop Diversified Economy in the Agricultural Co-operatives.
25. Food Grain Reserves.
26. Improve Housing Conditions.
27. Extermination of the Four Pests.
28. Strive to Eliminate Diseases That Do the Most Serious Harm to the People.
29. Protection of Women and Children.
30. Enforce the System of 'Five Guarantees', Preferential Treatment for Family Members of Martyrs and Disabled Revolutionary Military Personnel, and Care and Respect for Parents.
31. Eradication of Illiteracy, and Development of Cultural and Educational Undertakings in the Rural Areas.
32. Develop Broadcast Networks in the Rural Areas.
33. Develop Telephone and Postal Networks in the Rural Areas.
34. Develop Communications and Transport in the Rural Areas.
35. Improve the Commercial Network in the Rural Areas.
36. Develop Credit Co-operatives in the Rural Areas.
37. Develop the Enthusiasm of Demobilized Soldiers for the Socialist Construction of Rural Areas.
38. Raise the Socialist Enthusiasm of Youths in the Rural Areas.
39. Transform the Landlords, Rich Peasants, and Counter-revolutionaries and Other Bad Elements in the Rural Areas and Safeguard the Socialist Order of Rural Areas.
40. Urban Workers and Co-operative Peasants Must Help Each Other.

Most of the publication is couched in general terms of direction, exhortation and encouragement but, in a few instances, definite targets are set. Section 2, which deals with the increase of output of food crops, runs:

'In the 12 years starting with 1956, in areas north of the Yellow river, the Chinling Mountains, the River Pailung and the Yellow river in Tsinghai province, the average

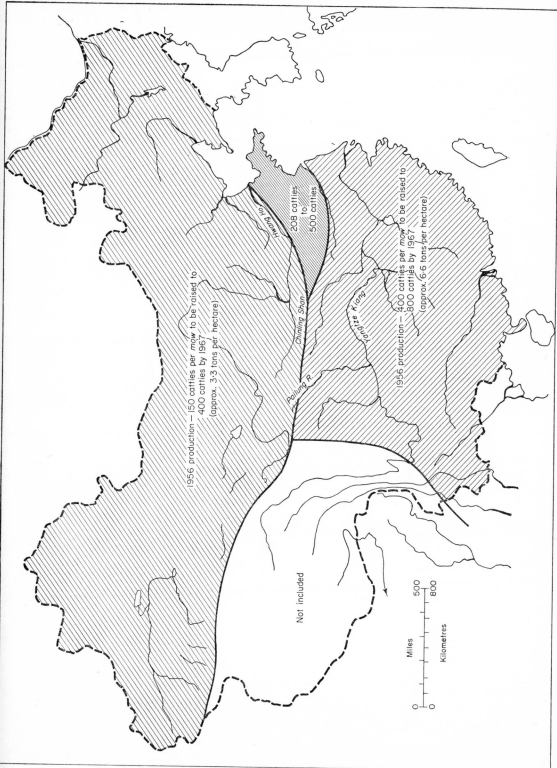

Map 9. *Twelve-year plan grain production zone targets*

annual yield of grain should be raised from the 1955 figure of 150 *catties/mow* to 400 *catties*. South of the Yellow river and north of the Huai river the yield should be raised from the 1955 figure of 208 *catties* to 500 *catties*. South of the Huai river, the Chinling Mountains and the River Pailung it should be increased from the 1955 figure of 400 *catties* to 800 *catties/mow.*'

In Section 6 it demands 'that each household in the countryside raise an average of 1·5 to 2 head of hogs by 1962, and 2·5 to 3 head of hogs by 1967.'

Successful communes, brigades and production teams often report their achievements, relating their yields to these targets.

In spite of the great emphasis, which the C.C.P. throughout has placed on the peasantry as basic to the revolution, it failed signally in the First and Second Five-year Plans to give adequate expression to this in the amount of capital investment it was prepared to assign to agriculture during this period. The planners concentrated their attention on the very rapid development of heavy industry[27]. During the First Five-year Plan the State Planning Commission planned to use 42,740 million *yuan* on capital development, assigning 24,850 million *yuan* (58·2%) to industry, mining and electric power and only 3,260 million *yuan* (7·6%) to agriculture, forestry and water conservancy*. This attempt at very rapid industrialization and the comparative neglect of agriculture was continued with greater intensity in the Second Five-year Plan, especially at its inception in the Great Leap Forward (1958–59). This and the succeeding years of bad harvests led to gross imbalance in the whole economy.

Apart from the assistance obtained from Russia between 1950 and 1954 in the form of loans (£500 million), which had been fully repaid in 1965, China has had to rely on its own resources in finding the necessary capital for development. This has had to come very largely from surplus agricultural production. Foresight, together with great economic experience and statistical information, neither of which were available to them, were required of the planners if wise utilization of capital resources was to be made. That experience was dearly bought during the hard years from late 1959 to 1962 when the series of bad harvests and economic disorganization forced the planners to review the whole position. The period 1959 to 1963 was one of retrenchment and re-orientation in the industrial field. A new order of priorities was instituted in which the needs of agriculture took first place, followed by light industry and heavy industry. Industry was called on to serve agricultural development and to give priority to agricultural equipment, particularly fertilizer plant, all kinds of agricultural tools, from tractors to hoes, and irrigation and drainage machinery. This has been the pattern of planning until the start of the Third Five-year Plan in 1966. This plan appears to be giving renewed emphasis to industrial development and has been ushered in by the upsurge of the 'Cultural Revolution' and the advent of the Red Guards. What impact this will have on agriculture in the near future remains to be seen.

---

* In 1952 the official exchange rate was 68,599 yuan to the £. In 1955 this was changed to the present rate of 6,859 yuan to the £.

REFERENCES

[1] HUGHES, T. J. and LUARD, D. E. T. 'Land Reform', *The Economic Development of Communist China, 1949–1958*, Oxford University Press, London, 1959
[2] MYRDAL, JAN. *Report from a Chinese Village*, Heinemann, London, 1965

REFERENCES

[3] ADLER, SOLOMON. *The Chinese Economy*, Routledge & Kegan Paul, London, 1957, Chap. VI

[4] *Co-operative Village, Kao Pei Tien*, Peking, Appendix

[5] WALKER, KENNETH R. 'Collectivization in Retrospect', *China Quart.*, No. 26, April–June 1966

[6] PERKINS, D. H. *Market Control and Planning in Communist China*, Harvard University Press, Cambridge, Mass., 1966, Chap. IV

[7] ACLAND, SIR RICHARD, *The Times*, 29th Sept. 1965

[8] 'Survey of a Commune', *Peking Review*, No. 10, Mar. 1966

[9] SHU TAI-HSIN. 'The Function and Power of Production Teams in Production Administration', *Kung-jen Jih-pao*, Peking, July 1961

[10] 'Survey of a Commune', *Peking Review*, No. 13, Mar. 1966

[11] *Far East Trade*, Oct. 1959

[12] HUGHES, RICHARD. *The Chinese Commune*, Bodley Head, London, 1960

[13] *China Reconstructs*, April 1965

[14] ROSE, J. 'Sinjao, a Chinese Commune', *Geography*, Vol. 51, No. 233, Pt. 4 (1966)

[15] DUTT, GARGI. 'Some Problems of China's Rural Communes', *China Quart.*, No. 16 (1963)

[16] *Far Eastern Economic Review Yearbook*, 1965

[17] CHAVANNES, E. *Les Memoires Historiques de Ssu Ma Chien*, 17th Treatise, Leroux, Paris, 1898, Chap. 29

[18] WANG CHEN. 'China's State Farms—Production Bases of Farm and Animal Products, *Peking Review*, April 1961

[19] MAO TSE-TUNG. *The Question of Agricultural Co-operation*, Foreign Language Press, Peking, 1959, pp. 22–23

[20] *N.C.N.A.*, Peking, May 1966

[21] *N.C.N.A.*, Peking, Sept. 1964

[22] DONNETHONE, A. *China's Economic System*, Allen and Unwin, London, 1967, Chap. 4 for a fuller treatment of State Farms

[23] *Jen-min Jih-pao*, Peking, Oct. 1964

[24] FEI HSIAO-TUNG. *Peasant Life in China*, Routledge & Kegan Paul, London, 1947, pp. 144–153

[25] TS'AI HSU. 'Sample Plots in Agricultural Production', *K'o-houch Ta-chung*, No. 9, Sept. 1964

[26] *National Agricultural Development Program*, (1956–1967), Peking, April 1960

[27] WALKER, K. R. A Chinese Discussion on Planning for Balanced Growth—A Summary of the Views of Ma Yin-Ch'u and His Critics, *The Economic Development of China and Japan*, C. D. Cowan (Ed.). Allen, London, 1964

AGRICULTURAL PRODUCTION

PRODUCTION, production and ever more production is one of China's most urgent needs if a rapidly growing population is to maintain and increase its intake and if the aim of industrialization is to be achieved. There are two roads which lead to this desirable end and both must be followed simultaneously. On the one hand, every effort must be made to bring more land under cultivation, and on the other, better use must be made of the land already under cultivation.

EXPANSION OF THE AREA UNDER CULTIVATION

Opportunities for the extension of cultivation within China Proper, i.e. the 18 Provinces* of old China, are limited. This is the region which has been densely settled throughout the centuries and in which more than 80% of the population lives. In the present state of knowledge, very little land suitable for cultivation has been left undeveloped. In fact development in some areas has been pushed beyond rightful limits; forests have been cleared where they should have been left standing, notably in south and central China; hilly grasslands have been ploughed where they should have been left for grazing, as in the dry lands of the north-west. Much of this marginal land, in the past, has been cultivated only intermittently, coming under the plough during periods of population pressure and reverting to waste when numbers have been decimated as, for example, by the recurrent famines of Shensi, Shansi and the North China Plain or by political unrest and civil war as in the T'aiping Rebellion (1850–1864) when, it is estimated, some 20 million people were killed. The turmoil of the first half of the present century has not been conducive to agricultural expansion.

With the peace which followed 1949 and the development of the co-operatives, there has been considerable inducement to extend cultivation. In the upsurge of enthusiasm in 1954 large areas of hill-land in south and central China were brought under the plough, often unwisely since ploughing in many instances was up and down the slope instead of following the contours, leading to immediate soil erosion and endangering the paddy fields below. More successful has been the extension of the terracing in the loess regions of the north-west, which has been possible under the advanced co-operatives and even more under the communes. The work of terracing requires overall planning of the whole hill slope or ravine, the co-ordination of a considerable labour force and the constant supervision and repair of all retaining walls. This was not generally feasible under individual ownership.

' "There was one well-to-do peasant here called Li Kuo-tung. He and his family tried to terrace the side of one small ravine. That family worked on that job for 50 years and

---

* Kansu, Shensi, Shansi, Hopei, Honan, Shantung, Szechwan, Hupeh, Hunan, Anhwei, Kaingsu, Chekiang, Kiangsi, Fukien, Kweichow, Yunan, Kwantung, Kwangsi.

failed. The trouble was that such a project has to be treated as a whole; the whole ravine must be terraced, otherwise . . . say you built terraces here" and he indicated a spot towards the mouth of a ravine, "but the farmer higher up fails to terrace his fields, then your terraces will be either undermined or destroyed by soil and water coming down on top of them from above".

'When we formed elementary and advanced farm co-ops there seemed to be a better chance of success. They had more manpower to deploy their mutual-aid teams and controlled a larger area, but still the job couldn't be done satisfactorily . . . but the communes planned the whole job here and co-ordinated its plans with the neighbouring communes. Naturally it consulted and took advice from the teams and brigades because they know their own lands better than anyone else. It unified the work of the brigades. So step by step we terraced the slopes and ravines. It was a lot of work. We built 170 kilometers of earth embankments. That meant moving 328,000 cubic metres of earth. We also rationalized the arrangements of plots by filling in and levelling up fields. We started with 15,000 small plots and ended with 9,000 larger ones.

'It is hard to over-estimate the importance of terracing. In this part of Chuwo *Hsien* there is no river water readily available for irrigation. Except for rain, snow and a small spring or two, water comes from underground cisterns where rainwater is collected, and from wells, some of them over 70 metres deep, from which water is drawn by windlass. So the main effort has been put into terracing as a means of soil conservation and of preserving every drop of water that falls from the skies, and meticulous cultivation of the terraces so as to retard evaporation'[1].

This work of terracing has been extended also in the wetter plateau land of the south-west (Yunnan and Kweichow).

The 'raised field' system, another method of bringing new land within China Proper into cultivation, has come into use in recent years. It is stated that in and around the region of the North China Plain (Hopei, Shantung, Honan, N. Kiangsu and Anhwei) there are areas of low-lying, swampy, saline and sandy land, which together comprise an area larger than the whole of France. The raised fields are created by digging drainage ditches on two sides of rectangular plots of land. The earth removed from the ditches is used to raise the level of the fields by anything from a few inches to over a metre. This not only prevents water-logging, but also helps to lower the water table and so avert salinization. The method is used for bringing new swampy land into cultivation and also for improving the yield of fields subject to water-logging and salinization. The work, which is arduous, demands a high degree of co-operation since it usually involves the construction of large drainage canals. Communes of northern Anhwei on the plain north of the Hwai-ho, claim that half a million of their members created 'raised fields' on 160,000 hectares of low-lying land in the winter and spring of 1965–66[2].

In recent years a considerable amount of land has been reclaimed along the coasts north of the Yangtze mouth. This is land which has been built up by the silt brought down by the Hwang-ho, Hwai-ho and Yangtze Kiang and has been enclosed by dykes in recent years. It extends far to the east of the old dyke, the Fan Kung Ti, built in the seventh century, A.D. This newly-acquired land is occupied mainly by State farms. The land nearest the seaboard is utilized for salt production and that further inland, which is less saline, is devoted to cotton growing[7].

A further source of increased acreage in China Proper has been the incorporation of graves into the arable lands. It has been estimated[3] that nearly 2% of the farmland of the country was occupied by family burials. Graves, sometimes measuring as much as 12 ft in diameter, were often sited in the middle of the best land, either as a mark of filial piety and/or by the decision of the geomancer. The communist requirement that all graves occupying valuable arable land be moved to wasteland has apparently been carried out almost universally and with little resistance. Confucianism, and with it ancestral veneration, had been on the wane for many decades and perhaps it was never as single-minded as was sometimes thought, as Han Su-yin indicates:

'Third Uncle, so prone to the past, addicted to tradition, ancestral veneration, the preservation of rites, must have found it a searing time. But later, in his autobiography, he wrote that he knew the burial grounds were profitable fields, that ancestral sancturies were selected for investment purposes and ways of consolidating the property system and that this business of veneration, selecting propitious spots in accordance with the wind and water diviner, was actually a functional way of acquiring land and of evading the more onerous agrarian and house taxes.'[4]

Virgin Lands

When we look outside China Proper to discover new lands that can be brought into cultivation, it is the North-East and eastern Inner Mongolia that immediately holds our attention. Here and here alone in the whole of China are vast steppelands of rolling fertile black earth. They are very sparsely populated and are capable of rapid development without preliminary costly reclamation expenditure. All three provinces of the North-East (Liaoning, Kirin and Heilungkiang) have, during the last 10 to 15 years, greatly extended their arable areas, but it is in Heilungkiang that the most spectacular gains have been made. Between 1952 and 1957 more than one-and-a-half million hectares were reclaimed, amounting to about 27% of the reclaimed land of the whole nation. Since then the movement has been greatly extended. Unfortunately there are no supporting statistics for this period. In 1957 there were already 36 state farms in Heilungkiang alone, farming 630,000 hectares, 36 public security farms and 13 military farms[5].

Partly for historical reasons, these virgin steppelands have remained untouched in the past. This was the land of the Manchus and was devoted mainly to nomadic animal husbandry. It was forbidden to the Chinese until the latter half of the nineteenth century. Its emptiness is also due to the long and severe winters, which, until the advent of modern farming techniques, made arable farming in this area precarious.

It is a region which requires careful husbandry since it could easily become another of the world's dust bowls. The strong, cold, dry north-west winter winds are a real menace. Great care will have to be taken to see that adequate wind screens are grown. According to all reports, the communes of the North-East are alive to this danger.

Wastelands

In addition to the virgin lands, which, generally speaking, can be brought under the plough with little or no preliminary capital expenditure, there are many outlying regions in Sinkiang, Tsinghai, Inner Mongolia and south-east Tibet, which are capable of development and which, in fact, in many instances are rapidly being developed. From an agricultural point of view they are all inhospitable and marginal and for the same reason, viz. lack of water. Given adequate irrigation facilities and agricultural know-how, most of them can be made to blossom as the rose in spite of the short growing period and hard, bitter winter, which are common to them all. Many hundreds of thousands of hectares of new arable land have been developed in the last 15 years in Sinkiang and Inner Mongolia and more recently in south-east Tibet. The numerous State farms in Tsaidam basin have opened up 20,000 hectares of wasteland since 1954. 'Tsaidam' means salt marshes[6]. More intensive animal husbandry has been fostered in Tsinghai and Inner Mongolia with the drilling of thousands of wells in the steppelands. These are considered more fully when dealing with Agricultural Regions, chapter V.

BETTER USE OF LANDS ALREADY UNDER CULTIVATION

Water Conservancy

Flood Prevention—A great deal of China's arable land has, throughout the centuries, been subject to flooding, which has reduced its productive capacity to a very considerable degree. The problem of flood prevention rested heavily on the shoulders of China's earliest emperors and throughout China's history the 'Son of Heaven's' mandate has resided partly in his ability to deal with floods[7]. 'If now I cannot overcome the floods, how can I meet the people's expectations'. In legendary times Emperor Yao (2357 B.C.) ordered his minister Yu to bring the unruly waters of the lower Hwang-ho under control. Yu's devotion to the task laid on him is remembered to this day and is held up as an example to Communist youth.

'Yu checked the overflowing waters. During 13 years, whenever he passed before his home, not once did he cross the threshold. He used his chariot for land transport; a boat for water transport; a kind of basket for crossing the marshes and crampons for crossing the mountains. He followed the mountains in separating the nine provinces; he deepened the river beds; he fixed tribute according to soil capacity; he made the nine roads usable; he damned the nine marshes and surveyed the nine mountains'[8].

There are records of floods going back over 2,000 years, but unfortunately these are not of great value as there is no objective standard for what constitutes a flood. Officials, reporting to emperors, or to their superiors, have been influenced by all sorts of considerations such as tax relief in time of calamity. Also, provincial records are not of comparable duration, some being over the whole 2,000 years and others only a few hundred years. Nevertheless, the records do give a clear picture of a country constantly menaced by inundation.

The almost universal method of containing the rivers in China has been that of building higher and ever higher dykes. Yu, however, even in those early years, was aware of the danger of this method and he knew the value of 'dividing and ruling'. He divided the then lower Hwang-ho (now the notorious Hai-ho and its tributaries) into nine channels, re-uniting them at their outlet into the Pohai. It was this example which Li- Ping (255–206 B.C.) and his son, Li Erh-lang followed with such marked success in dealing with the flood water of the Min Kiang in west Szechwan[9]. The work that these two men carried out has served successive generations for more than 2,000 years and still functions today. It therefore deserves fuller treatment.

The Min Kiang descends steeply from the Chunghsia Shan of west Szechwan, falling some 9,000 ft in 200 miles. As it issued out on to the Cheng-tu plain at Kwanhsien it spread its load of rock and silt in a wide fan, reducing it to a desert waste of marsh and swamp over an area of 3,000 sq. miles. In winter it is merely a tranquil stream, 50 yards wide and 6 ft. deep, but melting snow and summer rains swell it into a turbulent river more than half a mile wide.

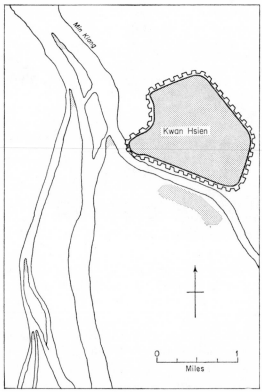

Figure 4.1. Water divide at To Chiang Weir

Li Ping, Governor of Cheng-tu, set about bringing this Min River to heel, a task which would tax the modern engineer with all his mechanization. The method Li used was to divide and subdivide the river *ad infinitum* by constructing arrowheads of rock mid-stream, thus diverting the waters into previously constructed channels. The first divisions are shown in *Figure 4.1*, and the whole network, in which the water of the Min and Lu are mingled, is shown in *Map 10*. Control and diversion was furthered by the construction of barrages composed of 'sausages' or 'bolsters' of boulders some 25 ft long and 2 ft in diameter held together by cases of plaited split bamboo, which can be broken up at will[10]. The work has been extended during the centuries, especially during the Yuan dynasty under Kublai Khan, when many of the channels were faced with stone, but method and technique have remained essentially the same down to the present day. The whole scheme has demanded a high degree of co-operation from governor down to peasant, both in its operation and maintenance. It is a matter of astonishment that it has continued to function uninterruptedly through more than 20 centuries in spite of civil wars, revolutions and disasters, and it deserves to rank as one of the wonders of the world. It has converted an area of desert waste into one of the most fertile and densely populated agricultural regions of the world.

Carved on the rocks above the gorge at Kwanhsien are Chinese characters meaning 'Dig the beds deep, keep the dykes low', Li Ping's famous dictum and *modus operandi*. Had this lead been able to be followed from early days throughout China, much of the

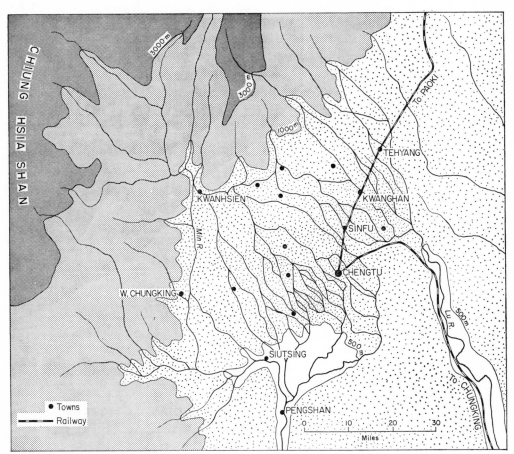

Map 10. Li Ping's irrigation channels, Cheng-tu Plain

disastrous flooding would have been avoided, but it was quite impossible of achievement. Most of the conservancy work was altogether too vast. The only method of river containment practicable, particularly on the flood plains of the great rivers, Hwang, Hwai and Yangtse, was that of dyke building.

Nowhere has the problem of flood control been more pressing than on the North China plain where the Hwang-ho issues from the gorges between Tungkwan and Sanmen.

Formerly an arm of the sea, the plain itself is the product of the Hwang-ho. Over countless millennia the river has poured out its detritus and the process still goes on for the region between Shantung and Shansi uplands is a geo-syncline, whose base is steadily sinking as further alluvial deposits are laid down. The sediment is now over 2,800 ft thick[7].

The Hwang-ho meanders across this plain, a sluggish, shallow stream in the winter but, during the few summer months, a mighty, menacing, heavily silt-laden river, very liable to change course. In order to harness this giant, thousands of miles of dykes have been built along its banks during the course of Chinese history. Usually these have been built well back from the actual bed, leaving a course between 5 and 8 miles wide in the belief that therein lay safety. In so far as the dykes have been successful in their work of containment, the result has been that the silt, which otherwise would have been spread broadcast over the plain, is deposited in the river bed, thus raising it. This, in its turn, has necessitated the raising of higher dykes and so on. In due course the river bed has become higher than the surrounding land. Consequently, if, when the river is in spate, the dykes fail to hold, the countryside is inundated and the waters fail to find their way back into the river course when levels fall. If the breach is serious, the river may drastically change its course as it has done on no less than nine occasions, at times finding an outlet to the sea north of the Shantung Peninsula, and at others south of it.

Immediately south of the lower Hwang-ho and with a scarcely perceptible watershed between, lies the Hwai-ho basin, which shares only in a slightly lesser degree the same flood menace. More than once the Hwang-ho has broken its banks and mingled its waters with the Hwai, finding a common outlet through the Hung-tse Hu into the Yellow Sea. The two have even emptied into the Yangtze mouth. The last occasion of the Hwang-ho flowing into the Hwai was in 1938 when the banks of the Hwang were deliberately cut by the Kuomintang forces in an attempt to stem the Japanese invasion. Some 21,000 sq. miles of arable land were flooded, causing the death of an estimated 900,000 people.

The lake-studded middle Yangtze basin (Hupeh, Hunan and Kiangsi) and the low-lying delta area are both subject at times to severe flooding, as in 1931 and 1954. They do not present such immediate and pressing problems as the Hwang-ho and the Hwai-ho, but in all these regions, quite apart from misery, disease and loss of life that accompany them, these floods are responsible for immense loss in agricultural production.

'It is estimated that 34,000 square miles in the middle and lower Yangtze Basin were flooded in 1931. Most of this was arable land, and at that time under crops, mainly rice. We may reckon that some 25,000 square miles or 16 million acres or approximately 100 million *mow* were lost to cultivation in that year. In terms of food this meant a loss of 250 million *tan* (1 *tan* equals 133 lb.) since one *mow* produces an average of $2\frac{1}{2}$ *tan*. Losses of this calibre have been the rule rather than the exception throughout the centuries.'[7]

Since 1949 the People's Government has bent every effort to meet this flood menace. In early days it entered the fight with supreme self-confidence in the assurance that, given the will and enthusiasm, these giants could soon be conquered. In that spirit much was actually accomplished, but quite soon the problems of water conservancy were viewed more soberly and realistically[11]. The approach has been at all levels and is an outstanding example of the slogan 'walking on two legs', i.e. a combination and integration of great modern engineering projects, such as multi-purpose hydro-electric schemes, initiated and carried out by central authority and smaller, local projects planned and executed by the communes with little or no Government assistance. The attack has also been by all means at their disposal, including large modern dam building, the continuance of dyke building great detention basins, large and small dredging, drainage and irrigation works.

GREAT MODERN ENGINEERING PROJECTS

The Hwai Basin

The central authorities rightly turned their attention first to the Hwai basin, which, as we have noted, was in a chaotic state as a result of the cutting of the Hwang-ho dykes by the Kuomintang in 1938, thus dislocating its whole drainage system.

After the repair of the breached dykes and the return of the Hwang-ho to its own bed, work was started in 1951 on the Hwai itself. Nearly 1,200 miles of dykes were repaired and rivers were dredged. Several detention reservoirs in the lower reaches were made. A new outlet from the Hungtse Hu to the sea was cut. This is the Peh Kiangsu Canal, which is 100 miles long and has tidal gates. It has the treble purpose of drainage, irrigation and navigation.

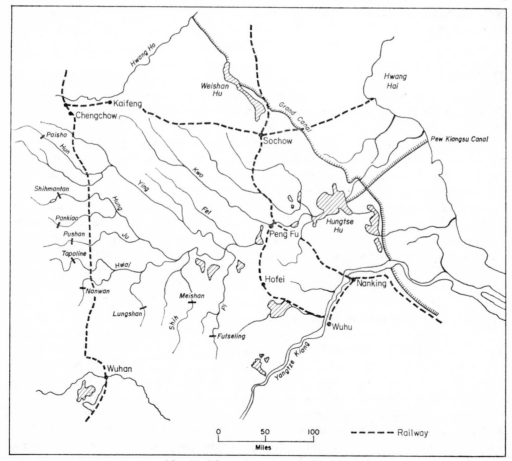

Map 11. Water conservancy in the Hwai basin

Control of the upper reaches of the Hwai and its many tributaries came under comprehensive planning. In all, 27 reservoirs high up in the hills are contemplated. Between 1951 and 1957 seven of these were completed: at Paisha on the Hun river, Pankiao on the Nanhung, Shihmantan on the Peihung, Paishan on the Ju, Tapoling and Nanwan on the Hwai. These are all in the north-west or west and their dams are comparatively low, being between 100 and 120 ft high. Since 1957 three much larger dams on the southern tributaries have been built at Lungshan, Meishan and Futseling. The dam at Meishan is 276 ft high, has a storage capacity of 2,000 million m^3 and irrigates 230,000 hectares[12]; that at Futseling is 230 ft high. All these works are multi-purpose and generate hydro-electric power to a greater or lesser extent.

Recently, further dams have been constructed on the southern right bank tributaries and the whole co-ordinated into one of China's biggest water conservancy schemes, known as the Pi-Shih-Tang Irrigation system. This co-ordination was begun in 1958. By it, in 1959, 60,000 hectares were irrigated; by 1966 this figure had reached 306,000 hectares which were served by 2,000 km of canals, together with countless auxiliaries. 80,000 hectares were added in the autumn and winter of 1965/66[13], and the work is continually being extended. As a result of these conservation works, the vast arable lands of the Hwai basin are much more secure from flood and drought than formerly[14]. Nevertheless, exceptional summer rains and typhoon visitation still can give rise to great anxiety.

The Hwang-ho

Although it has been the Hwai, which has called forth the earliest water conservancy efforts, it is the Hwang-ho which poses the trickiest problems and demands the greatest effort.

The river, which is some 3,028 miles long and has a catchment basin of 250,000 sq. miles, rises in the Bayan Kara Shan (15,000 ft) of north-east Tibet and flows as a mountain torrent above Lanchow. Between Lanchow and Wuchung in Ningsia it descends on to the Inner Mongolian plateau and is less torrential although still of considerable strength. At Wuchung it starts on its northward course, known as the Great Bend, across the Ordos Desert. Here it is a sluggish, meandering, shallow river with a very gentle gradient of about 1 in 5,000. At Hokochen, the point where the river turns sharply south, it enters the loess region and completely changes its nature. It cuts down through the thick, soft loess and becomes much narrower and faster flowing. It is in this sector that it becomes so heavily silt-laden. Right and left bank tributaries contribute their heavy yellow loads until, in summer, the river takes on the appearance of a thick soup. Some idea of the difference in this respect of the various reaches of the river can be gained from the following figures of maximum load. At Lanchow it carries only 3 kgm/m^3; between Wuchung and Hokochen it still carries only 6 kgm/m^3. Between Hokochen and Yumen the figure rises very rapidly and by the time it reaches the Tungkwan gorges it is carrying 580 kgm/m^3. 89·1% of the total silt is contributed in this reach between Hokochen and Tungkwan. It is estimated that 3,700 ton of soil/km^2 is lost annually from the loess region[15]. This is 27 times greater than the world average which is 137 ton/km^2. The silt load of the Hwang-ho is 34 times greater than that of the Nile. After it leaves the gorges it descends on to the North China Plain, receives no further tributaries below Chengchow and loses momentum. It deposits some 40% of its heavy load in its own bed in this sector before reaching the sea.

The problem of conservation of the Hwang-ho is further complicated by the nature of its rainfall. At least four-fifths of the precipitation over its middle and lower basins fall in the four summer months, resulting in a great change in the river's summer and winter levels. The rain often falls in torrents, which accentuates its erosive power, particularly in the loess region. To add a further complication, this is the area with the greatest annual variability of rainfall, giving it its notoriety as the most famine-prone part of China.

It was with such factors as these in mind that the State Council commissioned the Hwang-ho Conservancy Committee to examine and report on the control of the river. With the help of considerable Soviet technical assistance, it carried out a very extensive geological and geographical survey and presented its report to the First National People's Congress on July 18th 1955 under the title 'Report on the Multi-purpose Plan for Permanently Controlling the Yellow River and Exploiting its Water Resources'.

The scheme, as its title implies, has several purposes in view. The main objective is the control of the Hwang-ho's flow, thereby stopping flooding; it also aims at providing ample irrigation water and thus greatly increasing agricultural production throughout the basin. The generation of hydro-electric power is intended to assist irrigation works and also provide industrial power wherever large dams are built. Finally, it is proposed eventually to make the river navigable for vessels of 500 ton from its mouth to Lanchow. The planners have concentrated attention on the middle reaches of the river lying between Kweiteh in eastern Tsinghai and Sanmen in Honan. The whole plan is expected to take 50 years to complete.

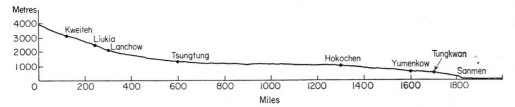

Figure 4.2. Section of middle reaches of Hwang-ho

The main feature of the comprehensive plan is, in the words of the report, 'what we call the Staircase Plan for the Yellow River. By this we mean a plan to build a series of dams on the main river so that the levels form a sort of staircase. This plan divides the middle reaches of the river—from the Lungyang Gorge above Kweiteh in Tsinghai to Taohwayu at Chengkao in Honan—into four sections and utilizes each of them in keeping with its special characteristics'.

The top step or level of the staircase is from the Lungyang Gorge to Tsungtung, near Wuchung; the second from Tsungtung to Hokochen; the third from Hokochen to Yumenkow; the fourth from Yumenkow to Taohwayu. In other words, it is utilizing the four natural divisions we have noted above. Within these sectors, the planners envisage constructing four great multi-purpose projects, to be built by the central government. These are to be supported by 44 secondary dams, undertaken by the central and local authorities together, and these, in their turn, are to be supplemented by thousands of minor dams and works, which are the responsibility of the *hsiens* and communes alone. Two further secondary dams on the plain below Taohwayu are planned.

When the plan is completed there will be two great multi-purpose dams in the top level, one in the Lungyang Gorge at Kweiteh and the other at Liukia. That at Kweiteh is intended to serve Sinang and eastern Tsinghai and that at Liukia, Lanchow and district. The dam at Liukia has already been completed, forming a reservoir of 4,900 million m³. It is capable of reducing the maximum flow of the river from 8,330 m³/sec to 5,000 m³/sec. It has a 107 m high head of water and a hydro-electric capacity of 1 million kW and an annual average output of 6,600 million kWh. Because it is sited in a sparsely populated area the formation of the reservoir has necessitated the resettlement of only 27,000 people.

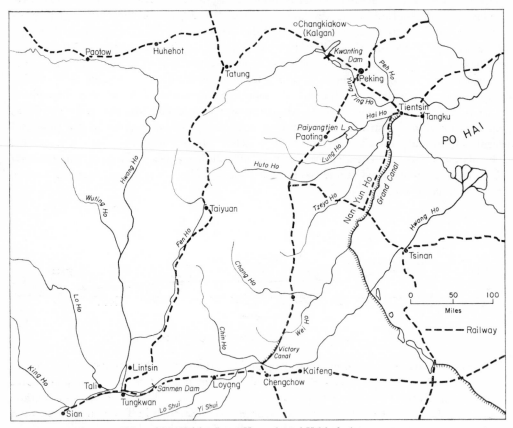

Map 12 (a). Lower Hwang-ho and Hai-ho basins

The dam at Tsungtung and the secondary dams between it and Hokochen—the section with a very gentle gradient—are intended to serve mainly irrigation and drainage works and to improve navigation.

It should be noted that no large multi-purpose project is planned in the third, i.e. loess sector from Hokochen to Yumenkow. The engineers and geologists have decided that 'for geological and geographical reasons the building here of large dams and reservoirs is impracticable'.[15] Below Yumenkow the river valley becomes much broader, but at the confluence of the Wei and the Hwang at Tungkwan the course turns sharply east and again enters gorges. At the eastern end of these is the Sanmen Gorge, which was chosen as the site for the biggest and most important of the multi-purpose projects. At this point two rocky islets stand in the middle of the river, dividing it into three gateways, known as 'The Gate of Man', 'The Gate of the Gods' and 'The Gate of Ghosts'. These three passages have been closed by a dam 90 m high. The resulting reservoir, when full, will have a head of water 350 m above sea level and will have a capacity of 36,000 million m³, second only in size to the Kuibyshev reservoir. The lake extends as far north as Lintsin on the Hwang-ho and to the west of Tali on the Wei-ho. This is a very densely populated region. When the reservoir is full it will necessitate the resettlement of 600,000 people, but during the first phase only half that number has had to be moved.

The Sanmen Dam is clearly the most important contributor to the whole conservancy scheme. Its most important function is the control of the summer flood waters as they issue on to the plain. It is estimated that the reservoir itself can reduce the heaviest imaginable flow from 37,000 m³/sec to 8,000 m³/sec. 'If ever extraordinary floods occur at Sanmen Gorge and in the Yi-ho, South Lo-ho and Chin-ho, tributaries of the Yellow river east of the Sanmen Gorge, the locks at Sanmen Gorge can be closed to hold back all flood waters from above the gorge for four days.'[15] The reservoir is also called upon to step up the flow of water to the North China Plain during the winter months, thus raising the level for irrigation and maintaining an adequate level for navigation.

The Sanmen was planned to have a hydro-electric capacity of 1 million kW with an average annual output of 9,800 million kWh, providing power for the industries of Loyang, Chengchow, Sian and Kaifeng. The plans and machinery were to be provided by U.S.S.R. Most unfortunately, disagreements and tensions between Soviet Russia and China arose before the installation of this machinery was completed, with a result that Russian plans and technicians were withdrawn and this side of the project has not yet been finished, a great disappointment and handicap and not the least of the reasons for the continuing ill-feeling between the two countries.

Several of the 44 secondary projects have been completed. It is difficult to ascertain the precise number. Notable dams have been built on the Wei-ho at Paoki Gorge, where 113,000 hectares are now irrigated with the help of the power developed at the dam. There is another on the Wutung-ho, right bank tributary of the Hwang-ho in the heart of the loess. A big dam has been built on the King-ho, left bank tributary of the Wei, forming the Tafowszu reservoir, which has a storage capacity of 1,500 million m³, generates 20,000 kW and irrigates 216,000 hectares.

However, attention has been focused less on these secondary dams, which are built as joint projects of central and local authorities, than on the small efforts, which rely entirely, or almost entirely, on commune man power, capital and initiative. The Report called for the construction of '215,000 works to protect the heads of gullies, 638,000 check dams, 79,000 silt-precipitation dams and small irrigation projects to water 4,760,000 *mow* of farmland, build 300 earth dams across gullies and repair 4,300 km of roads in gully areas.'[15] It is this local work that has been pursued so energetically in the loess region during the autumn and winter months by commune, brigade and production teams. Emphasis has been placed on soil retention. Small dams are built and small reservoirs formed, which, when filled with silt, as they quickly are, are turned over to cultivation and other dams built. Such is the immense silt load which descends each year that, until the supporting projects of afforestation, grassing, terracing and irrigation have become widespread and firmly established, the life of even the large reservoirs is likely to be short, as the Report admits:

63

'The Sanmen Gorge reservoir will last 50 to 70 years—perhaps even longer—thanks to its large storage capacity, the silt detaining dams on the tributaries of the river and, above all, to the work on water and soil conservation in the middle reaches. By that time, as a result of a series of other measures, the disasters brought by the Yellow River will have been greatly reduced. As for the difficulties that may arise in power generating, irrigation and navigation as a result of silting up of the reservoir, they will be comparatively easy to deal with.'[15]

The cost of the first phase of the whole project up stream from Sanmen is scheduled at £780 million.

Flood prevention measures below the Sanmen dam consist of control of the Lo Shui and Yi Shui, right bank tributaries and the Chin-ho, left bank tributary of the Hwang-ho. This control is in the form of dams, reservoirs and quite extensive irrigation works in their upper reaches. It should be noted that these three rivers are the last to join the Hwang-ho, which, for the next 600 miles, meanders across the plain to empty into the shallow and rapidly filling Po-hai.

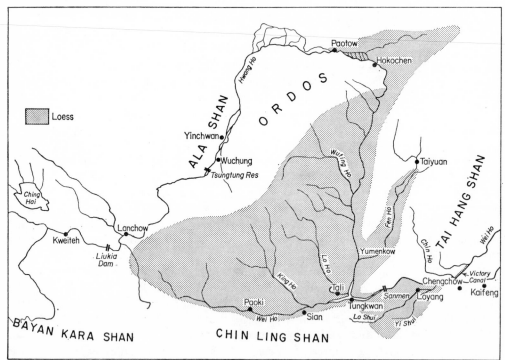

Map 12 (b). Hwang-ho water conservancy

In the middle 1950s the Victory Canal was cut, linking the Hwang-ho to the Wei-ho (not to be confused with the Wei-ho of Shensi and Kansu). The Wei-ho is a tributary of the Nanyun-ho, whose lower reaches, below Lintsing, have been canalized and form the final stretch of the Grand Canal. By means of the Victory Canal some water can be diverted into the Wei in time of need.

64

Since 1949 a great deal of work has been devoted to building, repairing and strengthening the dykes along the banks of the Hwang-ho. At particular danger spots, the dykes have been raised and faced with stone. Care has also been given to the extermination of burrowing animals, such as foxes, which have done much to weaken the dykes in times past.

The Hai-ho and its Tributaries

The group of nine rivers in the northern half of the North China Plain, which the legendary Yu is reported to have subdued more than 3,000 years ago, has been giving trouble continually over the last 600 years during which it is reported to have flooded no less than 383 times. In 1939 Tientsin was under water for a whole month. Virtually the entire river system of Hopeh drains eastward from the Taihang Shan and Wutai Shan and unites with the Hai-ho in a single outlet, through Tientsin, to the sea at Tangku. These rivers, so prone to flood in summer, often run nearly dry in spring, just when water is most needed for seedlings.

A good deal of work to rectify matters was carried out between 1949 and 1963 and new concerted schemes have been going on since 1964 under the name of the 'Heilungkiang' project. Scores of reservoirs have been built in the upper reaches of the rivers, extensive river dredging operations have been carried out and a new outlet for Paiyangtien Hu has been cut. It is reported that 400,000 commune members were engaged on this work in the slack winter season of 1965/66[16].

Flood control of this plain has been greatly helped by the construction of the Kwantung Dam in the Western Hills on the Yungting-ho to the north-west of Peking. The Yungting joins the Hai-ho a few miles above Tientsin and, until this big earth dam was built, contributed its unwelcome summer quota. The dam is 150 ft high and has a capacity of nearly 3,000 million m^3. In addition to flood prevention, it provides drinking water and hydro-electric power for Peking, and irrigation water for 1,300,000 hectares[17]. Flood control has been further assisted by the construction of a conduit from the Miyun reservoir, 40 miles north-east of Peking[18].

The North-East (Manchuria)

Water conservancy in the North-East has been developed in the past by the Japanese mainly with an eye to the generation of power rather than flood control.

During their occupation of the country between 1931 and 1945 the Japanese built the big Fengmen Dam on the Sungari river, mainly to serve the growing industry of Kirin. During the war (1938–45) the dam was neglected and began to leak badly. Since 1949 it has been restored and extended and now has a storage capacity of 12,000 million m^3 and a hydro-electric capacity of 567,000 kW, which ultimately is to be raised to 850,000 kW[19]. Even in its reconstituted and extended form it has proved inadequate to control the floods on the plains of Kirin and below. Therefore two further reservoirs, one on the Lalin and the other on an infeed of the Fengmen, were planned and are probably now completed.

When the waters of the Heilungkiang (Amur) rise earlier than those of the Sungari, as they frequently do, they tend to check the outlet of the latter in much the same way as the Yangtze checks the outflow of the Han in summer. This results in widespread flooding, particularly on the plains lying between the Ussuri and the Sungari. As we have seen, the North-East, particularly Heilungkiang, is one of the main regions of agricultural

development and settlement. Therefore adequate water conservancy is a matter of urgency,
To meet the problem further multi-purpose dams and reservoirs have been constructed on
the Mutan-kiang and on the Nun and Nomin above Tsitsihar.

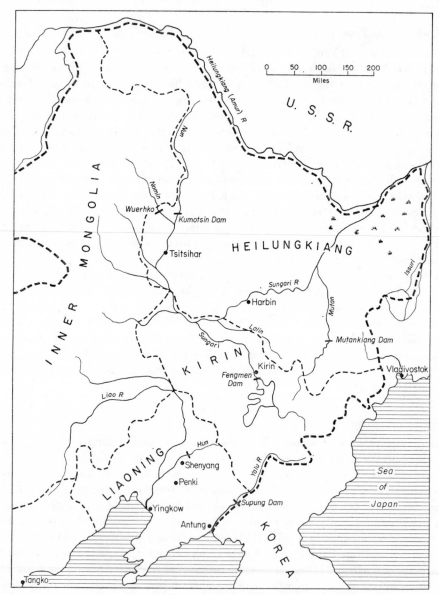

Map 13. North-east water conservancy

Less attention has been given to water conservancy further south in Liaoning, partly
because flooding is a somewhat less pressing problem, and partly because the call for
hydro-electric power is less insistent owing to the abundance of coal resources in the area.

66

One large retention reservoir has been built near Fushun on the Hun-ho to protect the prolific soya-bean growing region of the lower Liao, and another is planned.

Right on the border between Korea and China is the Supung Dam on the Yalu river, built by the Japanese, primarily for power purposes for the industrial region to the north and also for Antung, but also serving some flood control and irrigation functions. It was the approach of U.N. forces to this dam during the Korean War that created such anxiety and brought the Chinese into the war on the North Korean side.

The Yangtze Kiang

The Yangtze Kiang is a larger river than the Hwang-ho. It is 3,494 miles long and has a catchment area of some 714,000 miles^2, nearly three times that of the Hwang-ho. Nearly one-third of its course lies in the Tibetan plateau. It then descends rapidly and flows through three successive basins, the Red Basin of Szechwan, the Middle Basin of Hukwang (Hupeh, Hunan and Kiangsi) and the deltaic region of Anhwei and Kiangsu. Being farther south than the Hwang-ho, it comes under the influence of the summer south-east monsoon to a much greater extent. In consequence, rainfall throughout its entire length, although revealing the same seasonal changes as the Hwang-ho, is much heavier and is not subject to the gross variability from year to year that we noted in the north. This is further reflected in the greater volume and velocity of the Yangtze, which, in the summer of 1954, poured past Wuhan at a rate of 83,000 m^3/sec as compared with the Report's estimated 'greatest imaginable' outflow of the Hwang-ho at Sanmen of 37,000 m^3/sec.

The Yangtze is fortunate in that it has no long, sluggish middle course through desert; nor does it flow through a region of easily eroded loess. Although its silt load in summer is great—it is estimated that 5,000 million ft^3 of silt pass Wuhan annually—its volume and velocity are so much greater than the Hwang-ho that it is able to carry the greater part of its load to its mouth. It is difficult, without actually witnessing it, to realize the might and power of the Yangtze in summer at Wuhan, where it is a mile wide and 600 miles from the sea. In winter, at low water, the river is a mere 6 ft or so deep at this point. In summer it is a great leviathan, usually about 50 ft deep and moving at an average velocity of nearly 6 knots. Thus we are not faced here with the phenomenon of a river whose bed has been built up above the level of the surrounding land, nor with a river which, in its lower reaches, is liable to change of course.

As it flows across the Red Basin it is a fairly well-graded river. At Wanhsien it enters the famous Yangtze gorges. Here the river cuts through the Ta Pa Shan in a series of narrow gorges, sometimes only 200 yards wide, over a distance of 100 miles. At Ichang the river descends quickly on to the lake-studded Middle Basin of Hukwang. Hukwang is the composite name for the two provinces of Hupeh, (north of the lakes) and Hunan, (south of the lakes). Kiangsi is also included in the Middle Basin. The Yangtze here receives one large left-bank tributary, the Han and two large right-bank tributaries, the Siang and the Kan. Before reaching the Yangtze the two latter flow respectively into two large lakes, the Tung Ting and the Poyang, which now are silted and shallow but still prove valuable natural flood water regulators. The river is bordered throughout this section by hundreds of lakes, large and small, many of which become incorporated in the main stream in time of summer spate. When Abbé Huc journeyed up the river in the summer of 1845 he reported it to be 10 miles wide, and his accounts were discredited in consequence but, in fact, it does attain this width in places where river and lakes combine.

Although there is not the same flood menace or the same urgency for flood prevention as in the Hwai and Hwang basins, nevertheless it is very important that big works of water conservancy be undertaken if large areas are to be brought under more regular cultivation and disasters such as the floods of 1931 and 1954 are to be averted.

A most ambitious plan to control the flow at the Gorges has been under survey for some years. It is proposed to build a 400 ft dam in the Wushan Gorge at Sanhsia, near Patung. This would impound a great lake stretching upstream for 150 miles to Chunghsien, and thereby regulate flow from Ichang to Shanghai; the gorges would be made navigable for 10,000 ton vessels and 15 million kW would be generated. Another large dam is to be built at Ipin and there are to be subsidiary works on the Min, Kialing and Fow. The work, which will be very costly, is planned to be carried out between 1970 and 1975[20].

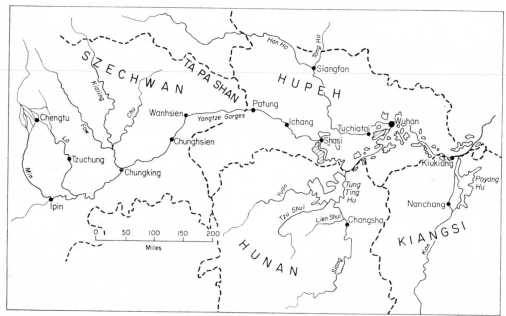

Map 14. Yangtze Kiang water conservancy

Humbler, but none the less considerable, projects were undertaken in 1954 and 1956 in the Middle Basin itself. They took the form of the construction of two large water-retention basins, one to relieve pressure in time of spate on the Yangtze itself and the other on the Han. In 1954 an army of 300,000 workers (men and women, mainly peasants) in 75 days built dykes in the angle of the land between the Yangtze and the Tung Ting Hu at Shasi to form a basin into which the waters of the Yangtze could be deflected in time of need and thus relieve pressure until the emergency had passed. The basin has a capacity of nearly 7,000 million m³ and an area of 355 sq. miles. It is empty most of the year and can be used for cultivation, but must be held in readiness to receive flood waters in summer. A similar basin has been built in the angle between the Han and the Yangtze just above Hanyang at Tuchiatai. This is particularly necessary as the Han becomes very narrow as it approaches its confluence, causing a piling up of waters at the bottle-neck and frequent flooding in this region during the summer. Two storage dams have been built on the Han, one near Siangfan at the junction of the Han and Tang-ho, and the other on the Saitzu, a tributary of the Han. Their respective storage capacities are 8,000 million m^3 and 500 million m^3.

More recently, both in the Middle Basin and in the deltaic region of the Yangtze and also in South China, attention has been concentrated more on co-ordinated large-scale works of irrigation and drainage than on big multi-purpose water conservancy schemes. These can be dealt with more appropriately under that heading.

Irrigation

Irrigation and Drainage—We have been discussing the big multi-purpose water conservancy works, whose primary purpose is flood control. Irrigation of the land surrounding the reservoir in nearly every case is a second objective. After the dam has been built and the reservoir filled, a great deal of auxilliary work in the form of canals, channels, sluicegates, etc. has to be done. In the early years this side of development was often neglected. Many reports from planners, especially before the formation of communes, complained that only 20 to 30% of the water made available by the reservoirs was actually being used. Bigger local organizing units were necessary if this auxilliary work was to be done successfully, especially in view of the general lack of mechanical digging aids and the reliance which has to be put on man-power. That things were not altogether satisfactory in this respect, even in 1965, is shown by the report of the National Conference on Water Conservancy held in September, 1965:

'The Conference was of the opinion that, for some time to come, emphasis should be laid persistently on building small water conservancy projects, while the big and medium sized ones should be built according to necessity and possibility, in a planned manner, step by step, and to the point.

'Our country has vast territories. The natural conditions in one place may differ entirely from those of another and may change every year. When designing and building water conservancy projects, therefore, these differences and changes must be taken into close consideration.'[21]

Irrigation has become the focal point in agricultural development and production since 1959. It figures prominently in the Eight-point Charter, which directs the attention of all agriculturalists to eight essentials: soil conservancy, irrigation, fertilizers, seed selection, rational close planting, better field management, better tools, i.e. mechanization, pest control. Later, a ninth point, the prevention of waste was added.

Eight-point Charter
Shui—water conservation
fei—fertilization
t'u—soil conservation
chung—seed selection
nai—dense planting
pao—plant protection
kung—tool improvement
Kuan—field management

69

Irrigation works, with which drainage must be included in many instances on the plains, have a dual purpose. On the one hand, they are an insurance against far too prevalent crop failure and, on the other, a means of greatly increasing agricultural acreage and output, enabling two or more crops to be taken annually where only one is possible in dry farming.

Clearly it is impossible and undesirable to attempt to record all the work that is being done in this field all over China's vast territories. Reports are continually coming in from all localities of achievements, many of considerable size and extent. All that can be done is to quote typical examples, illustrating the different methods that are being used or tried in differing geographical environments. With this in mind, we have classified them generally under three headings: arid regions, hilly lands and plains, although it is not always possible to draw a clear line of demarcation between them.

Irrigation in Arid Regions—For many centuries there have been pockets of population in the oases around the Taklamakan desert in the Tarim Basin. These communities rely on the melt water from the snowfields and glaciers of the Kunlun and T'ien Shan. Their continued existence through history has depended on how climatic changes and political security have allowed them to make use of these water resources[22]. The oases mark the lines of ancient imperial trade routes, notably the Silk Road, and are the sites of towns which have existed for more than two millennia. Others have been overcome by desert sands and have decayed. The irrigation works of the extant oases communities have been greatly expanded since 1949 and some of the derelict sites have been revived by the construction of new works, new canals, channels and sluices. A major disability of the region has always been the loss of water in the channels through seepage. This has largely been overcome by lining the beds of the channels with cobbles. Since the formation of the communes, the former irregular plots, together with the newly developed land have been reorganized into precisely arranged rectangular plots of 6 to 12 hectares, surrounded by intersecting channels, which allow an even and controlled distribution of water. The plots are lined by shelter belts of trees, two, three or four rows deep. The many State farms of this region, started largely by the P.L.A., are irrigated in the same way and have the same appearance. It is stated that, between 1949 and 1964, the irrigated area of this region has been increased nearly threefold[23] and large increases continue to be reported annually.

The farmers of the Turfan depression obtain their irrigation water mainly by wells from ground water. In the lowest lying parts of the depression they have developed the Persian and Afghanistan method of *karez* irrigation, i.e. by cutting long, horizontal tunnels into the hillsides, thus tapping the water table and leading the water out by gravitation.

Medium size dams with sluices are being built on many rivers descending the northern slopes of the T'ien Shan and irrigated farmland is being developed there. But the main interest in Dzungaria is centred on the extension of well boring to serve animal husbandry on the steppeland.

Two distinct types of water conservancy have been developed in Inner Mongolia and the northern tip of Ningsia Hui Aut. Region. As we have seen, along the great bend of the Hwang-ho the standard canal-channel-sluice gate type of irrigation has developed. Irrigation works of the Ningsia area date back to the Ching dynasty (221 B.C.). Since the construction of the Tsingtung reservoir they are being extended and are now known as the 'Yellow River Irrigation System'. In addition to the 200,000 hectares of farmland fed by

70

gravitational irrigation here, more than 12,000 hectares of arid upland have recently been brought into cultivation by pumping. The water is lifted between 15 and 50 ft above the level of the supply canals. Previously well-digging had been tried and had failed on account of the high saline content of the underground water making it unsuitable for irrigation[24].

Another area on the Hwang-ho, developed mainly by the China International Famine Relief Commission in 1929, lies between Paotow, Saratsi and Hokowchen. This also is being greatly extended. Care has to be taken in all these areas that adequate water is available to prevent alkalization of the soil. There are some swampy parts where drainage, rather than irrigation, has to be undertaken.

Once away from the river and surface water, particularly on the northern slopes of the Hara Narin Ula and the Ying Shan, the type of water conservancy changes to well-digging and boring, which was carried on in a rather haphazard fashion until the late 1950s. Since the formation of the communes this well-digging has been more rational. In 1963 a team from Nanking University—the base from which Lossing Buck conducted his research in the early 1930s—consisting of several hundred geologists, geographers, biologists and meteorologists carried out a comprehensive survey of the Inner Mongolian grasslands. They found and tapped abundant water on the lava plateau, which will make possible the opening up of 200,000 km^2 of arid grassland for stockbreeding[25]. Water conservancy of Inner Mongolia north of the highland rim is rightly being directed to the development of animal husbandry, which in many parts is losing its nomadic character.

Another fairly arid region where modern well-digging has been developed is in the loess of the Wei basin, Shensi. Here it is reported that 23,000 pump-operated wells, each capable of irrigating 100 *mow* (17 acres), have been opened on the plains and 160 deep wells in the hills. As a result 171,000 hectares are now under irrigation, representing 20 per cent of the cropland of the province[26].

Irrigation in Hilly Lands—The time-honoured method of irrigation, which has served the rice growers in the hills over the centuries, has been to build a retaining pond at the head of the valley and to lead the water down from terraced field to terraced field or to rely simply on a sufficiency of rain at the right time. This still remains true for very many parts, but the problem is now being attacked in two new ways.

The first method, and the one which is being used in most upland districts up to the present, has been possible only since communes have enabled the co-ordination of big, local labour teams. It is either to build a reservoir or tap the river high up in its course and to build a large main canal of considerable length. This canal is led around the contours of the hills and by aqueducts over valleys, distributing water to the countryside en route. It is a method demanding both engineering skill and capital.

Two outstanding examples of this method may be quoted. The Red Banner Irrigation Canal of Shansi has received much publicity as an example of self-reliance. It is, in fact, a network of canals, based on the upper reaches of the Chang-ho. By means of three main canals of over 100 km in length it leads water through the mountainous region of the Tai-hang Shan and irrigates 22,000 hectares of dry upland. It has involved much tunnelling and bridging with innumerable aqueducts and culverts. Stone from the mountains has been used in preference to concrete in construction because it is cheaper and nearly all the work was done with human labour and simple tools. The total cost was 13 million yuan of which only 4·3 million was borne by the central authorities, the rest being found by the communes[27].

The second example is that of the Shaoshan Irrigation System, built in Hunan in the region of Mao Tse-tung's childhood. This, again, is a hilly region subject to drought. Its main canal, which is 174 km long and some 30 m wide, has three large aqueducts, the longest of which is 530 m, and seven tunnels with a total length of 2·8 km. It is navigable for boats of 30 ton, serves for fish breeding, power generation and irrigates 66,000 hectares. It was built in 10 months and, like the Red Banner Canal, mainly man power and small tools were used in its construction[28].

Recent experience in Szechwan has caused its engineers to turn away from these schemes of large canals. Up to 1955 reliance was placed on building nearly 10,000 small or medium ponds on the flat land and in the hills, but they proved unsatisfactory. Being small, they dried up quickly and water was not available when most needed. Moreover, they tended to occupy valuable arable land. Between 1955 and 1962 it was the policy to build large reservoirs having good storage but this, in its turn, also proved unsatisfactory for it was found that the distribution of the water from the reservoirs was too difficult. Fields are widely scattered and the undulating land necessitates long canals. This led the Szechwanese to the conclusion that gravitational irrigation in hilly land was not viable. Therefore, in 1963, they turned to a third experiment which, it is claimed, is proving a success. The essence of the scheme is to build large numbers of small stone dams in rivulets and streams, holding back small reservoirs, larger and lower than the previous ponds. Water is then lifted by pumps from these reservoirs as required, the power being supplied by small hydro-electric stations, which abound in Szechwan. This method is styled 'the integration of pumping and storage . . . with chief emphasis on electro-mechanical irrigation.'[29]

It is claimed that the small stone dams have the added advantages of controlling the flow of streams, thus serving the big hydro-electric plants. Moreover, they occupy stream beds rather than arable land as did the ponds. Finally the supporters of the experiment claim that it is much cheaper than canal irrigation even at its best: 'The average construction costs in terms of per *mow* of irrigated acreage, for the different kinds of principal water conservation installations are: reservoirs ¥. 51·70; ponds in hills and on plains ¥. 10·30; stone dams ¥. 8·50. For every 100 yuan of investment, the effective irrigated acreage is 1·93 *mow* in the case of reservoirs, 9·7 *mow* in the case of ponds, and 11·76 *mow* in the case of stone dams.'[29]

However, this experiment will have to be tried out for a much longer period before any useful generalization can be made, for Szechwan's topography and climate differ markedly from the rest of the country.

Irrigation on the Plains—The method of watering the fields of the North China Plain, used over the centuries, has been that of well irrigation. Water has been raised from shallow brick or stone-lined wells by man or donkey power or by windmill and distributed by hand over the fields or through small channels, using 'dragon-backbone' treadles[7]. All these are still widely used but are steadily being replaced by deeper wells, using asbestos, iron or cement pipes for lining. More and more of the slow, hard manual work is being done, and done more efficiently, by small diesel or coal gas pumps.

An interesting experiment is being carried out along the lower reaches of the Hwang-ho where 20 syphon irrigation systems have been installed, introducing paddy-rice cultivation

(a)

(b)

(c)

(d)

Water conservancy: (a) *Heinanchiang Hydro-electric Station, Yangtze delta, designed and built by the Chinese;* (b) *paddy fields in Hainan;* (c) *small diesel pump on barge on irrigation channel;* (d) *trunk irrigation canal, Shaoshan, Hunan*

73

to the area for the first time. Taking advantage of the elevated level of the river bed, syphon pipes lift water from the river over the dykes to the surrounding fields. Irrigation and drainage here must be carefully co-ordinated if alkalization is to be avoided. Water, after use for irrigation, must be given an outlet otherwise the underground water level rises, leading to alkalization of the soil. Properly used, the syphoned water dilutes the alkalis and frequent changes of water in the fields help to carry off the harmful salts. In the dry season when the water in the river is low, the system is being reinforced by diesel or electrically-powered pumps. In the first large-scale attempt at rice growing in this way, 33,000 acres have been irrigated. This method has the advantage of being cheap and easy to install and requiring no motive power to operate. It is thus well within the financial means of any production brigade[30].

Extensive areas of China's vast plains lie at such low levels that, during the rainy season, the water table is at the surface and liable to flood, while during the dry season, growth may stop for lack of water. These areas, which comprise some of the most fertile land, need drainage and irrigation facilities if they are to produce to their fullest capacity.

The region, where these conditions are most clearly seen, is the Pearl river delta, a low-lying area subject to both flood and drought. Flooding occurs when the three rivers West, North and East are abnormally full in summer, and the situation becomes really serious when this coincides with especially high tides in the estuary, occasioned, may be, by the presence or proximity of a typhoon. In the past, embankments and dykes have been built to meet these dangers. In the four years, 1959 to 1963 a big conservancy campaign was carried out. It included extensive dyke strengthening, the building of retention reservoirs and sluices, and the installation of 2,600 electric pumping stations, generating 246,000 h.p., part of the duties of these being to keep the low-lying land drained during the five summer months when 80% of the rain falls. This region lies within the tropics and has a 12 month growing season provided adequate water is available. During the seven dry months the function of the pumping stations is reversed and irrigation is the order of the day[31]. The years 1963 and 1964 provided very severe tests of this new system. It stood up well first to the prolonged drought of 1963, when Hongkong's water shortage was such that its inhabitants were rationed to four hours water on each fourth day only. Then, in 1964, when Kwangtung experienced its heaviest recorded rainfall, most of the fields were saved from disastrous flooding. It is estimated that 70% of the 3,300,000 hectares of rice-growing farmland in the area now have guaranteed irrigation and drainage facilities[32].

The Pearl river delta provides the best example of a powered irrigation and drainage network, but it is by no means the only area that has developed such a network. Kiangsu and Anhwei in the Yangtze delta provide very similar topographical conditions, as also do wide stetches of lowland around the Tungting Hu and Poyang Hu in Hunan, Hupeh and Kiangsi. In all these, extensive dyking has been reinforced by the ever-increasing reliance placed on either diesel or electrically-powered pumping. A great deal of use is being made of the small 8 h.p. diesel motor, which can easily be moved to the desired spot by man-power or by boat along the irrigation and drainage channels. Hupeh farmers sing this song in praise of their 8 h.p. diesel motor:

> Four men carry our motor,
> To run it only one is needed.
> On the hillside or the plains,
> High or low our fields are watered.

74

Fertilizer

A great deal of land in China which is being farmed today has been under cultivation for some 2,000 years.   By great industry and careful adherence to traditional methods, fertility has been maintained fairly well over all these centuries. Admittedly the standard of return in terms of effort expended has been low and has tended to decrease during the last century as population and land hunger have increased.

Fertility has been maintained almost entirely by the application of organic matter of which night soil, i.e. human excreta, has formed—and still forms—the preponderating part.   Other ingredients have been animal manure, mainly pig, composting of all waste matter, ashes, bones, feathers, mud from ponds and some green manure.   The latter has not been widely used, especially in the densely-populated areas, as it entailed the use of land urgently and immediately needed to produce food.

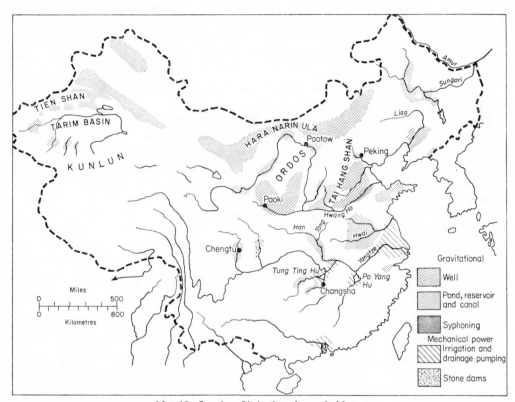

Map 15. Location of irrigation schemes cited in text

Night soil, to be an effective manure, must be carefully maturized.   Every village, every hamlet, virtually every household in the country had its *kang*, a huge earthenware container, let into the ground, for this purpose.   Every morning from every town and city there emerged a long train of coolies carrying buckets of night soil into the country, an unpleasant, laborious and inefficient business as Guiseppe Regis points out. 'Given the very low average active fertilizer content of material used, viz. from 15 to 45 times less than that of chemical fertilizer in the more common compounds, the labour involved in the collection, preparation, transport and spreading of these natural materials is enormous.'[32]   Conversely, it must be remembered that the heavy summer rains lead to leaching.   There is, therefore, some virtue in the repeated top dressing of night soil throughout the season as compared with the single annual dressing much of which may be quickly leached into the subsoil. Moreover, this universally accepted method of fertilization came under condemnation as a great breeder of disease, causing greater loss than gain.   Nevertheless, while communes are giving greater attention to more hygienic use of night soil, it remains the chief source of fertilizer.   In a recent Peking article it was stated that 'if all night soil is fully utilized, its fertilizing power will be equal to more than 10 million ton of ammonium sulphate'[33].

All the big Chinese cities are now developing modern sewage facilities but, as might be expected, only in conjunction with the use of the effluent on the land.   This is a new field for Chinese scientists and therefore one fraught with some danger to health.   In most instances, at present only the first step in the biological treatment of the sewage is done at the sewage plant, the effluent then being channelled direct to the rice fields instead of to ponds for oxidation.   Industrial waste water, the disposal of which is assuming growing importance, is required to undergo the necessary treatment in factories before being liberated for irrigation[34].

Pig breeding, largely as a means of producing manure, has been urged most strongly on production teams and individual peasants.

The value and importance of green manure has been stressed in recent years and now, with the development of the larger production units of brigades and teams, it is more possible of rational implementation.   Milk vetch and cow vetch appear to be the most widely sown.   They produce a very heavy crop of up to 70 ton/hectare in the south.   They are especially effective when ploughed into acid, saline and sandy soils, giving much-needed organic matter.   In north China sweet clover is sown in spring between rows of winter wheat and ploughed under after the summer wheat harvest.   Sesbania, grown in parts of the Hwang-ho basin, serves as basic fertilizer for cotton.   Throughout China there has been a spectacular increase in green manure crops, the area rising by 660,000 hectares in 1964 and 1,300,000 hectares in 1965.   In rice-growing Chekiang and Kiangsu, there is now on average 1 hectare of green manure crop to every 2 hectares of paddy fields, which, if supplemented with some chemical fertilizer and farmyard manure, provides sufficient basic fertilizer[35].

Production and use of chemical fertilizer received little attention before 1949[36].   With few exceptions, it was beyond the means and the know-how of the peasants.   Before liberation, peak production was 230,000 ton in 1941.   In 1949 only two chemical works at Nanking and Talien were functioning, producing some 20,000 ton of ammonium sulphate between them.   By 1952 production had recovered nearly to the 1941 peak level.   Under the First Five-year Plan (1952–57) three big plants were built at Kirin, Taiyuan and Lanchow, mainly with foreign equipment.   The first and largest of these was at Kirin, which drew on the trained personnel throughout the country, proceeded to train its own workers, and thereafter to train for the rest of the country.   It is reported that between 1958 and 1963 Kirin Chemical Co. has trained 23,000 skilled workers for a score or more chemical plants. Four more large factories at Shanghai, Kaifeng, Canton, and Chienchiang in Kweichow were added in 1963–64, bringing the total to seven large nitrogenous plants each with an annual capacity of over 100,000 ton.   In the first half of 1965 a further dozen large or medium (10,000 ton p.a. capacity) factories were built, but these have proved quite inadequate to meet the growing demand. In consequence, there has been a countrywide building of small and medium size plants. By 1964 they numbered over 150 and accounted for about 30% of the total output of which about one-third was nitrogeneous and the rest phosphates[37]. The small plants range between 2,000 and 5,000 ton p.a. capacity, concentrating mainly on liquid ammonia production[38]. These small concerns come under criticism on account of their high production cost per unit. A synthetic ammonia plant with an annual output of 800 ton, enough to meet the needs of 13,000 hectares, can be built by a commune in 4 to 6 months, but its subsequent production costs amount to $163 per ton as compared with $74–$82 in large plants[39]. However, against this must be placed the saving in distribution and the relief to China's hard-pressed railway and road transport.

Plant at Tanyang, Kiangsu was built in 1965 for the specific purpose of making, by a new process, ammonium bicarbonate, which is claimed to be nearly as effective as ammonium sulphate and cheaper. Its virtues are that it does not acidify or harden the soil; its shortcomings that it evaporates and disintegrates quickly. Therefore it is not a satisfactory product for large-scale production at a big plant since it would require storage and long transport haulage. It is, however, eminently suitable for small plant, which supplies local needs and is especially acceptable in south China for double cropping paddy, where it is used as soon as manufactured[37].

China is now successfully producing urea. Shanghai has succeeded in making the quality of steel necessary to resist the high corrosion and pressures occasioned by the process. The first urea factory, the Wuching Chemical Works, Shanghai has a 36 m high tower for recovering carbon dioxide and has a big compressor. Its production is estimated at 350,000 ton p.a.

The estimated output of chemical fertilizers for the whole of China in 1965 was about 9 million ton, although a Hong Kong estimate placed it as low as 5 million ton. The 1966 production will possibly reach the 12 million mark, more than half of which will be produced by small local plants built by local capital. Tientsin is now producing complete sets of machinery for fertilizing plants[40].

In spite of this great increase in the production of fertilizer within the country, in 1964–5 China figures as the world's largest importer, when imports were about 410,000 ton[41].

Seed Selection

Better seed selection is one of the most promising fields for the increase of agricultural production. The steadily decreasing yields per *mow*, which have been marked over the last century, have, in no small measure, been due to the poor strains from which the crops have been grown. This is not to say that the peasant has not been conscious of the advantages accruing to good seed. A common rural saying is 'One grain of superior seed, one thousand grains of good food', but, far more often than not, he has had Hobson's choice. He has had to take his seed from his own previous crop and seldom has he been able to hold back the best for next year's sowing. Moreover, his opportunities for proper storage of seed have rarely been available. Prior to 1949 there had been some research and experimenting at a few centres, notably at the Agricultural College, University of Nanking, but in comparison with the size and needs of the country, these were entirely inadequate.

After 1949 the Chinese Academy of Agricultural Science and the Agricultural Scientific Research Institute were formed. The former now has branches in every province and from them has spread a network of some 1,700 centres of seed breeding and seed propagation at *hsien*, commune, production brigade and even production team levels. As a result, it is claimed that new and rejuvenated strains have replaced the old over more than half the sown land of China.

Naturally the main work has been concerned with the five main grain crops, rice, wheat, maize, kaoliang and millet, together with soya beans and cotton. More recently it has extended to root crops and oil-bearing seeds. Experimenting in this field has been country-wide, often effectively at brigade and team level. A few examples will have to suffice to give some idea of the work that is being done. Reports seldom, if ever, are of controlled experiments and contain no record of the accompanying degree of irrigation, amount of fertilizer, etc. but rather of the results after a new strain has been used and tested under normal conditions over a wide area.

Rice has probably received more attention than any other cereal. What is looked for is a high-yielding plant with low stalks, which are not easily bent by wind or rain, and one which tillers early for it is on this tillering that increase in the number of spikes or ears depends. Late tillering is worse than useless since it increases foliage without producing concomitant grain and merely restricts light. Different qualities are required for early and late crops in double cropping, and again for late single crop rice in the Yangtze valley, where it is in rotation with winter wheat or barley. A strain which has received great acclaim in Central China is known as 'Nung k'en 58', or by the farmers as 'three-eights' because of the claim that it yields 800 *catties/mow* (approx. 6·6 tons/hectare), 800 *catties* of straw/*mow* and 80% greater yield than other strains[42]. It has a high tillering rate, resists lodging and withering, ripens 5 days earlier than its rival, 'Lao Lai Ching', and has the further virtues of being white and tasty and of greater volume when cooked. This is just one of dozens of strains being produced to meet the very varied climatic and soil conditions in which rice is now being grown.

Wheat is receiving only slightly less attention than rice. The main demands here are for seed which ripens quickly and is more resistant to disease. Two new and favoured strains are 'Neihsiang 5' and 'Neihsiang 36', named from the *hsien* in Honan in which they were developed. They have a high disease resistance and high yield, averaging 400 *catties/mow* (3 ton/hectare), which is the target set for north China in the Twelve-year Plan for Agri-culture (see p. 47). Another strain, 'Taitzu No. 30', produced after several years of testing for farmers in Tsinghai, which is 2,000 to 3,000 m above sea level and has only 120 frostless days. This is a cross between the local, early ripening hardy strain and a later ripening, bigger yielding strain. It ripens in 104 days and thus commends itself to western regions, which have a short growing period.

Millet and kaoliang are both hardy crops, resistant to drought and disease. The main aim of the seed grower, therefore, is to increase the yield. Old strains, for the most part, pro-duced only one ear per stalk. The new sorghum, 'Hsiung Yueh 253', it is claimed, is many-headed and yields 1,000 *catties/mow* (approximately 8·2 ton/hectare).

Vigorous efforts to introduce hybrid maize throughout the country have so far met with only limited success. Although hybrid strains yield up to 30% higher than ordinary maize, they do not breed true. It is necessary to produce double cross seeds each year as the strain loses its hybrid vigour after the second year. U.S. hybrid seed has been tried but does not adapt well to Chinese conditions[43].

Mechanization

If the Chinese peasant of the 1940s could have been transported back 2,000 years in time to the Han dynasty, he would have found his counterpart using much the same tools as himself. The hoe, the sickle and the iron-tipped plough were, and still are, the main instruments used on the land and of these the hoe figures most prominently. Further, apart from the fact that the hoe is made of iron instead of stone, it differs little from the main tool of his neolithic forebears. It is only since 1949 that a real revolution in agricultural tools in China has begun to take place.

Mechanization and the widespread use of better agricultural tools forms an essential part of the communist plan of socialist industrialization, as the following quotation from Mao shows: 'Only when socialist transformation of the social-economic system is complete and when, in the technical field, all branches of production and places wherein work can be done by machinery are using it, will the social and economic appearance of China be radically changed . . . If, in a period of roughly three five-year plans, we cannot fundamentally solve the problem of agricultural co-operation, if we cannot jump from small-scale farming with animal-drawn farm implements to large-scale farming machinery . . . we shall fail to resolve the contradiction between the ever-increasing demand for marketable grain and industrial raw materials and the present generally poor yield of staple crops. In that case our socialist industrialization will run into formidable difficulties; we shall not be able to complete socialist industrialization.'[44] Later the C.C.P. called for mechanization of agriculture in these rather cryptic terms: 'work for a minor solution within four years, get an intermediate solution within seven years and achieve a major solution within ten years.'

It is possible to discern fairly well-marked steps in such progress as has been made towards mechanization since the People's Government came into being. The period from 1949 to 1952 was one of rehabilitation in which production was concentrated on small and traditional tools. Peasants had to make the best use they could of their old tools. During the First Five-year Plan (1952–57), when industrialization was getting under way and new factories were coming into production, 'walking on two legs' was the order of the day. Nearly all the new agricultural machinery produced went to the newly-formed State farms, while the developing co-operatives had to be content with semi-mechanization, the use of more and better hand and animal drawn tools produced largely in the local hsien and co-op. workshops. It was only after the farmers had pooled their land in the co-operatives that mechanization began to become viable. Then followed the Great Leap Forward (1958–59) during which there was a considerable increase in production of tractors, etc. only to be succeeded by two years of confusion or 'consolidation' in the industrial sphere. Since 1963 industry has been directed largely in the service of agriculture. Consequently all kinds of equipment from ploughs and carts to tractors, combines, bulldozers and irrigation pumps have become increasingly available, although in no way approaching satisfaction of the total needs of the countryside.

It is not surprising that it is in the north-east, north-west and on the North China Plain that mechanization has progressed most rapidly and most intensively for these are the regions which lend themselves best to large-scale farming and where the majority of State farms and larger combines are to be found. Farms in these regions have received priority as tractors and farming machinery have begun to come off the lines of the growing number of factories. No. 1 Tractor Works, Loyang was the first to come into production in 1958. Since then large tractor centres have been developed at Tientsin, Nanchang, Anshan, Shenyang, Hangchow and Wuhan[45].

In a country the size and complexity of China, a great variety of machines is necessary if the needs of the various parts are to be met. During the First Five-year Plan many models, mainly of the heavier type, were imported from the Soviet Union, Czechoslovakia, Hungary and Roumania. Since 1960, these imports have fallen steeply and China now looks almost entirely to its own factories for supply. In early years production was greatly handicapped by lack of the vast variety of different qualities of steel which go to the making of a tractor[46]. In consequence, the quality of early models was not up to standard. The great efforts made in recent years in the steel industry to produce high quality steel of all grades has resulted in marked improvement. There are now 13 different types of tractor in production in China, ranging from big 100 h.p. bulldozers down to small hand-pushed cultivators. Of these eight are specifically for agricultural use. The 'Hung Ch'i' (Red Flag) and 'Tungfanghung' (East is Red) are the most popular of the caterpillar type and are mass-produced. The 'Hung Ch'i' (100 h.p.) is the heaviest and is made in Anshan. It is used for the roughest work and is specially adapted for opening up virgin land in the North-East. The 'Tungfanghung' (54 h.p.) is manufactured at No. 1 Tractor Plant, Loyang and is used for the general, heavy farm work—ploughing, harrowing and combine harvesting. Three out of four of the four-wheel tractors are in mass production. They are the 'T'ieh Niu' (Iron Ox), 45 h.p., made in Tientsin; the versatile 28 h.p. 'Tungfanghung' (East is Red), which can be adapted for cotton and maize cultivation, is made at No. 1 Tractor Plant, Loyang and the 'Fengshou' (Bumper Harvest) 35 h.p. made at Hangchow. The fourth, 'Leap Forward', 20 h.p. is still in the experimental stage. Wuhan specializes in the production of a hand tractor, the 'Worker-Peasant' of 7 h.p., which is light and easy to operate. Because it is so manoeuvrable, it is especially suitable for terraced paddy fields and small plots. Canton has developed the 'Kweifeng 10', a 10 h.p. hand tractor, which is specifically built to deal with the hard clay rice fields. With it the farmer can plough 1 hectare in 8 h, at least five times as much as he can do with a water buffalo[47]. Shenyang is now producing a hand cultivator of 3 h.p.

In the North-East, land of large-scale farming and State farms, it is claimed that one third of the land is now ploughed by tractors and that the resulting produce per farm-hand is many times greater than the communes still using traditional methods[48]. State farms accounted for 32% of total tractors, 50% mechanical farm tools, 82·5% combines and 68% motor cars for heavy-duty agricultural purposes[49]. In 1949 there were only 1·2 tractors in the whole country and these were all imported. In 1958 the figure was 45,330 and in 1966 it probably stood at over 200,000 with more than 2,200 State tractor stations. However, in spite of this spectacular rise, it is a very long way from satisfying the country's needs. In a report in 1963 it was estimated that there were 1,300 million *mow* (approx. 87 million hectares) of land that could be worked by machines and that an annual output of 200,000 tractors (15 h.p. units) would be necessary to meet this need. It is hoped to achieve this output in 20 to 25 years[50]. In 1962 less than 10% of China's ploughland was being worked by mechanical methods in the modern sense of the term. Only in very recent years has sufficient attention been paid to the provision of machine spare parts, to the establishment of adequate repair shops and to the training of sufficient skilled personnel—an error common to nearly every country in the early stages of its industrial development.

Buffalo harrow

Walking tractor from Wuhan plant

Rice planting old and new

For the most part, Chinese farmers have, to date, had to be content with what is termed semi-mechanization, which includes anything from rubber-tyred carts and barrows to animal-drawn drills, threshers and rice transplanters. From the point of view of total produce and numbers employed, of China's two agricultural 'legs', this semi-mechanized one is still far more important than the fully mechanized. A great deal of skill and ingenuity has gone into the invention and production of innumerable small agricultural implements. It is difficult to appreciate, without actually experiencing it, the advance achieved by so simple an innovation as the introduction of rubber tyres replacing the iron rims of the carts in the north, and the ball-bearing bicycle wheels, replacing the old wooden, squeaking wheels of the barrows of the south. Not only are they much more efficient, being so much easier to move, but also they do not furrow or rut the dirt paths and roads to the same extent. The old iron-tipped wooden plough has now largely been replaced by the modern plough, the share of which turns a deeper and better furrow than the old. In the North-East, where crops are grown on ridges, which allow more earth to be exposed to the warmth of the sun, the new ploughs are modelled on the share and mould board of the British plough[51]. Man- and animal-drawn five-row seeders or drills for flat land and three-row for hilly land, double-row wheat and cotton cultivators, hand threshing machines replacing old flailing methods, hand-pumped sprayers and fertilizer dressers are now being widely used and are being produced almost entirely at local *hsien* or commune workshops.

One of the most important of these semi-mechanical inventions has been the rice trans-planter, which should, in time, eliminate the back-breaking toil of hand-transplanting of rice seedlings. The first of these machines, the 'Liling No. 2, Hunan', appeared in 1956. It is simple and can be made by any skilled carpenter. It has been succeeded by the 'Nan 105B, Nanking', which is more complicated, factory-made and animal-drawn. It is estimated that, by hand, one man can transplant half *mow* with 15,000 clusters of seedlings in a day. Using the 'Liling' one man can transplant 3 to 4 *mow* and, using the 'Man 105B' one man and one animal can transplant 30 *mow*. The first big rice-transplanter factory has now come into production. It makes the new 'Kwangsi-65' type, which thrusts five clusters of rice seedlings into the mud at a time and is adjustable[52]. A further advantage of these machines is that they speed up the work. Transplanting of rice from seed bed to paddy field should be done in a 10 day period. Delay leads to low yields, hence the tremendous pressure of work at these times[53].

In spite of all this activity, a vast amount of agricultural work is still being done with old, antiquated tools and complaints are heard that even these in some parts are in such short supply that some members of production teams are unable to earn the labour points of which they are capable through lack of these simple tools[54].

Plant Protection

It is quite impossible to estimate with any degree of accuracy the loss of production in China through pest and plant disease ravages but, throughout the centuries, it assuredly has been very great. In some locust-infested areas, for example, it has, at times, amounted to virtually the whole crop. At long last concerted efforts are being made to stop this breach in the production dyke. Scientific research and widespread education of the peasant are being brought to bear. Attack on the problem is being made on three main fronts: better methods of cultivation, which help to destroy the pests, increasing use of insecticides and fungicides and the production of more disease resistant strains.

The locust menace, which has so often ravaged the provinces of the north, is now being tackled with some vigour. The increasing availability of insecticides and the collectivization of the economy combine to make the attack more effective. Peasants in every commune in the most badly affected province, Honan, have had special training in locust control and every production team has the responsibility of reporting immediately any sign of infestation. The whole commune can then go promptly into action, dusting insecticides over large areas to kill nymphs and young locusts before they put on wings. Efforts are also being made to control the sandy, alkaline areas beside the Hwang-ho, where the locust winters[55].

Similarly, in the lower Yangtze provinces there has been a successful campaign against the water snail, but with this difference, that this is protection for the human beings and animals, who produce the food rather than protection of the plants themselves. The water snail is the host of the blood fluke, which causes schistosomiasis (snail fever), a debilitating disease. Where the fever has been eliminated, a big increase in agricultural produce and livestock breeding follows[56].

China, herself, is now producing a wide range of chemical insecticides and fungicides. Naturally, the greatest attention has been focused on the needs of the great staple crops and mention of two or three of these must serve to give some idea of the work being done.

The Rice Borer, which on average causes 15–20% damage to the rice crop, is the main enemy in the Yangzte paddy lands. It has been found that thorough winter ploughing and weed clearing is effective, especially if this is reinforced by later spraying and the use of special lamps at night to attract the borer moths. The use of phosphorus fertilizer, promoting early maturity of the plant helps to repel the borer[57].

Two new fungicides, *p*-amino benzene sulphonic acid and sodium *p*-amino benzene sulphonate, have been found effective in combating wheat rust in the north. These are both harmless to man and beast[58]. Nevertheless, the most effective remedy lies in the promotion of resistant strains.

Cotton throughout China is troubled by the red spider, which has developed a resistance to the phosphoric insecticides used until recently. Now tedion is being successfully used instead[59].

The red ant (tetramorium quineense falreijus), which is a natural predator on the sugar cane borer, is now being systematically introduced in the southern cane growing areas. It is also being introduced to combat maize, rice and sweet potato borers[60].

Another pest which causes much damage is the army worm, so called because the larvae assemble and migrate from field to field. It is also known among the southern farmers as the 'night thief' because of its night activities. The old peasant method of finding and destroying the eggs was not effective and has been replaced by dusting with 5% DDT and 1% 666 powder[61].

These are but a few of the many instances of the growing interest in and use of modern methods of pest control. It will be many years yet, however, before supplies of insecticides are sufficient to meet the needs of the country or knowledge of their best use has spread universally.

Close Planting and Deep Ploughing

The 'Eight Point' Charter calls for close planting and deep ploughing as a means of achieving greater output per *mow*. During the First Five-year Plan much experimenting was done in this field, the results of which led, for a time, to fanatical optimism, for the very high yields which could be obtained under laboratory conditions were given universal validity. For example, 5,000 *chin* of winter wheat per *mow* were raised in North China by intensive, experimental methods on a few small plots. In the wild enthusiasm then obtaining, some planners jumped to the conclusion that this order of production could immediately be achieved throughout the country. Any idea of 'diminishing returns in agriculture' was ridiculed and 'the productive capacity of the land is unlimited' was affirmed[62]. On this basis the 'three-three' system of agriculture was proposed whereby the crop-growing area was actually to be reduced. One third of the land was to be under crops, one third to be afforested and one third to be left to lie fallow.

'If more than 10% of the winter wheat fields planted this year will produce 5,000 *chin*/*mow*, the sowing area of wheat may be duly reduced next year. If the per *mow* yield of grain crops can be universally raised to a level ranging between 3,000 and 5,000 *chin*/*mow*, the sowing area for grain can be reduced from 1,800 million *mow* in the country to less than 600 *mow*.'[62]

Note the disparity between this estimate and the targets of the Twelve-year Plan (p. 49). Happily more realistic and prudent councils quickly prevailed.

Close planting and inter-row planting is being increasingly practised, but its success clearly depends largely on the amount of fertilizer available and the quality of ploughing. The old Chinese plough seldom turned the earth to more than a depth of 4 in. The new ploughs, provided adequate power is available, can turn an 8–10 in furrow. Unfortunately, the too-quick and too-wide (an adoption of the Russian type plough) has not been a great success. Experience in south China has shown that light yellow oxen are not strong enough for this work. The Agricultural Development Program called for deep ploughing to a depth of 10–30 in, depending on the nature of the soil, to be carried out at intervals of 3 years. It is claimed that, by the end of 1958, 133 million acres had been so treated. However, Philips and Kuo[39], writing in 1961, stated: 'There are recent indications that the policy may be changing since it seems to be recognized that these techniques aid agricultural production only under certain conditions and that their over-emphasis may produce negative results.' Deep ploughing may be valuable in some instances in the south, where some plant food, lost through leaching, may be recovered. On the other hand, deep ploughing in the paddy lands may be disastrous if the iron pan, the thin impervious layer, which retains the water, is broken.

Field Management

Under this heading comparatively little has been written specifically of the 'Eight Points', possibly because it could be made to embrace nearly the whole gamut of agricultural production. Most of what should be included, such as the rotation of crops and the techniques of cultivation, receives some treatment in Chapter V which deals with agricultural regions.

We have touched briefly on the efforts being made to wean the peasant from his reliance on the old Agricultural Calendar (see Fei Hsiao-tung, Agric. Dev. p. 19). Closely associated with this is the peasant's reluctance to abandon his cherished customs, festivals and superstitious beliefs, which, in the eyes of the planners, are obstacles to modern agricultural practice and must be eliminated as quickly as possible—a task that is proving by no means easy.

Under this heading there is a call for constant and greater frugality. 'Attention should be paid to acclaiming exemplary cases of being high cost conscious, of leading a frugal life, and of increasing savings and family accumulation of wealth . . . All wedding and funeral ceremonies and other social parties should be held in the simplest manner in rural areas. An effort should be made to change all irrational customs and habits.'[63]

The 'ever-filled' granary in old China was a concept and a sign of good government. Today all communes and brigades are urged to have up to one-and-a-half years' reserve of grain for emergency use. A great difficulty in this connection is adequate storage. In the north, the grain is stored in great piles under matting. This is sufficient cover during the dry winter, but not in summer, nor does it give protection against the ravages of rodents, grain moth, mites and weevils which do great damage. Better granaries are being built and a new, aluminium phosphide fumigating agent is being widely used[64].

Partly as an application of communist educational theory of combining study with practice, partly to increase agricultural production, partly to meet the problem of shortage of schools and teachers, and partly to meet the demand for more qualified clerical personnel in the communes, there has been a great extension in rural areas of the work-study school, whereby boys and girls in middle schools divide their time between academic subjects and work in the fields. Since the growth of advanced co-operatives and communes, there has not been sufficient clerical staff to fulfil all the accountancy demands attendant on their complex activities. This is one of the basic reasons for the inadequacy of Chinese statistics. Conversely, from below there have been constant complaints of indiscriminate, bureaucratic

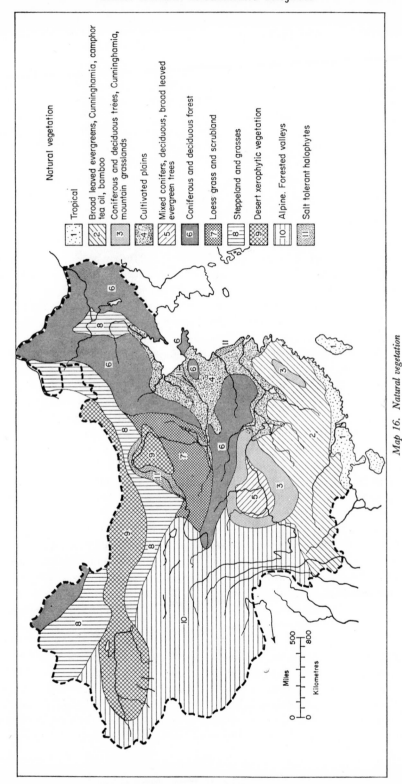

Map 16. *Natural vegetation*

Natural vegetation

1. Tropical

2. Broad leaved evergreens, Cunninghamia, camphor tea oil, bamboo

3. Coniferous and deciduous trees, Cunninghamia, mountain grasslands

4. Cultivated plains

5. Mixed conifers, deciduous, broad leaved evergreen trees

6. Coniferous and deciduous forest

7. Loess grass and scrubland

8. Steppeland and grasses

9. Desert xerophytic vegetation

10. Alpine. Forested valleys

11. Salt tolerant halophytes

Miles

Kilometres

demands for the completion of endless and needless forms, which have led to irritation and carelessness[65].

Forestry

Map 16 shows most of China Proper and the North-East with woodland cover. A line drawn from Yunnan to Heilungkiang effectively divides the country into two natural regions, the dry, treeless west and the wet, forested east. Even the cultivated plains of the east would largely be covered with trees if the land had no human occupation. But the map, useful in giving a reminder of natural conditions, gives quite a false picture of the forestry situation as it exists today.

When the Chinese began their expansion southwards from the largely treeless loess region in Ch'in (221–206 B.C.) and Han (206 B.C.–A.D. 220) times, they encountered the densely forested areas of the Chu and Yueh peoples in the lower Yangtze, described by Ssu-ma Chien as 'a large territory, sparsely populated, where people eat rice and drink fish soup, where the land is tilled with fire (i.e. ladang cultivation) and hoed with water; where people collect fruits and shellfish for food.' These were lands where the arduous work of forest clearance had to be done before traditional cultivation could begin and these were the conditions which faced the colonists everywhere in their southward movement. Thus the forest was regarded as an enemy and this has coloured the Chinese farmer's attitude to woodland right down to the twentieth century. As population increased, so destruction of the wooded lands continued far beyond the needs of clearance for cultivation. The uplands have furnished him with fuel, first with wood from the trees and then with grass, which has replaced them, for, in spite of the wide-spread abundance of coal, these are the only fuels which will serve his brick cooking stoves. It is interesting to speculate on what the effects would have been had an acceptable coal-burning stove been introduced at some time in China's history. The farmer also burns off his hillsides in winter for the ash, which, in theory, is washed down to the cultivated fields below by the summer rains. The burning also provides better young fodder for his animals. Another reason advanced for the clearance of the hillsides, at least in the southern half of China, is that it deprives robbers and wild animals of cover; the latter certainly still do considerable damage to crops[66]. But these have been poor returns compared with the disastrous soil erosion which forest clearance has engendered.

The result of this deforestation over the centuries is that, instead of the 30% tree cover, which in the opinion of Soviet experts, is necessary for adequate climate and soil regulation, China has a mere 5%. Su Ming[67] estimated that in 1950, of a total of 933 million hectares only 50 million hectares were forest land, or just over 5%. Philip and Kuo placed it at 8% and compared it with U.S.S.R. 33·9%, U.S. 32·6 and India 21·6%. Moreover, this remnant of forest is, for the most part, remote and inaccessible.

Afforestation

Since 1949 there have been serious and sustained efforts to promote afforestation in all parts of the country. It was realized that, if success were to be achieved in this field, the masses of peasants must be educated to appreciate the value of forests, that well-forested hills, by retaining water after heavy rain, prevent violent spate and so regulate the flow of the rivers, thus curbing flood, drought and soil erosion. In the drier west the value of the shelter belt in controlling wind and shifting sand had to be demonstrated.

Throughout the twentieth century realization of the importance of afforestation had been growing in informed circles. 'Arbor Day' was instituted and the value of trees taught in some schools. Once a year school children proceeded from school to the countryside, carrying young saplings, which they planted on the hillsides. Equally regularly each winter women, armed with their little bill-hooks, would emerge and strip the hills not only of their saplings but also grass and even roots in their search for fuel, thus vitiating any good that might have been done. Even if seedlings or saplings escaped this treatment, their chances of survival were minimal, since seldom was any after-care expended on them. With this experience in mind afforestation authorities have attempted mass education on the techniques of tree planting and after-care.

The division of the ownership of land into small plots is inimical to good forestry, which usually flourishes under large ownership. Prior to 1949, uncultivated areas adjacent to villages were regarded as belonging to the village generally, although there was no legal ownership. Consequently there was rarely much sense of responsibility. Chances of successful afforestation have been greatly enhanced by the joint ownership of land, which has come with the co-operatives and the communes. However, the following extract shows that the problem of ownership and care still demands attention:

'Party committees of all levels should correctly solve concrete problems peculiar to different localities according to Party policies and local conditions, and more properly arouse the enthusiasm of various quarters for afforestation. The main concern should be the correct handling of the problem of ownership in the collective economy. Today, there still exist some wasteland, sandland, grassland, and morasses between *hsien*, communes, and brigades whose ownership remains to be determined, with the result that when afforestation is carried out, these areas are often unattended. In these types of areas, ownership should be promptly determined so as to insure rational benefits from afforestation. In the people's commune, too, decision should be taken as to what belongs to the communes, brigades, or production teams. In the meantime, commune members should be encouraged to plant trees in front and in the rear of their houses. A clear announcement should be made to the effect that whoever plants the trees will own them. In this way, the problem of firewood for commune members can be partially solved, the need for a small quantity of timber for the use of the family can be met, and the economic income of the commune members can be increased. The determination of forest ownership is an important problem in forest development.'[68]

Afforestation planning presents a further example of 'walking on two legs'. On the one hand, great shelter belts of 1,000 km and more in length have been grown in the north, especially along the line of the Great Wall, at the instigation of the central authorities. On the other hand, 'round the village forest belts' have been urged on all localities. To carry out this work thousands of seed nurseries have been established throughout the country and every spring concerted drives, involving hundreds of thousands of mainly young persons, have resulted in the planting of vast areas with trees. The altruistic and patriotic element in this work has made a considerable appeal to the youth of the country. In this way it is estimated that 9,780,000 acres were planted between 1949 and 1957 and it was planned that 2·6 times this amount would be added between 1957 and 1967[39]. Between 1954 and 1958 nearly 100 million acres were surveyed for forestry purposes, about half by ground methods and half by aerial survey. In spite of all the work done to date, it has raised the forest cover to only about 10% of the whole, and forestry is still regarded as a weak link in the national economy[69]. Bitter complaints are still heard of the inadequacy of training and after-care[70].

The main areas in which afforestation has been effective are:

(1) *The North-East.* Since 1953 a reported 946,000 hectares have been afforested in this region, mainly in the Ta Hingan and Siao Hingan, along which line a shelter belt of poplar, willow and sugar maple, known as a 'Great Green Wall', of 1,600 km was completed by 1958. Along these mountain slopes 300 nurseries, raising mainly Korean pine, Scots pine and Manchurian ash, have been established. The long, cold winter restricts the planting period to only one month from mid-April. More than 60% of China's felled timber comes from this region. The industry, which is now well mechanized, employs 40,000 full-time forestry workers, who felled and replanted 133,000 hectares in 1965[71].

(2) *North China Plain.* A great deal of planting has been done along the dykes of the Hwang-ho, helping to strengthen them, and over the sandy wastes left by earlier flooding, helping to bind the shifting sands and reclaim the land for cultivation. Here the shelter belts are generally grown in a rectangular, criss-cross pattern.

(3) *Loess Region.* In this region of natural grass and scrub, efforts are being made to grow Chinese fir, poplar and Himalayan cedar. Trees here need careful planting and early attention, but once established they thrive. In the neighbouring Yinchwan region of Ningsia Aut. Reg., which is known as the 'silvery land' on account of the alkali salts which form a glittering layer, 15 afforestation centres have been opened and considerable progress made, particularly in the towns, where streets are now tree-lined with aspen, weeping willow and Chinese wax trees, and in the irrigated areas, where spruce, golden larch, fast-growing oleaster, elms and poplars are grown.

(4) *Inner Mongolia and Sinkiang.* Here state farms are stated to have planted 14,700 hectares between 1950 and 1964. The belts, 3 to 5 trees deep, skirt the farms and fields, line the sand dunes, irrigation canals and roads. The trees are now 12 to 15 m high and observers report a reduction of wind velocity of 27 to 40%, evaporation reduction of 20 to 25%, and effective protection of crops within a distance of 250 to 300 m[72]. Similar work is being done by the communes which occupy the oases around the Taklamakan desert and the northern slopes of the T'ien Shan.

(5) *Szechwan.* The Red Basin, whose natural cover is rich and very varied forest, suffered severe deforestation during the Sino-Japanese War (1937–45). This has now, to some extent, been remedied. Reports state that around Cheng-tu and Penki, 10 million mulberry trees have been planted along the roads, rivers, canals and fields. With the building of the Cheng-tu Paoki railway and the improvement of road communications, the vast and former-ly inaccessible forests of north Szechwan have been opened for development. The forests here are of great variety, providing timber for many industries such as ship-building, musical instruments, sports equipment, fine furniture, etc. The new timber industry is being mechanized with funicular railways, cranes, and powered saws[73].

(6) *Central China.* The forests of Hunan, Hupeh and Kiangsi received particularly rough treatment during the long troubled years of revolution, civil war and Japanese invasion during the first half of the twentieth century. The forests of west Hunan and west Hupeh,

chief source of timber for the lower Yangtze basin, have been severely exploited with comparatively little re-afforestation after felling. This, to some degree, has been remedied since 'Liberation'.

(7) *South China.* On the hills, which form so large a part of south China, there has been much planting of tung oil, tea oil, Chinese chestnut, together with bamboo and many kinds of fruit. Along the sandy coast, coconut palms have been raised to help in anchoring the dunes. There has been some experimenting in the aerial sowing of pine seeds both here and in Kweichow[74].

Some indication of the progress in afforestation, which has been made in this region, is the emphasis which is now being made on the necessity for making fire lanes and taking fire precautions.

REFERENCES

[1] 'In Yangtan People's Commune', *Peking Review*, No. 10, Mar. 1966
[2] *N.C.N.A.* Hofei, 3 May 1966
[3] BUCK, J. LOSSING, *Land Utilization in China*, Commercial Press, Shanghai, 1937
[4] HAN SU-YIN. *The Crippled Tree*, Cape, London, 1965, pp. 34–35
[5] SUN CHING-CHIH (Ed.). *Economic Geography of North-east China*, Peking, 1959
[6] *N.C.N.A.* Sining, 26 April 1966
[7] TREGEAR, T. R. *A Geography of China*, University of London Press, London, 1965, pp. 251, 68–80, 216, 108, 94
[8] Book of Hsia (see Chavannes, E. *Les Memoires Historiques de Ssu Ma Chien* 17th Treatise, Canals and Rivers, Leroux, Paris, 1898)
[9] YAO SHAN-YU. 'Geographical Distribution of Floods and Droughts in Chinese History, 206 B.C.–A.D. 1911', *Far Eastern Quart.*, Aug. 1943
[10] LITTLE, A. *The Far East*, Oxford University Press, London, 1905
[11] CHI WEN-SHUN. 'Water Conservancy in Communist China', *China Quart.*, No. 23 July/Sept. 1965
[12] *N.C.N.A.* Hofei, 18 Mar. 1965
[13] *N.C.N.A.* Hofei, 15 May 1966
[14] CHI HO-TEH and CHANG YEN-FENG. 'Carving out Rivers in the Hills', *China Reconstructs*, Peking, July 1965
[15] TENG TSE-HIN. 'Report on the Multi-purpose Plan for Permanently Controlling the Yellow River and Exploiting its Water Resources', *People's China*, Sept. 1955, pp. 7, 12, 17, 15
[16] *N.C.N.A.* Tientsin, 9 July, 1966
[17] LINDSAY, T. J. 'Water Conservancy in China', *Contemporary China*, Vol. 1, 1956–7, Hong Kong University Press, Hong Kong, 1958
[18] *Peking Pei-ching Jih-pao*, 22 Nov. 1966
[19] *Far Eastern Trade*, May, 1958
[20] AFANAS'YESKIY, Y. A. *Szechwan*, Moscow, 1962
[21] *Peking Jen-min Jih-pao*, 9 Sept. 1965
[22] LATTIMORE, O. *Geographical Journal*, Vol. CX, Nos. 4–6 (1947) 180
[23] *N.C.N.A.* Urumchi, 31 Oct. 1964
[24] *N.C.N.A.* Yinchuan, 1 Sept. 1965
[25] *N.C.N.A.* Nanking, 14 June 1965
[26] *N.C.N.A.* Sian, 10 Sept. 1965
[27] *Peking, Jen-min Jih-pao*, 21 April 1966
[28] *China Reconstructs*, Aug, 1966; *N.C.N.A.*, Changsha, 5 Aug. 1966
[29] KUO TE-TSUN. 'An Investigation into the Construction of Small Stone Dams in Tzuehung Hsien', *Ching-chi Yen-chiu (Economic Research)*, No. 7, July, 1965
[30] *Peking Review*, No. 27, 2 July (1965)
[31] SU TSUNG-SUNG. 'Irrigation Renews the Land', *China Reconstructs*, Nov. 1964
[32] *N.C.N.A.* Canton, 17 Oct. 1964
[33] REGIS, GIUSEPPE. 'Developments in Chinese Agriculture', *Far Eastern Trade*, Jan. 1962; *Peking, Jen-min Jih-pao*, 5 Nov. 1965
[34] *K'o-hsueh Ting-pao (Science Journal)*, No. 2, 17 Feb. 1965
[35] *N.C.N.A.* Peking, 5 June 1965
[36] LIU JUNG-CHAO. 'Fertilizer Application in Communist China', *China Quart.*, No. 24, Oct./Dec. 1965
[37] KAO KUANG-CHIEN. 'Great Strides Forward in Fertilizers', *China Reconstructs*, Feb. 1965
[38] MacDOUGALL, COLINA. 'Industrial Upsurge', *Far Eastern Economic Review*, 30 Sept. 1965
[39] PHILLIPS, R. W. and KUO, L. T. C. 'Agricultural Science and its Application', *China Quart*, No. 6, April-June 1961
[40] MacDOUGALL, COLINA. 'Production Records', *Far Eastern Economic Review*, 29 Sept. 1966

[41] *Far Eastern Trade*, March 1966
[42] LI MEI-SEN and YEH CH'AO-LIN, 'Superior Strains', *Chung Kuo Ching-nein*, (*China Youth*), No. 8, April 1965
[43] *N.C.N.A.* Chengtu, 27 Nov. 1965
[44] MAO TSE-TUNG. *The Question of Agricultural Co-operation*, Foreign Language Press, Peking, 1956, p. 34
[45] *Far East Trade*, Vol. 21, No. 1, July 1966
[46] KUO, L. T. C. 'Agricultural Mechanization in China', *China Quart.*, No. 17, Jan./Mar. 1964
[47] *N.C.N.A.*, Canton, 1 June 1966
[48] *N.C.N.A.*, Peking, 31 Jan. 1966
[49] SHANG CHIH-LING and MU CHING-P'O. 'Fifteen Years of Agricultural Mechanization of State Farms', *Technology and Agricultural Machinery, No. 11*, Peking, 1964
[50] CHUN WEN. 'China's Farm Machine-building Industry', *Peking Review*, No. 26, July 1963
[51] CHING TAN. Machinery Especially for Chinese Farms, *China Reconstructs*, Aug. 1964
[52] *N.C.N.A.* Nanning, 14 Nov. 1965
[53] YANG MIN. 'Mechanizing Rice Planting', *Peking Review*, 5 July 1963
[54] *Lung-ts'an Chin-jung* (*Rural Finance*), No. 10, 21 May, 1965
[55] *N.C.N.A.*, Chengchow, 23 Oct. 1965
[56] *N.C.N.A.*, Nanchang, 20 Oct. 1965
[57] *N.C.N.A.*, Changsha, 16 May. 1965
[58] *N.C.N.A.*, Peking, 20 Oct. 1965
[59] *N.C.N.A.*, Wuhan, 20 Oct. 1965
[60] *N.C.N.A.*, Foochow, 20 July 1965
[61] *China Reconstructs*, 18 May 1965
[62] *Peking Review*, No. 42 (1958) 12, 13
[63] *National Agricultural Development Program* (1956–67)
[64] *N.C.N.A.*, Shenyang, 7 June 1965
[65] P'AN LING. 'What should we do with too many reports and forms?' *Nan-fang Jih-pao*, 5 June 1964
[66] FENZEL, G. 'On the Natural Conditions Affecting the Introduction of Forestry in the Province of Kwangtung', *Lingnan Science Journal*, No. 7 (1929)
[67] SU MING, 'Forestry in New China', *Jen-min Tsung-pao*, 16 Nov. 1950
[68] 'Make an Early Preparation for Developing the Afforestation Movement', Editorial, *People's Daily*, Peking, 15 Dec. 1964
[69] *People's Daily*, Peking, 6 Feb. 1966
[70] 'Forest Construction is a Key Measure for the Basic Solution of the Agricultural Question', *People's Daily*, Peking, 14 Nov. 1964
[71] *N.C.N.A.*, Harbin, 10 June 1965
[72] *N.C.N.A.*, Urumchi, 21 Jan. 1965
[73] *N.C.N.A.*, Peking, 18 Dec. 1965
[74] *N.C.N.A.*, Kweiyang, 29 May 1965

5

AGRICULTURAL REGIONS

DIFFERENCES of altitude and rainfall combine to divide China into two parts which are not far from equal in area. To the north and west lie the great plateau lands of Tibet, Inner Mongolia and Sinkiang, the eastern boundary of which roughly marks the 15 in isohyet. Lands to the west become progressively drier and lands to the east progressively wetter. This isohyet also approximates quite closely with the Great Wall which divided 'China Proper' of the 18 provinces from the outlying imperial lands; the China of the *Han Jen*, the Men of Han or true Chinese from the barbarians of the outer regions. When Ch'in Shih Hwang Ti (221–206 B.C.) built this wall, his object was not only to check the entry of the barbarians into China, but also to dissuade the Chinese frontiersmen from moving outside, for this meant passing from a settled, agricultural economy into a nomadic, pastoral way of life[1]. Thus, our first big division is one which stretches across the entire land from south-west to north-east, separating pastoral from arable farming.

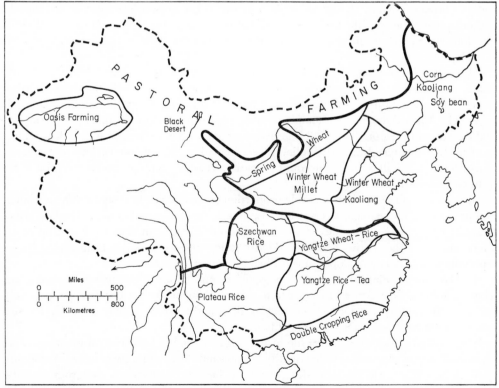

Map 17. Agricultural regions. (After Lossing Buck)

91

The arable region itself can be divided into two almost equal parts by a line running from west to east from the Nan Shan in Kansu, through the Chin Ling Shan and Funiu Shan to the sea. This is a line of great geographical significance. It divides the geologically older north from the younger south; climatically the north is drier and warmer than the south; northern soils are alkaline in contrast to the acid soils of the south; dry farming, with comparatively little irrigation, producing wheat and millet, contrasts strongly with the wet rice paddy which is general in the south. Even the people show different characteristics. Generally speaking, the Han Jen of the north are taller, slower and more phlegmatic than the shorter, volatile T'ang Jen of the south[1].

The further subdivision of these arable lands has followed quite closely those made by Lossing Buck in his *Land Utilization in China* on the basis of the outstanding crop or crops of the area, which will serve as a focal point for detailed discussion of all the agricultural activities of the district. Most of these areas are larger than the British Isles and consequently have considerable variety within their borders.

PASTORAL FARMING

The grasslands of the north-west, which support the pastoral activities, occupy about two-fifths of China's territory. Big differences of altitude, climate and topography are responsible for great variations in type and productivity. These grasslands stretch from eastern Inner Mongolia to the Pamirs in west Sinkiang and from the U.S.S.R. border at Altai to the Indian border at Lhasa. Large areas, such as the Takla Makan, are pure desert and are without population, but the greater part of the region is steppeland, and can be divided into four zones, which, although they have a common grassland denominator, vary considerably in character[2].

(1) Eastern Inner Mongolia and Heilungkiang on the east facing slopes of the Ta Hingan Shan. These are the most luxuriant of the pastures, lying on the wetter, eastern-facing slopes of the mountains and receiving some effect of the summer south-east monsoon.

(2) The Inner Mongolian high plain, lying north of the Yin Shan, Hara Narin Ula and the Kansu Corridor. This land is undulating; its winters are longer and colder and it is more arid than eastern Inner Mongolia. It is estimated to contain 860,000 km^2 of grassland, of which less than half is used on account of aridity. It becomes progressively less productive from east to west.

(3) Sinkiang contains a considerable proportion of true desert, notably the Takla Makan and parts of central Dzungaria. Over 60% is, in fact, virtually uninhabited. The best grasslands lie on the mountain sides of the Kunlun and T'ien Shan above the ring of oases, which surround the Tarim basin, in the Ili valley and around the Dzungarian basin, especially on the northern slopes of the T'ien Shan and Altai Shan.

(4) The Tibetan Plateau as a whole is too frigid and too arid to bear much good grass. There is some good pasture in the eastern part of Tsinghai, but it becomes progressively poorer as the country becomes higher, rockier, drier and more desolate in the west. Pasture is also good in south-east Tibet around Lhasa.

From earliest times the mode of life in these grasslands has been basically nomadic. It has varied largely in response to the quality of grass and the availability of water. Generally speaking, the more arid the land the greater has been the movement, the group or tribe sometimes moving 10–20 times in a year over distances of 150–200 km. As might be expected, the nearer the approach to settled communities, as, for example, along the elongated oases of the northern bend of the Hwang-ho, the less nomadic has been the way of life and a transitional zone of semi-pastoralist, semi-arable farmer is to be found.

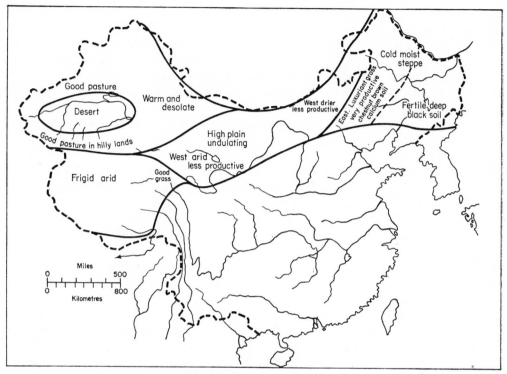

Map 18. Grasslands of the north

Until recently most of these lands have been occupied by leagues and banners owning only tribal allegiance. Law and order and the rule of a central government have been lacking. There was considerable banditry and cattle rustling[3]. In consequence, the use of the pasture has generally been wanton and competitive leading to over-grazing and deterioration. Both winter feed and winter shelter have been inadequate, resulting in disease and the ravages of predators, notably wolves. Animal husbandry has been primitive, conservative and backward. Thus annual losses have always been very great and population of men and animals has tended to remain stationary.

With 'Liberation' in 1949, some measure of central control over these vast outlying areas began to be possible. Old tribal sovereignty has been abolished. Boundaries of territory have been established and the rights of use of land have been fixed with a view to eliminating unplanned and reckless grazing, and the reduction of friction. Old league and banner organizations have been retained alongside the coming of co-operatives and communes. These reforms were a necessary first step towards achieving, as in the U.S.S.R., the general aim of a planned and settled pastoralism instead of nomadism, and also the promotion of much greater animal productivity. Even so, the idea that the pastures are very wide and that it does not matter whether their use is fixed or not, dies hard.

To open up the grasslands properly and scientifically, comprehensive surveys must be carried out in the hydrographic, geological, ecological and pedological fields. Already much work has been carried out over wide areas. A large research centre, covering all aspects of pastoral life and including the Chinese Grassland Research Institute, the Institute of Zoology and the Institute of Botany, has been established in Inner Mongolia and is doing valuable work[4]. During the years 1950–1965 much effort has been expended on convincing the pastoralists of the value of careful grazing. Seasonal and rotational grazing has been used in a rough way by herdsmen for a long time. It now needs mapping and planning so that pastures may be closed and the grasses properly nursed, to allow them to tiller and seed. The Icechao League of Inner Mongolia now closes specified parts of its pasture-land regularly between May and August[2].

Great attention has naturally been focused on increasing water supply. Surveys have revealed wide areas, particularly in Inner Mongolia, that have abundant underground water, which is being increasingly tapped by the sinking of thousands of wells. Between 1949 and 1963 it was reported that more than 20,000 wells were sunk in Inner Mongolia alone. These include 100, some 300 ft deep, equipped with power pumping machinery[5]. Drinking water for human beings and herds is now much more plentiful; in many areas water is available for the irrigation of fodder crops (clover), for green manure and for the afforestation of dunes by growing artemisia and other drought-resisting plants and trees, so regenerating failing pastures[6]. The Alashan Left Banner, occupying a notoriously dry area with no rivers, reports that it has sunk 2,200 new wells and tapped 380 springs, thus converting 8,900 km² of dry grassland into good pasture and enabling the communes to grow fodder crops of clover.

Much of the best pasture in Sinkiang is high up in the mountains of the Kunlun, T'ien Shan and Altai. In the Kunlun rich grasses lie above the loess-covered moraines of the lower slopes[1]. Here and on the north and south slopes of the T'ien Shan the pastures are fed by the melting snows from above. In Dzungaria the influence of Siberia is greater than in the Tarim; snowfall is greater and rainfall increases with altitude. In the Altai a belt of steppe lies above an expanse of desert and semi-desert. Above the grasslands is a belt of forest, composed largely of Siberian larch and white birch, whose bark is useful in souring milk. This is a great hunting area (wolf, fox, sable, ermine, bears and wolverines). Above the forests are the alpine meadows on which the famous Altai horses are bred. The Ulyungui Nor and the Irtish river abound in fish and waterfowl. With the improvement in communications these are beginning to be exploited commercially.

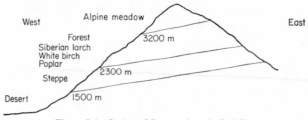

Figure 5.1. Section of Dzungaria and Altai Shan

Sheep and goats, roughly in equal proportions, are by far the most important, the most ubiquitous and most numerous animals reared on the grasslands. Cattle, horses and camels

94

follow in that order, and these are more specialized territorially. In addition to the Altai horses mentioned above, the Ili valley is famous for its fine breed of 'San-ho' horses, which are very hardy and strong and are reputed to be able to travel 30–40 km /day for days on end. Bactrian camels are reared in large numbers in the Kansu Corridor, a region which grows an abundance of shrubs and wild plants relished by camels. It is reported that there are now more than 40,000 camels in this area[7].

There is a sharp differentiation of numbers, kinds and distribution of animals between the true pastoral zone and the semi-pastoral, semi-arable zones. Pastoral regions rear only sheep, goats, cattle, horses and camels. Semi-pastoral, semi-arable regions have a much smaller proportion of sheep and a considerable number of pigs, together with some donkeys and mules.

Distribution of Livestock, Inner Mongolia

	Sheep & goats %	Cattle %	Horses %	Camels %	Pigs %	Donkeys %	Mules %
Pastoral zone	81·1	13·8	4·1	1·0	—	—	—
Agric. & agric./ pastoral zone	58·9	19·4	2·8	0·1	13·3	5·0	0·5

There are no comprehensive figures of animal population for the whole of the pastoral region, but there can be no doubt that, over the last 15 years, numbers have increased enormously, so much so that warnings against blindly doing so have been issued. In 1946 it was estimated that there were 8 million head of livestock in Inner Mongolia. In 1962 the figure stood at 32 million[9]. In 1965 it was reported that 11,260,000 head of young

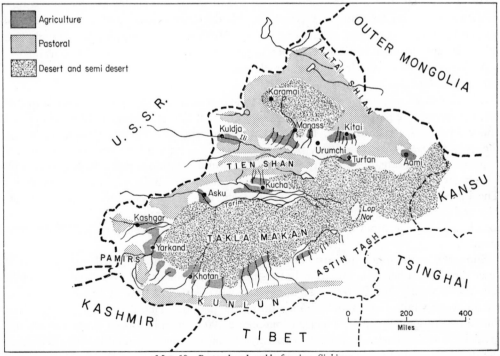

Map 19. Pastoral and arable farming, Sinkiang

animals had been added during the breeding season, bringing the estimated total to 40 million head. Tibet was estimated to hold 10 million head, an increase of 600,000 over 1964. This figure probably includes the 3·6 million lambs reported to have been born in 1965 in Tsinghai[10].

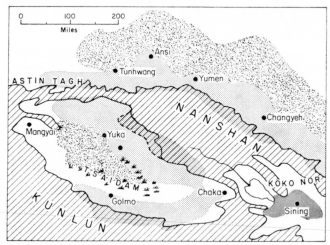

Map 20. Pastoral and arable farming, Tsinghai

There are several reasons for this rapid increase of stock. Apart from the great improvement in water facilities and the increased storage of winter forage, far greater care is now being expended on the animals themselves. Paddocks and sheds, giving shelter against winter blizzards—the great killer—are now widespread. The dipping of animals and injections are cutting down the incidence of disease. Many women have been trained to serve with the mobile veterinary units, which move over the steppeland, fulfilling a valuable educational function in animal husbandry.

The experimenting in and introduction of new breeds is having a profound effect on the life, not only of the pastoral people, but also on those of the settled regions of Sinkiang and Inner Mongolia. In Sinkiang, the development of the first fine-wool breed of sheep, the *gungnais*, was started in 1954, producing a large animal giving delicious mutton, a high propagation rate, adaptability to differing natural conditions and a high-grade wool. This latter quality is forming the basis of a rapidly developing indigenous woollen industry. The introduction of Romney Marsh and Lincoln Long-wool pedigree sheep into Inner Mongolia, has, among other things, resulted in the increase of the yield of wool per sheep to 3 km, about five times the previous yield. There are now several million head of this breed[11].

Similarly, in the sphere of cattle breeding, the crossing of short-horned bulls with local cows through artificial insemination has resulted in a big increase in beef and a threefold increase in milk yield. Crossing Heilungkiang cows with Puichow bulls has achieved a rise in average milk yield from 553·5 kg during the period of lactation to 2,705·5 kg in the fourth generation. By 1965 in Inner Mongolia, 2,500 women had been trained in animal artificial insemination[11]. In Tsinghai experimental farms have been established, attempting the domestication of wild animals, including deer, whose antlers are the source of drugs used in traditional Chinese medicine. The cross-breeding of the domesticated Tibetan sheep with the hardy, wild breed (*ovis ammon dotvina*) and the domesticated yak with the wild yak are two experiments which are proving successful[12].

As a result of the big increase in milk, reports state that Inner Mongolia now has 17 major milk processing factories, producing powdered and condensed milk, butter, lactose and cheese, and an increasing number of meat canning factories[13].

Mechanization in the pastoral areas is still in its initial stages. Pumps for wells, and shearing machines are steadily being introduced. Horse-drawn forage harvesters and rakes are now widely used in the better pastures and in large communes; where the supply of water is such that extensive forage crops are grown, tractors are in use[14].

Nevertheless, the National Livestock Breeding Conference, 1965, while reporting an increase of 10 million head of improved breeds, stated that 'compared with farming of the land . . . the breeding of large animals is still a weak link in agriculture'[15]. Draught animals are in short supply and are still urgently needed throughout China.

Within this vast region of pastoralism or emptiness lie a few pockets of settlement, most of which have been in existence for 20 centuries or more. They are, with few exceptions, oases situated in the more arid parts of the area.

Most notable is the ring of oases in the Tarim Basin, which surround the Takla Makan. They lie at the foot of the Kunlun, Astin Tagh and Tien Shan, which enfold the basin. Each oasis is sited on a river descending from the snow and ice fields above and at a point below the piedmont gravel, which the river has deposited as it fanned out on to the plain. Thence the river continues for varying distances until it is lost in the desert. Such are the sites of Charchan, Keriya, Khotan, Yarkand, Kashgar, Aksu and Kucha, cities through which the Imperial Silk Route and Imperial Highway passed in the days of the Han dynasty (206 B.C.–A.D. 220) ascendency. They existed then, as they still do today, solely by virtue of the water supply from the snow-capped mountains above and are surrounded by inhospitable desert[1]. Farther north, on the northern slopes of the Tien Shan and Bogdo Ula, there were small settlements on the steppeland at Urumchi, Kitai and Manass, ports of call on the caravan route to the Dzungarian Gate.

It is these settled centres and the regions immediately around them that have undergone so great a change since 1949. The census of 1953 showed Sinkiang as having a population of 4,874,000, of which 4,198,000 were Turkic and only 300,000 Han Chinese. Of the Turkic people, 3,640,000 were Uighurs and 475,000 Kazakhs. There are smaller numbers of Kirghiz, Mongols and Huis. In 1964 the Uighur population was given as 4 million. The Han population was stated to have risen to 2,600,000, an average increase of 255,000 a year, due almost entirely to immigration[16].

This enormous influx of Chinese is located largely in Dzungaria in and near the old settlements and new towns along the northern slopes of the Tien Shan and Bogdo Ula. This immigration is the result of a set Government policy, which has two main aims. One aim is to sinicize this outlying region, which is essentially Moslem in religion and culture, and so make more secure a weak frontier. The other aim is the opening of a promising outlet for China's ever-growing population. Given modern engineering and technological resources, this is a region, which is capable of great development in spite of its aridity and extremes of climate. Schomberg in 1932 estimated that from one-third to one-half of Sinkiang's water ran to waste and that, with proper conservation, it could irrigate up to 20 million acres of barren land.

When the civil war came to an end in 1949, the large contingents of the Peoples Liberation Army (P.L.A.), stationed in Sinkiang and deeply steeped in revolutionary ideas, were converted into a Production and Construction Corps. Ever since, it has devoted its energies and skills to all kinds of reclamation and construction work, including big projects of water conservation, reclamation of saline lands, the establishment of state farms and communes, afforestation and the building of railways and highways. As the projects have been completed, large numbers of the Corps have been demobilized and have settled on the farms or in the new towns and factories, which they have built. Their places have been taken by a constant flow of recruits to the P.L.A. and school leavers (15–22 years) from China Proper who volunteer for 3 years service in the area[17]. It is claimed that this Corps alone has reclaimed more than 10 million *mow* of virgin land, has established over 100 state farms and built many complete systems of industry[18]. It is difficult to arrive at an accurate assessment of what has been accomplished in the settled areas in the years since 1949 as reports are often confused and confusing, but there can be no doubt that a great deal has been achieved and revolutionary changes have taken place in the agricultural and industrial fields.

Because of the preponderant Turkic composition of the people of Sinkiang and the independent nature of the Uighur people, the formation of co-operatives and communes has been introduced with some circumspection. Great care was taken to reassure the pastoralists that their means of subsistence, i.e. yurts, personal belongings such as utensils, rugs, saddles and trappings for horses, together with a sufficient number of horses for transport, would remain in their private ownership[17]. Whether this reassurance will ultimately carry conviction and achieve conversion of the Uighurs to the new way of life, time alone will tell. Nevertheless, communes now appear to be the universal pattern of rural organization. Roughly a twofold development can be distinguished: the extension of old, existing oases in the periphery of the Tarim Basin in which the Uighurs predominate and the establishment of new towns and villages on the northern slopes of the Tien Shan where the people are mainly Chinese.

By utilizing the waters from the many rivers from the Kunlun, by building reservoirs and constructing thousands of kilometres of canals, the old oases of Keriya, Khotan, Yarkand and Kashgar have been expanded beyond recognition. They have pushed northward into the desert and extended laterally east and west, filling much of the empty desert space which formerly separated them. Along this southern edge of the Tarim Basin 42 new oases have been established, opening up 53,000 hectares (approx. 800,000 *mow*) to new cultivation. Around Khotan alone 40 new villages have been set up by 45 communes[16]. The old towns have developed modern industries and now have the amenities of modern cities. Kashgar, which had a population of 30,000 in 1949, is now a city of over 100,000. Freeberne[16] quotes the following description of the growth of a new town, north of Kashgar:

'Atushi, capital of the Kezlesu Khalkhas Autonomous *Chou* in western Sinkiang, has emerged with several other towns on the stretch of wilderness ringed by towering mountains on the edge of the Great Gobi Desert [Tahla Makan]. Today it has a population of tens of thousands, with all the amenities of a modern township—office buildings, factories, hospital, cinema, department store, bank, post office and schools.'

Immigrant Chinese are mainly responsible for the establishment and growth of the rural settlements, the hundreds of new villages and the many new towns, e.g. Shihhotzu, along the northern slopes of the Tien Shan. It is here that a great number of the state arable and state stock-breeding farms have been carved out of the arid land. The state farms, with their large 50–80 acre fields, ringed with shelter belts of trees, are highly mechanized. There are now 76 state-owned tractor stations in the area, controlling nearly 5,000 tractors (15 h.p. units). The grain crops consist of winter and spring wheat, hybrid maize, millet and kaoliang with some rice. The claim is made that Sinkiang is now self-sufficient in grain. Commercial crops are cotton and sugar beet. Cotton-growing is centred in the newly developed area of the Manass river and its production is six times greater than it was in 1949. Sericulture is also increasing both here and in the Tarim oases.

The vast agricultural expansion has been accompanied by equally rapid industrialization. Modern industry in towns, which formerly boasted only handicrafts, have grown with phenominal rapidity. Industry is based on the oil fields of Karamai, the coal fields of Urumchi, Hami and Kuldja and on thermal and hydro-electric power. More than 500 modern plants have been built, concerned with oil refining, iron and steel, machine building, electric power, textiles (notably woollens and cotton), cement and chemical fertilizer[20]. Urumchi, the capital, has grown from a population of 80,000 in 1949 to at least 400,000 in 1962. Thirty-nine new motor roads, totalling more than 3,000 km now connect the arable with the stock-breeding areas and it is claimed that 85% of the rural communes are now linked. by regular motor services[21].

Lying north of the Tien Shan, but cut off from the rest of Dzungaria by the Boro Horo Ula, is the comparatively small but important valley of the Ili River, which flows westward to Lake Balkhash. It lies open to U.S.S.R. Kazakhstan and to western climatic influences. It is occupied by Kazakhs and Uighurs, whose racial and cultural affinities lie westward rather than eastward. It is wetter and more fertile than the rest of Sinkiang and a large part of its population is engaged in arable farming and therefore settled. Its high production of wheat and other grain has earned for it the title of 'the granary of Sinkiang'. The pastoralists, who are mainly Kazakhs, are now becoming settled. In addition to the famous Ili 'San-ho', horses, mentioned above, they raise large numbers of sheep and goats. The valley has good deposits of coal. With this coal as its base and Kuldja, the capital, as its centre, a considerable and varied industry, which includes iron and steel, machine building and textiles, has developed recently.

South-east of Urumchi and south of the Bodo Ula is the amazing Turfan Depression, which, in the heart of a plateau 3,000–4,000 ft above sea level, is itself some 900 ft below sea level. It lies in the midst of true desert and experiences great extremes of diurnal and annual temperature. Being virtually rainless, its water is derived from the snow-capped Bogdo Ula and its cultivation is dependent entirely on irrigation, which is part surface irrigation and part *karez*. In view of the dryness of the atmosphere, the *karez* irrigation, being underground, greatly reduces loss by evaporation[1]. Its chief crop is fruit, of which grapes are outstanding. Natural conditions are particularly favourable to viticulture. High day temperatures increase the sugar content of the grapes, while cold night temperatures keep them soft and juicy. The chief vineyards are in the 'Emerald Amidst the Land of Fire' valley, where many varieties of grapes are grown, the most famous being the white seedless grape from which the finest sun-dried raisins are produced[22]. Cotton and grain are other important products; 8,000 hectares of wheat were reported to have been harvested in 1966, an estimated increase of 10% over the previous year's yield[23]. Sericulture is also practiced successfully.

99

Apparently the Uighur population has been successfully organized into the usual pattern of commune, brigade and production teams and is reported to have increased its vineyards by 1,000 *mow*.

The north and north-west of Tibet, known as Chang Tang, is an arid, frigid and barren plateau, the greater part of which is over 16,000 ft high. It is virtually unpopulated. Levels descend towards the south-east and east to an average of about 12,000 ft and it is here that the main grasslands are found.

The main stock-breeding area is around Nagchuhu, about 130 miles north-east of Lhasa. This region supports 6½ million head of stock out of a Tibetan total of 16 million and is highly regarded on account of its high survival rate. In 1964, 1·23 million lambs survived out of 1·4 million born[24]. This has been due largely to the rapid extension of veterinary services in the outlying regions and to the introduction of a new vaccine, which is said to be most successful in combating 'nyker', an infectious sheep disease most virulent in the bitter winter. The Tibetans are now organized into stock-breeding co-operatives.

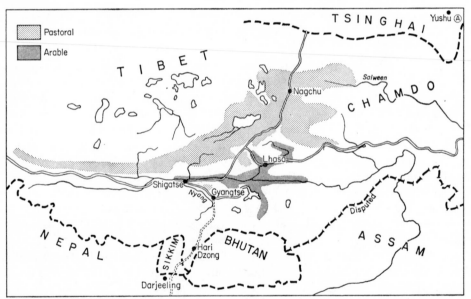

Map 21. Pastoral and arable land south-east Tibet

Arable farming is confined to the lower, warmer valleys in the south-east in the Lhasa, Shigatse, Gyangtse area. The cultivation of barley and wheat is reported to have been widely extended since 1951 under the influence of better tools, water supply and co-operation. *Tsamba*, made from barley, has become the staple diet. Tea, which formerly was transported from Szechwan in brick form by coolie labour, now enters in larger quantities by the motor highway. This trade has not yet been ousted by local production which is increasing. The first plantation of 10,000 shrubs was planted in 1952 and now produces four acceptable grades[25]. A lively exchange of pastoral and arable plus consumer goods is said to exist now between the stock-breeders of the north and the agriculturalists of the south.

In 1952 Tsinghai's farming activities were almost entirely concerned with pasture. The only arable farming possible was in the extreme east of the province in the lower-lying area around Sining. Fine-fleeced and coarse Tibetan and Mongolian sheep were reared on the slopes of the Astin Tagh and Nan Shan, producing 19,000 tons of fleece per annum. Yaks were reared around Koko Nor. These, the best mountain pack animals, are capable of carrying 150 kg loads for distances of 30–40 km/day. They give rich milk and produce good meat. Tsinghai's big, hardy South Tibetan horses are well known. Bactrian camels are bred in considerable numbers around the Tsaidam[26].

Since 1952 all these activities have continued and increased, but the region has undergone radical change. The discovery of oil and coal have led to the rapid development of roads. Between 1949 and 1964, 15,000 km of motor road have been built, cutting transport time to one-tenth and cost to one-fifth. This has had considerable effect on pastoral and arable farming and has produced much the same results as we have noted in Sinkiang and Inner Mongolia, i.e. the establishment of communes, the extension of irrigation, the reduction of nomadism, the growth of settled arable farming and the establishment of industries associated with farming.

Arable farming around Sining, which is now a modern city of 210,000 inhabitants, has been greatly extended. A new early-ripening spring wheat, 'Chinchun No. 1', has been evolved to cope with the short growing period of not more than 120 days, and yields of 6 ton/hectare are now obtained on the irrigated land on the Tsaidam plateau[27].

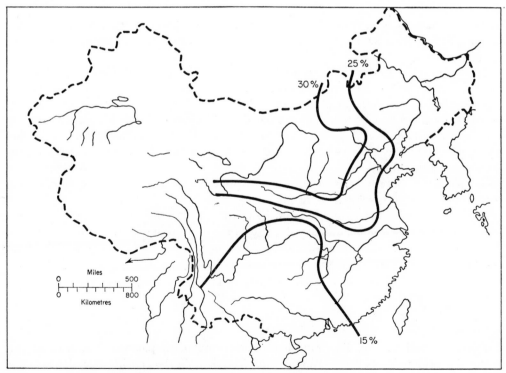

Map 22. Percentage variability of annual precipitation from the mean

The revolutionary changes we have noted in agriculture in these vast pastoral lands of Sinkiang, Inner Mongolia and Tibet have impinged on and revolutionized every aspect of life. The rapid advance of irrigation and the growth of forage crops is steadily reducing nomadism and the herdsman is deserting his *yurt* for a house, a settled life and all that it entails. Even if he is still nomadic, the old *yurt* is giving place to a new plastic type, which retains all the features of the traditional domed tent, made of felt with its collapsible lattice framework. The plastic has many advantages over the felt type. Its outer covering is of artificial leather, lined with foamed plastic. The lattice is made of plastic tubing and the rigging of caprone ropes. The windows are of organic glass and the floor is covered with plastic sheeting. It has greater resistance to insects and moisture, is lighter, more durable and has better insulation and ventilation[28].

The herdsman's sheepskin clothing is giving way, at least in summer, to textiles of wool and cotton. His diet is now more varied than formerly and his stock of consumer goods, which often includes a radio set, is greater. A considerable amount of education has been introduced, mainly through travelling schools and 'part study–part work' schools in which study time is varied according to the pressures of agricultural work. The subjects taught, in addition to political ideology, are reading, writing, simple arithmetic and farming, according to the particular circumstances. Travelling libraries are making their appearance. Finally, mobile clinics, concentrating on preventative medicine, are raising health standards.

ARABLE FARMING

Spring Wheat Region

Now moving to China Proper and the regions of arable farming; these are classified and labelled according to the most characteristic crop or crops of the area and serve as a basis for discussion of all the agricultural activities.

It is appropriate to start with an analysis of the Spring Wheat Region as it marks the zone of contention between pastoral and arable farming. As already remarked (p. 91), the boundary between these two ways of life coincides closely with both the 15 in isohyet and the line of the Great Wall. Throughout the centuries the Chinese farmer has tried to push northward and north-westward and there to establish his fields and farms. Time and time again he has been pushed back, not so much by the hostility of the 'barbarians', the lawless nomadic tribesmen, although their resistance and predatory raids have been by no means negligible, but rather by the unyielding climatic barrier, which makes arable farming bitterly hard and precarious. It remains to be seen how successful modern technology will be in overcoming the natural hazards. This is a region of great extremes of temperature, with a growing period of about 6 months, a low rainfall of 15 in or less, which, in addition, is most unreliable. Between two-thirds and three-quarters of its precipitation falls in the 3 summer months, June to August, and is liable to fail approximately one year in three.

	Jan.	Feb.	Mar.	April	May	June	July	Aug.	Sep.	Oct.	Nov.	Dec.
Saratsi Temp. °F	5	15	32	47	64	69	73	70	57	44	24	5
(3,078′) Rainfall in	0·1	0·2	0·3	0·3	0·9	1·8	3·9	2·9	2·0	0·6	0·1	0·1
Lanchow Temp. °F	20	24	39	53	61	70	73	62	49	49	37	25
(5,105′) Rainfall in	0·2	0·2	0·2	0·6	1·2	1·1	4·0	5·9	2·6	0·6	0·0	0·1

Pierre Teillard de Chardin, travelling on one of his many palaeontological excursions along the Hwang-ho between Paotow and Ningsia (Yinchwan) in 1923, laments the encroachment of the farmer into this area in these words:

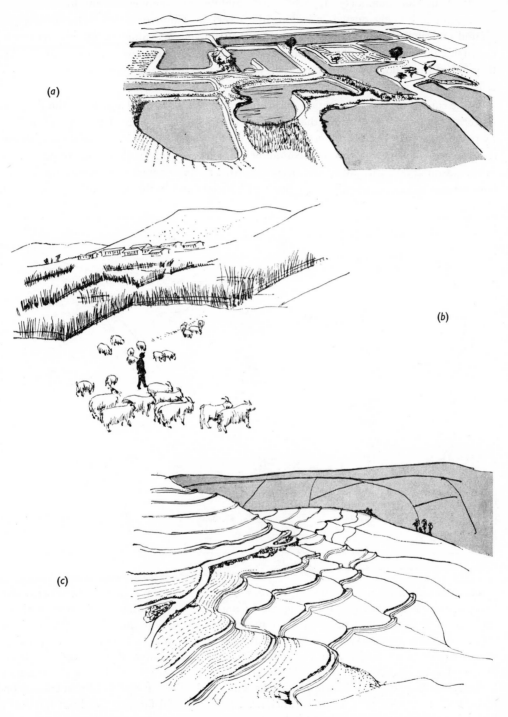

Contrasting land use: (a) Kwantung fish ponds; (b) Mongolian pasture; (c) loess terracing

'We are in Mongolia, a country whose true landowners—shepherds living in their yourts—are gradually being ousted (all along the river) by Chinese settlers, who scratch the ground and spoil the country far more than they enhance its value (because by recklessly destroying the age-old soil of the steppes and by cutting down the few trees that still remain, they loosen the sand, cause the formation of dunes and generally accelerate the terrifying erosion of these parts.'[29]

In the early days of rehabilitation and socialization between 1949 and 1952, the People's Government sought to reassure the pastoralists against the inroads of the agriculturalists by proclaiming a policy of 'protect pasturage, prohibit reclamation'[3]. Since then, with the development of co-operatives and communes and the sinking of thousands of new wells in the pasturelands, this policy has been discarded to some extent and encroachment has gone on apace, most markedly to the north of Huhehot and in the Ala Shan region.

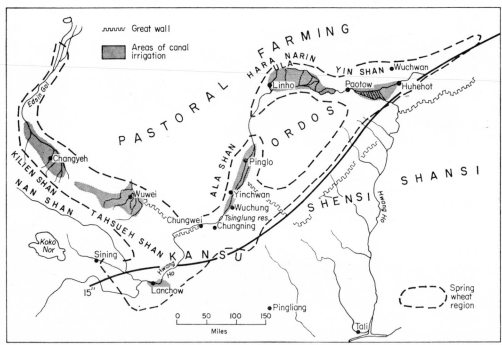

Map 23. Spring wheat region

The main intensive arable farming is concentrated in the three oases in the northward bend of the Hwang-ho, two of which are of ancient origin, dating back to Han times (206 B.C.–A.D. 220) and all of which have undergone renovation and great extension since 1956. The oases around Wuwei and in the Edsin Gol have also been developed. Utilizing the snowfields of the Kilien and Tahsueh Shan, the irrigated area of these oases has been increased from 120,000 hectares in 1949 to 410,000 hectares in 1964 and the total farmland in the Kansu Corridor has risen to 710,000 hectares[30]. All these areas rely almost entirely on irrigation. In a wide area around Lanchow, where dry field farming has been the norm hitherto and where little irrigation has been practised, modern water conservancy is revolutionizing crop yield and a new strain of spring wheat, 'Taitzu 30' has been evolved. It is a cross between the local Lanchow-Sining hardy, early ripening small eared variety with a later ripening, big eared variety. It ripens in 104 days and is hardy. It is therefore suitable for use in Tsinghai, around Sining and is coming into general use[31]. Wheat yields vary from 40 to 200 *catties/mow* according to the availability of water.

The main food crops are spring wheat, millet, barley, rice and legumes. Potatoes are grown in the drier parts. In 1952 it was estimated that 88·3% of the cultivated land was devoted to food crops[3]. Spring wheat is the staple food of the people. It is sown towards the end of March and harvested in the middle or towards the end of July. Together with all the wheats of the north, it is a hard wheat, good for bread and noodles. Wheats tend to become softer the farther south they are grown. There is quite a quick transition from the spring wheat to the winter wheat zone. Yinchwan grows 99% spring wheat and Pingliang 99% winter wheat; the yield per *mow* is much the same for both types[3]. Millet is an insurance crop—insurance against the uncertain rainfall—for it is hardier than wheat, withstands drought better and will flourish on poorer soils. Sown at the beginning of May, it is reaped early in September. It is the staple cereal of the herdsmen. Barley grown here has a shorter growing period than spring wheat by about ten days. The production of rice in this region is determined by irrigation facilities and flourishes most in the Ningsia plain. Until recently most of the rice was planted direct, thus avoiding the back-aching labour of hand transplanting but achieving a lower yield. With the introduction of transplanting machines (p. 81) techniques are changing and direct sowing is disappearing. Rice, which here is 95% non-glutinous, is classified locally into 'big' and 'little'. The 'little' predominates because the 'big' is much more exacting in all aspects of its cultivation, requiring earlier sowing, better irrigation and green manuring. However, it does give a greater yield. Soyabeans, string beans, green beans and cow peas are the main legumes grown and form an important part of human diet. Black beans and peas are grown for fodder. This is a good fruit-growing region. Apples, pears, apricots, peaches and grapes all flourish and melons from Ningsia and Lanchow are well known. Trees grown in the region around Chungning bear fruit, which produces *Lycium Chinense*, which is used exclusively for pharmaceutical purposes.

The main cash crops are cotton, sesame, hemp, sugar beet and local tobacco. Cotton growing has had a chequered history over the last 50 years. It suffered heavily during the Sino-Japanese war, but in recent years has prospered. It is grown mainly in central Kansu, on the Ningsia plain and in the newly irrigated areas in the Kansu Corridor. Hemp has a similar distribution to cotton. Because it is deep-rooted and is resistant to wind and sand, sesame is widely grown. The seed produces a high yield of edible oil; 1 *catty* of oil is obtained from 3 *catties* of seed. The fibre is used for making sacking, coarse cloth, sandals and paper. It is also used as fuel. Sugar beet has a promising future. Since the introduction of a Russian variety from Sinkiang during the Sino-Japanese war, it has grown to be third in importance as a beet producer in China. It is yielding 4,000 *catties/mow* with a 11–16 % sugar content[32].

Within the arable farming areas of the spring wheat region there is a considerable amount of animal husbandry. We have already noted (p. 95) the differences in kind and numbers of animals raised in the pastoral and semi-arable, semi-pastoral regions. The more intensive the arable farming the greater these differences become. For religious reasons, the Mohammedan farmers, who are numerous in this region, concentrate more on rearing sheep, while the Chinese (Han) farmers are the hog raisers. Formerly one-tenth of the sheep and goats were slaughtered for their skins alone[3]. With the development of meat canning, a fuller use is being made of the animals. The main livestock regions are I-meng, the land bordering the Ordos desert and Wu-meng, the lands bordering, and to the north of, the Hara Narin Ula and the Yin Shan. Wu Ch'uan-chun and his colleagues estimated the I-meng as 7% cultivation, 20% shifting sand and semi-shifting sand dunes, 30% stationary dunes, 33% steppe, 10% mountains[3]. It is here that Chinese farmers, in recent decades in their extension of arable farming, have encroached on the steppe and in places have created a 'dust-bowl'. Wu-meng has been the scene of the greatest development of well digging and pastoral settlement.

Winter Wheat–Millet Region

Lying south-east of the Spring Wheat Region is the Winter Wheat–Millet Region. Its boundaries are the 15in isohyet on the north-west, the Chin Ling Shan and Funiu Shan on the south and the Taihang Shan and Wutai Shan, on the east, marking the steep descent on to the North China Plain. The whole area is a deeply-dissected plateau, but its old topography is masked by a layer of loess, which is coincident with nearly the whole region and which, in places, is more than 250 ft thick. It is the presence of this loess which has determined the pattern of life of the area throughout the centuries. As already seen

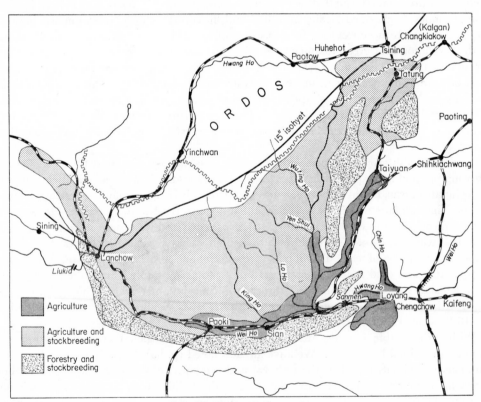

Map 24. Land use in loess region

106

(p. 1), the ease with which the loess can be worked was one of the main reasons for the early development of agriculture and the birth of Chinese civilization in this region. Since then it has been a leading factor in shaping agricultural activities, settlement, communications and housing, and is in no small way responsible for the precariousness of life here.

Loess is a very fine air-borne yellow and grey dust carried from the dry west. It has been laid down over thousands of years on successive growth of steppeland bunch grass, which has given it a vertical tubular character. This assists in the rise of ground water by capillary action, thus enabling cultivation on what would otherwise be impossibly dry land. Another of its characteristics is its vertical cleavage, which results in cliff formations, steep-sided valleys and gullies, giving it something of a mesa landscape and making communications difficult and circuitous. The constant passage of the heavy, iron-rimmed northern carts has resulted in the cutting down and wearing away of the soft, unconsolidated loess until the narrow roads are now often 20 ft and more below the surface of the surrounding land and are contained within cliff-like sides.

The inhabitants of the area have long utilized this vertical cleavage and ease of working of the loess for housing purposes. Caves are cut into the cliff sides and large wooden-framed doorways are fitted, giving dwellings which are warm and which afford good protection against the bitter winters, and being airy and cool during the hot summers. They have one serious defect. This region is subject to earthquakes, which, when they come, are disastrous for they easily shatter these cave houses, burying their occupants.

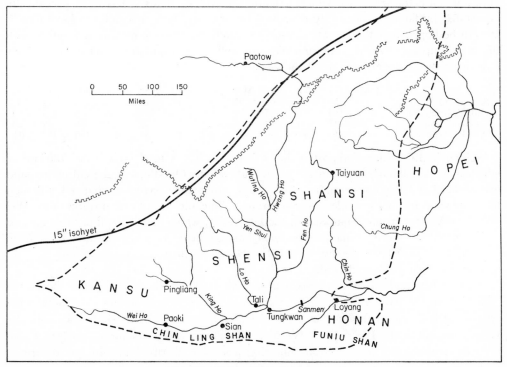

Map 25. Winter wheat–millet region

107

They also create enormous landslides and wreck havoc with the terraced fields so that famine is a normal successor. The earthquake disaster of 1920 resulted in a quarter of a million deaths[33].

Wherever the soft loess has been stripped of its natural steppe grass cover or wherever the farmer has failed to provide it with adequate terrace protection, it is subject to rapid and disastrous erosion. Although rainfall is sparse, it is normally fairly steady and gentle, but occasionally there are violent torrential downpours, which can do enormous damage, suddenly carving out great gullies, breaking down terraces and sweeping away fields. Terracing has always been an essential part of dry field, hillside farming in the loess, but it has seldom been adequate to meet both the gully and sheet erosion to which it has been subjected. Since the formation of the communes, strenuous efforts have been made to rectify this by raising the height of the terrace walls and changing the level of the fields so that they no longer slope downwards but are level or even dip inwards to the hillside. This has involved an enormous amount of human labour but, wherever it has been accomplished, it has proved most effective. However, some of the worst erosion has been in the east of the region in the Wutai, Heng and Taihang Shan, where the loess is very thin or absent. Here the natural vegetational cover should be forest, but deforestation in the past has been most destructive, reducing vast areas to bare and barren rock.

The Winter Wheat–Millet Region is notorious as the worst famine area in China. By far the greater part of its agriculture is dry field farming, and this has to rely on rainfall, which, at best is not plentiful. It shares with the Spring Wheat Region the handicap of unreliable and very variable seasonal rainfall, but except in the limited irrigated parts, does not share the insurance which irrigation provides. Thus it has been periodically devastated by famines, so vividly described by Mallory, in which millions have died[34]. It is to be hoped that the recent widespread water conservancy measures, together with the great improvement in communications, enabling the rapid transport of relief, have now made such disasters a thing of the past.

	Jan.	Feb.	Mar.	April	May	June	July	Aug.	Sep.	Oct.	Nov.	Dec.
Sian Temp. °F	33	39	50	63	75	82	86	82	72	63	44	35
(1,095′) Rainfall in	0·4	0·3	0·6	1·7	2·0	2·8	3·3	5·0	1·6	1·6	0·3	0·4
Taiyuan Temp. °F	19	27	41	54	67	73	78	73	64	50	35	24
(3,051′) Rainfall in	0·2	0·1	0·5	0·6	0·9	1·7	4·2	3·8	2·0	0·6	0·2	0·2

Writing in 1951, Shen[35] reported that this region had a total area of 380,730 km² of which only 82,880 km², or about 22%, was cultivated. One-third of the cultivated land was terraced and only one-tenth irrigated. These proportions have now changed, although to what extent it is not possible to say accurately. The ancient irrigation works of the Wei and King Valleys around Sian, and in the Fen valley, which had fallen into disrepair and were renovated by the China International Famine Relief Commission after the famine of 1932, have now been greatly extended[1]. However, they still constitute only a small proportion of the cultivated land.

Winter wheat and millet are the two chief crops grown in the dry fields, whether in the valleys or on the terraced hills. Winter wheat is grown to some extent over most of the region but is densely cultivated in the Wei valley from Paoki to its confluence with the Hwang-ho and in the Fen valley. Wheaten flour, from which northern bread (*mien pao*) is made, is the staple food. Proso-millet has a similar distribution, with the difference that there is no dense production in the Fen valley. Some kaoliang is grown in the upper

Wei and upper Fen valleys and in the extreme north of the region. Also the extreme north is the most important oat-growing area of China, where it is an important fodder crop. Some rice is grown under irrigation in the middle Wei valley and in the Lo valley around Loyang. Rape is widely and thinly distributed with some concentration in the middle Wei. Cotton is the outstanding economic crop. It is centred in the Wei valley around Sian, Sienyang, Sanyuan, Tali and in Honan in the Lo valley. The frost-free period is only 180 to 190 days, therefore the earlier maturing Chinese varieties are preferred to the longer staple American Upland varieties.

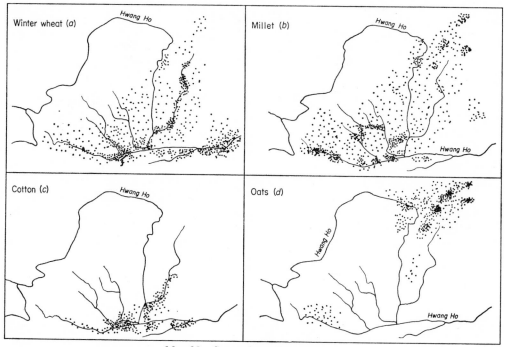

Map 26.   Crops, winter wheat-millet region

Winter Wheat–Kaoliang Region

This region embraces the whole of the North China Plain. Its western boundary is the steep edge of the Shansi plateau and its eastern boundary the Po Hai and the Hwang Hai (Yellow Sea). Its southern border has no clear physical feature to mark it. The course of the Hwai-ho is taken as an arbitrary line, indicating the transitional zone between the wheat-growing north and the rice-growing south.

The vast, flat or gentle undulating plain is built of immense alluvial deposits, together with loessial air-borne material, each of which continues to make its annual contributions, the former through flooding rivers and the latter by dust storms, which plague the north[1]. The flatness of the plain, which is virtually treeless, is interrupted only by the Shantung mountains.

This is one of China's densely populated regions, peopled almost entirely by Han Jen, 80% of whom are engaged in agriculture. They are settled in innumerable hamlets and villages, large and small—a shape of settlement, which has not been fundamentally altered by the changes to commune organization in the last 15 years. In other respects, however, land reform and the coming of co-operatives and communes have been revolutionary. Communal ownership of the land has resulted in a great increase in the size of fields, which, previously under individual ownership or tenancy, had usually been from half to one acre. This, in its turn, has materially affected much of farming techniques. For example, this

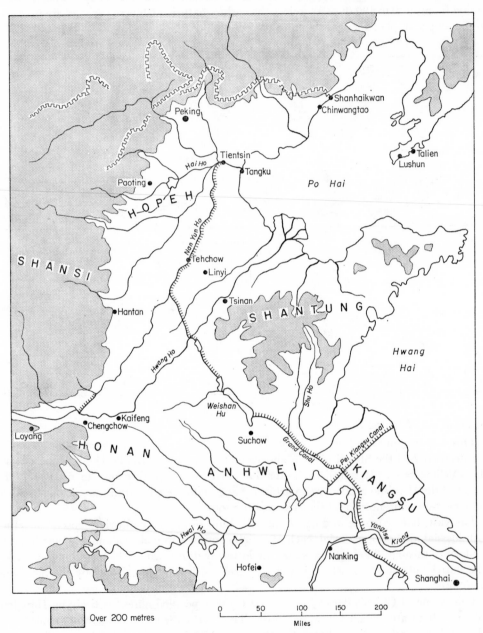

Map 27. North China and Hwai-ho flood plains

110

increase in the size of field has made mechanization or semi-mechanization of farming possible and this possibility has been further enhanced by the wide-spread construction of high-tension lines, carrying power to irrigation, etc. Nevertheless, apart from state and demonstration farms of the region, such development is still only in its initial stages in many parts.

The farmer of the North China Plain has two main enemies, flood and drought. Flooding stems mainly from the Hwang-ho, Hwai-ho and Hai-ho. Measures to meet this danger have been dealt with under 'Water Conservancy' (pp. 59–65). Drought, while not so devastating as in the Winter Wheat–Millet Region, is, nevertheless, a constant anxiety and danger. The time-honoured method of meeting this menace has been the sinking of wells and raising water either by man-power or animal-power (usually donkey). When drought has been severe, wells have often proved inadequate to permit the sowing of crops or their maintenance and famine has ensued. Only about 10% of the land was irrigated and there was little terracing. This would still appear to be the general pattern if the following report from Jenhsien *hsien* in 1966 can be taken as typical of the North China Plain, although it reveals that more co-ordinated effort than formerly can be brought to bear to meet drought when it does occur.

'Rainfall was inadequate in Jenhsien *hsien*, Southern Hopei Province, all through sowing to harvesting. When the time for sowing came, the fields were covered with a thick layer of dry earth. Ten thousand out of 14,000 hectares of wheat fields had no irrigation facilities to fall back on . . . The Jenhsien *hsien* Committee of the Communist Party organized study of what Chairman Mao said about conquering difficulties . . . The anti-drought battle went ahead with revolutionary determination. Members of the Yungfuchuang commune dug wells and sowed wheat in time. Within a few months, the communes in the *hsien* had built 27,000 new wells, renovated 6,500 old wells and dug 95 ponds. Ten thousand hectares of arid farmland was brought under irrigation. Thus the people have not only won the battle against drought this year but have created conditions for stable harvests in the future'[36].

The main food crops are winter wheat, kaoliang, foxtail millet, barley, soyabeans and sweet potatoes. This region is the great wheat granary of China and more than 150 million people living in the area depend upon wheat as their staple food. It is sown in September as soon as possible after reaping the summer harvest of soyabeans, kaoliang or millet. Traditionally it was harvested at the Tuan Wu Festival, on the fifth day of the fifth month of the Chinese calendar, i.e. towards the end of May. Adherence to the old agricultural calendar, to a large extent, no longer obtains. Gone, too, are many of the old techniques such as pulling the grain instead of reaping but, owing to differences of knowledge, techniques, management and soils, there are very great differences in output of wheat per *mow* as between different communes, brigades and teams, sometimes amounting to more than 10 times. High output production brigades are those which achieve a yield of over 300 *catties/mow*. However, a good deal of experimenting is going on and these standards appear to be undergoing a change. New strains, such as the 'Shan Nung 205', 'Peking 8', 'A Fu' and 'P'ing Yuan', suiting different local conditions, have been evolved. More attention is being given to the right time of planting so that full advantage can be taken of the autumn sun and temperature, thus promoting tillering before the winter onset. Because soil temperature on salt and alkali soils is some 2°C lower than in the case of ordinary soil, sowing must take place 10 days earlier; this entails more careful pest control. In view of the emphasis, which, in China, during recent years has been placed on the import-ance of chemical fertilizer, the following extract from the report on wheat-growing by the Crop Culture and Cultivation Research Institute, Chinese Academy of Agricultural Science in November, 1965 is instructive:

'In areas comparatively lacking in fertilizer resources, stress is laid on the application of basic fertilizer and seed fertilizer . . . Where the soil has a low degree of fertility and is lacking in effective phosphorous, application of phosphorous fertilizer as basic fertilizer has a marked effect of causing seedlings to grow strong, promoting branching before winter, and raising output.

'In districts where fertilizer is more abundant, some areas had in recent years applied chemical fertilizer to the exclusion of peasant household manure. This led to increasing hardening of the soil. Though the quantity of fertilizer applied increased with the years, yet the output of the land did not rise. In view of this, the practice of depending solely on chemical fertilizer was overcome. Peasant household manure began to be used as the main fertilizer, and it was used in combination with chemical fertilizer.

'This is a matter of direction concerning the application of fertilizer . . . But peasant household manure has a low content of effective nutrients, and it produces its effect slowly, unable to meet promptly the maximum demand of wheat plants for nutrition. By applying peasant household manure in rational combination with chemical fertilizer, it is possible both to raise output per *mow* rapidly and to nurse soil fertility continuously.'[37]

Rust is the chief wheat disease in the north and, to date, no really satisfactory rust-resisting strain has been bred. Red mold, which causes severe damage in years of higher temperature and greater humidity, is a much greater menace to wheat in the Yangtze valley than in the north.

A notable social change has occurred with regard to women's labour. Formerly, wheat threshing was the first outdoor women's work of the year in the north[38]. Today, women work in the fields at all times on an equal footing with men.

Kaoliang (Chinese sorghum) ranks second in importance to wheat. This plant, which grows to a height of 7–8 ft, carries a closely-bunched head of several hundred grain, each grain being about the size of a sweet pea. It is well suited to the area because, like millet, it can withstand severe drought and is not easily destroyed by flood. It is a coarser food than wheat, but it forms a very important item in the people's diet and gives a heavy yield per *mow*. Its tall, strong stalk is valuable for wattle and daub building, fencing and roofing. It is also used extensively for fuel. New hybrid kaoliang has been grown on demonstration plots in Honan, yielding 4·27 ton/hectare. The same strain grown in an area waterlogged for 1 month yielded 2·25 ton/hectare, a 60% improvement on local strains[39]. Kaoliang is often planted between widely-spaced rows of wheat in order to obviate the problem that kaoliang needs to be planted before the harvesting of wheat, if a satisfactory crop is to be obtained. In like manner cotton also competes with wheat. Sweet potatoes are a heavy crop and also form an important item in the peasants' diet. They are included in official records as grain on a ratio of four parts potato equal one of grain.

With the expansion of irrigation there is a noticeable tendency to grow rice rather than wheat, especially in the Hwai valley and southern Shantung, where it is reported that 'low-lying lands formerly suitable only for sorghum, sweet potatoes and other dry crops, are now growing rice with an average yield of 3 ton/hectare'[40]. Saline, waterlogged land, which has been drained in the Linyi district north of Tsinan, has been turned into paddy. This preference for rice is not surprising since the average rice yield per acre is $2\frac{1}{2}$ ton as compared with 1 ton of wheat. However, it must be remembered that rice requires a great deal more care in its cultivation.

Other food crops are corn, soyabeans and peanuts. A great variety of vegetables is grown, including cabbage, spinach, turnip, onion, cucumbers, melons, squashes, beans and peas. These are grown principally on the peasants' private plots.

Cotton is by far the most important economic crop of the region. The main producing areas are western Shantung, southern Hopei and Honan. Most of the cotton grown is of short staple, Chinese varieties of less than 1 in staple, but these have a high lint yield. In spite of all efforts to encourage the increase of quality and quantity, the output of cotton still lags behind the constantly increasing demand. There is a persistent 'contra-diction', i.e. competition, between cotton and grain for growing space[41]. Saline lands bordering the Po Hai have been brought into cotton cultivation. By careful cultivation and the addition of fertilizer and pond and river bed mud, soils containing as much as 3·17% salt have increased their yield from 10 *catties* ginned cotton per *mow* to 80 *catties* or more[42].

Corn–Soyabean–Millet Region

The terminus of the Great Wall is at Shanhaikwan on the Po Hai. This marks the narrowest point of the coastal plain, which leads from the North China Plain to the North-East, as the former province of Manchuria is now called, and which is divided into three provinces, Liaoning, Kirin and Heilungkiang. This corridor leads from the flat, alluvial plains of the Hwai, Hwang and Hai into a vast country of undulating steppeland, bordered on the west by the Tahingan Shan and on the east by the densely forested East Manchurian Mountains. The steppeland is covered, for the most part, by a rich chernozem soil. It is open to the influence of the south-east monsoon and, in consequence, has a summer maximum of rainfall, most places receiving an annual precipitation of between 20 in and 26 in, with a considerably heavier fall in the east than in the west. Winters are long and bitter as a result of the north-west winds from the Siberian high pressure. The region stretches about 1,000 miles from north to south and thus there is a considerable difference in temperature between north Heilungkiang and south Liaoning. There is a growing period of 120–150 days according to latitude, but the long summer days, with 14–16 h of sunshine, compensate this to some degree.

	Jan.	Feb.	Mar.	April	May	June	July	Aug.	Sep.	Oct.	Nov.	Dec.
Talien Temp. °F	23	26	36	49	66	69	75	77	68	57	41	28
(315') Rainfall in	0·5	0·3	0·7	0·9	1·7	1·8	6·4	5·1	4·0	1·1	1·0	0·5
Shenyang Temp. °F	9	14	28	46	60	70	76	74	62	48	29	14
(144') Rainfall in	0·2	0·2	0·8	1·1	2·2	3·4	6·3	6·1	3·3	1·6	1·1	0·2
Harbin Temp. °F	−2	5	24	42	56	66	72	69	58	40	21	3
(525') Rainfall in	0·2	0·2	0·4	0·9	1·7	4·1	5·8	4·2	2·2	1·2	0·4	0·2

When the pastoralist Manchus descended on China in the seventeenth century and overthrew the Ming dynasty, the North-East was a sparsely populated area. Succeeding Manchu emperors endeavoured to keep it closed to the Chinese and for a long time it remained a prohibited area[1]. However, Chinese famine pressures leading to uncontrollable waves of migration, Russian penetration into Siberia along the Amur River calling for colonization and manning of the Chinese frontier, and Manchu need for agricultural

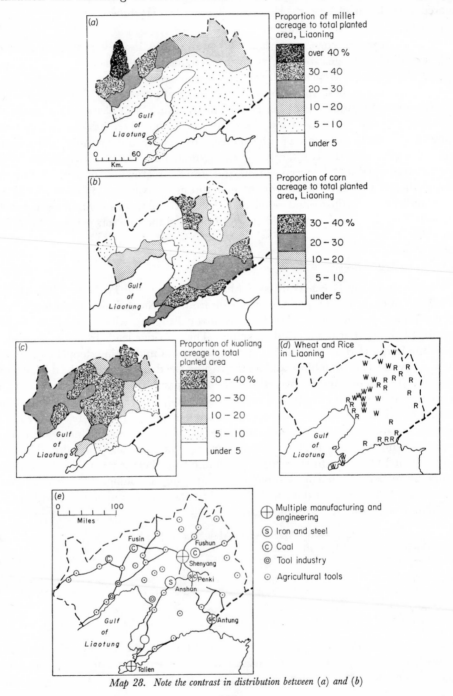

Map 28. *Note the contrast in distribution between (a) and (b)*

114

labour, combined to break down this prohibition[43]. By 1907 all legal barriers to immigration into the North-East had disappeared. There was an annual seasonal migration of labour, mainly from Shantung and Hopei, approximately half of which remained each year to settle. Population was estimated at about 34 million in 1930, and 1957 census figures were:

Liaoning	24,095,000
Kirin	12,550,000
Heilungkiang	14,780,000
	51,425,000

The population is overwhelmingly Han in composition. The 600,000 or so Manchus are mainly in the upper Sungari area in Heilungkiang, the region from which they originally moved to conquer Ming China. There are 220,000 Koreans, skilled rice-growers, concentrated in south-east Kirin around Yenki. Some 38,000 Mongolians occupy the grassland slopes of the Ta Hingan Shan in the west and are engaged in animal husbandry, and 45,000 Mohammedans are mainly urban dwellers, engaged in commerce and industry. In spite of the great increase during the last 20 years, the country remains under-populated in face of the ever-increasing demand for man-power in industry and agriculture[44].

In view of its proximity to China Proper and its more temperate climate than the other two provinces, it is not surprising to find that Liaoning is the most densely populated and

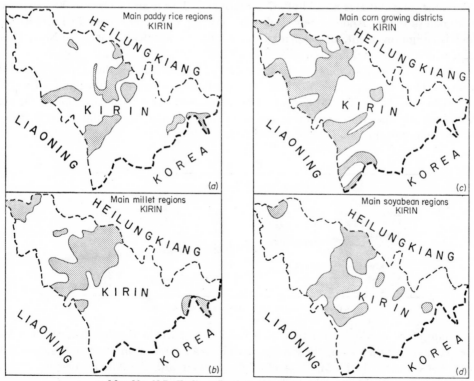

Map 29. N.B. Kaoliang distribution almost identical with millet

the most important agricultural part of the North-East. Of its 24 million inhabitants, 8·5 million are urban, and of these 80% are concentrated in the conurbation centred in Shenyang. This exercises a considerable influence on the agricultural pattern of the North-East. Intensity of cultivation and unit output tend to decrease northward and the size of farm tends to increase. Thirty-three per cent of the land in Liaoning is cultivated. No comparable figures are available for Kirin and Heilungkiang, but it is certain that the proportions are a good deal less. Irrigation and drainage works, which are being extended to all cultivable parts of the North-East, are most advanced in Liaoning. Much of the lowland of the lower Liao and Hun, which is subject to flooding, has been brought under control. It is reported that half the rural communes are now served with electric power and pumping stations[45].

A general pattern of grain crop distribution can be discerned. Millet and kaoliang tend to be grown in the somewhat higher and drier western parts, whilst rice is grown mainly in the south-east and in the coastal areas. Some winter wheat is grown in central Liaoning, but it is not a popular crop owing to its comparatively low unit yield. Its production has been urged on communes because it provides year-round work. The growth of spring wheat is increasing in Heilungkiang.

Millet and kaoliang still constitute the principal food of the farming population, but the steady growth in the standard of living is shown in the increasing demand for rice and wheat. Experiments by Prof. Kung Chi-tao have led to the evolution of a new strain of kaoliang, bearing several clusters in place of the usual single cluster, which all mature at the same time and give a yield of 3·7 ton/hectare. This is an increase of 50–100% over other good strains[46]. Another new strain, the 'Hsiung Yueh 253', ripens in 130–140 days, which is an improvement, although it compares unfavourably with that of the North China Plain, which ripens in 120 days.

Corn has a longer growing season than millet or kaoliang and is therefore grown in the lowlands. The most important producing area is a belt stretching from the plain of Liaoning northward into the lowland of Kirin and Heilungkiang. This is an extension of the corn belt, which stretches from Szechwan right across the North China Plain. Some idea of the importance of this crop can be gained from *Table 5.1.*

Table 5.1. Percentages of Sown Area

	Kirin (1957)	Heilungkiang (1957)	Liaoning (1958)
Rice	6·2	3·1	7·5
Corn	19·7	20·7	31·5
Kaoliang	15·5	10·4	9·0
Millet	18·3	16·3	10·6
Wheat	1·1	12·8	0·8
Soyabeans	20·0	20·9	15·0
Cotton	—	—	4·2
Peanuts	—	—	3·4

Compiled from *Economic Geography of North-east China*

In spite of its northerly situation, rice has been grown in the North-East for a long time. Its main region is along the south-eastern Korean border from the Liaotung peninsula to the Yenki district in Kirin. It is closely associated with the Korean people, who are regarded as experts in a method of rice-growing peculiar to the region. Great claims

116

have been made for recent experiments in rice-growing made by Korean farmers in Kirin, which have raised the yield from 2·2 to 3 ton/hectare by old methods, to a new average of 4·9 ton/hectare[45].   This has been achieved partly by nursing early rice seedlings under plastic sheeting and so avoiding frost, and partly by irrigating rice paddies only at night, using water warmed by the sun during the day and so maintaining a higher night temperature. But these experiments, which have been carried out over 3,300 hectares, have not been controlled for they have been accompanied by better manuring, better seed selection and close planting.   Therefore it is not possible to measure how much of the increased yield is attributable to the 'Korean Method'.

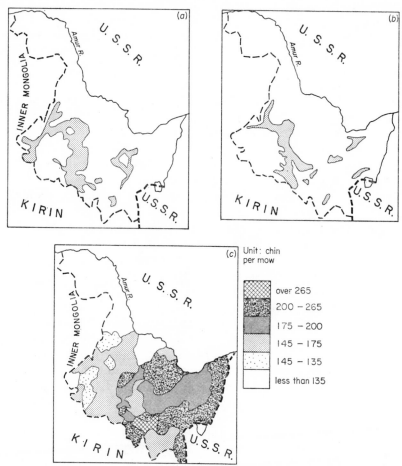

Map 30.   Heilungkiang: (a) distribution of sugar beet and flax; (b) distribution of soya beans; (c) average unit yield for grain during first five-year period

Rice-growing has been extended north right into the Sungari and Nun river valleys where the crop is being cultivated by more extensive farming methods than in the south. This is due, in some degree, to the Shenyang production of the 3 h.p. or 7 h.p. walking tractor, suitable for paddy fields.   Here in the north there is an abundance of farmland and a shortage of labour.   Rice is planted in rows more than 1 ft apart—the conventional method farther south is to plant rows 6 in apart—thus enabling weeding to be done by animal or walking tractor. It also has the advantage of giving better ventilation and admitting more sunshine[47].

The soyabean, which shares first place with corn and millet, is grown in every province in China but is more important here than anywhere else. It is a very important part of Chinese diet. Bean curd (*tu fu*) in some shape or form is served at most Chinese meals. *Tu-chiang*, a fluid expressed from soyabeans, has, for centuries, formed a valuable baby and invalid food. The oil, obtained by crushing, is used universally as a cooking oil. The residue, in the form of large round cakes, is a valuable cattle food.

When the North-East was under Japanese rule, the export of soyabeans from that region was of great importance, especially during World War I, when it was in great demand for making explosives. Manchurian export of soyabeans at that time stood at over 4 million tons p.a. Since World War II, the United States has undertaken production and this export trade has fallen, but Chinese production has been maintained and absorbed for home use. The North-East is still the most important producing region, and one-fifth of the planted area of Kirin and Liaoning is devoted to it. It is usually grown in a three-crop rotation with kaoliang and millet and is sometimes interplanted with corn. The extension of rice-growing tends to push the cultivation of soyabeans into the rolling hills of the west. In spite of the importance of the crop in the past, cultivation methods have been poor and unit yield low. Application of chemical fertilizer and the introduction of better seed in recent years have helped to raise the standard in the North-East. A new strain, 'Feng Shou 4', has a higher yield, but like so many higher bearing strains is more prone to disease, although it is more resistant to drought and pests.

Peanuts (groundnuts), grown mainly in south Liaoning and the lower Liao valley, are second only to soyabeans as a source of edible oil. Like soyabeans, their cultivation has been backward but shows a similar recent improvement.

Of the economic crops of the North-East, cotton and sugar beet now vie with each other in importance. The main cotton-growing area is in the Liaoning plain, along the Liao river itself, in the Luta peninsular and in the south-west around Chinchow. It has the comparatively high yield of 132 *chin* of ginned cotton per *mow* and an average staple of 23–24 mm. It faces problems of spring drought and high precipitation in late summer during the ripening season. Sugar beet is grown mainly in Kirin on the Sungari plain where it is the most important economic crop. In 1958 it still occupied only 1% of the planted area, but since then this has been greatly increased together with local sugar refineries. In 1959–60 output was reported as 250,000 tons, which represented 3·5% of the national output, placing it seventh in the national scale. Flax is grown in quantity in the Sungari valley. Liaoning is one of the chief producers of flue-cured tobacco, producing 6·3% of the national total in 1958. Tussah silk, which is produced from silkworms reared on chestnut-leaved oak, mainly in east Liaoning, suffered a near eclipse in 1948 when pre-war peak production of 200,000 *tan* of dried cocoon fell to 10,000 *tan*. Its production in 1957 was reported to be approximately 1 million *tan*.

Fruit-growing is becoming an important agricultural activity, especially in Liaoning, where apple-growing is increasing very rapidly. It is stated that it now produces 80% of the whole of China's output. The humid oceanic influences, significant diurnal temperature changes and sufficient sunlight combine to produce apples of fine quality. Pears are second in importance. Good grapes are grown in Luta peninsula.

Heilkungkiang is the province in which the greatest number of state farms has been established and the greatest degree of mechanization has taken place. In all, 36 such farms are now in existence and 453,000 hectares of virgin land have been brought into cultivation. Nearly all these have been started by veteran soldiers of the P.L.A., who have later been joined by younger people. It is reported that all have been set up 'in accordance with the Nanniwan revolutionary spirit of self-reliance', i.e. following the pattern of the brigade of the 8th Army in the early 1940s, which was sent to Nanniwan, near Yenan to open up wasteland[48].

Reports on the Chiayin State Farm set up in March, 1964 in the north of Heilungkiang state that it has now 740 workers. 'They made conscious efforts to break away from the pattern borrowed from abroad for the running of State farms. They decided, for instance, not to build modern residential quarters like those of the cities and thus risk becoming divorced from the masses of the peasants . . . At first all the leading functionaries and the workers lived in tents. They began reclamation work while still building dwellings and roads. They made no special arrangements with any building department but erected all the dwellings and other buildings themselves. Now everyone on the farm lives in simple housing similar to that of the nearby villages. They all lead a frugal life.'[49]

Thus these northern State farms present a different appearance from many of the southern ones. 'Thousands of settlements now make a patchwork of this former desolate area and every farm has its own schools, clinics, shops, clubs and other services.'

The main crops grown on the State farms, which are highly mechanized, include spring wheat, soyabeans and corn. There are some State farms engaged in animal husbandry, which has been, and still is, the livelihood of the Mongolians, who occupy the western foothills of the Ta Hingan Shan. Estimates credit Heilungkiang alone with 5·9 million hectares of pasture and 1·65 million hectares of wasteland suitable for grazing. The main animal breeding region is in the Nun valley, where horses are most important. This contrasts strongly with Liaoning where more than 80% of the large animals are yellow oxen and donkeys needed for draught purposes.

Table 5.2. Principal Crops of Liaoning (in 100 billion chin)

	1949	1952	1957	1958
Rice	3·40	5·99	13·03	20·08
Corn	17·04	25·16	34·58	83·04
Kaoliang	29·66	38·64	39·93	16·80
Tubers	2·99	4·19	7·79	11·15
Soyabeans	8·13	11·07	15·34	19·71
Cotton	0·82	5·50	2·24	4·07
Tobacco	0·03	0·45	0·38	0·50
Apples	1·00	1·70	3·33	4·34
Tussah Silk	0·41	1·06	0·66	0·88

Compiled from *Economic Geography of North-east China*, p. 86

Szechwan Rice Region

We now move south of the Chinling–Funiu Shan line, which until recently, divided the wheat-growing north from the rice-growing south. We have seen that, as irrigation facilities develop, there is an increasing urge and ability to grow rice farther north. There is no corresponding tendency to extend wheat-growing farther south. All five of the remaining agricultural regions have rice as their staple crop, the differentiating factor or factors being either the manner or amount of the rice grown or the nature of subsidiary products.

Szechwan is a huge province, which can be divided topographically from north to south by the 3,000 m contour. The western half constitutes the eastern part of the Tibetan plateau, which is deeply incised by the Yangtze (Kinsha) Kiang and its left bank tributaries. To the east lies the rich Red Basin, bounded on the north by the Mitsung Shan and Tapa Shan and on the south by the Talou and Fangtou Shan, which form the northern edge of the Yunnan-Kweichow plateau. Here, in this land-locked depression, deep deposits of red sandstone were laid down in cretaceous times. It is these deposits which give the basin its name. It has a general level of some 500–1,000 m above sea level. It slopes from north to south down to the trough of the Yangtze. Szechwan, meaning 'Four Rivers', gets its name from the four main left-bank tributaries, which flow from north-west to south-east.

The land-locked nature of the Red Basin imparts a surprising and unique climate to the region. Here, in the heart of a land mass, a comparatively equable climate is found, freer from extremes of temperature than Shanghai, 1,000 miles to the east on the sea coast. The main reason for this freedom is the protection afforded by the northern ring of mountains against the bitter outflowing winds from the winter Siberian high pressure.

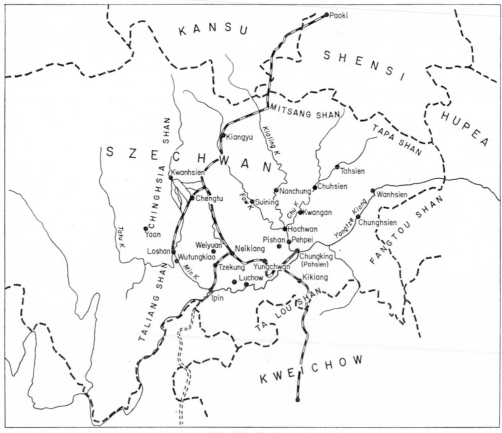

Map 31. Szechwan

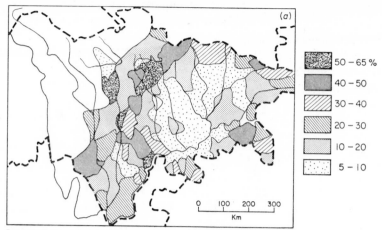

Percentage of corn to total crop acreage

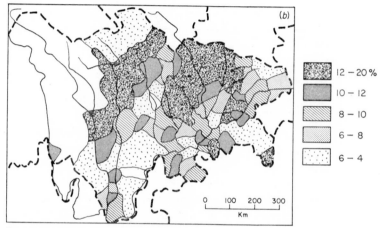

Percentage of wheat to total crop acreage

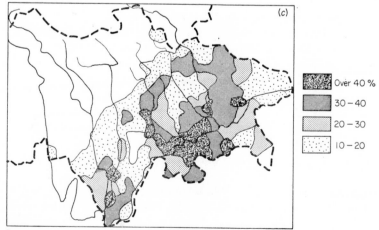

Percentage of rice acreage to all crops in Szechwan

Map 32. Szechwan

The Red Basin is also known for its cloudiness and high humidity, which is reflected in the local saying that 'when the sun shines, the dogs bark' and the fact that Szechwan's southern neighbour is called Yunnan, meaning 'South of the Clouds'. As a result, the Red Basin has a long growing period of 11 months and produces a great variety of agricultural products. It is said, with near but not absolute accuracy, that Szechwan can grow everything that is grown in China.

	Jan.	Feb.	Mar.	April	May	June	July	Aug.	Sep.	Oct.	Nov.	Dec.
Chengtu Temp. °F	44	46	55	63	70	76	78	78	71	64	56	46
(1,560') Rainfall in	0·2	0·4	0·6	1·7	2·8	4·1	5·7	9·7	4·1	1·8	0·4	0·1
Chungking Temp. °F	47	50	58	67	74	79	82	84	76	67	59	50
(755') Rainfall in	0·6	0·8	1·4	4·0	5·5	7·1	5·6	5·1	5·8	4·6	2·0	0·9

It was estimated that in 1957–58 some 13·5% of the total area of the province or 114,990,000 *mow* was arable land. Of this 83·1% was devoted to grain production, 55,380,000 *mow* or just under half was paddy, and 59,610,000 *mow* was under dry crops[50]. Some idea of the relative importance of the main crops can be gleaned from *Table 5.3*.

Table 5.3. *Szechwan Crop Output* (10,000 *piculs*)[50]

Date	Rice	Wheat	Corn	Sweet Potato	Cotton	Rape-seed	Sugar Cane
Prewar (1936 Estimate)	15,631	3,685	2,954	5,654	38	—	2,500
1949	18,464	1,990	3,003	3,460	30	307	1,121
1952	21,007	1,795	2,950	4,059	83	379	2,518
1957	27,374	3,276	4,269	6,365	140	553	3,445

It is interesting to note that the production of rice had risen considerably in 1949, whereas figures of production for nearly every commodity in the country for that year were at their lowest ebb. The reason for this is that from 1936 and throughout the Sino-Japanese war there was a continual migration from the east in Szechwan resulting in a great increase in demand and production of rice. It is now the country's greatest producer.

Rice is grown under irrigation in the hills and on the plains. The efficiency of irrigation varies very considerably in different areas. We have seen (p. 56) something of the ancient irrigation system of the Chengtu plain. It is here and in the Yangtze valley around Chungking that the highest yields per hectare are obtained. This is achieved by taking an early rice crop, a late autumn rice crop and a spring catch crop, usually of vegetables. Some account (p. 72) has been given of the experiments in irrigation that are being made in the hilly lands where water conservancy is most backward. It is reported that, in 1958, 11% of the paddy land was still relying on storing water in the fields themselves, a most precarious method. The Red Basin grows more rice than it needs for local consumption and therefore exports a fair amount to the north by the new railway to Paoki and by boat down the Yangtze. The accompanying maps of rice, wheat and corn acreage show an interesting localization of distribution, intensive rice-growing being concentrated in the lowlands to the south and south-east, and wheat and corn in the uplands of the north and west.

The important food crops of the dry farmland area are wheat, corn and sweet potato. The drive during the last 10 years has been to bring these dry fields under irrigation. Insofar as this has been achieved, yields have been for the most part doubled. About three-quarters of the wheat grown is winter wheat. Almost the entire crop of wheat and corn is consumed within Szechwan itself.

Szechwan is one of the country's major corn producing areas. Recently the communes have undertaken the mass production of double-cross maize, which has a 30–40% higher yield per hectare than local strains, but requires a yearly production of double-cross seed otherwise it loses its hybrid vigour[51]. In common with so much of the poorer land of China, sweet potatoes form the staple food of the peasants of the dry upland farming areas.

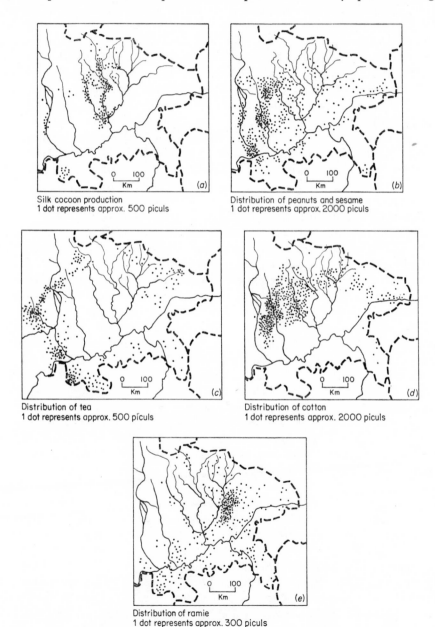

Silk cocoon production
1 dot represents approx. 500 piculs (a)

Distribution of peanuts and sesame
1 dot represents approx. 2000 piculs (b)

Distribution of tea
1 dot represents approx. 500 piculs (c)

Distribution of cotton
1 dot represents approx. 2000 piculs (d)

Distribution of ramie
1 dot represents approx. 300 piculs (e)

Map 33. Szechwan

Szechwan's main economic crops are oil seeds, cotton, sugar, tobacco and fibres[52]. Of the oil producers rape-seed is by far the most important, occupying more than one-third of the economic crop acreage. Rape is a winter crop on paddies and in the dry corn fields and thus is very widely distributed throughout the Red Basin. Peanuts and sesame are also grown alternatively with corn and produce a large amount of vegetable oil. The acreage under cotton increased considerably to 2·3 million *mow* during the Sino-Japanese war. This trend has continued; the acreage had more than doubled by 1958 and now occupies about one-third of the land devoted to economic crops. Its growth is concentrated in the Chengtu plain and in the north-west. Attention has recently been given to developing a strain which matures early in order to avoid the unfavourable autumn rains, thus raising former low yields to 37 *catties/mow*[50]. Sugar cane production ranks second to Kwangtung or third if Taiwan is included. Introduced from Fukien in A.D. 1670, it prospered until the beginning of the twentieth century, since when it has had a chequered history. It has now recovered. Although natural conditions are not as favourable as those of Kwangtung, heavy crops are reaped. Planting takes place in February and March and the crop is harvested between November and April. In recent years sugar-beet has been successfully introduced. In 1964, 8 big or medium-sized (300–500 ton/day capacity) and 112 small (15–30 ton/day capacity) refineries were either built or improved, doubling the refining capacity of the province[52]. Tobacco is grown on some 700,000 *mow* of which about one-third is in the Chengtu plain. It is virtually all sun-dried and finds a ready market throughout the rest of China. Ramie (*ssu ma*—silky flax) and hemp (*ho ma*) are the two chief fibres, the production of which stands second only to Hupeh. Ramie is grown mainly east of the Kialing Kiang. Tea production is concentrated in the foothills of the Tibetan plateau. Although green tea and a small amount of black tea are produced, by far the most important is the 'border' or brick tea, a coarse, rough mixture of leaves and stems grown mainly for export to Tibet and Mongolia. It is pressed into slabs or tiles about 5–6 in square and half an inch thick, making it suitable for transport, formerly on the backs of coolies but, happily, today largely by lorries. The production of green (unfermented) and black (fermented) tea is increasing rapidly to meet the needs of the province.

Sericulture in Szechwan is said to date back to the Chin dynasty (221–206 B.C.), made famous in the Shu brocades and Pa satins. In addition to the mulberry trees, which flourish in the Szechwan climate and on which the silk industry is based, the province is rich in oak trees. Experiments are going on in the use of the oak leaf as feed for silkworms. A record production in 1925 of 700,000 *piculs* (1 *picul* = 133 lb) of dried cocoons gave 70,000 *piculs* of reeled silk. Due to Japanese competition and internal disorder, production fell to 100,000 *piculs* of cocoons in 1949. By 1958 a partial recovery had been made, 250,000 *piculs* being produced, representing 15–20% of the national output[50].

The province has a great variety of fruit, ranging from tropical to temperate. Bananas, pineapples, oranges, tangerines, dragon eyes, and lichee are grown in the lower, warmer valleys of the south, while apples, peaches, pears and plums are grown mainly in the higher, cooler north-west, the southward flowing rivers providing the main means of transport.

It is estimated that about 18% of Szechwan is forested. The main stands are in the west and in the upper reaches of the Min, Tatu and Fow rivers. The forests here range from evergreen broadleafed and deciduous trees below 2,500 m, to spruce and fir up to 3,500 m. Above this height there is alpine meadow and little tree growth[50].

The forests of the Mitsang Shan and Tapa Shan in the north and east are composed mainly of Huashan pine, green kang, chestnut oak and cypress. On the lower slopes, below 1,000 m, there is a variety of oil-bearing trees, wood oil (*tung yu*), tea oil and tallow. Of these the wood oil is by far the most important commercially. It forms the basis of paints and varnish and has figured prominently in the export trade, especially to U.K., throughout the twentieth century. It also has many domestic uses, including waterproofing oiled cloth (*yu pu*) and the preserving of all river craft. In recent years the cultivation of wood oil has received more careful attention, resulting in marked improvement in output. It is grown almost exclusively in the eastern half of the Red Basin, east of the Kialing Kiang.

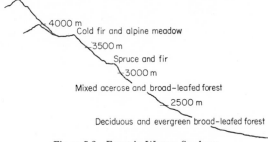

Figure 5.2. Forest in Western Szechwan

Szechwan is reputed to have the highest cattle population of all the provinces of China. In the Red Basin the cattle are almost exclusively draught animals, chiefly yellow oxen and water buffaloes. These have been greatly increased since 1949, together with pigs, which are reared for their meat and also as a source of manure. On the broad, natural grasslands of the highlands of the north-west, there is pastoral farming, including the raising of horses and yaks.

Table 5.4 Szechwan Livestock (10,000 head)

	Hogs	Oxen*	Buffaloes
1936 estimate	900	140	200
1949 ,,	1,019	392	236
1952 ,,	1,378	471	219
1957 ,,	2,500	482	237

*Includes yaks and milch cows

Yangtze Rice–Wheat Region

The fertile lower Yangtze basin, drained by the main river and its great tributaries, the Han, Siang and Kan, contains six important provinces, Kiangsu, Anhwei, Hupeh, Hunan, Kiangsi and Chekiang, which together have a population of about 180 million people or nearly one-third of the whole of China.

Although the area has many common geographical and agricultural features, it has been divided into two regions largely to emphasize the virtual disappearance of wheat production south of the Yangtze. Throughout the entire area rice is by far the most important food crop grown. North of the Yangtze in Kiangsu, Anhwei and Hupeh approximately 33% of the food-crop acreage is devoted to rice, 28% to wheat, 10% to barley, 9% to corn and 6% to sweet potatoes. South of the river in Hunan, Kiangsi and Chekiang, the proportions are approximately 70% devoted to rice, 7% to wheat, 5% to barley, 3% to corn and 4%

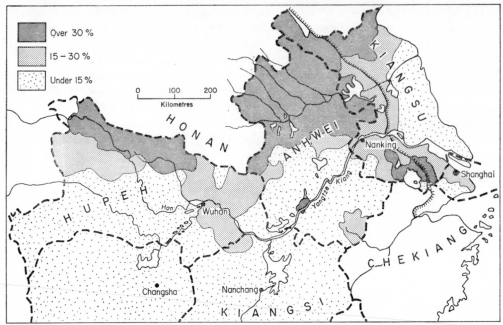

Map 34. Percentage of cultivated land under wheat. (Compiled from 'Economic Geography of Central China 1960 and Economic Geography of Eastern China' 1961. *Institute of Geography Chinese Academy of Sciences)*

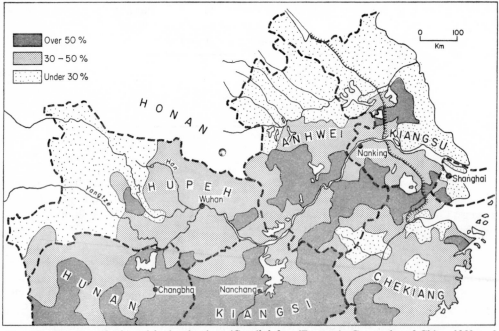

Map 35. Percentage of cultivated land under rice. (Compiled from 'Economic Geography of China 1960 and Economic Geography of Eastern China' 1961. *Institute of Geography Chinese Academy of Sciences)*

to sweet potatoes. When actual grain outputs are compared, the contrasts are even more arresting[53] (see page 51). The three northern provinces which form the Rice–Wheat Region produced, in 1957, 407 million *tan* (1 *tan* = 50 kg) of rice and 95·9 million *tan* of wheat, which respectively represented 60% and 14% of the grain output, while the three southern provinces of the Rice–Tea Region produced 438 million *tan* of rice and only 9·2 million *tan* of wheat, which respectively represented 85% and 1·8% of the grain output.

The main summer crops of the Rice–Wheat Region are rice, sweet potatoes, peanuts, sesame, cotton, fibres and tobacco. The winter crops are winter wheat, barley, peas, beans and green fertilizer. Nearly all the agricultural land of the region is double cropped. When grown in succession to rice, barley has a slight advantage over winter wheat in that it matures somewhat earlier, thus giving more time for ploughing and puddling the paddy in preparation for transplanting the rice seedlings. Barley is used for human consumption much more readily in central China than in Europe. While the acreage under corn in this region is not nearly as great as rice or wheat, the introduction of new hybrid strains has resulted in greatly increased output.

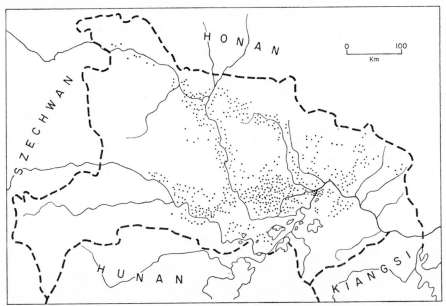

Map 36. Hupeh cotton production distribution. (*From* 'Economic Geography of Central China', Institute of Geography, Chinese Academy of Sciences

When it is remembered that the Yangtze valley has been the main source of agricultural raw materials for export during the last 70–80 years, it is surprising to learn that only about 7% of the total cultivated land in this region is devoted to economic crops, i.e. crops other than food grain. Of the economic crops cotton is by far the most important, occupying about half the acreage. The main growing areas are Kiangsu and Hupeh. Hupeh was one of the chief cotton producers before 1936 and led the country in 1928 with an output of 4·2 million *tan* of lint. This fell to less than 1 million *tan* in 1949, but subsequently recovered and in 1947 Hupeh was again producing 4·5 million *tan* with an average yield of 100 *chin/ mow*. The main growing areas are in the Yangtze-Han plain between Ichang and Wuhan and along the lower valley of the Han. Because cotton must be planted in April and wheat is not harvested until May, it is a common practice in Hupeh to interplant cotton and wheat. However, because of their earlier maturity, barley or oats is preferred in rotation with cotton. The average length of staple is 0·7–0·8 in. Most of the cotton is processed in Hupeh. No. 1 Cotton Mill, Wuchang was established with the latest Lancashire machinery at the turn of the century. No. 2 Cotton Mill has been built recently and has all the most modern equipment. Kiangsu's main cotton-producing areas are in the Yangtze delta between Shanghai, Wusih and Nantung and along the coast. The coastal strip is largely land reclaimed from the sea over many centuries; its soil is saline. Cotton, being a plant which is more tolerant to salt than most others, has therefore been developed in this area, the former large private farms now being taken over by state and commune[1]. Yields from saline lands have been very small in the past. However, by meticulous cultivation, which has included thorough draining of the saline land which is usually very subject to water-logging, by ploughing in winter and collecting the accumulated surface salt after the thaw in the spring, by constant harrowing, weeding and fertilizing and, finally, by expert seed selection, production from soil containing as much as 3·17% salt has been raised from 10 *catties* of ginned cotton to 84 *catties*/*mow*[41]. Cotton processing is centred in Shanghai.

The main fibres produced in the Rice–Wheat Region are ramie, hemp and jute. South-east Hupeh is China's leading producer of ramie (*ssu ma*) with an output of 350,000 *tan* in 1957, which comprised about one-third of the country's total production. This is still 40,000 *tan* less than the pre-war peak. Ramie is the Chinese equivalent of linen and provides a very acceptable cloth for wear in hot, humid, summer days in Central China. There are three harvests a year in May, July and October. Better cultivation and processing is necessary to meet the rising demand. Many areas in the Yangtze delta are admirably suited to the growth of jute on account of the high summer water-table. Production has increased greatly in the last decade to meet the rapidly-rising demand.

Vegetable oils produced from rape-seed, sesame and peanuts form a large proportion of the economic crops of the region. Of these rape-seed is clearly the most important and has a very wide distribution. Rape, which is a winter crop, matures earlier than wheat or barley and thus gives more time for rice preparation. Its production, therefore, tends to increase with the extension of rice production. Peanuts usually are grown on dry lands and on newly rehabilitated sandy wastelands, and do not compete with grain crops. Sesame is a summer crop, which alternates with wheat, barley, beans and peas. It has a poor resistance to heavy rainfall and therefore its production tends to decrease southward[53]. Some 250,000 *tan* of good quality wood oil (*tung yu*) is produced annually in west Hupeh from trees grown round homesteads, around fields and along roads.

The area around T'ai Hu in Kiangsu and extending into south and west Anhwei has for long been one of the most important sericulture regions in China[54]. Between 1929 and 1932 it enjoyed a period of great prosperity when more than 1 million *mow* were under mulberry orchard. Thereafter it encountered difficulties. During the Sino-Japanese War sericulture was discouraged and silkworm strains, in consequence, were weakened. This, together with the increasing competition of synthetic fibres, had resulted by 1949 in a fall of production by at least 50%. Since 1949 there have been big efforts to revive the occupation, but there is keen competition from food crops for the low-lying plains in this densely populated area. Efforts are therefore being made to establish sericulture in the somewhat higher land around Nanking and Chinkiang, and also to develop the tussah wild silkworm on the scrub-oak woodland of that area[55]. Six schools of sericulture have been started on the slopes of the Tapiehshan in an endeavour to introduce the most modern techniques[56].

A small amount of tea is grown in the uplands along the southern border of Kiangsu and south Anhwei. It is of excellent quality, known as 'Po-lo-chun', which is one of China's six famous teas. A large new State plantation has recently been opened for the development of black tea for export.

Since 1949, the amount of land devoted to tobacco growing in Anhwei has been extended from 60,000 to 300,000 *mow* (1957). The yield is reported to have been raised from 50 to 100 *chin/mow*. It is planted after the wheat harvest in late May and harvested between late August and late September.

Of the large livestock in the Rice–Wheat Region approximately 85% are oxen and water buffaloes. Horses and mules decrease in numbers towards the southern borders of the region. Although numbers of oxen and buffaloes are large, estimated at more than 7 million in 1957, they are still inadequate for draught work on the farms. Hogs are ubiquitous and, following the national drive in recent years, have greatly increased in numbers. Some sheep are reared in north Anhwei and north Hupeh. In Kiangsu the breeding of angora rabbits as a secondary village occupation has developed rapidly recently. The wool is sent to Shanghai mills for manufacture into jerseys and scarfs for export to the U.S.S.R. and East Europe.

	Jan.	Feb.	Mar.	April	May	June	July	Aug.	Sep.	Oct.	Nov.	Dec.
Shanghai Temp. °F	38	39	46	56	65	73	80	80	73	63	52	42
(33') Rainfall in	2·0	2·3	3·4	3·7	3·6	7·4	5·9	5·7	4·7	3·1	2·0	1·3
Hankow Temp. °F	40	43	50	62	71	80	85	85	77	67	55	45
(118') Rainfall in	1·8	1·9	3·8	6·0	6·5	9·6	7·1	3·8	2·8	3·2	1·9	1·1

Rice–Tea Region

The Rice–Tea Region contains within its borders three fertile alluvial basins, the flood-plains of the Siang and Yuan around the Tung Ting Hu in Hunan, that of the Kan Kiang around the Poyang Hu in Kiangsi and that of the Sinan around Hangchow Wan in Chekiang. The climate begins to assume a sub-tropical character, especially in the southernmost parts, and as a consequence the growing season is lengthened.

	Jan.	Feb.	Mar.	April	May	June	July	Aug.	Sep.	Oct.	Nov.	Dec.
Changsha Temp. °F	43	46	51	63	71	79	86	86	77	66	55	43
(295') Rainfall in	1·8	3·8	5·8	6·1	7·8	8·8	4·8	5·2	3·4	3·6	3·1	1·8
Wenchow. Temp. °F	47	47	53	61	69	77	83	83	77	69	64	51
(10') Rainfall in	1·8	3·4	4·9	5·5	7·0	9·9	7·5	9·4	8·0	3·2	2·1	1·6

A glance at the food crop statistics is sufficient to emphasize the all-important position that rice occupies in the sustenance of the people south of the Yangtze. About 70% of the cultivated land is devoted to rice and this forms 85% of the total food output for the three provinces, Hunan, Kiangsi and Chekiang, which make up this region. In rice production, Hunan ranks second only to Szechwan, which is nearly three times bigger and has nearly twice the population. In 1957 Hunan produced 193 million *tan* of rice. Thus, it is able to produce more than it needs and exports considerable quantities eastward down the Yangtze.

We have seen something of the efforts that are being made to modernize and extend irrigation, especially around the Tung Ting and Poyang Lakes (see p. 68). Nevertheless much of the paddy, particularly in south and west Hunan, is still irrigated by old 'mountain

129

pool' and 'flat pool' methods. These pools vary in size, but none are really large and few are adequate. The 'flat pools' are usually shallow and entail lifting water to the fields. This is done painstakingly and rather inefficiently by the old methods. It will be many years yet before the lifting is everywhere replaced by diesel or electric pumps. In Hunan rice is the summer crop, followed usually by a later autumn crop of beans, buckwheat or sweet potatoes. In favourable conditions a third crop of rape-seed or green fertilizer is reaped. Recently there has been an increase in the double-cropping of rice in the Ningpo and Wen-chow districts of Chekiang. It is maintained that, given adequate irrigation and labour facilities, climatic conditions in Chekiang are everywhere suitable for double-cropping, followed by a green fertilizer crop (*astragalus sinicus*)[55].

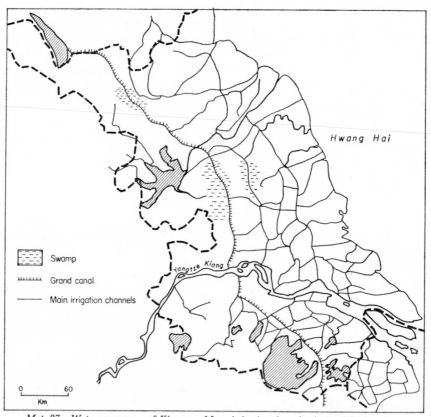

Map 37. Water conservancy of Kiangsu. Many irrigation channels also used for transport

Tea, which has been the national beverage since at least the eighth century, is the outstanding economic crop of the three provinces[1]. Chekiang ranks first and Hunan second in national production, raising 466,000 *tan* (one-fifth of the national output) and 370,000 *tan* respectively in 1957. The tea export trade suffered a shattering blow in the 1880s, when Indian and Ceylon teas, grown on large plantations and processed under careful super-vision, swept the western market—a blow from which China's tea trade has never properly recovered. However, such is the importance of the domestic market and demand that the

130

loss of the export trade was a comparatively minor matter. The natural conditions of the three provinces are well suited to tea production. They all enjoy a long frost-free period. High summer temperatures, abundant summer rain and high humidity and deep soil on well-drained hills ensure rapid leaf growth. Both green and black teas are grown, much of which has been of poor quality, due to the fact that production has been in the hands of individual small peasant farmers to whom tea-growing has been a secondary occupation. Larger plantations and specialization, consequent on the formation of co-operatives and communes, should bring improvement in quality and quantity. Some of Hunan's coarser qualities are made into brick tea for transport to Tibet, Mongolia and U.S.S.R. Kiangsi produces 'Ning Hung' and 'Fou Hung' red tea in the Siu Shui valley.

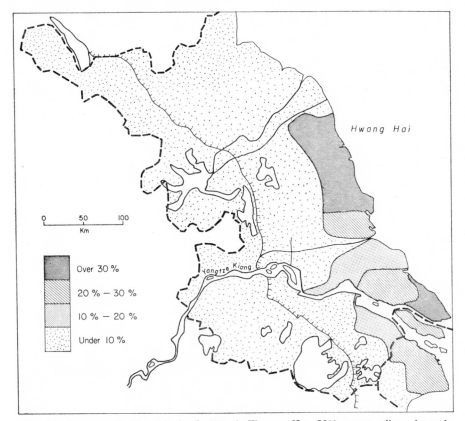

Map 38. *Percentage of cultivated land under cotton in Kiangsu. Note* 30% *category saline and sparsely populated. (Compiled from* 'Economic Geography of East China', Hua Tung Ching Chi Ti Li. Ed. Sun Ching-shih)

The great activity in sericulture in southern Kiangsu, noted above, is extended southward with even greater intensity into Chekiang, which has always been China's greatest silk producer. As in Kiangsu, sericulture is one of the chief secondary occupations of the villages.

'Silkworm production in this province is divided into four periods—spring, summer, autumn and late autumn. Of these the period for the spring silkworm is the most important, as more than 75% of the year's cocoons are produced during this time. In spring the mulberry leaves are particularly juicy and tender, and the climatic factors, such as temperature and humidity, are also ideal for silkworm culture. Furthermore, man-power use for spring silkworm culture does not conflict with farming activities.'[55]

Like Kiangsu, sericulture in Chekiang has suffered the same setbacks of suppression during the Sino-Japanese War and the competition of synthetic fibres and production has not yet reached the pre-war peak. In 1957 there were 1,730,000 *mow* of mulberry orchards in the province and 490,000 *tan* of cocoons were produced. Increasing care is being given to silkworm egg selection and to the improvement of mulberry orchards.

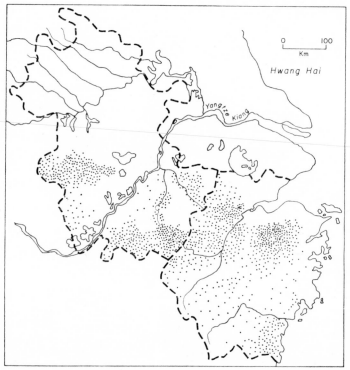

Map 39.   Distribution of tea in Anhwei and Chekiang.   (From 'Economic Geography of East China'. Hua Tung Ching Chi Ti Li. Ed. Sun Ching-shih)

Cotton production is of less importance south of the Yangtze than north. In Chekiang the main growth is on the plain to the north and south of Hangchow Wan. Here the usual rotation is two years of rice and one of cotton, the pattern of which is: first year, wheat, barley, rape or other winter crop, followed by cotton; second year, winter green fertilizer crop, followed by late-maturing rice; third year, further green fertilizer crop, followed by double-cropping rice[53]. The cotton crop is sent mainly to Shanghai for manufacture, but some spinning and weaving is done in Hangchow. Of the fibres, ramie and hemp are produced in Hunan and Kiangsi, while jute is more important in Chekiang.

Nearly 60% of the economic crop acreage is devoted to the growth of vegetable oils. Rape-seed, as usual, is by far the most important and is widely distributed over the whole of the region. A good deal of sesame is grown in Kiangsi.

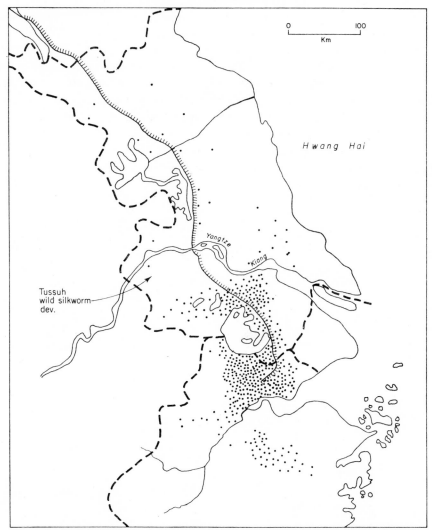

Map 40. Distribution of silkworm cocoon production in Kiangsu and Chekiang Provinces (each dot equals 1,000 shi tan). (*From* 'Economic Geography of East China'. Hua Tung Ching Chi. Ed. Sun Ching-shih)

Much of the natural forest has been cleared from the uplands of the region, but considerable reserves still remain in the remoter parts. The densest forests are in west Hunan in the middle and upper reaches of the Yuan Kiang and the south-eastern side of the Siang Kiang, producing fine stands of 'Ch'en' cedar and 'Yao' cedar and 'Ma-wei' pine, which is in much demand for mining and railway ties. In 1957, 1·8 million m³ were cut, of which about two-thirds was cedar and one-third pine. A great deal of this was exported down the

133

river to Hupeh and east China. Hunan also produces excellent rapid-growing bamboo, which, in addition to its thousand and one uses in handicrafts, paper making, umbrellas and many kinds of household utensils, is also finding an extended use in building construction[55]. The character of the forested uplands changes gradually eastward through Kiangsi to Chekiang. Cedar gives place to pine (*pinus massoniana*), fir, chestnut, camphor and pseudo-sassafras. Bamboo, on the lower slopes, continues to be of great importance industrially. Chekiang is one of the richer forest provinces with an estimated 57 million *mow* of woodland in 1958, which represents about 37% of the land area. Considerable care and attention is being given throughout the whole region to afforestation of the uplands; in Chekiang 780,000 *mow* are reported to be planted with wood oil (*Aleurites cordata*).

Fruit production has received remarkable impetus during the last two decades. The growing of citrus fruits (oranges, tangerines and grape fruit), peaches and pears figures largely in the west in Hunan and Kiangsi, especially around the lakes. In Chekiang, fruit production extends to loquats, apricots, strawberries, walnuts, dates and chestnuts as well. Some sugar cane is also grown.

Map 41. (a) Rape-seed production in Hunan (each dot equals 1,000 tan)—note main production along river valleys; (b) tea production in Hunan (each dot equals 500 tan)—note main production in uplands

Throughout the whole of the Rice–Wheat and Rice–Tea Regions freshwater fishing makes an important contribution to food production. This is dealt with in a later section.

South-west Rice Region

Yunnan and Kweichow, which together comprise the South-west Rice Region, form the most remote part of China Proper. For the most part it is a plateau of a general height of some 4,000 ft, but higher in the west and deeply incised with steep valleys. It was into this land that the many and varied tribes, who occupied the middle Yangtze valley, were pressed by the Chinese *Han Jen* of the north as they expanded southward between 200 B.C.

134

and A.D. 900. Consequently, of the 36 million people who today occupy these lands, nearly one-third are what are termed 'minorities'. Of these the chief is the Puyi, numbering about 1,250,000 at the 1953 census, followed by the Pai, Tai, Hani, Tung, Miao, Ka-wa, Hai, Na-hsi, La-yu, Chingpo, Yao and many others. They have had little contact with the Chinese until recently and, for livelihood, have followed generally 'slash and burn' agriculture and hunting. Population becomes increasingly rural (more than 90%) and decreasingly dense (less than 40/km²) westward.

It is surprising that there has not been more intensive Chinese occupation of the region, for in many parts it has a most attractive and equable climate. Yunnan, meaning 'South of the Clouds', is noted for its warm, dry, winter days with its clear sunny skies. In summer it has ample rain, particularly in east and west. The centre has something of a rain shadow. 'From October to April, tropical continental air masses move southward. The Yunnan Plateau is controlled by west-bound currents that are warm and dry. The whole plateau enters into its dry season. After April the tropical continental air masses move northward. South-westerly wind currents from India and south-easterly seasonal winds from the Pacific Ocean separately control the east and west areas of the plateau, bringing rich rains'.[50] East Kweichow is lower, cloudier and colder in winter and has a more equable distribution of rainfall than Yunnan. The whole region enjoys a long growing period but, owing to its mountainous character, is handicapped by the small proportion of cultivable land as is shown on *Maps 42(a)* and *44(a)*.

	Jan.	Feb.	Mar.	April	May	June	July	Aug.	Sep.	Oct.	Nov.	Dec.
Kunming Temp. °F	48	51	60	66	70	72	70	70	66	63	56	49
(5,940′) Rainfall in	0·5	0·5	0·6	0·7	3·8	6·1	9·4	8·2	5·4	3·6	1·7	0·6
Kweiyang Temp. °F	37	42	53	63	71	72	76	77	68	57	53	47
(1,070′) Rainfall in	1·0	1·1	0·9	2·0	7·0	8·1	9·0	4·1	5·4	4·2	2·0	0·6

In spite of its favourable climate, this south-west region has the unenviable reputation of being the most backward agriculturally in China Proper. This undoubtedly is due, to some extent, to its remoteness and isolation, to the poverty of soil and to the limited amount of cultivable soil, but it is equally certain that it is also the result of human factors. It has been noted above that an appreciable proportion of the population is tribal, which, until recently, has had little impact on agriculture. Since 1949, the People's Government has been assiduous in its attempts to integrate these people into the body politic and economic. This has been done by granting local self-government to the tribal *chou*, by sending well-qualified cadres to assist in development* and by forming 'Institutes of Minorities' in many large cities, the largest being in Peking. To these institutes, the local leaders are sent for training in administration and in modern agricultural and industrial practice. In this way the establishment of co-operatives and communes in these backward areas has been quicker and more successful than might reasonably have been expected. Another reason for the backwardness of agriculture has been the degenerate social state of the Chinese population itself. Absentee landlordism, uncharacteristic laziness and love of ease, exploitation of women's labour and general addiction to poppy growing and opium smoking have all been contributary causes[57]. Land reform, the prohibition of poppy-growing and opium smoking and the emancipation of women have gone a long way towards social regeneration and the establishment of higher agricultural standards.

* Fei Hsio-tung, an eminent sociologist, has done much to assist in the development of these people and was their representative in Peking for many years.

135

Rice is the most important grain crop grown. Although the acreage devoted to corn rivals it, the yield per *mow* from rice was more than twice as great in 1957. Rice-growing is concentrated in the south and south-east of the region, where 92% of the production is paddy and 8% upland rice. There are big differences in unit yield as between districts, depending on cultivation methods, many of which were reported as being poor and slipshod in 1957, average yield being only 150–200 *chin/mow*. Where water supply is adequate, rice is followed by a winter crop of wheat, barley, rape or beans, but too often fields have, unnecessarily, been left fallow during the winter. Reports since 1957 indicate that, with the extension of irrigation, the situation has changed materially. A network of 180 electric pumping stations has been built round the Tien Chih lake, Kunming since 1958, serving 13,000

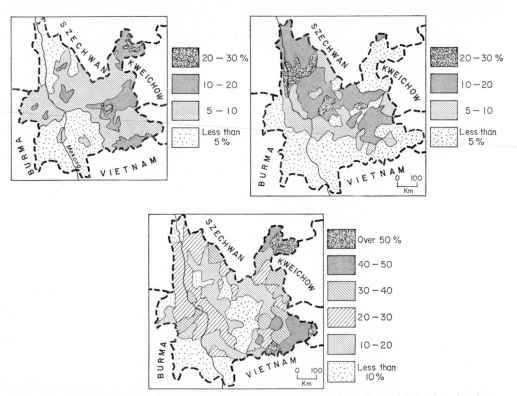

Map 42. (a) *Percentage of cultivated land in Yunnan—note small percentage in deep valleys and high ridges of south west, and high percentage on central plateau and Yangtze valley; (b) percentage of wheat to cultivated land in Yunnan; (c) percentage of corn to cultivated land in Yunnan. (Compiled from 'Economic Geography of South-west China,' Peking 1960)*

hectares and guaranteeing them against drought, which is the main hazard in central Yunnan. A new rice strain, 'Wannung No. 1', developed at Kweiyang on an experimental farm, bids to raise production per *mow* to over 500 *chin*[58]. One other example must suffice to indicate the change taking place in the remoter tribal regions. Reports from Te-Hung Tai and Chingpo Autonomous *Chou*, which has a population of 400,000 composed of Tai, Chingpo, Pengling, Lisu and Achong nationalities, claim that 54% of its farmland is now fully irrigated, served by more than 60 electric power stations. Hillsides have been terraced and a diversified economy developed, which includes summer rice and winter wheat, the growing of pineapples, bananas, papaya and citrus fruit, tea and coffee-growing and the rearing of pigs[59].

Maps 42(b) and 44(b), (c) show a clear zoning of the three main grain crops, rice in the south-east, corn on the central plateau and wheat in the north-west. Rape-seed, grown in winter and heavily cropped on the central plateau, is the most important of the oil seeds. Soyabeans also are widely grown and are usually planted between the rows of corn on the uplands. They are grown here mainly as a food and not for oil extraction.

Both provinces have an excellent climate for tobacco, the main production of which is concentrated on the central plateau. Tobacco stock is good and recent improvement in methods has raised the yield to 245 *chin/mow*. Some indication of the importance placed locally on this crop can be gleaned from the fact that a special middle school has been opened in Kweiyang and offers two courses, one for tobacco cultivation and the other for food crops.

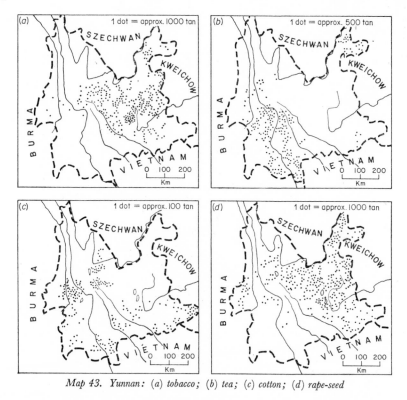

Map 43. Yunnan: (a) tobacco; (b) tea; (c) cotton; (d) rape-seed

Cotton, which in the past was not extensively grown and was of poor quality, is now being rapidly developed. A successful long staple strain has been bred, which, if sown in November instead of March, flowers before the heavy rainy season. Formerly much of the crop was spoiled by the June rains, which harmed pollination and promoted excessive vegetational growth to the detriment of the boll. Yields of 1,500 kg/hectare (about 80 *chin/mow*) are reported[60].

Karst country, Kwangtung　　　　　　　　　　*Liukia gorges, Hwang-ho*

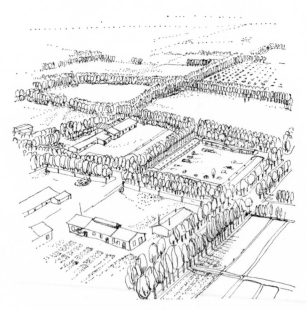

Sinkiang State Farm

Tea is grown in Yunnan and Kweichow. The main producing areas are the district west and south of Erh Hai and in the hills south of the Yangtze in the extreme north-east. Green tea forms the bulk of the output, but black and brick tea are also grown. Yunnan's production, 180,000–190,000 *tan* in 1958, is about double that of Kweichow. A little seri-culture is practiced, the silkworms being raised mainly on oak leaf. The production of sugar cane, which has suffered in the past from the long winter-spring aridity, is getting a new lease of life as irrigation develops.

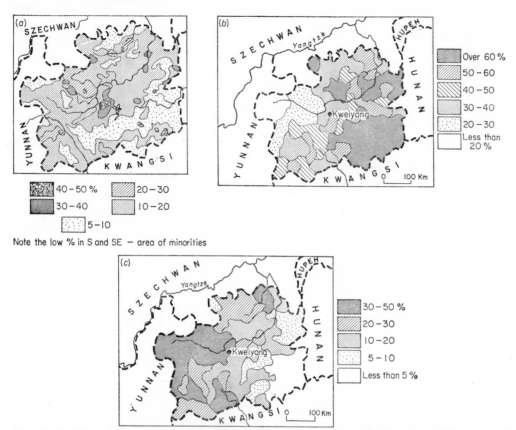

Map 44. Kweichow: (a) percentage of cultivated land; (b) percentage of paddy to total cultivated area; (c) percentage of corn crop to total cultivated area. (Compiled from 'Economic Geography of South-west China,' Peking 1960)

Second only to Szechwan, this South–West Rice Region is one of the richest forest areas of China Proper, the remoter the district, the finer the forest. In the north-west, crypto-meria, Lohan pine, red and white birch predominate. On the central plateau the main stands are pine, fir, cypress and oak, while in the lower south and south-east broad-leafed trees of oak, maple and poplar and bamboo groves mark the valleys. A great deal of the natural forest has been destroyed in the settled districts. For this reason, afforestation is being urged on all communes. In addition to quick-growing fir, wood-oil trees are being extensively planted.

Like Szechwan, this region received large numbers of migrants, fleeing westward before the Japanese forces between 1936 and 1945. As a consequence, agriculture and industry were advanced. Progress over the 21 years between 1936 and 1957 is shown in the following tables:

Table 5.5. *Agricultural Products* (10,000 *tan*)
(Compiled from *Economic Geography of South-west China*)

	Rice	Wheat	Cotton	Tobacco	Peanut	Rape	Sugar cane	Cattle	Buffalo	Hog
								Livestock (10,000 head)		
Yunnan										
1936	3,498	613	4	—	24	107	—	49	54	276
1949	4,439	322	1	4	13	46	508	185	95	—
1952	5,132	392	5	11	17	42	609	208	108	371
1957	7,124	617	7	61	61	90	1,509	303	139	652
Kweichow					Corn					
1936	3,177	120	5	22	1,587	—	—	57	60	142
1949	4,221	66	3	26	1,201	49	—	154	70	288
1952	4,748	102	5	32	1,480	73	—	170	76	360
1957	6,720	405	5	99	2,231	165	—	250	92	615

Table 5.6. *South-west Rice Region Grain Crops, 1957*
(Compiled from *Economic Geography of South-west China*)

	Acreage planted 10,000 mow	% of total	Yield mow	Total output 10,000 tan	% of total
Rice					
Yunnan	1,593	27·3	447	7,124	57·0
Kweichow	1,342	26·6	501	6,720	63·9
Wheat					
Yunnan	501	8·6	123	617	4·9
Kweichow	405	8·6	100	405	3·9
Corn					
Yunnan	1,388	23·8	193	2,672	21·4
Kweichow	1,131	24·1	197	2,231	21·2
Barley					
Yunnan	312	5·4	92	283	2·3
Kweichow	161	3·4	96	155	1·5
Sweet Potatoes					
Yunnan*	277	2·4	245	682	2·7
Kweichow†	221	2·3	286	637	3·0
Beans and Peas					
Yunnan	542	4·6	112	656	2·7
Kweichow	118	1·3	77	91	0·4
Economic Crops, 1957					
Rape-seed					
Yunnan	276	4·7	54	94	
Kweichow	378	8·1	44	165	
Peanut					
Yunnan	54	0·9	113	61	
Kweichow	13	0·3	143	19	
Tobacco					
Yunnan	91	0·8	85	73	
Kweichow	92	0·9	108	99	
Cotton					
Yunnan	38	0·7	18	7	
Kweichow	37	0·4	17	6	
Fibres					
Yunnan‡	14	0·3	62	9	
Kweichow§	11	0·2	56	6	
Sugar Cane					
Yunnan	30	0·5	5,078	1,500	
Kweichow	5	0·1	3,801	176	

* Potatoes and yams   † Sweet and Irish potatoes   ‡ Mainly hemp   § Mainly ramie

140

Double-cropping Rice Region

This region covers roughly the provinces of Fukien, Kwangtung and Kwangsi. Geologically it consists mainly of igneous and metamorphosed formations in the east from which overlying sedimentaries have been largely eroded and extensive limestone formations in the west, giving rise to fantastic karst scenery. For the most part the region is hilly and even mountainous, the only areas at all comparable to the wide, alluvial plains of the Yangtze and Hwang-ho being the flood plain of the lower Si Kiang.

The whole region enjoys tropical or sub-tropical temperatures, which, given adequate water, ensure a growing season of 12 months. There is a marked and heavy summer maximum of rainfall.

	Jan.	Feb.	Mar.	April	May	June	July	Aug.	Sep.	Oct.	Nov.	Dec.
Canton Temp. °F	56	57	63	71	80	81	83	83	80	75	67	60
(49′) Rainfall in	0·9	1·9	4·2	6·8	10·6	10·6	8·1	8·5	6·5	3·4	1·2	0·9
Foochow Temp. °F	53	52	56	64	72	80	84	84	76	67	59	50
(66′) Rainfall in	1·8	3·8	4·5	4·8	5·9	8·2	6·3	7·2	8·4	2·0	1·6	1·9

While the population of Fukien and Kwangtung is predominantly Chinese, it is distinguished from the Han Jen of north China. The people of the south refer to themselves as T'ang Jen or Men of T'ang, the dynasty (A.D. 618–907) during which the south was firmly and extensively settled. The people have their own distinctive dialects of Cantonese and Fukienese, although, of course, they have the same written language as the north. In the west, however, only 11·4 million out of a total of 19·4 million are Chinese, the remainder being minorities, who, as in Kweichow and Yunnan, were pushed into the hills by the advancing Chinese. By far the largest of these people is the Chuang, who number over 7 million. For this reason, the People's Government has established here the Kwangsi Chuang Autonomous Region. Other important tribes are the Yao (484,000), Miao (219,840), T'ung (148,424) and Yao-lao (44,666). In addition there are considerable numbers of 'boat people', living on the water in the river estuaries and along the rugged coast. Most of the Chinese emigration to Malaysia, Indonesia and Borneo in times past has been from this double-cropping rice region, and it is from these emigrants that considerable remittances are still received.

As its title indicates, the characteristic crop is rice, to which 68% of the planted area is devoted. Most of the lower-lying land, having adequate water facilities, grows an early and a late crop of rice, followed by an over-wintering crop of wheat, peanuts, beans or green manure. To do this the late crop must follow the early in quick succession. There is a local saying 'In the morning, yellow; in the evening, green', indicating that the standing ripe rice is reaped in the morning and that, by evening, the same fields should be green with the transplanted seedlings of the new crop. This is an exaggeration, but it serves to emphasize the need for getting the second crop in as quickly as possible. Late planting means a poor yield, hence the need for the rational use and economy of labour, especially at peak times in rice cultivation. Officials are called away from their offices and students from their desks at such times, but such help as they can give is probably small when compared with the increasing mechanization in the rice fields that is taking place in the form of transplanting machines and tractors for reaping and ploughing. The new powered rice transplanter, which is a great improvement on the machines of 1958, transplants 12 *mow* of seedlings in a day. The new rotary tiller, drawn by a 35 h.p. tractor, works well in muddy paddy fields and it is claimed that the new, long-distance spray, having a 15 m jet, keeps the rice borer infestation down to 1% and is considered revolutionary. It is to the production of this kind of agricultural machinery that industry has been directed since 1960, but there is no clear report of how widely it is now in use.

The great efforts that have been expended in extending irrigation and drainage in this region have been directed primarily to furthering rice production. Under a long-range plan, reservoirs have been built on the Tung (East) Kiang, most unruly of the three rivers (Si, Tung and Peh), thereby relieving the strain on the plains below during typhoons and heavy rains. In the low-lying Pearl river delta, 1,200 electric pumping stations guarantee 460,000 hectares of farmland against flood and drought[61]. Of Kwangtung's 30 million *mow* of farmland 24 million *mow* are now said to be well irrigated. Similar claims are made for the more restricted arable areas of Fukien and Kwangsi. The latter, owing to its limestone formations, is more prone to drought. Thousands of wells are being sunk, tapping the abundant underground supplies of water[62]. Since 1958 20,000 hectares of land have been reclaimed from the sea in the Pearl river delta area by means of building massive dykes, and much of this land is already harvesting double-cropped rice[63]. The work and capital throughout is attributed almost entirely to the communes.

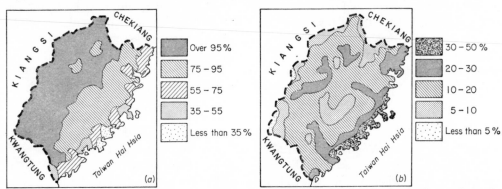

Map 45. Double-cropping rice: (a) percentage of total crop area planted in rice in Fukien—note almost exclusive rice cultivation in uplands; (b) percentage of cultivated land to total land area. (From 'Economic Geography of South China'. Ed. Sun Ching-chih)

Much attention has also been focused on the development of a short-stalked variety of rice which will stand up to the heavy downpours and the high winds experienced in the south. High tillering varieties, developing many spikes to each plant, have recently been bred and yields of 7–7½ ton/hectare are now generally being achieved. Cultivation has been further aided by extensive building of chemical fertilizer plant. Kwangtung alone now has 32 large and small plants, which produced more than 500,000 ton of fertilizer in 1964[64].

Wet rice is often rotated with dry crops—wheat, beans, taro—to allow the surface of the rice fields to be baked by the sun, which, it is held, improves soil fertility. Taro is an important crop in this connection. It has a long growing period and is therefore interplanted with fast-growing vegetables such as beans, cucumbers, pai tsai (cabbage), followed by jute seedlings and potatoes when the taro leaves wither. In this way as many as five or six crops can be harvested in a year.

Wheat plays a small part in the remaining grain crops. Corn is produced in appreciable amount only in Kwangsi. Tubers, mainly sweet potatoes, are an important part of the general diet.

Oil seeds occupy more than half the area devoted to economic crops. Peanuts are by far the most important, followed by sesame. Rape-seed has, only recently, come into prominence. The tropical character of the region is emphasized by the fact that coconut and palm oil, tea oil, cassia, citronella oil and aniseed oil are all produced there. Kwangsi is an

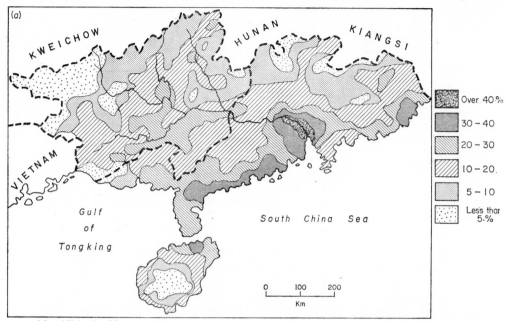

Map 46(a). Double cropping rice: proportion of cultivated land to total land area Kwangtung and Kwangsi.
(*From* " Economic Geography of South China ". Ed. Sung Ching-Chi)

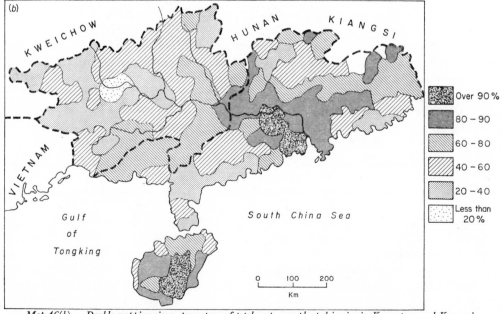

Map 46(b). Double cropping rice: percentage of total crop area planted in rice in Kwangtung and Kwangsi.
(*From* " Economic Geography of South China ". Ed. Sung Ching-Chi)

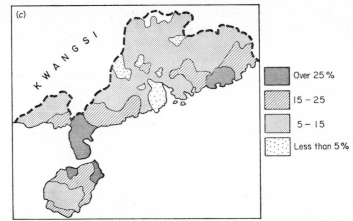

▓	Over 25%
⁄⁄	15 – 25
░	5 – 15
∴	Less than 5%

Map 46(c) Double cropping rice: ratio of sweet potatoes to cultivated land area in Kwangtung.
(From 'Economic Geography of South China'. Ed. Sung Ching-Chi)

important producer of wood oil and tea oil, ranking second respectively to Szechwan and Kwangtung in the national scale.

The cultivation of sugar cane is rapidly increasing. Natural conditions throughout the region, and particularly in Hainan, are very favourable. Kwangtung, which is the biggest producer, raised its output over the previous year by 100,000 ton in 1964–65. The cane yielded 11·1% sugar of which 77% was No. 1 grade. Cane yield in Fukien is reported as 75 ton/hectare. The most important producing areas are the Chu Kiang (Pearl river), Han Kiang around Swatow, the coastal region between Foochow and Amoy and northern Hainan, where the two most important varieties are 'East Java 3016' early ripening and 'Formosa 134' late ripening. It has been found that interplanting in alternate rows of sugar cane and peanuts raises the yield of both and this is now practised on a wide scale. The peanut tubercles are able to assimilate nitrogen from the air and so enrich the soil. After the pods are gathered the vines and leaves are ploughed in. The peanut plants also reduce evaporation and so conserve water for the canes[65]. A great increase in sugar refining has accompanied the rise in cane production. In 1965, Kwangtung alone had 7 large and 28 medium refineries with an annual total sugar output of 40,000 ton[66].

Although lying outside the Rice–Tea Region, Fukien enjoys national fame as a tea producer on account of its 'Wu-yi' and 'T'ieh-kwan-yin' varieties. As might be expected, the main tea gardens are in the north-east, contiguous to the Chekiang gardens. The climate gives a long growing period, permitting picking during 10 months of the year. Although tea culture methods have made marked advances recently they are still somewhat primitive[67]. There has been an increase in coffee-growing in recent years, but the amount is still very small.

Sword hemp (*Bryophyllum Houghtonii*) and sisal are both grown in Kwangtung. The former is a tough fibre, resistant to sea water and is therefore good material for fishing nets. It is also valuable industrially for the manufacture of motor tyres, conveyor belts, etc.[68]. Some ramie is grown. Jute, which is planted in March and reaped in September, is grown along the river banks. It is usually followed by a late rice crop and then a catch crop of vegetables or green manure. A small but increasing amount of Sea Island cotton is grown in the south.

Sericulture is practised mainly in the lower Si Kiang basin and the Pearl river delta.

144

Fast-growing white mulberry enables seven to eight pickings to be made in the year, with a result that Kwangtung produces one-eighth of the entire country's cocoons. Many varieties of wild silkworm are raised in west Kwangtung and Kwangsi on oak and camphor leaves[68].

The variety of fruit grown in this region reveals its tropical and sub-tropical nature. In addition to the vast quantities of citrus fruits (oranges, tangerines, pomelo and grape fruit) that are grown and exported, melons, longans, lichees and olives are produced in

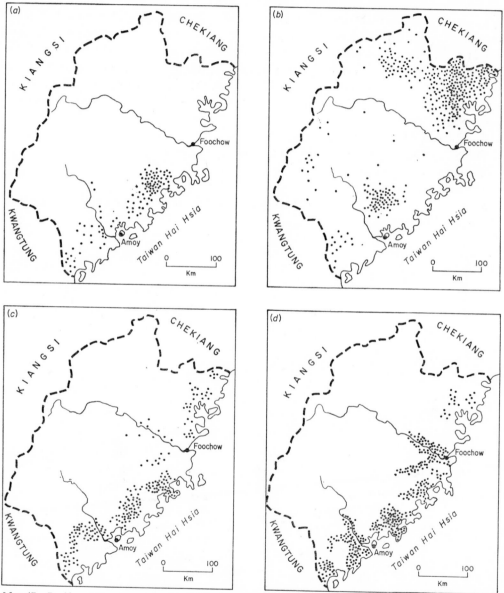

Map 47. Double-cropping rice region: (a) distribution of sugar cane in Fukien (each dot equals approx. 100,000 tan); (b) distribution of tea in Fukien (each dot equals approx. 200 tan); (c) distribution of jute in Fukien (each dot equals approx. 500 tan); (d) distribution of fruit in Fukien (each dot equals approx. 3,000 tan)

145

the river valleys and alluvial plains. Papaya, bananas, mango, pomegranates and betel nut are grown in the south and in Hainan. Pineapple, which demands little from the soil and can be successfully cultivated on quite steep hillsides, is now being extensively cultivated. Transportation and storage of fruit is improving and the canning industry is increasing very rapidly.

A natural vegetational cover of tropical and sub-tropical forest should cover much of the region. It has, however, undergone widespread deforestation in the past centuries and, in consequence, the land has suffered severe erosion[69]. It is estimated that some 61,000 sq. miles or 27·5% of the total land area of Kwangtung is so affected. In recent years strenuous efforts have been made to educate the peasantry in the value and care of forests, and large areas have been afforested. Pine, fir and eucalyptus, together with bamboo, are the main trees planted. These are fast growing and are fit for cutting in 10 years. The following lines are an example of the custom now so much in vogue in China of turning to song and verse to mark any achievement:

The forest in Chieh Shou is green and luxuriant.

The mountains are covered with verdant bamboo and trees.

To protect the forest well,

We hasten to open fire lanes[70].

Since 1949, there has been a rapid increase in the development of rubber plantations, especially in Hainan.

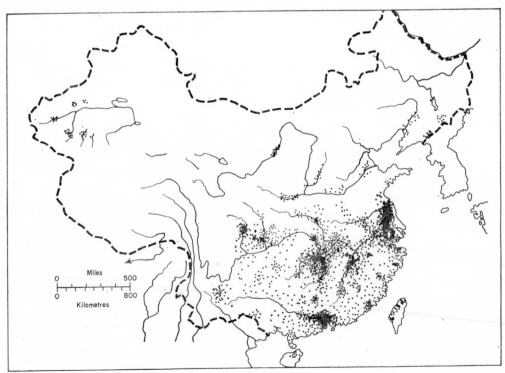

Map 48. Rice

146

Virtually all the large livestock of this region are used for draught purposes. As might be expected in so intensive a rice-growing area, water buffalo form a larger proportion (nearly 50%) than farther north. The national campaign to increase hog raising has been most intensive in the Double-Cropping Rice Region since its emphasis is so much on the production of manure. It is reckoned that one hog produces between 2,000 and 3,000 *chin* of manure annually, which may be instrumental in producing an additional 200 to 300 *chin/mow* of rice. Since the formation of co-operatives and communes, peasants have been urged to raise pigs collectively. That there has been some struggle and resistance to propaganda in this field is shown by the fact that by 1964 only about 30% of the hogs in this region were raised collectively, the rest being raised on private plots either indirectly for the collective or for individual households. In the latter case manure would not find its way to the paddy fields. Clearly there is a strong temptation to breed pigs privately. 'Some rich peasants, seriously affected by the spontaneous tendency towards capitalism, tried their utmost to play down the role of collective hog breeding[71].'

Table 5.7

| | 1949–52 | | 1957 | |
| | *Planted area* | | *Planted area* | |
	10,000 *mow*	%	10,000 *mow*	%
Food Crops				
Rice				
Kwangtung	7,030	83·9	7,271	72·4
Kwangsi	—	—	3,391	60·4
Fukien	215	76·9	221	71·4
Wheat				
Kwangtung	110	1·3	359	7·6
Kwangsi	—	—	391	5·2
Fukien	15	5·6	24	7·9
Corn				
Kwangsi	—	—	833	14·8
Tubers				
Kwangtung	1,085	13·0	1,863	18·6
Kwangsi	—	—	627	11·2
Fukien	40	14·5	45	14·6
Economic Crops				
Sugar Cane				
Kwangtung			176	24·1
Kwangsi			56	13·2
Fukien			37	17·1
Peanuts				
Kwangtung			378	51·9
Kwangsi			236	55·4
Fukien			111	50·9
Rape-seed				
Kwangtung			—	—
Kwangsi			35	8·2
Fukien			45	20·8
Fibres				
Kwangtung (hemp and ramie)			34	5·8
Kwangsi (jute and ramie)			12	2·9
Fukien (jute and ramie)			10	4·3
Tobacco				
Kwangtung			37	5·1
Kwangsi			15	8·4
Fukien			10	4·3

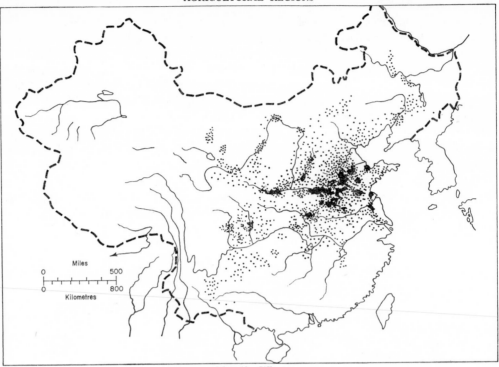

Map 49. Wheat

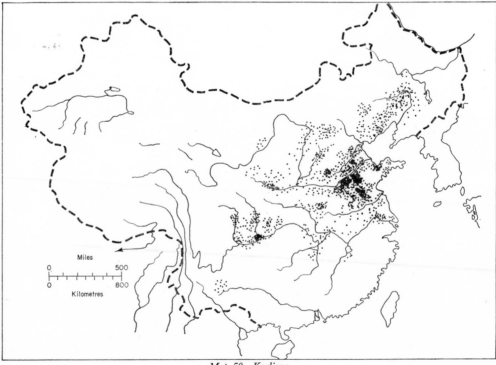

Map 50. Kaoliang

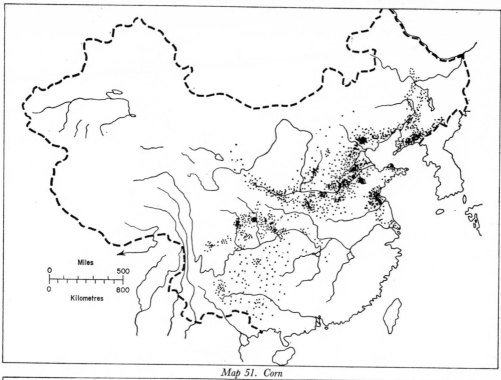

Map 51. Corn

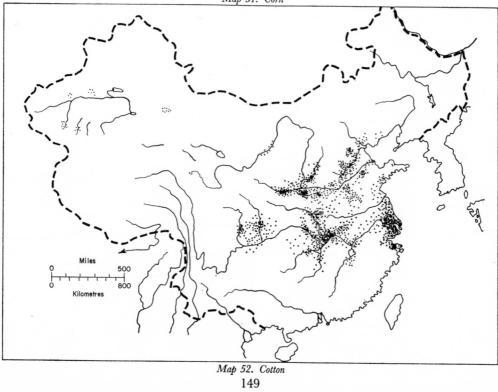

Map 52. Cotton

149

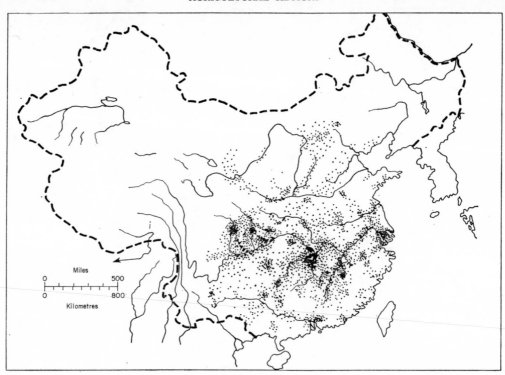

Map 53. Rape-seed

Table 5.8. Crop Production (million ton)

Year Peak	Total grain	Rice	Wheat	Misc. grain	Potatoes (4:1)	Soyabeans	Cotton lint	Rape-seed	Peanuts	Sugar cane
pre 1949	150	52·5	23	—	—	9·84	0·84	1·75	2·76	3·25
1949	113	38·3	13	36	10	4·24	0·44	0·73	1·27	2·64
1950	132	50	15	—	—	—	0·71	—	—	—
1951	145	59	16·8	—	—	—	1·04	—	—	—
1952	164	68·4	18·1	52	16	7·9	1·30	0·93	2·32	7·12
1953	167	70·4	18·1	51	17	8·03	1·18	0·88	2·1	7·21
1954	170	69·7	23·2	49	17	7·5	1·06	0·88	2·77	8·59
1955	183	75	—	55	19	7·6	1·50	0·97	2·92	8·11
1956	199	82	—	53	20	8·5	—	0·94	3·33	8·67
1957	193	81·7	23·7	54	21	8·4	1·63	1·00	2·34	13·18
1958	220	—	—	—	—	8·7	—	—	2·78	—
1959	250	—	—	—	—	9·6	—	—	—	—
1960	—	—	—	—	—	—	—	—	—	—
1961	—	—	—	—	—	—	—	—	—	—
1962*	178	80·6	20·8	54	24	—	—	—	—	—
1963*	179	78·4	21·8	55	24	7·8	1·0	0·5	1·9	—
1964*	181	82	23·5	54	22	8·6	1·25	0·7	2·3	—
1965*	180	84·9	21·5	53·4	20·1	6·8	—	—	2·3	—
1966†	180 (250‡)	—	—	—	—	—	—	—	—	—
1967†	190 (230§)	—	—	—	—	—	—	—	—	—

* Unofficial estimates (probably on the conservative side). (From *F.E.E.R. Year Book 1965* and *F.E.E.R. No. 186*, 21 July, 1966).
† *Current Science* Vol. VI (1968) No. 12.
‡ T. A. Close, F.E.E.R. 5 January 1967.
§ Anna Louise Strong, estimate in *Letter from China*, Foreign Language Press, Peking, 15 January, 1968.

Table 5.9. Food Crops

| | Planted area | | | Total output | |
	10,000 mow units	% Total crop acreage	% Food crop acreage	10,000 tan	% Food crop
Rice					
Rice–Wheat Region					
Kiangsu	3,269	22·5	30·6	13,422	57·0
Anhwei	3,372	22·4	28·2	12,190	53·1
Hupeh	3,253	29·6	40·5	15,111	68·9
Rice–Tea Region					
Hunan	5,669	55·2	69·8	19,333	86·1
Kiangsi	4,414	53·9	80·5	12,474	91·3
Chekiang	2,443	39·2	59·7	11,945	76·5
Wheat					
Rice–Wheat Region					
Kiangsu	3,164	19·6	26·6	3,148	13·4
Anhwei	4,021	26·1	33·7	4,010	17·5
Hupeh	1,734	15·8	21·6	2,438	11·1
Rice–Tea Region					
Hunan	500	4·9	6·2	301	1·3
Kiangsi	226	2·8	4·1	114	0·8
Chekiang	468	7·5	11·4	513	3·3
Barley					
Rice–Wheat Region					
Kiangsu	1,102	6·8	9·3	1,341	5·7
Anhwei	—	—	—	—	—
Hupeh	873	7·9	10·9	894	4·1
Rice–Tea Region					
Hunan	221	2·2	2·7	137	0·6
Kiangsi	106	1·3	1·9	71	0·5
Chekiang	304	4·7	7·4	377	2·4
Corn					
Rice–Wheat Region					
Kiangsu	938	5·8	8·9	1,751	7·4
Anhwei	—	—	—	—	—
Hupeh	692	6·3	8·6	1,194	5·4
Rice–Tea Region					
Hunan	249	2·4	3·1	276	1·2
Kiangsi	26	0·3	0·5	35	0·3
Chekiang	239	3·8	5·8	514	3·3
Sweet potatoes					
Rice–Wheat Region					
Kiangsu	532	3·3	4·5	1,034	4·4
Anhwei	1,132	7·5	9·5	323	14·1
Hupeh	285	2·6	3·5	895	4·1
Rice–Tea Region					
Hunan	40	0·4	0·5	67	0·3
Kiangsi*	296	3·6	5·4	729	5·3
Chekiang	266	4·3	6·5	1,650	10·6

* Tuber, 90% sweet potatoes.

Table 5.10. Economic Crops, 1957

	Planted area			Total production
	10,000 mow units	% All crops	% Econ. crops	10,000 tan
Cotton				
Rice–Wheat Region				
Kiangsu	1,084	6·7	66·7	400
Anhwei	300	—	28·8	—
Hupeh	875	8·0	53·7	454
Rice–Tea Region				
Hunan	121	1·2	21·2	43
Kiangsi	109	1·3	12·5	52
Chekiang	113	1·8	21·5	—
Ramie				
Rice%–Wheat Region				
Kiangsu*	45	0·3	2·8	—
Anhwei*	51	—	4·9	—
Hupeh	33	0·3	2·0	35
Rice–Tea Region				
Hunan	25	0·2	4·4	18
Kiangsi†	29	0·4	3·3	65
Chekiang‡	77	1·2	14·7	—
Rape-seed				
Rice–Wheat Region				
Kiangsu	210	1·3	12·9	—
Anhwei§	645	—	61·7	—
Hupeh	264	2·4	16·2	106
Rice–Tea Region				
Hunan	294	2·9	51·6	111
Kiangsi	515	6·3	59·1	103
Chekiang	246	3·9	46·9	—
Sesame				
Rice–Wheat Region				
Kiangsu	—	—	—	—
Anhwei	—	—	—	—
Hupeh	309	2·8	19·0	210
Rice–Tea Region				
Hunan	22	0·2	3·8	11
Kiangsi	135	1·6	15·5	59
Chekiang	—	—	—	—
Peanuts				
Rice–Wheat Region				
Kiangsu	251	1·6	15·4	—
Anhwei	—	—	—	—
Hupeh	111	1·0	6·8	276
Rice–Tea Region				
Hunan	50	0·5	8·8	76
Kiangsi	68	0·8	7·8	115
Chekiang	25	0·4	4·8	—
Tobacco				
Rice–Wheat Region				
Kiangsu	—	—	—	—
Anhwei	41	—	3·9	—
Hupeh	—	—	—	—
Rice–Tea Region				
Hunan	16	0·2	2·8	16
Kiangsi	—	—	—	—
Chekiang	—	—	—	—

* All fibres, including jute, hemp and bast.   † Ramie and jute.
‡ Jute.   § Vegetable oil crops, including peanuts and sesame.

REFERENCES

[1] TREGEAR, T. R. *A Geography of China*, University of London Press, London, 1965, pp. 52–58, 65–67, 287, 285–294, 290–291, 73–76, 216, 270–272, 252, 131–132

[2] CHIA SHUN-HSUI. 'Grass Plains', *K'o-hsuch Ta-chung* (*Popular Science*), No. 9, Sept. 1964

[3] WU CH'UAN-CHIN *et al*. *Economic Geography of the Western Region of the Middle Yellow River*, Peking, 1956 (U.S. Joint Publications Research Service)

[4] *N.C.N.A.*, Huhehot, 28 July 1965

[5] *N.C.N.A.*, Huhehot, 27 Nov. 1964

[6] *N.C.N.A.*, Huhehot, 15 Mar. 1966

[7] *N.C.N.A.*, Lanchow, 22 Aug. 1965

[8] *Economic Geography of Inner Mongolian Autonomous Region*, U.S. Joint Publications Research Service, 1957

[9] T'ANG YI-JEN, 'Animal Husbandry's Place in the National Economy', *Hsin Chien-she* (*New Construction*), No. 12, Dec. 1964

[10] *N.C.N.A.*, Peking, 8 June 1966

[11] *N.C.N.A.*, Huhehot, 5 Feb. 1965

[12] *N.C.N.A.*, Sining, 11 Feb. 1965

[13] *N.C.N.A.*, Huhehot, 8 Sept. 1965

[14] *N.C.N.A.*, Huhehot, 2 Aug. 1965

[15] *People's Daily*, Peking, 10 July 1965

[16] FREEBERNE, MICHAEL. 'Demographic and Economic Changes in the Sinkiang Uighur Autonomous Region,' *Population Studies*, Vol. XX, No. 1, 1966

[17] *N.C.N.A.*, Peking, 28 Jan. 1965

[18] *Far Eastern Economic Review*, 16 Nov. 1965

[19] *N.C.N.A.*, Urumchi, 9 Oct. 1965

[20] *N.C.N.A.*, Urumchi, 18 Dec. 1965

[21] *N.C.N.A.*, Urumchi, 23 Sept. 1965

[22] CHANG HUNG-WEN. 'Grapes in the "Land of Fire",' *China Reconstructs*, Peking, June 1963

[23] *N.C.N.A.*, Urumchi, 22 June 1966

[24] *N.C.N.A.*, Lhasa, 3 Sept. 1965

[25] *N.C.N.A.*, Lhasa, 22 Feb. 1965

[26] KAHMYKOVA, V. G. and OVDIYENTO, L. KH. *Geographical Survey of North-west China*, Moscow, 1957 (U.S. Joint Publications Research Service)

[27] *N.C.N.A.*, Sining, 6 June 1966

[28] *N.C.N.A.*, Huhehot, 2 June 1965

[29] TEILLARD DE CHARDIN, P. *Letters from a Traveller*, Collins, London, 1957, p. 81

[30] *N.C.N.A.*, Lanchow, 14 Dec. 1964

[31] *N.C.N.A.*, Sining, 4 May 1965

[32] *N.C.N.A.*, Huhehot, 10 Nov. 1964

[33] CRESSEY, G. B. *Land of the 500 Million*, McGraw-Hill, New York, 1955

[34] MALLORY, W. H. *China, Land of Famine*, American Geographical Society, New York, 1926

[35] SHEN, T. H. *Agricultural Resources of China*, Cornell University Press, Ithaca, New York, 1951

[36] *N.C.N.A.*, Paoting, 17 July 1966

[37] *Preliminary Scientific and Technical Summing up of Bumper Wheat Harvests in 1965*, Crop Culture and Cultivation Research Institute, Chinese Academy of Agricultural Science; *Peking Kuang-min Jih-pao*, 16 Nov. 1965

[38] YANG, M. C. *A Chinese Village—Taitou, Shantung*, Routledge & Kegan Paul, London 1946

[39] *N.C.N.A.*, Peking, 26 June 1965

[40] *N.C.N.A,.* Tsinan, 17 July 1966

[41] *Chung-huo Nung-yeh K'o hsueh* (*Chinese Agricultural Science*), No. 3, 15 Mar. 1965

[42] *People's Daily*, Peking, 9 Feb. 1965

[43] LATTIMORE, O. 'Chinese Colonization in Manchuria', *Geogrl. Rev.*, 1932

[44] SUN CHING-CHIH (Ed.). *Economic Geography in North-east China*, Peking, 1959. (English Transl.). Research and Microfilm Publicity Inc., Annapolis, Maryland

[45] *N.C.N.A.*, Shenyang, 8 April 1965

[46] *N.C.N.A.*, Shenyang, 1 April 1965

[47] *N.C.N.A.*, Shenyang, 25 Nov. 1964

[48] *N.C.N.A.*, Harbin, 13 Jan. 1966

[49] *N.C.N.A.*, Harbin, 14 Sept. 1966

[50] SUN CHING-CHIH (Ed.). *Si-nan Ti Ch'u Ching-chi- Ti-li* (*Economic Geography of South-west China*), Peking, 1960

[51] *N.C.N.A.*, Chengtu, 27 Nov, 1965

[52] *N.C.N.A.*, Chengtu, 22 July 1965

[53] SUN CHING-CHIH (Ed.). *Economic Geography of Central China*, Peking, 1960

[54] FEI HSIAO-TUNG. *Peasant Life in China*, Routledge & Kegan Paul, London, 1947

[55] SUN CHING-CHIH (Ed.). *Economic Geography of East China Region*, Institute of Geography, Chinese Acad. Sci, 1961

[56] *N.C.N.A.*, Hofei, 17 Nov. 1965

[57] FEI HSIAO-TUNG and CHANG-CHIH-I, *Earthbound China: a Study of Rural Economy in Yunnan*, University of Chicago Press, Chicago, 1945

[58] *N.C.N.A.*, Kweiyang, 31 Jan. 1966

REFERENCES

59 *N.C.N.A.*, Kunming, 13 Dec. 1965
60 *N.C.N.A.*, Kunming, 26 Nov. 1965
61 *N.C.N.A.*, Canton, 23 Oct. 1964
62 *N.C.N.A.*, Nanning, 21 April 1965
63 *N.C.N.A.*, Canton, 7 Aug. 1965
64 *N.C.N.A.*, Canton, 28 Dec. 1964
65 *N.C.N.A.*, Canton, 8 Sept. 1965
66 *N.C.N.A.*, Canton, 14 Mar. 1965
67 SUN CHING-CHIH (Ed.). *Economic Geography of South China*, Peking, 1959
68 LIANG JEN-TS'AI, 'Economic Geography of Kwangtung', *Academia Sinica*, 1958
69 FENZEL, G. 'On the Natural Conditions Affecting the Introduction of Forestry in the Province of Kwangtung'; *Lingman Sci. J.*, No. 7, 1929
70 *Nan-fang Joh-pao*, Canton, 28 Oct. 1964
71 *Nung-lin Kung-tso T'ung-hsm (Agricultural and Forestry Work Bulletin)*, No. 6, 6 June 1964

6

COMMUNICATIONS AND TRANSPORT

BEFORE embarking on an analysis and description of recent developments in communications in China, it will be as well to be reminded of some of the underlying geographical factors in this field. The mere distances involved are enormous. As the crow flies, it is about 2,000 miles from Canton to Tsitsihar in Heilungkiang; about the same distance from Peking to Kashgar in western Sinkiang; some 1,750 miles from Peking to Lhasa, and 1,500 miles to Kunming. Relief or climate makes access to some parts very difficult. This is particularly true of the Tibetan plateau, whose great height and the innumerable ridges, which have to be crossed, make travel most arduous and hazardous. The intervening deserts between China Proper and Sinkiang tend to isolate the outlying west. Long winters and frozen rivers have, until recent years, made access to the remote North-East difficult for a large part of the year. Within China Proper there are some districts in which difficulty of movement is notorious. The loess region of Shensi, with its deep, steep-sided valleys enforcing long and arduous detours, is a case in point. Another example is the rugged land which separated Szechwan from Yunnan. Until the construction of the Burma Road, it was quicker and easier to journey from Chengtu to Kunming by going down the Yangtze to Shanghai, then by sea to Haiphong, thence by rail to Kunming rather than attempt the perilous direct route.

In spite of the immense distances and difficulties, vigorous and efficient emperors in the past have been successful in holding the huge Chinese empire together over long periods. This could be done only by the establishment and maintenance of adequate communications, thus enabling administrative contact with the outlying parts to be sustained. The Han (206 B.C.–A.D. 220), T'ang (A.D. 618–907), Yuan (1279–1369) and Ch'ing (1644–1911) were all successful in doing this, at least in their earlier years. Marco Polo, writing when the Yuan (Mongol) dynasty was at the height of its power, gives a glowing description of the efficiency of post houses and posting, stating that, in emergency, messages could be carried 125 miles in a day[1]. As soon as the emperor and court became effete and communications were allowed to deteriorate, the empire began to fall apart and break up.

Much of the trade was in the form of tribute to the emperor and travelled along the imperial routes to the capital of the time[2]. Most notable of these was the Imperial Silk Route through Kansu and Sinkiang, which was also the main road followed by Chinese pilgrims to India and by which Buddhism entered China.

Throughout the centuries there has been a marked contrast in the means of transport used in north China and those used in the south. In the drier, less wooded north, carts drawn by horses, mules, donkeys and camels, have been the main method of moving goods, most rivers being unnavigable. Dr. Needham has pointed out the early advances made by the Chinese in the use of equine tractive power by such inventions as the stirrup, breast-strap and collar harness[3]. For movement over desert and semi-desert regions bactrian camel caravans have been the main means used. Farther south in the wetter, forested

155

regions, reliance has been placed almost exclusively on man's shoulders and legs by means of the carrying pole, wheelbarrow and sedan chair, wherever water transport could not be used. Roads, for the most part, were mere paths, occasionally paved with stone slabs but, more generally, were mere earth tracks, which became deeply rutted by the wheelbarrows in wet weather.

With the expansion southward during the T'ang dynasty and the consequent shift of the economic heart of the country into the Yangtze basin, the movement of bulky tribute grain over long distances to the northern capitals presented an increasing problem. This grain was essential to the life of government, court and army. The problem gave rise to an era of canal building, which produced the New Pien Canal from the Yangtze near Nanking to Kaifeng and so to Changan (Sian), the then T'ang capital, and later, in the Yuan dynasty, the Grand Canal from the Yangtze to Peking[2].

MODERN DEVELOPMENT

Railways

Lines of communication and means of transport remained essentially unchanged for 2,000 years, from the Han dynasty until the latter half of the nineteenth century when western intrusion was beginning to make itself felt.

The first railway to be built in China was a short, narrow gauge (2 ft 6 in) line between Woosung and Shanghai. It was built with foreign capital and with foreign enterprise and opened in 1876. It met with official and local peasant opposition and, in 1877, its rails were torn up and shipped to Taiwan. Official opposition sprang from the deep-seated conservatism of the Imperial Court and the intense hatred and fear of foreign aggressiveness; while peasant opposition stemmed from the widespread necromantic belief in 'feng shui', the spirits of wind and water which were believed to reside in the land, especially in high places. These spirits were disturbed at one's peril and the well-being of the whole countryside might thereby be endangered. 'Feng shui' was a factor, which developers of railways, telegraph and mines found they had to reckon with seriously since it could easily be evoked by anyone whose interest it was to hinder development. The author remembers how, in the early part of the twentieth century the building of a mission hospital at Anlu had to be re-sited on a less socially-favourable spot because the buildings on the chosen site would have over-topped the pagoda and so upset the 'feng shui'. Apart from one or two small mining lines in Honan and Hopeh, no further attempt at railway construction was made until the closing years of the nineteenth century.

The defeat of China by Japan in 1894 and the general belief that China was on the verge of disintegration was the occasion of a campaign of intrigue, known as 'the battle of concessions' in which most of the great powers of the day scrambled and schemed to obtain concessions and spheres of influence in which they might operate in China. It was the jealousies between these powers that helped to keep the tottering Ch'ing dynasty from falling until 1911. Russia (and later Japan) obtained preponderating influence in Manchuria; Germany in Shantung around Tsingtao; France in Yunnan next to her colonial territory in Indo-China; Great Britain around Tientsin and Shanghai and in the Yangtze valley.

Then followed a spate of railway building between 1900 and 1920 as the table below shows. More than 6,000 miles of track were built during those years, very largely with foreign capital. Belgium secured building concessions out of proportion to its size partly because, being small, the Chinese Government considered it less menacing than the rest[4].

By skilful negotiation the Chinese secured that ownership and administration rested with their government.

Main Railway Lines (1900–1923)

	Opened	Mileage
Peking–Mukden (Shenyang)	1903	525
Peking–Hankow	1905	755
Tientsin–Pukow	1912	629
Peking–Kalgan–Tatung–Paotow	1909	468
	1915	
	1923	
Shanghai–Nanking	1908	193
Shanghai–Hangchow	1908	171
Lunghai (Suchow–Tungkwan)	1916	515
Canton–Kowloon	1911	112
Taiyuan–Shihchiachuang	1907	151
Tsingtao–Tsinan	1904	256
Yunnanfu (Kunming)–Laokai	1910	289
Manchuria		
Chinese Eastern (5 ft gauge)	1903	1,081
South Manchurian	1903	519

Apart from the Peking–Mukden line, which was built largely with British capital, all Manchurian railways were the work of Russia and Japan during this period. The Russians short-circuited their Siberian railway by a line running from Chita, via Mancholi, Tsitsihar and Harbin, to Vladivostock and built up a network in the north, which was known as the Chinese Eastern Railway. This, and a system Russia developed in the south, the Southern Manchurian Railway, were of 5 ft gauge. When Japan defeated Russia in 1904, she took over this southern network and, in 1907, converted it into standard gauge. When she annexed Manchukuo in 1931–32, Japan took over the entire system[2]. Between 1916 and 1928 the country was divided and in the hands of war-lords. Although some railway building continued, this disturbed period is notable rather for the deterioration of track and rolling stock. There was another burst of building under the Kuomintang between 1928 and 1936, bringing the total length of track (including Manchukuo) to over 12,000 miles. Unhappily this was followed by 10 years (1936–46) of war with Japan and then 3 years of bitter civil war between Kuomintang and Communists, which left communications throughout the country in a parlous state, further accentuated by the destruction of bridges, culverts, rolling stock and permanent way as the K.M.T. retreated. Of this meagre existing mileage (12,036), '3,726 miles were lost through the Japanese invasion of Manchuria in 1931 and 6,566 miles were lost or destroyed during the first five-and-a-half years of the Sino-Japanese war'[5].

Railway Development in Communist China

Sun Yat Sen, in his later years, was very conscious of the part that railways must play in the modernization of his country. During World War I he sketched a building programme, which envisaged 100,000 miles of track. He returned to the subject in his 'San-min Chu-ih'.

When they came into power in 1949, the Communists had clear ideas as to the position of the railways in their policy of creating a modern, industrialized state. The railways were to serve in the wide dispersal of industry. Founded originally largely on foreign capital and initiative, nearly three-quarters of the country's industry was located in the coastal regions and thus was, in some degree, a symbol of erstwhile imperialist dominance. Moreover, from a strategic point of view, dispersal of industry would render the country less vulnerable in time of war. Railway development was also essential to national integration, to the drawing together of the outlying, under-developed regions and to the assurance of unified political control. Finally, railway development was imperative if the vast reserves of raw materials, which these regions contained, were to be opened up and made accessible.

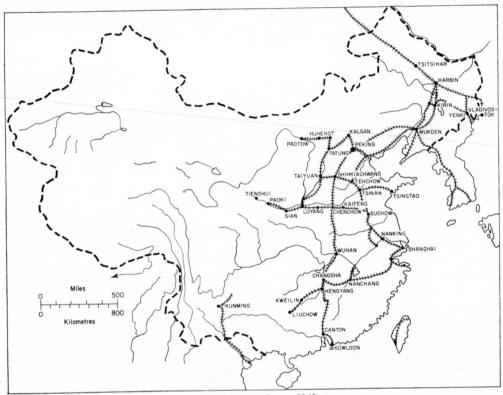

Map 54 (a). Railways, 1949

Some idea of the importance attached to railway development can be gathered from the fact that, in 1953, under the First Five-year plan, 17·1% of the total state investment capital was allocated to communications, 13·3% going to railways and the remaining 3·8% to all other forms of transport. The actual planning and construction of new lines after 1949 follows closely the ambitious plans of Chang Kia-ngau, Nationalist Minister of Communications in 1942 for railway expansion at the end of the Sino–Japanese war. He envisaged the building of some 14,300 miles of track, but unfortunately was never able to implement his plans[5].

Between 1952 and 1960 the following new main lines were opened:

North and North-west—The Lunghai Railway, which had been carried to Tienshui, west of Paoki before 1949, was extended to Lanchow, which was rapidly becoming a large industrial centre. From this base at Lanchow, a new line of over 700 miles, known as the Sinkiang Friendship Line, has been constructed across the intervening steppeland and desert into the Tarim Basin and Dzungaria to the Sinkiang capital, Urumchi. This railway has clear economic and political purposes. Until complete pipelines are laid, the railway is the only economical method of delivering the oil from the Karamai field of Dzungaria to the east. It also provides an outlet for the increasing raw materials and finished products of the region. Its political *raison d'etre* is to bring the Uighur, Kazahk and Kirgiz population consciously within the national fold and to enable the central government's writ to run. It was also intended to be a link with its communist neighbour and it was planned to join with the Soviet Kazahkstan line from Ayagur, through the Dzungarian Gate. Unhappily discord between the two countries has brought building to a stop and the Chinese line ends at Manass.

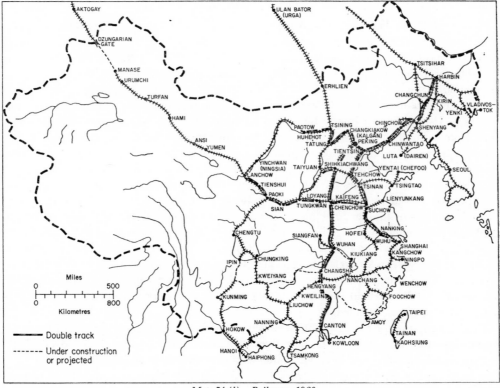

Map 54 (b). Railways, 1960

A line has been built from Lanchow to Sining. This is to be extended into the Tsaidam to tap the oil and other mineral resources, which have recently been discovered. A railway from Tsining northward to Erlien links with the Outer Mongolian line to Ulan Bator and so to the Siberian railway, thus providing a direct route from Siberia to China Proper.

159

A further important extension is that from Paotow to Lanchow, following the course of the Hwang-ho and opening up the growing oases of the region.

West—The two big cities of Szechwan, Chengtu and Chungking have been joined by a rail running through Neikiang. However, it was the completion of the line from Chengtu to Paoki, thus linking Szechwan with the Lunghai Railway and the north, that excited national enthusiasm. This line had been planned and partly surveyed by the Nationalist Government, but credit for its final achievement rests with the People's Government. It proved a difficult engineering undertaking, involving an immense amount of tunnelling and bridging through the Chinling Shan, which divides Szechwan from Shensi.

Two further lines have been built from Chungking. One links it with Kweiyang, capital of Kweichow and the other runs via Neikiang to Ipin. Both these lines will eventually be continued to Kunming.

South—The Henyang-Kweilin line was quickly extended for 260 miles from Liuchow to the Vietnam border at Pingsiang, thus giving rail communication with Hanoi. This was opened in October, 1951. In 1955 a branch from this line at Litang was built to Chankiang, which is rapidly becoming an important southern port.

South-east—Both Foochow and Amoy are now linked by rail to the Yangtze valley. Following their respective river valleys of the Min and Kiuling, their tracks join at Shakikow and meet the Nanchang–Hangchow line at Yintang. Built rapidly for military purposes to meet possible menace from Taiwan, these railways, nevertheless, have considerable economic usefulness.

It is significant to note that, apart from the short line built from Wuhan to the steel works at Hwangshih—a line to be continued eventually to Kiukiang—and the projected line from Kingtihchen to Wuhu, no railway construction has been undertaken in the lower Yangtze valley in spite of its great economic importance. This is an eloquent comment on the value of this great river as a line of communication and transport.

Very few new main lines have been opened in the north-east since 1949. The region was already served by a more complete network than existed anywhere else in China. Some 250 miles of lumber lines have been built in the extreme north in the Ta Hingan and Siao Hingan mountains. The main development in the north-east has been the double-tracking of the main line from Harbin to Shenyang. Similarly, all the main lines of the south, the Peking–Hankow–Canton, the Tientsin–Pukow, Peking–Paotow and the Lunghai from Suchow to Lanchow have been double-tracked, this rendering them far more capable of carrying the heavy load they have been called upon to bear. Even so, serious bottlenecks have not been avoided.

The railway building programme sketched above has been carried through with great speed, urgency and energy. The initiative and enthusiasm shown have not always been accompanied by adequate surveying and engineering. This has resulted in mistakes involving considerable renovation work. The planners clearly had intended the pace of railway construction to be continued throughout the Second Five-year Plan, for 20·9% of national capital investment was allocated to communications of which three-quarters was to be devoted to railways. In fact, the railway building programme slowed down after the Great Leap Forward (1958); emphasis since has been laid on improvement and upkeep of existing lines. Even during the First Five-year Plan, one-third of the capital allocated to the railways was ear-marked for renovation and one-fifth for rolling stock[5].

Table 6.1. *Length of Railway Tracks Laid.* (*From* Ten Great Years, Peking, 1960)

		Total	New lines	Restored lines	New double-track lines	Restored double-track lines	Special purpose lines
Period of Rehabilitation of National Economy							
	Total	12,090	7,513	1,749	1,833	995	4,451
	1950	808	97	427	—	284	172
	1951	1,021	743	138	—	140	185
	1952	1,233	480	605	—	148	236
First Five-Year Plan	Total	3,062	1,320	1,170	—	572	593
	1953	706	587	—	14	105	494
	1954	1,132	831	—	49	252	283
	1955	1,406	1,222	39	87	58	458
	1956	2,242	1,747	285	206	4	866
	1957	1,166	474	150	538	4	569
Second Five-Year Plan	Total	6,652	4,861	474	894	423	2,670
	1958	2,376	1,332	105	939	—	1,188

Note: In addition to the above figues, 4,400 km of narrow gauge tracks for forest railways were laid between 1950 and 1958

A marked change in railway construction took place during and after the Great Leap Forward, a change which provides an outstanding example of 'walking on two legs', i.e. the support of central schemes by local effort. The need for some form of transport of raw materials to the hundreds of thousands of local 'back yard' blast furnaces led to the construction of all sorts of local 'railroads' of greatly varying efficiency and ingenuity, ranging from Emmett-like contraptions of wooden or cast-iron rails and converted lorries as locomotives, to trackless trains on pneumatic wheels. Most of these faded out with the collapse of the ill-fated Great Leap, but many also formed the basis for subsequent feeder lines, sponsored by communes and of much greater value and efficiency. Richard Hughes, writing of these, says 'Cast iron rails used in Anhwei province withstand a pressure of up to 50 ton/metre and the commune-made locomotives can run on them at a speed of 35 km/h.'[7] Although they have now been largely replaced by road transport, they have served a useful purpose, particularly as their construction formed no charge on the national investment fund.

Table 6.2. *Rapid Increase in Volume of Goods Carried by Modern Means of Transport* (thousand tons). (*From* Ten Great Years, Peking, 1960)

	Total goods carried	Carried by railways	Carried by motor vehicles	Carried by ships and barges
Pre-1949 peak	—	136,650	8,190	12,640
1949	67,130	55,890	5,790	5,430
1950	115,690	99,830	9,210	6,650
1951	135,060	110,830	14,120	10,110
1952	168,590	132,170	22,100	14,320
1953	212,270	161,310	30,940	20,010
1954	264,670	192,880	43,030	28,750
1955	278,430	193,760	48,960	35,700
1956	372,150	246,050	79,130	46,960
1957	411,710	274,200	83,730	53,770
1958	633,760	381,090	176,300	76,360

The pre-war peak of railway freight is quoted[6] as being 40,400 million ton-km. This figure fell to 18,400 million in 1949 and then rose steadily and rapidly year by year to 185,520 million ton-km in 1958. No figures have been published since that date. Although it is certain that this rate of increase in freight carried has not been maintained, the absolute amount of goods carried has continued to rise. Railways are still by far the greatest transporters.

Table 6.3. Freight Turnover by Modern Means of Transport (million ton-km)
(From Ten Great Years, Peking, 1960)

	Total	Railways	Motor vehicles	Ships and barges
Pre-1949 peak	—	40,400	460	12,830
1949	22,980	18,400	250	4,310
1950	42,690	39,410	380	2,900
1951	59,340	51,560	570	7,210
1952	71,540	60,160	770	10,610
1953	93,010	78,140	1,300	13,570
1954	113,830	93,240	1,940	18,640
1955	125,120	98,150	2,520	24,440
1956	152,060	120,350	3,490	28,210
1957	172,930	134,590	3,940	34,390
1958	236,400	185,520	6,960	43,910

Ever since 1949 the railways have been called upon to do more work than that for which they are technically fitted. The most difficult period was during the Great Leap Forward when transport demands were increased almost overnight. Since then, the big development of road transport, and the emphasis which has been laid on regional development by communes, has relieved pressure. Undoubtedly the Cultural Revolution activities and free transport accorded to the Red Guards between July, 1966 and January, 1967, when millions of young people were transported again placed considerable strain on the railways. Owing to continued Cultural Revolution factionalism, China's railways were placed under military (P.L.A.) control in September, 1957. Nevertheless, serious disruption in communications in some regions has continued to exert an adverse influence on industrial production.

Roads

There was comparatively little change either in routes used or the vehicles passing over them during the 2,000 years from the Early Han dynasty to the beginning of the twentieth century. The roads for wheeled traffic in the north were mere dirt tracks to which no attention to upkeep was given. In the south, the narrow paths, which served as roads for wheelbarrows and pedestrians, were occasionally paved—usually the work of some rich landowner or virtuous widow 'earning merit'—but there was no attempt throughout the country at either maintenance or systemization except for short periods as, for example, under the Yuan dynasty, and even then the emphasis was on courier service rather than transport. All movement was slow and expensive. A journey of 20 miles a day by land was as much as could ordinarily be accomplished and it was arduous. A strong coolie, using a carrying pole, could carry a *tan* (100 *catties*) about 20 miles in a day. The normal method of payment was to provide the coolie's food plus a mere pittance of a wage. Nevertheless, it was a most expensive method of transport as Sun Yat Sen, in his 'San Min Chu

Ih' was at pains to point out with more fervour than accuracy, remarking that it took 10 days for 10,000 coolies to move 10,000 ton over 500 *li* (170 miles) while the same work could be done by train requiring only 8 h and the services of 10 men. A ton-kilometre per day could be regarded as the average work of a coolie carrier. 'Today in level and hilly areas engaged in subsidiary food production the amount of labour used for transport in the field represents about 35% of the total labour force. In mountainous areas it is about 60%.'[5]

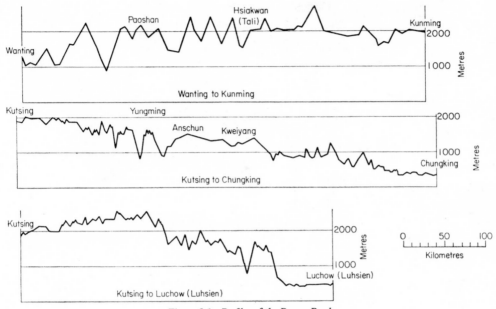

Figure 6.1. Profiles of the Burma Road

Automobiles began to be introduced into China during the second decade of this century. Their use was confined to the metalled roads within the concessions and the short, mainly dirt, roads a few miles around the cities. Between 1930 and 1936, the Nationalist Government carried out extensive road building, which was continued in west China during the Sino-Japanese war and included the spectacular Burma Road over the many north-south longitudinal high ranges and deep valleys, which divide Burma from Yunnan. After reaching Kunming from the Burmese border, this road forks, one branch running north to Neikiang and Chengtu and the other, via Kweiyang, to Chungking. With the end of hostilities, the section between Myitkyina and Paoshan lost much of its *raison d'etre*, but the remaining sections have served as the foundation of a road network for the south-west. The above profiles of the roads give some idea of the difficult terrain of these sections.

The years of civil war and chaos between 1946 and 1949 resulted in sad depreciation of existing roads. One report estimated that, in 1949, there were only 75,000 km of roads, most of which were barely usable for motor traffic[8]. Certainly, those of Central China over which the author travelled at that time were calculated to ruin any motor vehicle in the shortest possible time.

Home of old 'extended' Chinese family

Modern urban building.   Roads are wide and more than adequate for present motor traffic

From 1950 the People's Government embarked on a strenuous programme of road building, which has continued in intensity. Unfortunately there are no comprehensive figures of achievement in this field after 1958.

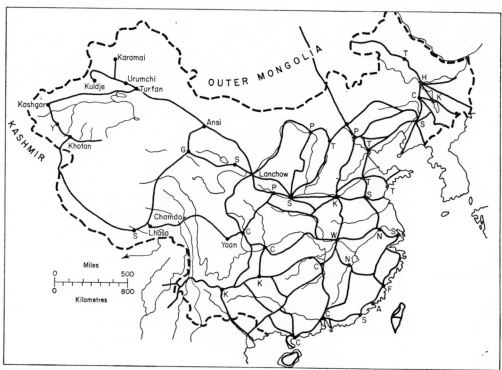

Map 55. Motor roads, 1958

Table 6.4. Length of New and Improved Highways (km). (From Ten Great Years, Peking, 1960)

	Total	New Highways
Period of rehabilitation of National Economy		
1950	15,463	450
1951	19,545	1,366
1952	11,168	1,940
First Five-year Plan		
1953	9,654	2,598
1954	7,164	3,824
1955	8,138	3,578
1956	89,717	55,930
1957	38,168	17,472
Second Five-year Plan		
1958	210,000	150,000
Total	409,017	237,249

Note: Figures for 1956 and after include lower grade highways.

As with railways, so with roads. The Central Government has undertaken the construction of the great arterial highways and has left the local roads to the initiative of the communes. The following are the great motor roads to outlying provinces and remote regions, which have been built since 1949:

(*a*) The Kansu–Sinkiang Highway follows the same route as the Sinkiang Friendship railway. From Lanchow it passes along the northern slopes of the Nan Shan through Wuwei, Changteh and the oil refineries of Yumen to Ansi. Here a branch swings south through Tunhwang, famous for its Buddhist caves and carvings, over the Tangching Pass at the western end of the Nan Shan, and so into the Tsaidam. From Ansi the road continues through the desert to Hami and the Turfan Depression. At Turfan the road divides, going north and south of the Tien Shan. The northern route passes through Urumchi and Manase and on to Ebi Nor. As it approaches the U.S.S.R. frontier it turns south to Kuldja, the heart of the Ili valley. The southern branch runs through Kucha and Aksu and all the oases of the northern rim of the Taklamakan desert to Kashgar; then it turns south to Yarkand and Khotan. The intention is to complete the circuit of the Tarim Basin through Charchan and Charkhlik, but it may be some time before this is done. This south-eastern corner of the basin is the least important economically and this, combined with the engineering difficulties of shifting sand, wind and the crossing of torrential rivers descending from the Kunlun, is likely to postpone action.

(*b*) The Khotan–Lhasa route leaves Khotan to cross the Kunlun by the Karakoram Pass. Following the northern slopes of the Karakoram mountains, it passes through the disputed territory of north-eastern Kashmir and along the Tsangpo or Brahmaputra, via Gartok and Shigatse to Lhasa. Most of this road is through very high and bleak country. The mountains, the rarefied air and low temperatures, often below $-20°$ C, make road building hazardous and most arduous. Difficult tasks, such as building this road and the road along the southern edge of the Tarim Basin are undertaken by the PLA Engineering Corps, which is famed for its toughness[9].

(*c*) Lhasa is now linked by motor road with Chengtu through some of the most difficult country. Like the Burma Road, it has to cross large numbers of north-south ranges and valleys, but it has to contend with much greater heights and attendant constructional and maintenance difficulties occasioned by snow and rock falls. Between Chamdo and Kinsha Kiang (Yangtze) most of the road runs at a height of between 3,000 and 4,500 m. Its highest pass is 4,889 m. As it descends from the Tibetan Plateau it crosses the Tatu river by a new steel bridge, which has been built close to the chain bridge, rendered famous by its dramatic capture during the Long March. It is now possible to travel by bus from Chengtu to Lhasa, taking about 2 weeks on the journey instead of at least 6 months before the road was constructed. The purpose of the road is primarily political, bringing south-east Tibet and the many indigenous tribes of western Szechwan within Central Government control. However, the increasing flow of goods is proving that the road has economic value. It also makes possible the fuller survey of a region of great potential mineral wealth.

(*d*) Leaving Lhasa, the Lhasa–Sining Highway traverses the desolate and sparsely populated Tibetan–Tsinghai plateau until it descends into the Tsaidam. This section of the road, although very high (3,000–4,000 m) does not have to negotiate deep, longitudinal valleys and ranges as does the Lhasa–Chengtu Highway. The road turns eastward at Golmo and, skirting the Ching Hai (Koko Nor), runs to Sining and Lanchow. Again, this

166

is a road the purpose of which is primarily political. Nevertheless, the building of a road network based on the highway has done much to develop the industrial potential of Tsinghai especially its oil and coal. It is reported that in 1949 there were only 472 km of rough road near to Sining. In 1964 there were 15,447 km of motor road, which have cut transport time to one-tenth and cost to one-fifth[10].

(e) Linking with Sining and Lanchow is the recently constructed motor road from Lanchow, via Ahpa, to Chengtu. It follows a route through 142 km of high mountains and gorges, the line which constituted the Red Army's severest ordeal on its Long March. The road forms part of the highway network, which is being built in west Szechwan and Tibet in order to make close contact with the minorities.

Apart from the great trunk roads, which have been the responsibility of the Central Government, a great deal of road development has been carried through in all the provinces by local authorities. The pattern of development has been much the same throughout. The commune, often with some technical and material help from the State has constructed a main motor road through its territory, linking with similar roads by its neighbours. Production brigades have then been responsible for building 'country roads' leading to the villages and hamlets. These roads, which usually have little metalling, are fit for trucks in fine, i.e., dry weather. There can be no doubt that, in this way, local markets have been greatly widened and stimulated[11].

Bridges

Closely associated with the modern development of railways and roads has been a great upsurge in bridge building. It is strange that, although China in the past has figured so little in road building, yet its engineers have pioneered in bridge building. Joseph Needham describes how Li Ch'un built the first segmental arch bridge across the river at Chaohsien, Hopeh in A.D. 610. This is a beautiful structure, which is still standing and, since its recent repair, is in full use. China also was 1,000 years ahead of Europe in the building of suspension bridges. In the Sui dynasty (A.D. 581–818) bamboo cables were used for this purpose, but in succeeding centuries these were replaced by iron chains[3].

Modern bridge building received its initial impetus from railway development at the beginning of the century. The Hwang-ho was bridged just north of Chengchow in 1905 to carry the Peking–Hankow railway and at Tsinan to carry the Tientsin–Pukow railway. Apart from these two, no other outstanding bridge was built before 1949, although, of course, a great many smaller structures were constructed as the railways developed.

Bridges were a major casualty in the Sino-Japanese war and in the subsequent civil war, particularly during the final defeat and withdrawal of the Nationalist forces. The broken bridges were repaired or rebuilt at great speed during the years of rehabilitation (1950–52). Thereafter an ambitious programme of new building was undertaken. The most outstanding achievement to date has been the construction of the Yangtze Bridge at Wuhan, providing at the time of building, the only dry crossing of the river from west Szechwan to its mouth. The Yangtze, nearly a mile wide at this point, seriously interrupted railway communication between the Peking–Hankow and the Wuchang–Canton lines. For more than 30 years plans for connecting the two by bridge had been discussed and surveys of the river made, but no action was taken. With the aid of Soviet engineeers and technicians the work was undertaken. A two-decker bridge, carrying a double-track railway below and a six-lane road above, was completed in 1956—no mean engineering

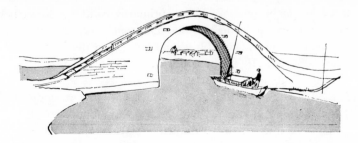

*Arch bridge of Kiangsu
and Chekiang*

Bamboo cable bridge of Yunnan

*The Yangtze bridge, Wuhan (1956) carries
a double rail track below and a six-lane
motor road above*

168

feat when one remembers the width of the river and the 45 ft change in water level between summer and winter. The Yangtze has since been again bridged at Chungking and an even more ambitious bridging plan was completed at Nanking in September, 1968.

The following is a list of major new bridges built between 1950–1958[6]:

Name	Place	Length (m)
Wuhan Yangtze River Bridge	Hupeh	1,670
Tungkwan Yellow River Bridge (temporary structure)	Shensi	1,070
Hunan–Kweichow Railway Hsiangkiang Bridge	Hunan	844
Shenyang–Shanhaikwan Railway Talingho Bridge	Liaoning	830
Fengtai–Shacheng Railway Yungtingho No. 1 Bridge	Hopeh	722
Lunghai Railway Hsinyiho Bridge	Kiangsu	700
Paotow–Lanchow Railway Sanshengkung Yellow River Bridge	Inner Mongolia	683
Peking–Paotow Railway Kweishui Bridge	Hopeh	663
Hunan–Kwangsi Railway Liukiang Bridge	Kwangsi	616
Peking-Canton Railway Changho Bridge	Hopeh	569
Fengtai–Shacheng Railway Yungtingho No. 8 Bridge	Hopeh	526

Since 1958 many more bridges have been constructed, including the first modern highway bridge in Tibet over the Tsangpo at Lhasa. This is a reinforced concrete structure, 730 m long and having 19 arches[12]. A big conference on bridge construction in the North-west was held in 1965, attended by representatives from Tibet, Sinkiang, Tsinghai, Kansu Ninghsia, Inner Mongolia and Shensi. These are the regions in which bridge and culvert building is especially difficult on account of high altitudes, low but concentrated rainfall leading to dangerous freshets, wide shallow river beds and unstable river courses, encumbered with large loads of silt and stones.

Water Transport

In primitive economic conditions movement by water is the easiest and cheapest form of transport. Where roads and adequate wheeled transport are absent it is often also the most comfortable. Consequently, in central and south China, where rivers are navigable for small craft over most of their length, this method of movement of goods and people has had great prominence. In deltaic regions, such as obtain in the lower Yangtze and Si Kiang, water transport has been by far the most important[13]. In north China, where rivers are less navigable, more wheeled transport is used, but even here rivers are used wherever possible, for example by inflated hide rafts on the middle Hwang-ho, which are floated down, deflated and returned overland to source in much the same fashion as on the Tigris in Babylonian times.

Canals

Relying as they did on the transport of tribute grain to support the Court and army at the capital, emperors from a very early date recognized the importance of water communications and engaged in canal building accordingly[2]. As Chinese domination extended further south and as greater and greater reliance was placed on the grain of the south, which became the economic heart of the country, so the need for water transport became more pressing. In consequence, the Sui emperor, Sui Yang-ti (A.D. 605) caused, at shocking loss of life, the New Pien Canal to be cut from the Yangtze to Kaifeng and so to his capital at Chang-an (Sian).

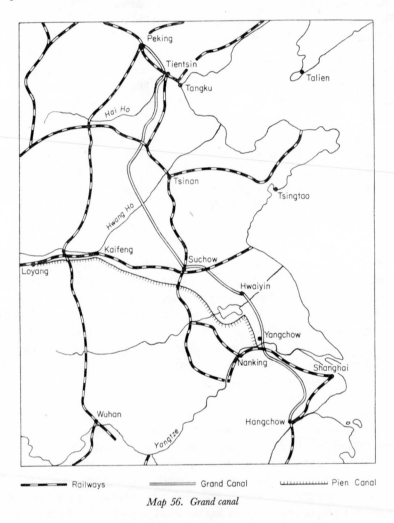

Map 56. Grand canal

When the Mongol (Yuan) dynasty was established (1279) and Kublai Khan moved the Imperial capital to Peking, the need for easy and quick transport of supplies from the south was even more pressing. Kublai Khan therefore ordered, in 1283, the cutting of the Grand Canal, linking Hangchow with Peking. This was the extension of a small, old canal, cut by a prince of the State of Wu (506 B.C.) between Tai Hu and Hangchow. The Grand Canal measures 1,700 km and links, from south to north, five rivers, the Chientang, Yangtze, Hwai Hwang and Hai. For many years it formed a main artery of communications from north to south, but constant maintenance was necessary because it cuts right across the flood plains of the Hwai and Hwang-ho and thus is subject to silting from their repeated inundations. The Grand Canal finally fell into disuse, except for local transport over short stretches, when the Tientsin–Pukow railway was opened in 1912. Canals are early victims of internal disorder. It was not surprising, therefore, to find the Grand Canal virtually useless in 1949.

With the development of the Hwang-ho conservancy schemes from 1950 onward, the Grand Canal naturally came under discussion and was incorporated as an integral part of the plans for flood control and drainage. Work began in 1958 on its renovation. It has been straightened, widened and deepened and a new course of 70 km has been cut. New modern locks and lock-gates have been constructed throughout its length. Formerly 50 ton barges were the largest that could be used; now 200–500 ton barges can sail on all sections; when complete, 2,000 ton craft will be accommodated. Its main use at present, apart from local traffic, is the conveyance of coal from north to south and grain in the reverse direction, although it is reported that, with the increasing productivity of the North China Plan, there is less need now for the transport of southern grain[14].

River Development and Shipping

Of China's great rivers, the Yangtze Kiang, with its tributaries the Han, Siang and Kan, ranks far above all others as a line of transport, both from the point of view of the area served and the amount of traffic carried. Second is the Sungari and then the Si Kiang. Neither the Hwang-ho nor the Hwai-ho figures high on the list, largely on account of the flooding which occurred so frequently in their lower reaches. With modern conservation, which has been and still is being undertaken, these two rivers are now increasing in value as lines of communication.

Something of the regime and the size of the Yangtze has already been seen (pp. 67–68). For many centuries it has been a busy artery for sailing junks, large and small, which, even in the winter when the river is at its lowest level, are able to ply from its mouth to Ichang. Here most river craft stopped, blocked by the series of gorges between Nanto and Wanhsien. The Chinese have a saying, 'The Way to Szechwan is as difficult as the way to Heaven', to describe the passage of these gorges, which could be undertaken by haulage by tracker teams along paths hewn out of the cliff sides—a perilous and arduous endeavour for tracker and boatman. The current through the gorges is terrifyingly fast and the channel beset with rocks and shoals. At the notorious Goat Horn Reef the river falls 7 m in 2·5 km and at one point the channel was only 30 m wide[15]. A graphic description of a passage of these 100 miles and more is given by Han Su-yin[4]. By the second decade of the twentieth century, powerful small steamers were able to make the precarious journey unaided by trackers, but their numbers were few and their impact not very significant.

A great deal of money and energy has been expended since 1950 in rendering this most difficult section of the river safer for navigation. 12·6 million yuan has been spent on dredging and clearing. More than 200 shoals have been cleared, innumerable rocks have been blasted and removed. The narrow channels have been widened and marked by buoys, and bank signals now make passage through the gorges possible by night as well as by day. By 1959 it was possible to make the return trip from Wuhan to Chungking and back in less than a week. Freight charges have been reduced many times with the introduction of tug and barge trains, which can now navigate the improved channels[16].

The nature of shipping on the Yangtze underwent a revolutionary change after 1860 through the establishment of treaty ports along the river and the opening of the river to international trade and foreign bottoms. Two British companies, Butterfield and Swire, and Jardine, Matheson began to operate along the river in 1872 and 1873 respectively and were closely followed by the newly-formed, indigenous China Merchants' Steam Navigation Coy., an important happening as it was the first instance of Chinese officials entering into commercial competition with foreigners[17]. Commenting on the special regulations governing shipping on the Yangtze, the China Year Book, 1925 stated 'In most countries inland navigation is reserved to the natives of the country. In China, however, the inland waterways are open to foreign navigation'.* This was an obvious cause of offence and complaint by the Chinese against foreign imperialism in spite of the very considerable increase in trade that it occasioned. Checked after the 1927 revolution, foreign shipping thereafter was prohibited up the Yangtze beyond Shanghai.

In summer when the river is in spate, ocean-going vessels of 10,000 to 15,000 tons, drawing more than 30 ft, can reach Wuhan, 600 miles inland. Navigation, however, must be carefully timed as a sudden drop in water level in late summer could leave such ships stranded with no chance of exit until the rise of water the following year. Regular steamships, plying up and down the river as far as Wuhan throughout the year, must be specially constructed to draw not more than 6 ft, such is the change in level between summer and winter. Clever designing during this century has enabled passenger-freight vessels of 5,000 ton to be built fulfilling these conditions.

Cheap labour conditions have militated against the introduction of modern wharfage equipment at the river ports. Loading and unloading of goods, has, without exception, been by man-power and carrying pole, a slow, hard job, especially in winter when the water is low and long ramps up the steep banks from the hulks, which serve as wharves, have to be climbed. Since 1950 these conditions have steadily been changed. Now all the major river ports are largely mechanized. Wuhan now has 40 modern wharves, served mainly by conveyor belts for loading and unloading. The change is especially noticeable and welcome at Chungkiang, which stands on cliffs above the river. Cable cars, chutes and overhead cables have now replaced much of the man-handling up steps and ramps[2].

For many years the marking of channels by buoys and lightships, from Shanghai to Wuhan, was well maintained. It deteriorated badly during the Sino-Japanese war and civil war and thus stood in urgent need of rehabilitation in 1949. Since then this work has been taken seriously in hand. It is reported that night navigation is now possible from Shanghai through the gorges to Ipin, the channel being marked by 2,800 buoys and bank signals based on the Soviet chain-signal system from Shanghai to Chungkiang. In 1959 the system was electrified[19].

The development of modern shipping and equipment on the Yangtze has been discussed above, but it should be remembered that the greater part of the goods moved up and down the river is still carried by native Chinese craft—small 'hwatzu', junks and rafts propelled by wind or man-power. These are undergoing rapid change. It is stated that between

* China Year Book, 1925, p. 1039

1960 and 1961 no less than 10,000 junks on the river were mechanized, 150,000 h.p. having been installed.

While the planners have expended a great deal of energy and money on the development of the Yangtze, it has by no means received exclusive attention. The navigability of the Sungari and Liao in the north-east and the Si Kiang in Kwangtung and Kwangsi have been greatly improved in the last 10 years. The numerous multi-purpose dams built in their courses have had increased navigability as one of their objectives. Moreover, many of the smaller rivers have been improved by the combined efforts of local communes. A case in point is the lower Wu Kiang as it descends from Kweichow to the Yangtze below Chung-king. The channel has been dredged and shoals removed so that, it is claimed, there is ten times as much traffic on the river as in 1949[20].

Coastal Shipping

China has some 14,000 km of coastline, which is strikingly different north and south of the mouth of the Yangtze Kiang. The south and south-east coasts are rugged and replete with deep, natural harbours. Mountains come down to the sea in most places and the few coastal plains are narrow. Consequently the hinterlands of ports along this stretch of coast tend to be restricted. Navigational hazards spring from sudden storms and typhoons and, in the past, from piracy rendered easy by virtue of many convenient hide-outs. Towns have tended to be comparatively small and the population traditionally has looked out-wards to the sea for a livelihood. It is mainly from Fukien and Kwangtung that China's seamen have come and from Fukien that the bulk of overseas Chinese derive.

Sharply contrasted is the coastline north of Shanghai, which, apart from that of the Shantung peninsula, is smooth and devoid of natural harbours. Any ports here are essentially man-made. This is particularly true around the Po Hai into which the Hwang-ho, Hai-ho and Liao-ho pour their loads of silt. It is significant that there is no coastal town of any size between the Shantung peninsula and Tientsin. Shipping in the Po Hai and Lioatung Wan is handicapped by the shallow waters and also by the off-shore dust storms, which can make navigation dangerous.

Coastal trading has flourished in the south from early days, but was much less active in the north. It received some impetus during the Yuan dynasty when Kublai Khan, employing a couple of ex-pirates as directors, organized regular sailings carrying grain from the Yangtze mouth to Taiku (Tientsin) to reinforce grain movement on the Grand Canal.

The opening of the Treaty Ports after 1840 was the signal for a big increase in coastal traffic in which British and Japanese shipping firms became particularly active. This growth continued for a whole century until the outbreak of the Sino-Japanese war in 1936, when all Chinese and many foreign vessels fell into Japanese hands and coastal shipping came to a standstill. At the end of the war China was virtually without modern river or ocean-going ships, and it was not until after 1950 that some recovery was made.

China was not without some experience in ship-building. Prior to the Sino-Japanese war most of the river steamers and a fair proportion of the coastal vessels were built in the yards at Talien (Dairen), the Kiangnan Shipyard, Shanghai and in the Hong Kong shipyards. In the early decades of this century the work was mainly under British super-vision, but after 1930 Chinese engineers were increasingly responsible. Nearly all the material used in construction came from abroad.

173

In order to meet imperative needs immediately after 1949, it was necessary to buy some vessels from abroad and to rely on foreign shipping for coastal trading. However, the People's Government quickly rehabilitated the former shipyards and brought them into production, concentrating at first on the building of river craft and coastal vessels. A Ship Research and Designing Institute has been established at Wuhan, specializing in passenger and cargo ships and tugs for the Yangtze. In 1965 the first small oil tanker of 3,000 tons for coastal service was launched. The shipyards at Shanghai are now building ocean-going ships up to 13,000 tons for which they have designed and produced successfully an 8,820 h.p. low-speed marine diesel engine, the largest yet in China[21]. It is claimed that all sea-going ships have now been fitted with radar equipment, wireless direction finders and sound-echoing detectors. These are very modest achievements by comparison with Japan's present massive production, but a start has been made on what appears to be sound lines. Needless to say, all Chinese passenger and cargo ships are state owned and controlled. Official overseas operations began in 1961[22].

Ports

Prior to 1949, Shanghai was by far the most important port of China and ranked sixth in world trade. The only others of real significance were Tientsin with its outport at Taku, Whampoa, the port for Canton and Dairen.

Shanghai's strength as a modern port lies in its great hinterland of the Yangtze basin. Its growth has been very rapid. In northern Sung times (1074) it appears in the records as a fishing village with a shipping officer to manage the taxation of Yangtze shipping. Later, in Ming times, it acquired a wall and fortification to meet the ravages of Japanese pirates, but it was still only a very small town in 1840, when, at the end of the Opium war, it was chosen as the site for a British concession, which was expanded into the International Settlement in 1863, from which its rapid development dates. It is interesting to note that its first factory, built in 1862, was a shipyard. Population soared. By 1865 it already was 690,000; in 1936 3,740,000 and in 1948 5,200,000. Shanghai today is a municipality, answerable directly to Peking. It has an area of 5,910 sq. km and a population of some 10 million, of which more than 6 million are within the city boundary[23].

After Liberation in 1949, there was an initial attempt to reduce and disperse some of Shanghai's population in accordance with the general policy of dispersal of the country's industry, but economic momentum and the natural positional advantages proved too strong and the policy was quickly reversed. Since then there has been a very rapid growth of industry, especially in heavy engineering, shipbuilding, chemicals and textiles, and the port has renewed its earlier activity.

Shanghai, from its earliest days as a modern port, has always had to face severe difficulties of silting, resulting from the Yangtze's heavy load, which persistently threatens to block the mouth of the small tributary, the Hwangpu, on which Shanghai stands. Only constant and efficient dredging can keep its outlet into the Yangtze at Woosung clear. For a big international port handling huge quantities of raw materials, Shanghai was singularly deficient in modern loading and unloading equipment before 1949. The reason for this was the abundance and cheapness of labour. Since then there has been a great deal of up-to-date equipment introduced and, consequently, a quickening turn-round of ships in the port.

Shanghai has retained its pre-eminence as the first port of the country, but other ports, old and new, have their place in the progress that has been made. All the major ports

174

have taken on a new look and all now have modern, mechanized loading equipment, better wharfage and road and rail communications.

Tientsin now has a new outport at Tangku. Formerly only vessels of less than 3,000 ton could enter the Tai-ho. The rest had to anchor at the bar at Taku, which, as a port, has now been virtually discarded in favour of the new harbour at Tangku on the left bank of the Hai-ho. Its construction was started by the Japanese during the 1936–45 war, but it was left unfinished with only two wharves capable of accommodating 3,000 ton ships. It is now complete with wharves large enough to take 10,000 ton vessels, warehouses, modern loading equipment, including coal conveyor belts, the latest dredging equipment and good railways. Tangku is thus more capable of serving the rapidly growing commercial

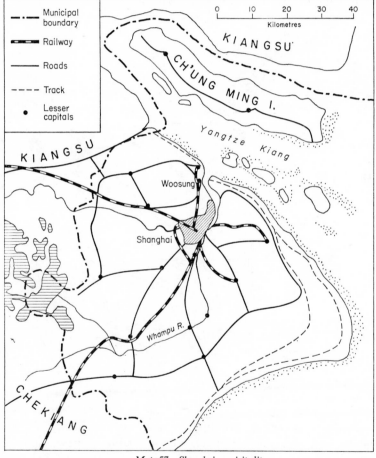

Map 57. Shanghai municipality

and industrial needs of Peking and Tientsin and of handling the bulk of north China's import and export trade. Similarly, facilities have been improved at Lushun (Port Arthur), Talien (Dairen), Hulutao, Chinwantao and Yingtow. Canton was formally opened to foreign ships for the first time in November, 1965. The river has been dredged and new warehouses and wharves, capable of handling ships up to 4,000 ton, have been built. Formerly all Canton's shipping was handled at Whampoa, 23 miles down stream.

An entirely new port has been constructed at Tsamkong (Chankiang) in Kwangtung, opposite Hainan. Formerly it had one small wharf for sailing and small passenger boats. It is now a modern harbour with wharves accommodating ships up to 10,000 ton.

Air

The Sino-Japanese war (1936–45) severely interrupted the development of civil air transport, which had begun early in the 1930s. There was some acceleration and progress between 1946 and 1949, but on the defeat and retreat of the Nationalist forces in 1949, the meagre fleet of civil planes was withdrawn to Hong Kong where it was impounded. A long legal battle over ownership then ensued. Thus the Communist Government found itself virtually without civil aircraft and with only primitive airfields.

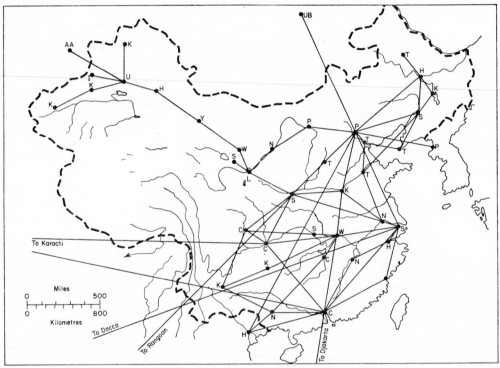

Map 58. Main air routes of China, 1966

Between 1950 and 1958 rapid progress was made, but air services, of necessity, were restricted to only the most pressing priorities. These consisted mainly of the transport of important political and economic personnel, such as leading cadres, engineers and technicians; topographical and geological teams and their equipment; aerial photography; the transport of fragile instruments, spare parts and urgently required machinery. Towards the end of this period, the needs of agriculture, such as the distribution of chemical fertilizer, pest spraying, the rapid transport of fish fry and the control of forest fires began to receive some attention. By 1958 most of the main cities had some air communication and a considerable increase in air traffic had been achieved.

Progress in Civil Aviation
(From Ten Great Years, Peking, 1960)

Year	Freight turnover (thousand ton-km)	Passenger turnover (thousand passenger km)	Total flight hours for industrial and agric. purposes (h)
1950	820	9,780	—
1952	2,430	24,090	959
1957	8,250	79,870	9,168
1958	13,310	108,990	17,845

However, it has been since 1959 that the main progress in development, co-ordination and organization of regular flights has taken place. Peking and Shanghai are the two great hubs from which routes to more than 70 Chinese cities radiate. These domestic routes cover over 34,000 km[24]. Most of the airfields are still not equipped for night flying so that nearly all flights are day flights. Newly established through routes from Shenyang to Sian via Peking and Taiyuan, and from Shenyang to Chengtu, are reported to take $7\frac{1}{2}$ h and $8\frac{1}{2}$ h respectively. Slow as this may appear by comparison with western standards, it is, nevertheless, a great advance in communication.

China now possesses three international airports, Peking, Shanghai and Canton, each fully provided with the necessary standard equipment for 24 h flying service. The routes operating in 1967 are to U.S.S.R., Mongolia, Korea, Vietnam, Burma and Pakistan[25]. Large turbo-propeller planes are replacing medium-sized piston planes. China is designing and producing its own planes although, as yet, these are not in sufficient supply.

Broadcasting

The constant propagation of Lenin–Maoist ideology lies at the very heart of Chinese Communist policy. It is not surprising, therefore, to find that adequate provision has been made for this essential modern means of communication of ideas. Every corner of China is penetrated. Every commune, every village, has its public receiver set and loud speaker. Chinese-designed and produced transistors are now widely available at a price which is within the means of a thrifty worker.

REFERENCES

[1] MARCO POLO. *The Travels of Marco Polo, the Venetian*, Bk. II, Ch. XX
[2] TREGEAR, T. R. *A Geography of China*, University of London Press, London, 1965, pp. 80–90, 79–80, 192–197, 68–80
[3] NEEDHAM, J. 'Science and China's Influence in the World', *Legacy of China* (Dawson, R., Ed.), Clarendon Press, Oxford, 1964, p. 271
[4] HAN SU-YIN. *The Crippled Tree*, Cape, London, 1965
[5] LIPPIT, V. 'Development of Transportation in Communist China', *China Quarterly*, 27 (1966) Quoting Chang Kia-ngau *China's Struggle for Railroad Development*, Day, New York, 1943
[6] *Ten Great Years*, Foreign Language Press, Peking, 1960
[7] HUGHES, R. *The Chinese Commune*, Bodley Head, London, 1960
[8] *Kung-lu (Highway)*, 10 (1964)
[9] *Min-tzu T'uan-chieh (National Unity)*, 10 (1964)
[10] *N.C.N.A.*, Sining, 11 Oct. 1964
[11] *N.C.N.A.*, Foochow, 28 June 1965
[12] *N.C.N.A.*, Lhasa, 20 Oct. 1965
[13] FEI HSIAO-TUNG, *Peasant Life in China*, Routledge & Kegan Paul, London, 1947
[14] *China Reconstructs*, July 1963
[15] *China Reconstructs*, Jan. 1965
[16] *Far Eastern Trade*, Dec. 1961
[17] LIN KWANG-CHIN. 'British-Chinese Steamships Rivalry in China, 1873-1885', *Economic Development of China and Japan* (Cowan, C. D. Ed.), Allan, London, 1964
[18] *Peking Reviews*, 17 (1966)
[19] *N.C.N.A.*, Chungking, 30 July 1965
[20] *N.C.N.A.*, Kweiyang, 20 June 1965
[21] *N.C.N.A.*, Shanghai, 13 Dec. 1965
[22] *Far Eastern Trade*, Nov. 1961
[23] *China Reconstructs*, Mar. 1962
[24] LING SHANG. 'Rapid Development of Civil Aviation', *Shih-shih Shou-ts'e (Current Events)*, 9 (1964)
[25] *Ta-kung Pao*, Peking, 4 Oct. 1964

7

POWER

POPULATION

THE discussion and analysis of China's population is deliberately included under the heading of Power in order to emphasize how big and important an element it has been, and still is, in China. In agriculture and transport, man, together with animals, has been virtually the only source of power. In fields throughout the centuries, he has worked individually or in small clan groups. On occasion, he has been mobilized into great labour armies to carry out some big national work, such as building the Great Wall under Ch'in Shih Hwang Ti, or the New Pien Canal in the Sui dynasty or the Grand Canal under Kublai Khan. The mobilization of such large numbers was possible only after the break-up of the feudal system at the end of the Chou dynasty (221 B.C.). It was nearly always compulsive, the exceptions being on occasions of emergency dyke repairs. These mobilizations have been accompanied by great hardship, cruelty and loss of life, and consequently are looked back on with loathing and hatred by the common people.

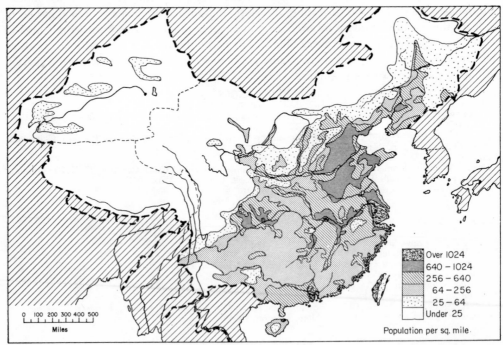

Map 59. China's population

The Chinese peasant is sturdy and tough, patient and persistent and, within wide limits, amenable to organization. When inspired and willing, he is capable of great endurance,

The carrying pole, and old heavy wheelbarrow are being replaced gradually by more efficient pneumatic tyred vehicles. Human energy is still the main source of power

as we have seen during the Great Leap Forward. Chinese Communist intention is to achieve a modern, industrialized state as quickly as possible, which involves mechanization in all its manifestations and breaking free from this reliance on man-power. This has been achieved to some extent in the modernization of transport, the building of integrated steel plant, the equipping of mines and ports, and in the mechanization of state farms, but viewed in the setting of the country's vast needs, only a beginning has been made. Most of the great reconstruction work so far carried out has, of necessity, had to be handled by human muscles and by the mobilization of vast numbers. Even the building of the big dams, such as San Men, has been largely the work of hoe, basket and carrying pole. The rapid construction of the Shasi and Tachiatai retention basins in the Yangtze were achieved by the mobilization of more than half a million workers, men and women from the localities, working with simple tools. Patriotic fervour, socialist propaganda and considerable care for the welfare of these armies appear to have made such mobilizations possible without arousing the deep-seated hatreds, which have accompanied all such previous mobilizations.

China's man-power has been notably increased by the emancipation of women, which has steadily been taking place throughout the twentieth century and which has gained great momentum since 1949. An important aspect of rural and urban communes has been the freeing of large numbers of women from household ties and chores on to the labour market. Women's equality of status with men in China carries with it the obligation to tackle even the same physical work as men and to carry the same responsibilities, from judges to tractor drivers. This has met with an amazing positive response and has increased the labour force enormously.

Numbers

In 1953, for the first time in Chinese history, a census of the people was carried out. Previously all figures of population have been estimates based on the number of households or on food consumption or salt consumption and, more recently, on postal material. The results of these estimates have shown great variation and have very little reliability. The necessity for reliable information on numbers in a modern state, especially in a planned communist society as compared with one of free enterprise, is obvious. Equally obvious are the difficulties of taking a census in a country so vast and of such variety as China. It is not surprising, therefore, to find that, in this first counting of heads, the Government used a very simple schedule of five questions[1]—too simple according to some experts. No attempt was made to carry through the census on any one single day, or to attempt a *de facto* numbering, i.e. the persons actually present at a particular place at a certain time. Instead the *de jure* method was used, i.e. recording those persons habitually present. When the census was published in 1954 and the total population for Mainland China was given as 582,603,417, nearly 100 million higher than the highest pre-1949 estimate (that by the Post Office in 1926), some outside observers were very sceptical as to its honesty and reliability[2]. There appears to be little reason for questioning the honesty of the figures although they have not the same accuracy as similar Western demographic statistics. In some outlying border regions, occupied by national minorities, the normal registration could not be undertaken and estimates had to be made. Other unusual elements of the 1953 census were the inclusion of the population of Taiwan, which, although at present politically separate, is regarded by both the Communist and the Nationalist governments as an integral part of China. Also included are the Overseas Chinese, i.e. Chinese settlers in foreign lands and students studying abroad.

Direct census registration of the Mainland	574,205,940
Borderland National Minorities estimate	8,397,477
Taiwan (1951 figures)	7,591,298
Overseas Chinese	11,743,320
Total	601,938,035

These figures, published by the Statistical Bureau in November, 1954 differ slightly from those of the Government Report in June, 1954. From 1953 to 1957 records were kept of changes in population and these were published by the Statistical Bureau. Since then they have ceased. It was the announced intention to conduct a second census in 1963, but this did not materialize.

Table 7.1. Population Distribution of Mainland China by Provinces (in thousands). (From Ten Great Years, Peking, 1960)

Province	1953	1957
Szechwan	62,304	72,160
Shantung	48,876	54,030
Honan	44,214	48,670
Kiangsu	41,252	45,230
Hopei	35,984	44,720
Kwangtung	34,770	37,960
Hunan	33,227	36,220
Anhwei	30,343	33,560
Hupeh	27,789	30,790
Chekiang	22,865	25,280
Kwangsi Chuang Aut. Region	19,560	19,390
Yunnan	17,472	19,100
Kiangsi	16,772	18,610
Shensi	15,881	18,130
Kweichow	15,037	16,890
Shansi	14,314	15,960
Fukien	13,142	14,650
Kansu	12,928	12,800*
Ningsia Hui Aut. Region	—	1,810
North-East		
Liaoning	18,545	24,090
Jehol	5,160	— †
Heilungkiang	11,897	14,860
Kirin	11,290	12,550
Inner Mongolian Aut. Region	6,100	9,200
Sinkiang Uighur Aut. Region	4,873	5,640
Sikang	3,381	— ‡
Chinghai	1,676	2,050
Tibet	1,274	1,270
Municipalities		
Shangahi	6,204	6,900
Peking	2,768	4,010
Tientsin	2,693	— §
Total	582,603	646,530

* Jehol incorporated in Lianning   † Sikang incorporated in Szechwan
‡ Tientsin incorporated in Hopei   § Ningsia withdrawn from Kansu

The distribution of the population is best appreciated by an examination of the accompanying population map and the provincial table below. The concentration in the east, in the North China Plain, in the Yangtze basin and along the south-east and southern coasts is most marked. The report states that 505,346,135 or 86·74% of the total population is rural, that is, living in hamlets, villages and small towns of 2,000 or less inhabitants. This proportion, as between rural and urban, has changed somewhat in favour of urban in the last 15 years, but it is still true to say that more than four-fifths of China's population is rural. There are great contrasts in density of population; in some rural regions the density is very great indeed, for example, in the irrigated areas of the Chengtu plain in Szechwan densities of 2,000 to 3,000 persons/sq. mile are not uncommon. Kiangsu, with an area of 107,300 sq. km, has a population of 41,252,192, giving an overall density of 384 persons/ sq. km, but in the rural river valleys there is a density of over 1,000/sq. km[3]. On the other hand, in many parts of the Tibetan plateau and in the Taklamakan the density is far less than 1 person/sq. mile.

Since 1949 there has been a big and rapid increase in urban population. Some indication of this growth is given by the report that in the 5 years between 1953 and 1958 the number of cities having more than 1 million inhabitants has grown from 8 to 15; those having 500,000 to 1,000,000 from 16 to 20 and those having 100,000 to 500,000 from 73 to 80[4]. The most striking growth has been in the new economic centres of the north-east and the north where there was a large absolute and relative increase. *Table 7.2* lists the cities of more than 500,000 in 1957. Since then no comparable figures have been published. Had they been, many more cities would now appear in it.

Table 7.2. Population of Cities having over 500,000 Inhabitants.
(Year-end of 1957 in thousands). (*From* Ten Great Years, Peking)

City	Population	City	Population
Municipalities directly under central authority		Kiangsu Nanking	1,419
Peking	4,010	Suchow	676
Shanghai	6,900	Soochow	633
		Wusih	613
Hopei			
Tientsin	3,200	Chekiang	
Tangshan	800	Hangchow	784
Shihkiachuang	598		
		Fukien	
Shansi		Foochow	616
Taiyuan	1,020		
		Honan	
Liaoning		Chengchow	766
Shenyang	2,411		
Lushun-Talien	1,508	Hupeh	
Fushun	985	Wuhan	2,146
Anshan	805		
		Hunan	
Kirin		Changsha	703
Changchun	975		
Kirin	568	Kiangsi	
		Nanchang	508
Heilungkiang			
Harbin	1,552	Kwangtung	
Tsitsihar	668	Canton	1,840
Shensi			
Sian	1,310	Szechwan	
		Chungking	2,121
Kansu		Chengtu	1,107
Lanchow	699		
		Kweichow	
Shantung		Kweiyang	504
Tsinan	862		
Tsingtao	1,121	Yunnan	
Tzepo	806	Kunming	880

Growth in Number of Big and Medium-sized Cities

Population	No. of cities	
	1952	1957
Over 5 million	1	1
3 to 5 million	—	2
1 to 3 million	8	11
0·5 to 1 million	15	20
100,000 to 500,000	81	90
Under 100,000	54	52
Total	159	176

The 1953 official census classified the people into ethnic groups or 'nationalities'. Of these the 'Han' (Chinese) form the preponderating group, numbering 547,283,057 or 93·4% of the whole. The report makes no attempt to differentiate between the northerners (Han Jen) and southerners (T'ang Jen) on whom we have already commented. Within their common culture, there are still marked differences of stature, spoken language, facial characteristics and temperament between north and south, of which one is very conscious when journeying between the two regions. The northerners are generally taller, slower and more phlegmatic than their more volatile compatriots of the south whence revolutions have more commonly emanated. Moreover, the northern Chinese are more homogeneous than those of the south, where the main admixture of other nationalities occurs.

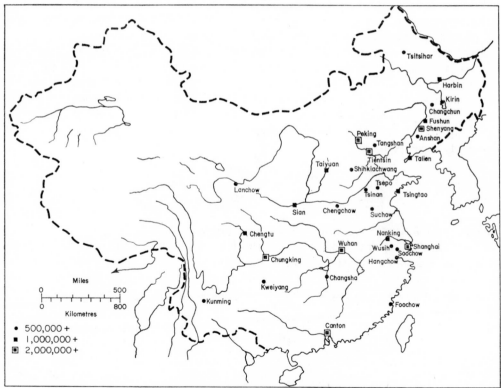

Map 60. Cities of over 500,000, 1958

These 'national minorities' number in all 35,320,360 or 6·06% of the whole. No less than 51 of them are listed in *Ten Great Years*. Where these nationalities are found in large numbers, they have been given some semblance of autonomy and self-government. The main examples are the Kwangsi Chuang Autonomous Region, where the Chuang people numbered 6,611,455 in 1953; the Sinkiang Uighur Autonomous Region, where the Uighurs numbered 3,640,125 and the Ningsia Hui Autonomous Region and the Inner Mongolian Autonomous Region, where the Hui or Chinese Moslems and the Mongols respectively form the majority of the population. Other important minorities are the Tibetans (2,775,622); the Yi (3,254,269) in the Szechwan-Yunnan borders; the Miao (2,511,339) in Kweichow and west Hunan; the Pu-yi (1,247,883) in south-west Kweichow; the Koreans (1,120,405) in the Yenpien Korean Autonomous *chou* in Kirin. The Manchus, who at the census numbered 2,419,931, now have no region of concentration and have become integrated throughout the country. It is instructive to note that, in addition to the Yi, Pu-yi and Miao, the majority of the smaller tribes or nationalities are found in the south-west in western Szechwan, Kweichow, Yunnan and west Kwangsi. The People's Government takes great credit for its treatment of these minorities, in its care for their economic well-being, the raising of their living standards, in educating them in local government, in raising the standard of literacy and in inventing a written language in those cases where none has existed previously. Institutes of National Minorities with this educative end in view are a feature of many large cities, notably Peking and Wuhan.

In common with some Asian countries, but contrary to Western experience, men in China outnumber women. In view of the importance placed, in the past, on male succession and the performance of correct ceremonies in ancestral worship by the male head of the family, it is not surprising that more value was placed on boys than on girls and more care was lavished on them. In times of famine, it was common practice among the poor people to abandon female babies and to sell their young girls to wealthier people. With the decline of Confucianism and the growth of Western standards, the status of women has risen during the last 50–60 years and with it, the chances of survival of female babies has improved, especially since 1949. The change, however, has not yet become apparent in the total figures of sex composition[5]:

Year	Total Population	Male	Female (thousands)
1949	548,770	285,140	263,630
1953	595,550	308,850	286,700
1957	656,630	340,140	316,490

Chinese living in Hongkong, Macao and abroad are not included.

However, Prof. Chandrasekhar quotes the following figures and, commenting, says 'The cultural modes favoured the male infant. These have now changed, and the change is reflected in the sex ratio of infants under three years. That the sex ratio becomes increasingly unfavourable to the female in the higher age groups is noteworthy'[1].

Sex Ratio at Various Age Groups

Age groups	Sex ratio Number of males per 100 females
0	104·9
1—2	106·2
3—6	110·0
7—13	115·8
14—17	113·7
18—35	111·5
36—55	106·8
56 and over	86·7

The age composition of a society or country has very considerable influence on its economic well-being. Other things being equal, the greater the proportion of its people who are of working age, the greater will be its productive capacity. Exactly what constitutes 'working age' is difficult to determine and differs from country to country and also within the same country. In China, children are brought into productive employment at an early age in rural areas. Moreover, Communist politicians and educators lay much emphasis on practical experience and very many schools—particularly middle schools—are run on a part-time study, part-time work basis. During the summer months an appreciable amount of work in the fields is done by boys and girls. It is therefore difficult to make clear-cut divisions between productive and non-productive ages, such as school-leaving at one end of the scale and retirement at the other. At the time of the 1953 census the age composition of China's population was[1]:

Age group (years)	Distribution %
0—4	15·6
5—9	11·0
10—17	14·5
0—17	41·1
18—49	45·4
50 and over	13·5

Comparable figures for U.K. in 1959 were

0—14	23·2
15—64*	62·3
65 and over†	14·7

* Men only 60–64 years. † Women of 60 years and over included.

These figures emphasize the youthfulness of China in 1953 with 86·5% of its people under 50 years of age.

Population Growth

China's population, until the seventeenth century, had remained fairly constant at a figure somewhere between 100 million and 200 million, held steady by the Malthusian checks of war, famine and pestilence. During the long peaceful reigns of the two great Manchu emperors, K'ang Hsi and Ch'ien Lung, the population grew rapidly to an estimated 300 million by 1850. It should be noted that during this period there was no concomitant increase in the amount of cultivable land. Hence, from this time on land hunger began to be felt and, as population continued to increase, it became acute in the twentieth century.

The 1953 census revealed that there were 582 million people living in the country; returns in 1957 showed this to have risen to 656 million, an annual increase of nearly 15 million. It is estimated that if the present trend continues, there will be 800 million Chinese in 1970 and over 1,000 million in 1980. The reasons for this explosion of numbers are not far to seek. To a very large extent the Malthusian checks have been removed. Since 1949 China has enjoyed a peace and political unity unknown in the previous 100 years. Threatened famine and its death toll have been averted by rationing of supplies and a more even and equitable distribution of food, made possible by the development of modern communications. Even more important has been the rapid extension of public hygiene and the cult of cleanliness throughout the country. During the early years after 1949, the authorities concentrated attention on preventive medicine. Training for doctors, during these years, was reduced from 6 to 3 years in order that this preventive side should be implemented.

The result has been that, while the number of births has remained fairly constant, the death rate, estimated at about 27 per 1,000 in the early decades of the twentieth century and 18 per 1,000 in 1952, had fallen to 11 per 1,000 in 1957 and is still falling.

Table 7.3. Crude Birth and Death Rates in Mainland China.
(From S. Chandrasekhar[1], by courtesy of Hong Kong University Press)
(Per 1,000 population)

Year	Birth rate	Death rate	Natural increases
1952	37	18	19
1953	37	17	20
1954	38	13	24
1955	35	12·4	22·6
1956	32	11·4	20·6
1957	34	11	23

The fall in infant mortality rates is even more striking. There are no reliable figures for these rates before 1949, but some estimates place infant deaths at nearly 200 per 1,000 population. In rural areas alone the rate stood at 138 per 1,000 in 1954. It had fallen to 109 in 1956. The infant mortality rate for the whole country, including the urban population, was down to 34·1 in 1957[1]. Figures for cities alone show a remarkable fall. For example, infant death rates in Peking, Shanghai and Canton in 1952 stood at 65·7, 81·2 and 47·7 per thousand. By 1956 these had fallen to 35·1, 31·1 and 25·1 respectively[1].

Such population changes pose the Government with problems. Orthodox Chinese communism is inflexibly opposed to the Malthusian theory of population, holding that China is well able to feed any increase in numbers that may occur and that increasing numbers, far from being a weakness, constitute the strength of the nation. Mao Tse-tung, with his faith pinned firmly on the masses and their support, has emphatically affirmed his belief in large numbers. 'I hope that these people will take a wider view and really recognize the fact that we have a population of six hundred millions, that this is an objective fact and that this is our asset. It is a good thing.'[7]

This optimistic and confident view continued until 1954 when some questioning began to arise since production was not increasing as rapidly as had been anticipated. A rather vacillating policy has since ensued. The first official suggestions of the desirability of some birth control came at the National People's Congress in 1954 when Shao Li-tze stated 'It is a good thing to have a large population but, in an environment beset with difficulties. it appears that a limit should be set'. He urged the advertisement of birth control by contraceptive methods. However, it was not until March, 1957 that Madam Li Teh-chuan, Minister of Health launched a full-blooded birth control campaign. Throughout the year great publicity was given everywhere to the use of contraception.

It was at this time that Ma Yin-ch'u, one of China's leading economists, published his paper, 'The New Principle of Population', in which, while stressing his opposition to the Malthusian theory, attacked the orthodox communist attitude to population questions. He contended that a high population and a high growth in numbers slows down economic development and that curbing of population growth was necessary in order to produce a higher quality of people. He advocated limitation by family planning and contraception on the one hand and much greater capital expenditure on the mechanization of agriculture, water conservancy and irrigation, mainly on small-scale works, in order to raise living standards. He argued that, with mechanization and automation, a big population was not necessary. In spite of his declared opposition to Malthusian ideas, he was denounced as Malthusian, his critics contending that, in China, there was a labour shortage and not the reverse, and meeting Ma's arguments with the doctrinaire statement 'Everyone knows— according to the viewpoint of Marxism and Leninism on the population question—that unemployment and surplus population are the production of capitalists, privately owning the means of production'.[8]

The Great Leap Forward followed shortly after in 1958–9. In the universal enthusiasm and confidence of these years control of numbers was lost sight of. It was the near-famine years of 1960 and 1961 which again focused attention on the question. Once again contraception was advised, stressing the need for family planning, the proper spacing of childbirth and the care of the mother's health, rather than the curbing of numbers. From 1962 onwards emphasis has been placed on late marriages. 'Planned childbirth and late marriage is the established policy of our country during the socialist construction period.'[9] The ages of marriage recommended are 23 to 27 for women and 25 to 29 for men. Earlier marriages are condemned on the basis that they are physically and mentally harmful to the health of parents and children and that they distract youth from study and productive work[10]. The advocacy of late marriage and smaller families has been vigorously preached throughout the country. As might be expected, it appears to be having greater success among the urban than the rural population.

COAL

Reserves

During the Middle and Late Ordovician era, the great Cathaysian geosyncline, which at that time stretched from the north-east to Indo-China, was divided by the raising of the Chin Ling axis from east to west. This axis has remained a permanent geographical factor ever since, dividing the country geologically, climatically, vegetationally, economically and even politically. At that time, land to the north of the axis was raised, while that to the south was deeply submerged. During the Carboniferous and Permian, great areas in the north were alternately submerged in shallow seas and continental shelves and raised above sea level. This is the period of the formation of the great coalfields of Shensi, Shansi, Hopei, Honan and the North-East. From the Permian onward, north China has not been deeply submerged. Comparatively small basins were below sea level in Tertiary times, when the immensely thick coal beds of Fushun and Fusin were laid down in the North-East.

Most of the coal of central and southern China is of secondary formation. There were some Carbo–Permian deposits along the northern periphery of the deep southern sea, but the great coalfields of Szechwan and the widely-scattered fields of Hunan, Hupeh, Yunnan, Kweichow and Kwangtung are of Rhaetic origin, when the whole of southern China had been uplifted[11].

There has been no publication of overall coal reserves since 1949, but the subsequent extensive geological surveys that have been carried out have doubtless raised considerably the figures published by Nelson Dickerman in 1948, which showed total reserves of over 283 billion metric ton, of which nearly 230 billion were bituminous. China is well served with reserves of some 45,870 million ton of anthracite and has comparatively little lignite. The 1934–1945 estimated reserves serve to give a fair general picture of coal distribution.

Table 7.4. *Coal Reserves and Production. (From* N. Dickerman[12], *by courtesy of* U.S. Bureau of Mines)

Province	Reserves 1934–1945 (figures in million metric tons)				Production 1944 (thousand metric tons)
	Anthracite	Bituminous	Lignite	Total	
N.W.					
Shansi	36,471	87,985	2,671	127,127	6,250
Shensi	750	71,200		71,950	650
Kansu	59	997		1,056	110
Ningsia	173	284		457	140
N.E.					
Heilungkiang		5,000	3,980	8,980	3,047
Kirin		5,581	478	6,059	6,117
Liaoning	36	2,606		2,642	10,940
Jehol		4,714		4,714	5,359
Chahar	17	487		504	9,300
N. China Plain					
Shantung	26	1,613		1,639	10,300
Hopei	975	2,088	2	3,965	12,000
Honan	4,455	3,309		7,764	300
Central China					
Hupeh	45	309		354	40
Hunan	741	552		1,293	550
Anhwei	60	300		360	1,250
Kiangsi	271	420	9	700	120
Kiangsu	25	192		217	1,100
Red Basin					
Szechwan	293	3,540		3,833	2,700
S.W.					
Yunnan	77	1,539	694	2,310	260
Kweichow	822	1,696		2,518	250
Kwangsi	45	1,111	1	1,157	200
S. and S.E.					
Chekiang	22	78		100	2
Fukien	147	6		153	30
Kwangtung	59	274		333	100
W.					
Tsinghai	240	584		824	—
Sinkiang		31,980		31,980	180

By far the most extensive reserves lie in the north-west of China Proper in the provinces of Shensi, Shansi, Kansu and Ningsia Autonomous Region. Much of the coal is hidden beneath sandstone and loess deposits, but lies exposed in large areas along axes running from north to south along both sides of the Hwang-ho, also to the north of Paotow and in some places in Ningsia. Huge reserves of good quality anthracite lie mainly to the east in Shansi, while the bituminous is mainly to the west. Happily there has been comparatively little tectonic movement in the region and, consequently, the coal seams are generally horizontal, thereby facilitating mining. Although the seams here cannot compare with the great thicknesses of the exposed beds in the North-East, they are, nevertheless, ample, varying from 10 to 40 ft.

The North-East ranks second in reserves, but has only about one-eighth of those of the north-west. Bituminous is distributed widely throughout the three provinces and lies exposed on the eastern and western edges of the Cathaysian geosyncline. Anthracite is virtually absent, but there are considerable deposits of lignite in Heilunkiang. Two Tertiary coal basins are located in Liaotung, at Fushun and Fusin, each having exposed coal seams of up to 400 ft thickness.

The reserves of the North China Plain (Shantung, Hopei and Honan) are also found along the west and east edges of the Cathaysian geosyncline, i.e. along the faulted edges of the Wutai and Taihang Shan, on the one hand, and the western scarps of the Shantung peninsula on the other. It is highly probable that there are rich coal deposits lying below the deep alluvium of the plain. Honan is the only province of the North China Plain, which has large reserves of anthracite. These are a continuation of the Shansi beds.

The statistical table of reserves reveals the great difference in wealth of coal that exists between north and south China immediately the Chin Ling Shan is crossed southward. The Rheatic beds of the Red Basin of Szechwan alone carry reserves which can bear comparison with those of the north. Szechwan's coal lies buried in the centre of the basin under Cretaceous red sandstone, but outcrops mainly on the periphery, particularly in the south and south-east, along the crests of the anticlines. The provinces of the south-west plateau (Yunnan, Kweichow and Kwangsi) have fair bituminous reserves quite widely distributed. Kweichow has fairly extensive deposits of anthracite. Eastward and southward the reserves become progressively poorer, especially around Fukien and Chekiang.

No figures of coal reserves for Inner Mongolia are available. The 1934–45 estimates for Sinkiang were 31,980 million tons and for Tsinghai 240 million tons of anthracite and 584 million tons of bituminous. Since then extensive geological surveys have been made in both these regions and there is reason to believe that these figures should be considerably increased. Sinkiang's main coalfields extend along the northern slopes of the Bogdo Ula from Manass to Kitai and in the Ili Valley, centred on Kuldja. There are abundant peat beds in Inner Mongolia.

Production

Coal has been in general use in China for cooking and smelting since the Sung dynasty (960–1279) when it was replacing charcoal[13]. Marco Polo reported with wonder the use of coal in these words: 'Throughout this province there is found a sort of black stone, which they dig out of the mountains, where it runs in veins. When lighted, it burns like charcoal, and retains the fire much better than wood; inasmuch that it may be preserved during the night, and in the morning be found still burning. These stones do not flame, excepting a little when first lighted, but during their ignition give out considerable heat.'[13a] Mine shafts over 100 ft deep were sunk and galleries were fitted with bamboo pipes for drainage and for pumping fresh air and evacuating gases.

Theoretically all soil and therefore all coal and minerals belonged to the State. However, some private exploitation in mining was permitted and during the Ming dynasty (1368–1644) there was steady growth of private enterprise. Nevertheless, it was always kept under close control by the scholar-administrator class. Towards the end of the dynasty, Emperor Wan-li clamped down on private mining in an edict which declared: 'It is no longer permitted to open private mines without authorization: the important thing is not to disturb the bowels of the earth.'[13]

The extraction of coal by modern methods did not take place until the beginning of the twentieth century. Mining corporations and companies, often combined Chinese and foreign ventures, obtained concessions from the Government and began operations. Most notable of these were the Japanese South Manchurian Railway Company's Fushun Collieries in 1907, the Peking Syndicate (1905) operating in Honan and the Kailan Mining Administration (1912), whose concessions lay in the region behind Chingwangtao[14]. Their development was part cause and part effect of the railway development of that period. For example, the Peking–Mukden Railway served and was served by the Kailan mines. The Peking–Hankow Railway followed closely the scarp slopes of the Wutai and Taihang Shan, pushing branch lines into the Shansi plateau to tap and develop the exposed anthracite of the edge. Coal exploitation was conditioned by communications and therefore was confined to the east. Shansi's great coalfields remained virtually untouched, except for shallow local mines, until the post-1949 development of railways in the region.

Methods of coal extraction have varied enormously, ranging from fairly advanced mechanization to an entire reliance on man-power. All mining has been influenced by the abundance and cheapness of human labour, which has militated against the introduction of machinery. Some large collieries were well mechanized and installed reasonable safety precautions, but in very many the conditions below ground were unspeakable, as described by George Cressey and as experienced by the author in Shihhweiyao, Hupeh, where the galleries were low and unpropped and were the beds of rushing streams, and where ventilation was practically non-existent. Since 1949 much attention and energy has been focused on improving all safety measures in mines[15].

Coal production rose gradually and somewhat unsteadily throughout the first half of the twentieth century:

Year	Tons	
1912	13,000,000	
1923	22,000,000	
1930	16,839,000	
1944	71,263,000	
1949	32,430,000	
1958	270,000,000	
1959	335,000,000	(planned)
1966	240,000,000	(estimated)
1967	190,000,000	('Current Scene', Vol. VI, No. 12 (1968) 6

The phenominal rise in output since 1949 reflects the great effort that has been put into industrial development. The dispersion of industry has had the effect of stimulating modern coal mining in many regions where previously it had been conducted on a primitive local scale. By 1958 it was reported that new pits, with a total annual output of 150 million ton had been opened since 1949. These included big developments at Kweisui, north of Paotow, Tatung and Taiyuan: also the rapid expansion in Sinkiang, east and west of Urumchi, to serve growing industrialization there. However, the same report voiced the complaint that too great a proportion of capital investment allocated to coal development was still going into the well-established north and North-East and so maintaining an imbalance in the distribution of industry[16]. While no comprehensive account of the coal industry has been published, the constant reports in newspapers and magazines of the opening of new pits and their capacities give some indication of the scope of development. For example a new mine shaft, designed and constructed by Chinese engineers and having an annual

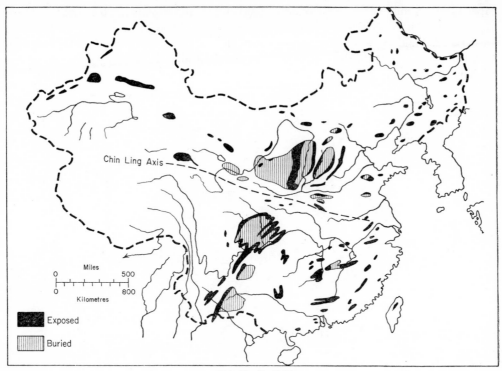

Map 61. Coalfields

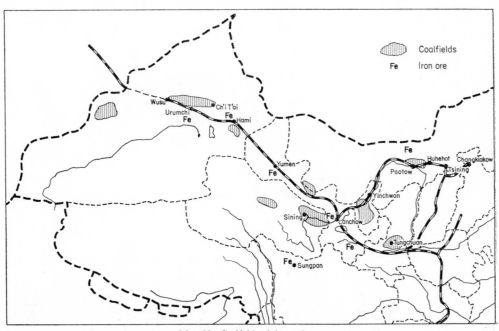

Map 62. Coalfields of the north-west

capacity of 1·8 million ton, was recently completed in the Kailan mining area[17].   Three new mines with capacities of 900,000, 1,200,000 and 1,500,000 ton p.a. were opened between 1958 and 1964 at Pingtingshan, south Honan, exploiting seams of coking coal up to 17 m thick.   All these three mines are mechanized and are to serve the needs of the Wuhan Iron and Steel Works[18].

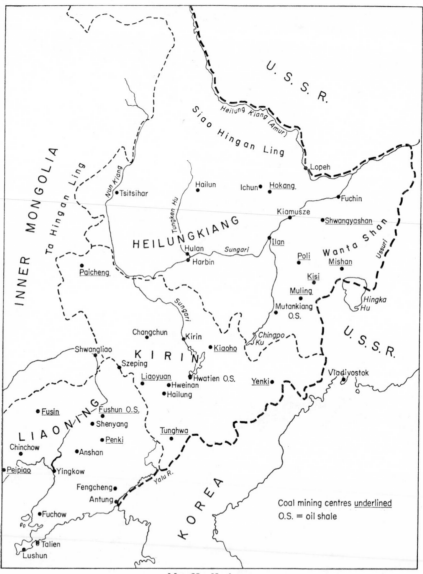

Map 63.   North-east

The North-East remains China's main coal producing area, which is not surprising in view of the ease with which much of it can be mined. Not only at Fushun and Fusin in Liaoning, but also at Hokang in Heilungkiang there are open-cast mines with coal seams of immense thickness. Fushun, which was first developed by the Japanese and has now been extended, is reported to be producing over 20 million ton annually. Here the coal seam, which varies between 120 and 360 ft in thickness, is overlain by layers of oil shale and green shale, which are used respectively for oil distillation and soap-making or water softening. The oil refinery, built by the Japanese, is sited immediately above the cut, which is some 4 miles long and 1,500 yards wide. The Fusin mines, which are similar in formation, are beginning to rival Fushun in output. Both are highly mechanized. Penki and Peipiao, also in Liaotung, in 1957 produced respectively 5 million and 2·8 million ton of good coking coal. Hokang's open-cast seams total 130 ft in thickness and produced 4·9 million ton in 1957. Other large Heilungkiang mines are sited at Kisi and Shwangyashan, which produced 5·8 million and 2·3 million ton respectively in 1957[19]. Smaller workings are at Mishan, Poli, Ilan and Muling. Kirin's most important mines are at Liaoyuan, which produced— 3 million ton of good industrial coal in 1957, and at Tunghwa where good coking coal is obtained.

Chinese claims have been made recently of the discovery of new coke-making methods by blending weakly-coking coals and so producing coke of greater strength and lower ash content than conventionally made coke. If these claims are substantiated, the discovery will be of great importance as China's supplies of good coking coal are limited in amount and distribution.

Undoubtedly the factionalism and labour strife during 1967–68 have had a serious effect on the production of coal, which accounts for about 90% of China's primary energy supply. Power shortages have occurred wherever industry had been dependent on coal-fired thermal generation.

OIL

The first recorded use of oil and natural gas in China comes from the Eastern Han dynasty (A.D. 25–220) when 'fire wells' were drilled at Ch'unglai *hsien* in Szechwan and the natural gas was used for the processing of salt. Towards the end of the Ming dynasty (1368–1644) wells at Chienwei, Szechwan, several hundred metres deep were being drilled[20]. Apart from this, however, no other development of oil resources appears to have taken place during the succeeding centuries.

Although the presence of oil in north Shensi at Yench'ang and at Yumen in west Kansu was known in the early twentieth century, little was done to develop it. Domestic lighting at that time was by oil lamps throughout the land. The fuel for these came almost entirely from American, British and Dutch companies. This rich market may have influenced American assessments of China's potential oil reserves in such statements as 'both the types of rocks and their genetic age in the greater part of China preclude the possibility of there being any petrol deposits worthy of exploitation'[21] and 'There is almost no possibility of petroleum deposit in the greater part of China.'[22] Almost complete reliance on foreign imports of oil continued until 1949. China's peak output before this was in 1943 when 320,000 ton were produced, as against 1,950,000 ton imported.

Since 1949, in concurrence with the general policy of industrial development, the attaining of national self-sufficiency in oil production has been a constant aim, borne out by the large amount of capital, which has been invested in this field. Extensive geological surveys and prospecting have been—and still are being—carried out. During the first 10 years after 1949, this work was greatly assisted by the U.S.S.R., which supplied many technologists, introduced advanced skills and survey techniques, and much oil-drilling machinery. This help was withdrawn abruptly in July, 1960 since when the Chinese have relied on their own resources to a large extent.

As a result of this prospecting, the oil situation has changed radically; new fields have been discovered and old fields extended. Estimates of reserves now stand at 2 billion ton, of which 90% is located in north-west China[23].

Karamai Field

The presence of oil in Sinkiang was known at the turn of the century but very little was done towards its development. Only a small amount was obtained from a few shallow wells —not enough even for the supply of local lamps. Between 1953 and 1957 the Russians played a big part in surveying and opening up a most fruitful field in the semi-desert of Dzungaria in the vicinity of Karamai, where reserves are estimated at 100 million ton. Production of oil from here rose rapidly from 330,000 ton in 1958 to 780,000 ton in 1959, and to an estimated 1,500,000 ton in 1963. Until 1959, oil from Karamai was transported by truck to the railhead. A pipeline of nearly 100 miles now links the field to Tushantzu where a refinery has been built. There are also smaller fields in the Tarim basin, along the southern slopes of the T'ien Shan at Kashgar, Aksu and Kucha and also in the Turfan Depression[24].

Yumen Field

Oil was discovered in the Yumen area in 1937, but it was not until after 1950 that its exploitation was energetically pursued[25]. Careful prospecting revealed a reserve five times as great as previously estimated. Extensive drilling has been carried out, resulting in greatly increased production. It is estimated that, in 1963, the output of the Yumen field was 1·8 million ton. Yumen has its own refinery with an annual capacity of 400,000 ton and is now linked by pipeline with the Lanchow refinery, which has a capacity of 1 million ton p.a.[23].

Tsaidam Field

A great deal of prospecting and experimental boring in the Tsaidam has revealed a most promising field of good quality oil. Production is increasing annually and a refinery with a capacity of 300,000 ton p.a., has been built at Leng-hu, just south of the Tangching Pass over the Nan Shan.

Szechwan Field

The early knowledge and use of natural gas in Szechwan indicated that this should be a profitable source of supply. Nevertheless extensive earlier prospecting proved fruitless. It was not until 1958 that efforts were rewarded in the discovery of good oil over a wide field in the Lower Jurassic and Triassic strata in the vicinity of Nanchung and Penglai, central Szechwan. This field is now being energetically worked; its output remains small by comparison with that of Yumen.

Taching Field

Much publicity has been given between 1965–66 to the opening up of a large new oilfield in the North-East. Work on it started in 1960 and it is now in production, promising a big increase in supplies. Curiously, no clear information has yet been released as to its exact

194

position beyond the fact that it is in steppeland and experiences bitter winter conditions. This, together with travellers' accounts, indicates that it probably lies in the Tsitsihar–Harbin region. Another large oilfield has been opened up in the region west of Chinchow, Liaotung.

The result of all this activity has been greatly increased production[24]

Year	Tons	
1943	320,000	pre-1949 peak
1949	122,000	
1950	202,000	
1952	436,000	
1955	966,000	
1957	1,410,000	
1958	2,260,000	
1959	3,700,000	
1960	5,500,000	
1961	6,500,000	
1962	7,500,000	
1963	8 to $8\frac{1}{2}$ million estimate	

The aim of self-sufficiency has not yet been achieved. It is estimated that about 62% of the oil consumed in 1960 and 70% of that used in 1963 came from domestic supplies. Until 1961 the greater part of the oil imports came from U.S.S.R. Since then there has been a marked decrease from that source and a corresponding increase in supplies from Roumania[24].

The main difficulties China has had to face in developing its oil supplies lie first in the position of the oilfields themselves, which, for the most part, lie in the remote west and north. Transport of oil by road or rail tanker is expensive and the only solution lies in pipelines. Some progress in this respect, as already indicated, has been made between Karamai and the railhead and between Yumen and Lanchow, but no report has yet been made of a pipeline network. In the early stages of development there was acute shortage of all kinds of surveying and drilling equipment and of technical 'know-how'. Russian aid in both these respects was invaluable, especially in the training of oil engineers and technicians. Since the withdrawal of Russian aid, the Chinese claim that they are now well able to cope by themselves, Yumen and Lanchow both now producing the necessary equipment and precision instruments[26]. Present difficulties are largely concerned with adequate refining plant. Crude oil production in 1966 was estimated at between 9 and 10 million ton, which was more than its refineries could deal with[27]. In recent years, complete refining plant has been urgently imported from Italy and West Germany. At the same time Chinese engineers are continually experimenting, evolving and adapting techniques germaine to local needs. They claim to have built a 'platforming' unit to obtain a large range of highly purified benzenes through the use of a catalyst containing platinum[28]. China's reserves of oil shale are estimated to be 21 billion ton.

The amount of oil obtained from oil shale is considerable. In 1963, 1·8 million ton of oil was obtained from Fushun alone. Other centres in the North-East are at Mutankiang and Hwalien. An open-cast mine yielding 1·5 million ton of shale annually has been opened at Mowming, south Kwangtung, which has a small refinery turning out gasoline, diesel oil and kerosene. The main oil shale deposits are found in the north-west, but as their location largely coincides with liquid oil, they are not likely to be exploited to any great extent at present.

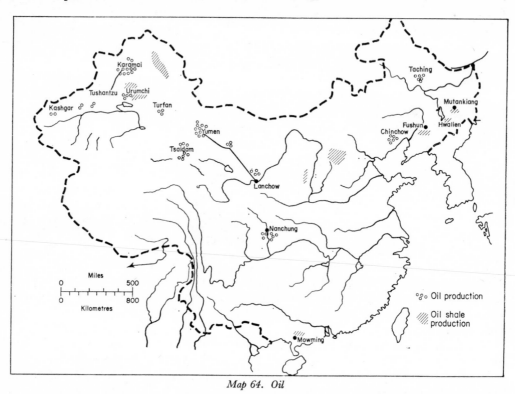

Map 64. Oil

With the rapid development in road building, an ever-growing production of cars and tractors and an increasing use of diesel locomotives, the demand for oil is also increasing rapidly. It remains to be seen whether domestic supplies will be able to keep pace with this increase. At present the annual consumption per head of its 700 million people is only 4 to 5 gal as compared with Japan's 130, U.S.S.R.'s 200 and U.S.A.'s 900 gal per head[24].

ELECTRIC POWER

Because of the ease of its distribution and its adaptability to the needs of industry and agriculture, the planners are relying mainly on the development and use of electrical power. In industry, it can be transformed to meet the needs of many kinds of production such as the special needs of aluminium manufacture and the new steel electrical furnaces. In irrigation and drainage work, electrical power is proving more convenient and dependable than the internal combustion engine. In the Pearl river delta more than 2,500 electric power stations for irrigation and drainage had been installed by 1965; 60% of the farm land of the Yangtze delta is irrigated and drained by electric power and the well water of the North China Plain is now lifted largely by the same means[29]. To this end China is attempting to follow the pattern of all modern industrial countries in building a number of power networks, based on a co-ordination of thermal and hydro-electric generation.

As might be expected in a country so vast and diverse, this development is uneven. The construction of grids, based on already established industrial and mining areas with large cities as centres, has gone ahead rapidly. Less developed areas are relying on medium and small plants, using local resources such as minor water power, small collieries and shallow deposits of natural gas, with a view to eventual linking. It is claimed that electricity is now available to most of the villages in over 1,300 of China's 2,126 *hsien* and that rural consumption of electricity is 25 times greater than it was in 1957[30].

Realizing that the generation of electric power is more quickly achieved and the plant cheaper to erect by the use of coal rather than water power, attention has been concentrated on the building of thermal plant. Even in the North-East, where hydro-electric power was more developed than elsewhere in China, it was estimated in 1959 that 68% of the electric power was thermally generated[19].

China's potential water power is enormous, one recent estimate placed it at 500 million kW[31]. Although great effort has been put into the development of this power since 1949, most of the water conservancy schemes have had flood control, irrigation and drainage as their primary objectives. The only hydro-electric power developed in China before 1949 was by the Japanese in the North-East, where two big dams were built. One at Fengmen, near Kirin at the head of the Sungari Reservoir, had a capacity of 850,000 kW when it was built, but the plant was partly destroyed and the dam damaged and neglected during the Sino-Japanese War. It was subsequently repaired and now has a capacity of 567,000 kW. The other dam was built at Supung on the Yalu river, and had a capacity of 600,000 kW. Since 1949 the Chinese have built three further dams in the North-East, each developing power: Kumotsin on the Nun Kiang, above Tsitsihar, developing 209,000 kW; Mutankiang, developing 383,000 kW; Tahoufang, near Fushun, which has a storage capacity of 1,970 million m³ but for which no kilowatt capacity is available.

In China Proper the outstanding development has been on the Hwang-ho. Two great multi-purpose dams have been built, one at Liuchia, above Lanchow and the other at Sanmen, below Tungkwan Gorge. Each has a capacity of 1 million kW. The completion of the generating plant of the latter suffered a severe setback by the withdrawal of Russian technicians in 1960. A further dam at the Lungyan Gorge, above Liuchia, is planned to serve the Tsaidam. A large dam at Kwantung on the Yungtung-ho serves Peking and district, but the actual output is not available. Among the many water conservancy projects in the Hwai-ho basin, the main achievement from a hydro-electric point of view is the dam at Futzeling, built in 1954, which develops 11,000 kW. All the above were built with Russian assistance.

Great publicity has been given to the completion in 1965 of the Sinan (Hsinan) Dam in Chekiang. It is 105 m high and has been built entirely to Chinese design and by Chinese workmen. It already has four 72,500 kW generators and can accommodate a further five, giving a total of 652,500 kW. It serves the power grid linking Hangchow, Shanghai and Nanking and also the farming population of the delta area[32]. Far-reaching plans for the Yangtze Kiang development have been mentioned on p. 68, but these projects have not yet been started.

NUCLEAR POWER

The explosion of nuclear bombs in the Taklamakan Desert in the vicinity of Lop Nor gives some indication of the great advance that Chinese physicists, engineers and technicians have made in these fields.

Growth of Electric Power. (*From* Ten Great Years, Foreign Language Press, Peking)
(million kWh)

1949	4,310
1950	4,550
1951	5,750
1952	7,260
1953	9,200
1954	11,000
1955	12,280
1956	16,950
1957	19,340
1958	27,530

REFERENCES

[1] CHANDRASEKHAR, S. *China's Population*, Hong Kong University Press, Hong Kong, 1959
[2] LIN NAI-JUI. 'Population Problems in China', *Contemporary China*, Vol. 1, 1956–57, Hong Kong University Press, Hong Kong, 1958
[3] HU HUAN-YUNG, *Wen Hui Pao*, 21 Mar. 1957
[4] WU YUAN-LI. 'Principal Industrial Cities in Communist China', *Contemporary China*, Vol. V, Hong Kong University Press, Hong Kong, 1961–62
[5] *Ten Great Years*, Foreign Language Press, Peking, 1960
[6] CHANDRASEKHAR, S. *Communist China Today*, Asia Publishing House, Bombay, 1962
[7] MAO TSE-TUNG. *On the Correct Handling of Contradictions Among the People*, Foreign Language Press, Peking, 1957
[8] COWAN, C. D. (Ed.) 'Ma Yin-Chi on Population', *The Economic Development of China and Japan*, Allen, London, 1964
[9] *Nan-fang Jih-pao*, Canton, 14 Apr. 1965
[10] FREEBERNE, M. 'Birth Control in China', *Population Studies*, Vol. XVIII, No. 1, 1964
[11] TREGEAR, T. R. *A Geography of China*, University of London Press, London, 1965
[12] DICKERMAN, N. 'Mineral Resources of China', *Foreign Mineral Survey*, U.S. Bureau of Mines
[13] BALAZS, E. *Chinese Civilization and Bureaucracy*, Yale University Press, New Haven, Conn, 1964
[13a] MARCO POLO. *The Travels of Marco Polo, the Venetian*, Bk. II, Ch. XXIII
[14] *China Yearbook*, Tientsin Press, 1925
[15] *Peking Review*, No. 17, 22 Apr. 1966
[16] *N.C.N.A.*, 27 Dec. 1958
[17] *N.C.N.A.*, 22 Oct. 1964
[18] Chi Cheng-ju. 'Opening a Vast Coalfield', *China Reconstructs*, Oct. 1964
[19] Sun Ching-chih (Ed.). *Economic Geography of North-east China*, Peking, 1959
[20] 'From Dependance on "Foreign Oil" to Basic Self-sufficiency in Petroleum', *Shih-shih Shou-tse (Current Events)* No. 8, 1964
[21] CLAPP, F. G. *Petroleum Science*, 1 (1938) 139
[22] ROGERS, W. S. S. *History of Industrial Development in U.S.*, 1941
[23] CHANG KUEI-SHENG. 'Geographical Bases for Industrial Development in North-west China', *Econ. Geog.*, XXXIX (1963) 341–350
[24] HEENAN, B. 'Chinese Petroleum Industry', *Far Eastern Economic Review*, Nos. 5, 13 and 16, 1965
[25] YEN ERH-WEN. 'Oil to Dominate Old China', *China Reconstructs*, Apr. 1966
[26] N.C.N.A., Lanchow, 24 Apr. 1965
[27] MacDOUGALL, COLINA. 'Production Reports', *Far Eastern Economic Review*, 29 Sept. 1966
[28] *N.C.N.A.*, Peking, 1 Sept. 1966
[29] PAO KUO-PAO. 'The Role of Electric Power in the National Economy', *Hsin Chien-she (New Construction)*, No. 4, 20 Apr. 1965
[30] *N.C.N.A.*, Peking, 16 Sept. 1965
[31] *Far Eastern Trade*, Jan. 1966
[32] *Peking Review*, 15 Oct. 1965

8

INDUSTRIAL DEVELOPMENT

DEVELOPMENT OF MODERN INDUSTRY

AT the beginning of the twentieth century modern industry in China was still in its infancy. By far the larger proportion of man-made articles in use by people throughout the land were produced by hand in small local workshops: agricultural tools, such as hoes and plough-share tips, and domestic utensils in local foundries and blacksmiths' shops; cloth by hand loom in cottages or small workshops; food processing and flour milling either in the home or local mill.

Such modern industry as there was, was distributed near the coast or along the banks of the Lower Yangtze, notably in the Treaty Ports at Shanghai, Tientsin, Wuhan, Hangchow and Wusih, and was involved mainly in mining and smelting, textiles, the processing of foodstuffs and public utilities (water and electricity supplies). Between 1895 and 1913 there were 136 foreign-owned firms and 549 Chinese-owned firms, which might be termed modern and which were engaged in these activities. The former contributed about 45%, of which nearly 50% was British and 25% Japanese, and the latter 55% of the total capital employed. The total capital involved amounted to between £30 and £35 million. Foreign interests were centred mainly on mining and smelting, followed by foodstuffs, textiles and public utilities. Chinese firms concentrated more on textile manufacture, then on mining and smelting, public utilities and foodstuffs[1].

Western European demand during World War I gave considerable impetus to Chinese industry. From that time on, until the outbreak of the Sino-Japanese War in 1936, industrial expansion was continuous, albeit fitful owing to political circumstances. Its location in China Proper remained along the littoral and along the Yangtze as formerly. From 1927 onwards, following the Northern Expedition, there was growing hostility towards foreign firms, all of which were regarded as products of imperialism, and industry fell increasingly into the hands of Chinese capitalists and *entrepreneurs*. The years 1945–1949 following the war were marked by civil war, political corruption and financial chaos due to inflation (see *Rise of Communism*, pp. 15–24). Industry was brought to its lowest ebb for two decades. Such was the inheritance the Communists entered into and out of which they have since attempted to build a modern industrialized, socialist state.

We have already examined at some length the steps taken to this end in the agricultural field. In the industrial and commercial sphere, six periods are clearly discernible between 1949 and 1967:

(1) 1949–1952 was a time of recovery and rehabilitation in every aspect of national life. In industry it meant the immediate halting of inflation, the taking of the first steps of Government penetration into control of industry, the control of banks and the establishment of Government trading companies, which took over the entire wholesale trade. Prices and wages were successfully pinned to an index based on five commodities: rice, flour, oil, coal and cotton[2]. Central control was firmly established and opposition, particularly that of

199

manufacturers and traders, was met by two campaigns, known as the 'three anti' and the 'five anti'. Recovery during this period was not assisted by the floods and poor harvests of 1949 or by participation in the Korean War, 1950. It was during these three years that the bases for the First Five-year Plan were worked out.

(2) 1952–1956. During this period, which largely coincides with that of the First Five-year Plan (1952–1957), a great deal of socialization of industry took place. By 1956, private enterprise in China had virtually ceased to exist except for a few small traders, having been taken under State-owned or joint State-private management[3]. Of the gross industrial output in 1956, 54·6% was produced by State-owned enterprises, 27·1% by joint State-private ownership, 17·1% by co-operative industry and only 1·3% by individual and private capitalists[4]. Nearly all produce from mine and factory was sold at the State or co-operative stores, which undertook distribution to the consumer. The individual handicraftsman or peasant was not allowed to sell his produce privately in a free market. This was a period of increasing bureaucratic control.

After 'Liberation' in 1949, it was the intention of the Central Government to carry out economic development of the country along the Russian pattern in a series of Five-year Plans. Accordingly, in 1952, the Finance and Economic Affairs Committee instituted the State Planning Commission, under the chairmanship of Li Fu-ch'un, which then formulated the First Five-year Plan[5]. Although the plan was launched and work started in 1953, it was not officially inaugurated until July, 1955, when Li Fu-ch'un made a speech to the First National People's Congress. Many reports of progress and achievement have been issued, but no comprehensive outline of the plan has been made public.

Some idea of the importance and emphasis placed on industrial development, as distinct from agricultural, social and cultural, can best be obtained from the proportions of capital allocated for investment in these fields between 1953–57: Industry 58·2%, Communications 19·2%, Agriculture, including water conservancy, 7·6%, Education and Public Health 7·2%.

Industries were grouped and placed under the control and direction of ministries of the Central Government: Electrical Power, Coal, Petroleum, Metallurgical, Chemical, Building Materials, Machine Building, Electrical Equipment, Timber, Textiles, Food Industry and Light Industry.

The total capital to be invested in all fields was 42 billion yuan or approximately £6,000,000,000. Of industry's share, 88·8% was destined for new construction and modernization in heavy industry—an indication of how small consideration was given to consumer goods and needs during the period.

The main objectives were the building of 694 important large factories and mines, of which 156 were to receive help from the U.S.S.R. and were to form the backbone of the whole industrial reconstruction. The 156 concerns covered all branches of industry. They included the extension of the already very large Anshan Iron and Steel Works, the building of new, integrated steel plant at Wuhan and Paotow and 17 other smaller plants, 15 electric power stations each with more than 50,000 kW capacity, 31 coal mines with more than 1 million ton p.a. capacity, a dozen or more machine, tractor and car factories, 23 new cotton mills, leading to an increase by 1·5 million spindles and 6 sugar refineries each with an annual capacity of 50,000 ton. The reasons given for small investment in light industry were that many existing works, such as cigarette factories, were working far below capacity and that such factories were dependent on raw materials, the increase in production of which would, of necessity, be slow*.

Planning of production was based on the fixing of annual targets for factories and works within each industry, a method fraught with many pitfalls. All planning requires close co-ordination between all branches of industry and must be backed by adequate information and a highly qualified and incorruptible civil service. Happily, during this period accurate information became increasingly available as the new State Statistical Bureau grew and developed a good professional standard. A highly qualified civil service was not immediately available and had to be developed by hard experience. In view of the corruption which ran through K.M.T. administration, the rapid achievement of a high standard of honesty was remarkable. Remarkable, also, was the quickly rising standard of technical efficiency, which was greatly helped by Russian aid and which resulted in the lowering of production costs, particularly in the iron and steel and mining industries.

(3) 1956–1958. There was considerable murmuring in agriculture and industry against so much central bureaucratic control. Consequently there was some relaxation and some free markets were reintroduced. In March, 1957, Mao Tse-tung made his famous 'Let a Hundred Flowers Bloom' speech to intellectuals, inviting freer criticism. This criticism came with greater force and volume than was anticipated. In spite of the undoubted achievements in production under the First Five-year Plan, the planners came under heavy criticism from C.C.P. academic economists, notably from Ma Yin-ch'u. Ma attacked the entire basis of target planning as being too crude and giving too little consideration of what was the optimum in each field, that over-centralization and bureaucracy led to loss of flexibility, and that departmentalism led to lack of co-ordination and the formation of water-tight compartments. He wanted more care and research and less haste before embarking on new schemes and new machines. He criticized the too rapid movement of industry away from the littoral into the interior as being wasteful of capital and skilled labour and advocated the greater use of price increases as an incentive to production—now known in China as 'economism'[6]. For his pains Ma Yin-ch'u was demoted and disgraced, and criticism suppressed. This period of relaxation of central control was short-lived, brought to an end by the Great Leap Forward and the sudden birth of the communes.

(4) 1958–1960. The Second Five-year Plan started in 1958 and, as with the First Plan, was accompanied by no overall or detailed blue-print of targets for the 5 years. The general aim was to increase the tempo of production; a slight change in favour of agriculture was indicated. 'In that year (1958), the Chinese Communist Party's Central Committee and Comrade Mao Tse-tung, having summed up the experience gained in the First Five-year Plan, put forward the general line of going all out, aiming high and achieving greater, faster, better and more economical results in building socialism. That general line inspired the whole Chinese people with still greater keenness and determination to rely on their own efforts and work energetically to make their country strong and prosperous . . . In the years 1958–60, investment in capital construction was greatly increased and far exceeded that in the whole First Five-year Plan'[7]. This was the mood which led to the fantastic and fanatical outburst of energy and enthusiasm, known as the Great Leap Foward. These upsurges of effort are an essential part of Mao's philosophy of struggle as the essence of life[8]. Its manifestation on the agricultural side was the creation of the communes. On the industrial side it took the form of the self-imposition of higher and ever-higher targets of production.

* Information from notes at an interview with Hsueh Po-ch'ao in Peking, December, 1955.

Emulation was the keynote. Peasants turned from their fields to iron smelting; Great Britain's steel production was to be surpassed by 1972, and so on. The movement had as its object 'communism in our time'. It was largely spontaneous and apparently no carefully organized planning preceded it. Near economic anarchy resulted. Although there was a great increase in production—the Second Five-year Plan was said already to have been fulfilled by 1960—it was unco-ordinated, and resulted in many casualties. Not least of these was the collapse of the Statistical Bureau, crushed under the weight of an inflow of over-optimistic and often quite unrealistic returns. Since this collapse, no firm figures of production for the whole country have been published, but only percentage increases.

(5) 1960–1963. The Great Leap Forward came to a sudden end and was succeeded by a policy of 'readjustment, consolidation, filling-out and raising standards'. It was admitted that 'during that period (1958–60) some new problems cropped up in our economic development. First, for three successive years, 1959–61, China was struck by exceptionally severe natural calamities—mainly prolonged droughts and serious floods and water-logging . . . Second, while all branches of industry registered increases in productive capacity during 1958–60, the rate of increase was not even. This caused certain discrepancies between industries producing raw and other materials and processing industries. . . . Third, in July, 1960, the Soviet Government unexpectedly withdrew all the 1,390 Soviet experts working in China, tore up 343 contracts and supplementary contracts on the employment of experts, and cancelled 257 items of scientific and technical co-operation . . . It was against that background and in view of the above-mentioned considerations that the policy of "readjustment, consolidation, filling out and raising standards" was formulated.'[7] Apart from the factors listed above by Fang Chung, the withdrawal of labour from agriculture during the 'Great Leap' was a significant contributor to the disorganization that followed. In addition to the acute food shortage, industry, especially light industry, suffered from lack of agricultural raw materials. Attention was therefore turned to the re-establishment of agriculture, which became a first charge on industry. As we have seen, industry was required to concentrate on the production of agricultural machinery, fertilizer and irrigation and drainage equipment. The proportion of capital investment going to agriculture and essential raw materials was considerably increased. Heavy industry was also directed to make strenuous efforts to strengthen its extractive side, and industry as a whole was required to increase the variety and raise the quality of its products. Finally, the policy looked to a better integration and co-ordination of the whole industrial system.

(6) 1964–67. Successive good harvests and annually increasing agricultural production since 1964 has caused attention to turn once again to the production of heavy iron and steel goods, to the formulation of a Third Five-year Plan and talk of another 'Leap Forward'. Another great revolutionary upsurge, known as the Cultural Revolution, took place throughout 1966. The motivation behind this new movement is complex and in some aspects obscure, but undoubtedly, in large measure it lies once again in Mao Tse-tung's insistence on struggle as the staff of life and in his fear that the young, on-coming generation, which has not known the hardships faced by the old guard, will become soft and revolutionary fervour lost. Hence the formation of the Red Guards. It remains to be seen how deeply their activities have affected the smooth development of industry.

Before turning to a detailed examination of the main industries, a brief glance at some of the economic and social handicaps suffered and advantages enjoyed by China in its present industrial development will be useful.

202

One of the great handicaps since 1949 has been the securing of adequate capital for its vast planned expansion. Apart from loans received from Soviet Russia in the early years, China has had to rely on her own resources. Russian help, £100 million in 1950 and £400 million in 1954, was only a small proportion of the £6,000 million budgeted for the First Five-year Plan. Nevertheless it was very valuable as the loans were supplied largely in the form of complete plant, enabling individual industries to start production quickly. For the rest, the Central Government has had to rely on internal saving derived from taxation, from domestic borrowing in the form of loans and bond issues and from profits of Government enterprises. In 1957 taxation accounted for just over half the revenue and state enterprises just under half. Loans, etc. amounted to a mere one-thirtieth. U.S.S.R. loans were short-termed and were repaid mainly in grain and agricultural raw materials. Since the strained relations between the two countries in 1960, China has had no outside assistance in capital, which accounts for the persistent propaganda on the need for 'self-reliance'.

It was only after the Boxer Indemnity money was utilized for overseas education that Chinese students went abroad in any significant numbers. Even so, comparatively few received education in industry or technology during the first half of the twentieth century. Consequently, China was ill-equipped with trained technicians, engineers and managerial personnel to undertake the tasks before it in 1949. Hence great effort has been put into the development of large technical colleges and institutes throughout the country. The natural industriousness and application of the Chinese has gone a long way already to offset this disadvantage and the initial shortage of trained personnel is rapidly being overcome.

The Chinese have long been an inventive people (see p. 8). This ability they have turned to good account in meeting the many industrial handicaps, which have confronted them through their lack of modern equipment. They have also made wide use of the advantage which socialized industry has over private enterprise in the freer sharing of new ideas and inventions. In agriculture and in industry, when a new method is evolved or a new machine or process invented, there is an eagerness to make it available as generally as possible.

Leading Industrial Centres

Anshan	Leading integrated iron and steel centre (rolled steel, seamless tubing, angle steel, rails, cables). Coal. Large Chemical Works. Cement.
Canton (Hwangchow)	Textiles. Machinery. Chemicals, Cement. Many new small works.
Changchun	Machine tools. China's biggest motor vehicle plant, making Liberator and Red Flag trucks, limousines.
Chengtu	Oil refinery with capacity of over 1 million ton p.a. Chemicals. Machinery. Textiles.
Chungking	Integrated iron and steel plant (steel ingots, rolled steel, low-alloy steel). Agricultural machinery. Lorries, vans and 40-seater coaches. Chemical fertilizers.
Fushun	Coal. Steel. Chemicals. Oil refinery (shale).
Fusin	Coal.
Hangchow	Textiles (silk and cotton). Chemicals.
Harbin	One of the major machine-building centres (hydro-turbines). Textiles, oil refinery.

203

Hofei	New small iron and steel works. Textiles.
Huhehot (Hu-ho-hao-te)	Woollens. New small steel works.
Hwainan	Major colliery. Chemicals.
Kirin	Chemical fertilizer. Steel. Oil refinery.
Kunming	Small iron and steel works. Milling and boring machines. Textiles. Chemicals.
Kweiyang	Coal. Iron and Steel. Textiles. Chemicals.
Lanchow	Large oil refinery. Oil equipment. Coal. Chemicals. Textiles (wool).
Lhasa	Small pharmaceutical factory. Turbine pumps. Fertilizer.
Loyang	Large car and tractor plant. Large ball-bearing plant. Oil refinery. Textiles (cotton).
Luta (Talien and Lushun)	Chemicals. Machinery. Shipbuilding. Textiles.
Maanshan	Coal. Iron and steel (rolled steel).
Nanking	Large motor vehicle plant. Machinery (gears, precision instruments, optical, transistors, medical). Chemical fertilizer and insecticides. Cotton cloth and yarn. Oil refinery.
Nanning	Rice transplanter factory.
Paotow	Integrated iron and steel plant.
Peking	Many medium and small factories. Textiles and synthetic fibres. Precision instruments. Chemicals.
Shanghai	Seamless steel tubing. Rolled steel. Tractors. Shipbuilding. Machinery. Precision instruments. Textiles. Synthetic fibres. Chemicals and fertilizers. Food processing.
Shenyang	Major heavy and light machine making (lathes of all kinds). Transformers. Big textile centre. Cement. Chemicals.
Sian	Steel. Machinery. Textiles. Chemicals.
Taiyuan	Integrated heavy iron and steel works. Chemicals. Machinery (casings). Textiles.
Tangshan	Steel and machine works. Textiles. Cement. Oil refinery.
Tatung	Steam and diesel locomotives. Coal.
Tientsin	Steel and rolling mills. Machine tools. Chemical fertilizer machinery. Textiles (spinning). Pharmaceutical products. Electrical instruments. Tobacco.
Tsingtao	Steel. Machinery. Textiles. Chemicals.
Urumchi (Tihwa)	Iron and steel. Cement. Agricultural machinery. Textiles. Nitrogenous fertilizer plant.
Wuhan	Integrated iron and steel works. Machine tools. Walking tractors. Agricultural pumps. Shipbuilding plate. Textiles. Tobacco.

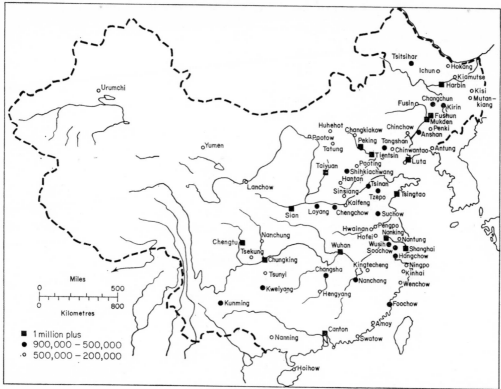

Map 65. Principal industrial cities in China. Note very rapid growth of cities of 500–200,000 in the far north-east. Absence of cities of over 200,000 in the west. (Compiled from Yuan-li Wu, 'Contemporary China', Vol. V, 1961–62)

IRON AND STEEL INDUSTRY

Iron Ore Resources

After his extensive travels and survey in China between 1870 and 1872, Baron von Richthofen was of the opinion that there were extensive iron ore deposits in the country. This opinion ran counter to the generally held view, that the quality and quantity of iron resources was poor in China, and was discredited. The seven reports on the Chinese Mining Industry, which were published between 1921 and 1948, each showed progressive increase in estimated iron ore reserves, rising from 677,899,000 ton in 1921 to 5,432,934,000 ton in 1948[9]. In spite of these figures, the opinion persisted that China was poverty stricken as far as iron resources were concerned. J. S. Lee declared 'It is quite clear that China can never be an iron-producing country of any importance.'[10] George B. Cressey, even as recently as 1955, could write 'There is enough to care for present needs but it is clear that China cannot equal the industrial countries.'[11] These low assessments may have been influenced by the fact that by far the largest reserves, i.e. those of Liaoning (387·5 million ton in 1921), are of a low iron content, which, at that time, was considered very near the economic margin. The deposits in the rest of the country, although less in quantity, were of good quality. The first proper survey of outlying regions of the north-west, and south-west were not undertaken until 1945.

205

Iron Ore Deposits and Iron Content, 1921. (Reprinted from Yuan-li Wu[9] The Steel Industry in Communist China, *by permission of* The Hoover Institution on War, Revolution and Peace, Stanford University. © 1966 by the Board of Trustees of the Leland Stanford Junior University
(thousand metric tons)

	Total iron ore deposits	Total iron content	Percentage
Liaoning	387,580	105,205	27·1
Chahar	69,200	36,200	52·3
Hupeh	52,666	29,780	56·6
Anhwei	50,000	25,125	50·3
Kiangsu	35,000	17,500	50·0
Shantung	29,920	14,138	47·3
Hopeh	22,279	9,234	41·4
Kiangsi	18,060	8,671	48·0
Fukien	7,500	3,650	48·7
Honan	3,400	1,640	48·2
Chekiang	2,300	1,050	45·7

The situation has altered materially since 1949. Extensive surveys have been carried out and new fields discovered. Although no official statistics have been published, it is certain that iron reserves now stand at a much higher figure than formerly. The old prognostics of a country destined to confine its industrial activities to light industry alone have been discarded and China is joining the ranks of heavy industry.

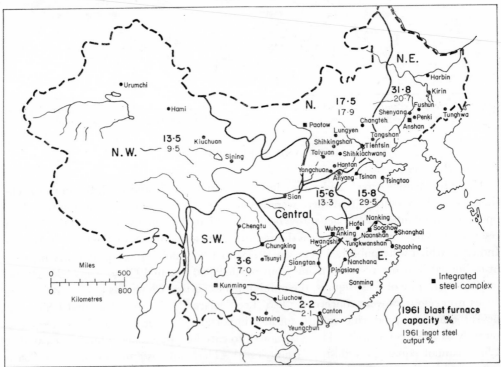

Map 66. Steel centres, 1964. (Compiled from R. Hsia, 'Changes in the Location of China's Steel Industry', C.Q. No. 17, 1964)

Geological prospecting between 1949 and 1957 is stated to have disclosed iron resources at 5,600 million ton and estimated reserves at between 12,000 million and 15,000 million ton, of which three-fifths have an iron content of 30 to 50%[12]. Recently, large iron ore reserves have been reported from east Szechwan, west Kweichow and in north-west Kansu and the Ho-hsi corridor.

Iron and Steel Manufacture

China's first essay into modern iron and steel production was carried out by a progressive viceroy, Chang Chih-tung, who, on his transfer from Canton to Wuchang, Hupeh, bought modern machinery (two blast furnaces and two converters) from Europe and founded the Hanyang Iron Works in 1894, two years before Japan built its first iron and steel works at Yawata. The main purpose of the works was the production of steel rails for the Peking–Hankow Railway. Excellent iron ore was available at Tayeh, halfway between Hankow and Kiukiang. Chang's venture was beset with difficulties from the start, the chief of which were lack of adequate capital, poor management, unsatisfactory supply of coking coal and inefficient transport, which consisted of junks. The concern was taken over by Sheng Hsuen-huai, who formed it into a private company, the Hanyehping Coal and Iron Co. Ltd. in 1908. Although Sheng discovered good coking coal at Pinghsiang in Hunan, the capital cost of developing adequate transport to Hanyang was crippling[1]. Throughout its activities, the lack of capital forced the company to borrow heavily. Between 1902 and 1913 no less than 16 loans were obtained from Japanese banks on the guarantee of continuing shipments of iron ore and pig iron. Thus the Japanese steadily gained control of the Hanyehping Co. Their interest was in the Company's iron ore, which was wanted for the development of their own works at Yawata—an interest they maintained until their defeat in 1945. When the author visited Shihhweiyao in 1948, millions of tons of Tayeh iron ore still lined the river bank, stacked awaiting shipment to Japan, which never materialized owing to U.S. submarine activity towards the end of the war. The world demand for iron and steel during World War I kept production at the Hanyehping works alive until 1919; thereafter it rapidly declined and virtually all smelting had ceased by 1925. Shanghai, during this period, developed a very active engineering and shipbuilding industry, which had very little impact on the indigenous iron and steel industry since practically all the steel used was imported from overseas.

Development of the vast resources of the North-East began soon after the Japanese acquired control of the South Manchurian Railway from the Russians in 1904[13]. The first iron and steel works were built at Penki in 1910; by 1918 30,000–40,000 ton of pig iron were produced. The building of these works at Penki was followed by the foundation of the Anshan Iron and Steel Works in 1919, which have since grown to such great proportions. The industry here was—and still is—well supplied with ample coal and raw materials. Most rapid development occurred after the Japanese annexation of Manchuria in 1931 and particularly after 1936 when the Manchurian Industrial Development Plan was inaugurated[14]. During the 12 years of occupation capacity and production were raised:

Year	Pig iron (ton)	Plant capacity (ton)	Steel production (ton)
1932	368,181	637,750	—
1936	633,393	637,750	344,000
1938	900,000	1,879,760	622,000
1943	1,726,700	2,500,250	837,000

By 1943, which was the peak year of production, there were nine modern blast furnaces in operation. There followed a rapid decline as the Allies gained increasing victory over the

Japanese during World War II. By 1945 work had ceased completely. While Russia was in control of the region (1945–48), she dismantled and removed a great deal of the plant, estimated at 70–80% and valued at U.S. $131 million[9].

As a result of the Sino-Japanese War all iron and steel-producing works in eastern China fell into Japanese hands. The K.M.T. Government and many industrialists retreated west into Szechwan and the south-west, carrying with them what equipment they could. With this and what could be brought in by the Burma Road, some iron and steel industry was developed, but it did not attain any great dimension.

Post-1949 Development of Iron and Steel

We have mentioned the great emphasis that was placed on the development of heavy industry in the First Five-year Plan (p. 200). This is reflected clearly in the statistics, which show the rapid and steady growth of output between 1950 and 1957. The figures also reveal the effect which the Great Leap Forward had on the industry. Disregarding the output of 'backyard furnaces', production of iron and steel was nearly doubled in 1958–59 by stupendous efforts on the part of workers. During the 'Great Leap' it is reported that some 2 million—the figure includes large numbers of rebuilds and replacements—blast furnaces, the majority of which were not more than 10 ft high, were built of mud brick and erected on any piece of waste land available, hence their name 'backyard furnaces'. Lack of adequate blast, reasonable ore and technical knowledge led to the production of about 3 million ton of metal, the vast bulk of which was useless except for the manufacture of simple agricultural tools, such as hoes. The fever, which sprang from the nation-wide desire to achieve industrialization immediately, died and in the confusion which followed, the furnaces were discarded. The better-built, medium sized plant, which was built during this period, has survived and is performing a useful function.

Production of Pig Iron, Ingot Steel and Finished Steel
(thousands of metric tons)

Year	Pig iron	Ingot steel	Finished steel	
1936	670	—	167	
1943	1,883	923	486	
1949	246	158	141	
1950	978	606	464	
1951	1,448	896	808	
1952	1,900	1,349	1,312	
1953	2,175	1,774	1,754	
1954	2,962	2,225	1,965	
1955	3,630	2,853	2,505	
1956	4,777	4,465	3,921	
1957	5,860	5,350	4,260	
1958	9,530	8,000	6,000	
1959	9,500	8,630	9,200	
1960	12,700*	12,000*	12,800*	*Includes 'backyard' production
1963	—	7–8,000	—	FEER estimate 28/2/63
1964	—	8–10,000	—	FEER estimate 4/3/65

In 1958 the C.C.P. Central Committee divided the country into seven economic regions. The iron and steel industry has played a major part since 1949 in this new locational pattern for industry as a whole. The extent and nature of the change is demonstrated in the following statistics given by Ronald Hsia[15].

Location of China's Steel Industry

Regional Distribution of Blast Furnace Capacity

Economic Region	1945* %	1953 %	1957 %	1961 %
N.E.	67·8	59·1	79·6	31·8
N.	19·7	25·1	14·4	17·5
E.	7·6	5·7	4·0	15·8
Central	0·3	0·8	0·5	15·6
S.W.	4·6	9·3	1·5	3·6
S.	—	—	—	2·2
N.W.	—	—	—	13·5

Regional Distribution of Ingot Steel Output

Economic Region	1945*	1953	1957	1961
N.E.	65·3	65·9	67·8	20·7
N.	30·5	24·4	10·7	17·9
E.	1·7	5·5	14·7	29·5
Central	0·6	2·1	4·1	13·3
S.W.	1·9	1·1	2·7	7·0
S.	—	—	—	2·1
N.W.	—	—	—	9·5

* Before Russian dismantling

North-East—The first steps taken after 1949 towards the rehabilitation of industry were centred in the North-East. New, fully automated iron and steel plant was imported from Russia to replace the plant removed in 1945. This was erected by Soviet experts at Anshan, and has become by far the greatest fully-integrated steel complex in China, comparable in size and efficiency to great Western complexes, such as Port Talbot, S. Wales. It contains 10 large blast furnaces. No. 10, the last to be built, has a capacity of 1,513 m³, includes smelting, rolling and finishing mills, and turns out a full range of products from heavy steel girders, rails and steel plates to seamless tubing of all sizes and for all purposes. During the First Five-year Plan it was virtually the only source of materials for the construction of other steel bases[16].

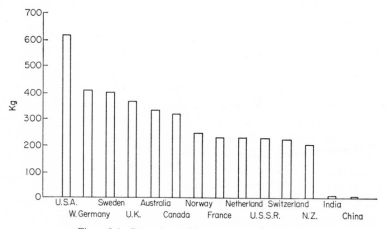

Figure 8.1. Per capita world consumption of steel, 1955

In the early years 1950–57, a great deal of the country's available capital and skilled personnel was concentrated on the development of this centre. Skilled workers from other parts of the country, notably Shanghai, were transferred here in the initial stages and much training was done by the Soviet experts. The withdrawal of Soviet technicians in 1960 was a setback which has been overcome. Anshan remains the main training and steel research centre of the country.

Closely associated with Anshan are the steel works at Penki and Fushun. By 1957 the three centres together had annual capacity of 5,670,000 ton of pig iron—more than double the Japanese peak capacity in 1943. In 1960, Anshan's capacity was 4,170,000 ton of pig iron and 5,570,000 ton of ingot steel. Other large steel centres in the North-East are at Kirin and Tunghwa.

Before 1960, attention was focused mainly on increasing quantity without due regard for the diverse needs of modern industry. Since then emphasis has been increasingly on quality, and Anshan's boast now is that it can meet the most exacting steel requirements and is making steel to thousands of specifications. Although the North-East steel production has continued to increase, its relative position has declined as the other economic regions have progressed.

North China—The Northern Economic Region includes Hopei, Shansi and Inner Mongolia. As the statistics show, it is an important area, producing nearly one-fifth of the country's ingot steel and having nearly one-fifth of its blast furnace capacity.

Its biggest works are at Paotow, the new complex, completed in 1961. This is based on good coking coal from Ta Ching Shan, iron ore from the rich fields to the north at Pai-yun-o-po and local limestone. Owing to the late start in building this complex and to the fact that it came into production just at the time when production throughout the country was being curtailed, its output has not yet been outstanding. The provinces of Hopei and Shansi, however, have many other recently-developed iron and steel centres, outstanding among which are the Iron and Steel Corporations of Taiyuan and Lungyen, which together had a blast furnace capacity of 2,550 m³ in 1961. Here, and particularly in the Eastern Economic Region, there has been a rapid development of converter steel, contrasting with Anshan's predominantly open-hearth steel. Writing of this, R. Hsia says: 'The speedy rise in the importance of converter steel originates from the campaign for small-scale production, which more than the introduction of overall planning has hastened the locational dispersion of China's steel industry.'[15]

East China—Shanghai, which was the only large steel centre in China which was really functioning in 1949, was scheduled under the dispersion of industry plan for reduction in size. As already seen, some of its trained personnel were transferred to the North-East, but this policy was soon reversed. Since then, Shanghai has continued to function and grow as a leading steel manufacturer. It does not rank high as a producer of pig iron. In 1959 No. 1 Iron and Steel Plant built two new furnaces of 255 m³ capacity, but between 1952 and 1957 it increased its ingot steel output from 75,000 ton to 480,000 ton. Whereas before 1949 it drew its raw materials and semi-raw materials from overseas, it now gets them mainly by water transport down the Yangtze. Much of its iron and steel making, which previously had been unco-ordinated, has now been integrated and it is producing high-quality alloy steels, steel plates of all grades, silicon sheet steel, zinc and tin plate, seamed and seamless tubes[17].

East China, which before 1949 had little iron and steel significance apart from Shanghai, has developed very rapidly since 1957. The main growth has been at Maanshan, Tungkwan-shan and Hofei in Anhwei, Nanking in Kiangsu and Tsinan and Tsingtao in Shantung, but there has also been development in a number of other smaller places. During the Sino-Japanese War the Japanese built a small iron smelting plant at Maanshan, based on the rich iron ore of the district. This has now been developed into a medium-size integrated iron and steel complex with a blast furnace capacity of 8,000 m³.

East China is now the leading region in the production of ingot steel. Overall planners are experiencing difficulty in achieving and maintaining a balance between the production of pig iron, ingot steel and finished steel. At present, ingot steel capacity is in excess of the other two[9].

Central China—Iron and steel production in this area, which had ebbed so low as to be virtually non-existent by 1949, has since revived to the extent that, in 1961, it possessed 15·6% of the country's blast furnace capacity and produced 13·3% of its ingot steel output. The revival has been due mainly to the establishment of the Wuhan Iron and Steel Corporation. This great new complex started production in 1958 and was completed in 1961. It is situated about five miles downstream from Wuchang on the right bank of the river. Its plant comprises the largest blast furnace in south-east Asia, very modern open-hearth ovens, rolling mills and refractory material plant, and has an annual capacity of 3 million ton of steel. Its main and subsidiary workshops cover 10 km². The Tayeh mines, which are the main supply of high grade iron ore (50–60%) have been extended and four new mines opened. The ore dressing plant has been modernized, froth flotation and magnetic separation methods for the separation of copper and iron have been installed and the railway has been electrified. Tayeh itself is a considerable ingot steel producer, having four open-hearth and four electric furnaces. Coking coal is obtained from the mines at Pinhsiang, Hunan; Siangtan, Hunan and Hwainan, Anhwei. A new field at Puchi, S. Hupeh, which will reduce transportation costs considerably, has recently been discovered. Iron and steel works have been built at Pingsiang, which, in 1960, had a total blast furnace capacity of 982 m³. Two new combines have also been established at Siangtan, Hunan and Anyang, Honan.

South-West—The development of the iron and steel industry in south-west China, which took place as a result of the Sino-Japanese War, has continued. The Chungking Iron and Steel Corporation, whose original plant came from Wuhan in 1938, considerably expanded its blast furnace capacity during the first two Five-year Plans. The industry here is based on good haematite ore from mines at Kikiang, south of Chungking, and at Kiangyu on the Chengtu-Paoki railway. There is good coking coal around Chungking at Kiangpei, Pahsien, Pishun and Hochwan. The mining is still largely from small pits and awaits fuller development[18].

The most notable expansion has been in Yunnan where the Kunming Iron and Steel Corporation, between 1958 and 1961, built four fairly large blast furnaces, the output of which has begun to rival that of Chungking. Kunming works are served by iron ore from Wuting, 40 km north-west of the city, and from Hwang-chia-tan, also by coal from I-ping-lang. It is intended that the Chungking and Kunming works be developed into fully integrated plant. Kweichow's iron and steel industry is centred at Tsunyi, north of Kwei-yang. Throughout the south-west region a fair amount of wrought iron is still produced by indigenous methods.

Although the pig iron output of the south-west is very small compared with that of the rest of the country, its ingot steel output is quite appreciable. However, the importance of the iron and steel industry of this region should not be measured so much by comparison of output with the northern and eastern regions as by the needs which it serves in this remote area and the saving of transport thus achieved.

South—The southern economic region consists of two provinces, Kwangtung and Kwangsi. It did not figure in iron and steel returns until 1961, when it had 2·2% of the country's blast furnace capacity and furnished 2·1% of its ingot steel output. Its main development is at Liuchow, Kiangsi, where a medium-size iron and steel complex has been built[19]. There is good grade iron ore to the south in the Hung Shui valley. The only supply of good coking coal comes from Fuchung, some 100 km to the east of the city. There is also an iron ore field at Shihlu on the west coast of Hainan, which is reported to have a reserve of 200 million ton of high grade ore (54–67%), easily worked and containing only a very small admixture of phosphate, sulphur and copper. This was opened up by the Japanese during the Sino-Japanese War and then produced 1·5 million ton p.a. If good coking coal can be found, this may well prove to be an important iron and steel centre in the near future.

North-West—The North West Economic Region consists of Sinkiang, Kansu, Shensi and Tsinghai. Like the south, its development has been very recent, but unlike the south, its growth has been very rapid indeed. The reason for this lies in the discovery of rich and extensive iron ore deposits in west Kansu at Chingtiehshan, on the basis of which a large integrated iron and steel complex has been built at Kiuchuan (Suchow), some 80 km east of Yumenshih. The Kiuchuan Iron and Steel Corporation is comparable in capacity and output to Paotow. Other centres of lesser importance but by no means insignificant have been established at Sian, Lanchow, Hami, Sining and Urumchi. In 1960 pig iron and ingot steel capacities, in thousand metric tons, were: Sian (500/450); Sining (400/300); Hami (800/600); Urumchi (800/600)[9]. This development bids to have profound influence on the life and character of the whole north-west region.

NON-FERROUS MINERALS

Recent systematic surveys are proving that China has large resources of non-ferrous minerals, and her potential reserves of tungsten, antimony, tin and molybdenum are now reckoned to be the richest in the world[20]. Great deposits of graphite, manganese, tin, lead, magnetite, gold and antimony were reported to have been discovered in 1957 in the North-East in the Heilungkiang valley. Certain minerals, such as mercury (mercuric sulphide or cinnabar), which is the source of Chinese vermillion paint and red seal-ink, have been known and worked for many centuries, but any exploitation of non-ferrous minerals has been—and for the most part still is—by small-scale indigenous methods.

The research arm of the Geology Department in Nanking University claims to have established a relationship between granite formations and minerals in China, the Caledonian period having an association with gold, the Indo-China and Yenshan periods with tin and the Yenshan period with tungsten[21].

Antimony

Stibnite, the source of antimony, is found in all the provinces of the south-west. The richest deposits are in Hunan and the biggest mine is at Hsikwanshan, west of Changsha. Antimony is a valuable alloy in the manufacture of pewter and of white metal, the much-favoured material for ornaments, trays and urns. It is important in casting printers' type because of its property of expanding at the moment of solidification, and in making bearing metal.

Formerly China was the world's largest producer. Pre-1949 peak production was in 1916, during World War I when 42,800 ton were produced. China's closest competitors at that time were Mexico and Bolivia. The main processing was centred in Hankow. Internal disorders led to decreasing production and finally, as a result of the Sino-Japanese War, China disappeared from the world market, which turned to the Americas for supplies. However, there has been a rapid recovery since 1949. In 1951, antimony exports were again 20,000 ton, the Hsikwanshan mines producing 12,000 ton. With the growing industrialization of the country, internal requirements will probably absorb the greater part of production.

Bauxite

Bauxite is fairly widely distributed throughout the country. Because the manufacture of aluminium is dependent on the supply of cheap and ample electric power, the exploitation of bauxite resources has been very limited in the past. Some development, based on cheap thermal power, occurred under Japanese rule at Penki and Anshan. The building of big multi-purpose dams, generating cheap hydro-electric power may lead to the growth of aluminium production, but the demands of power for irrigation and drainage are likely to have precedence for some time to come. Recently, good deposits of bauxite have been discovered in Kweichow. Their exploitation awaits the development of the Wukiang hydro-electric station.

Copper

In spite of the fact that the Shang and Chou dynasties are famous for their bronzes and that China for two millennia used copper coinage, the annual production of copper during most of that period amounted to a few hundred tons. Records show that the average production between A.D. 847 and 859 was 290 ton. New copper mines were opened in Yunnan by the Mongols during the Yuan dynasty (A.D. 1279–1368). These mines were greatly extended during the Ming dynasty (1368–1644) and by 1727 output had risen to 3 million *catties* (approx. 1,600 ton). The mines were worked by private enterprise under Government supervision through official yardmasters[22]. Production was not maintained. In the 1930s it had fallen to less than 500 ton p.a.

While it was realized that copper deposits were quite widespread, it was generally held that these were limited. The best ores (3–10%) are found in north-east Yunnan at Hwetseh (Tungchwan), in north-west Kweichow at Weining and in west Szechwan. In the North-East the biggest deposits are at Tienpaoshan, near Yenki, Kirin where the ores have a content of 1·7% copper, 6% zinc and 5% lead. Recent surveys have revealed that copper resources are much greater than previous estimates. Discoveries of copper sulphide in the Lanchow area are said to disclose reserves equal to those of Yunnan, and further reserves have been discovered in Ningsia. Total reserves are now reckoned to equal those of Chile.

Gold

Placer gold is reported to be widespread through China, the best deposits being in Heilungkiang, Kirin and Sinkiang. Any production is by indigenous methods and consequently is of negligible quantity.

213

Manganese

It is now estimated that reserves of manganese ore, which formerly were regarded as being very meagre indeed, are ample for China's needs and, moreover, are well located near the iron and steel centres, an important factor, as an average of 14 lb. of manganese is required for every ton of steel[23]. Manganese is distributed widely over southern China and in the North-East. Recently, further deposits, estimated at 700 million ton, have been discovered in Kwangsi[24].

The main producing centres in the south are at Siangtan, near Changsha, Loping near Tayeh, and Mosun and Kweiping in east Kwangsi. The large deposits near Chinchow, south-west Liaoning, were heavily worked by the Japanese, and produced about 10 million ton annually.

Marble

Throughout the centuries fine marble of many varieties has been in great demand for the building of palaces and temples. Examples are the 'white jade' marble so much in evidence in the bridges, steps and balustrades of the Imperial Palace and Altar of Heaven in Peking. The fine and beautifully marked marble of Tali, Yunnan is renowned throughout the country and now figures in foreign trade, Egypt being a keen buyer since 1949.

Mercury

The presence of mercury has been known in China for over 2,000 years and its working is one of China's oldest industries. During the nineteenth century more than 1,000 metric ton were produced annually from a belt of land some 60 miles wide and stretching from south-east Szechwan across Kweichow to western Hunan[25]. Production fell to between 130 and 470 ton p.a. in the early part of the twentieth century and continued to fall during the Sino-Japanese War. No production figures for the post-1949 period are available. The use of mercury in the past has been in the manufacture of vermillion paint and red seal-ink, China's colour for denoting felicity and happiness.

Nickel

Formerly Sinkiang was the only known Chinese source of nickel. This was of a very low grade and of little importance. The first deposits in China Proper were recently discovered in west Szechwan in conjunction with rich sources of mica and asbestos. Szechwan is proving to be one of the richest areas of non-ferrous minerals.

Salt

Salt has always been in short supply throughout the centuries, partly owing to transport difficulties and partly to its production being a government monopoly and therefore regarded as a revenue-raising medium. Today, in addition to increasing domestic demand, the requirements of modern chemical industry are emphasizing its importance and improved communications are making its transport from remote parts possible.

There are three main sources of supply. The coastal evaporation saltfields are sited in Hopei, Shantung, Kiangsu and Liaoning. Changlu, Hopei is the most important centre, producing 93·7% sodium chloride. The brine wells of Szechwan form a second source. Deep drilling in this region dates from the Earlier Han dynasty (206 B.C.–A.D. 24) and has continued to this day. A third and increasingly important source are the huge deposits from the dried lakes in the north-west, notably in the Ningsia Autonomous Region and in the Tsaidam of Tsinghai. 'Tsaidam' is the Mongolian word for 'Salt Marshes'. Here it is estimated that there are reserves of 26 billion tons. Writing of this, K. S. Chang says, 'Part of the 216 mile highway across the region has been built on a bed of salt and even the mile posts are made of salt chunks'[26]. There are vast quantities of potash at Ta-erh-lan and boron at Tatsaidam. Chinese geologists claim to have discovered in this salt lake four previously unknown borate minerals, viz. hungtsaoite (named after the geologist Chang Hung-tsao), carborite, hydrochlorborite and trigonomagneborite[27]. Borate minerals are increasingly important ingredients in high-energy fuels and in the metallurgical and chemical industries.

Tin

China's tin reserves lie in association with the Malayan tin belt. The biggest reserves are found in Kwangsi and extend into southern Yunnan and southern Hunan. The tin veins are associated with granite, which disintegrates and the tin is washed down into the limestone, where, in places, it forms a rich storage of high quality. Being, with copper, an alloy in the making of bronze, it has been worked from very early times. Much the same indigenous methods then used have continued to the present day. Only during the last decade or so have more modern methods begun to be used.

The main mining areas are at Kokiu, near Mengtsz, Yunnan and around Kweilin. During the twentieth century production has varied between 6,000 and 15,000 ton p.a. due to fluctuating world prices of tin and to the political state of the country. Peak production

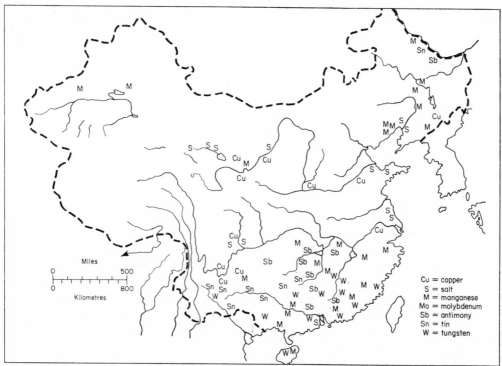

Map 67. Non-ferrous minerals. (While the south and north-east show a wealth of non-ferrous minerals, the blank areas do not necessarily denote a dearth, but only a lack of information)

was achieved in 1938 when 15,540 ton were mined. During the 1930s exports at times exceeded 10,000 ton. No separate figures are available for tin exports since 1949, but appreciable amounts of tin, mercury and antimony have gone to U.S.S.R. annually since that date.

Tungsten (Wolfram)

High-grade wolframite ores were first discovered in south Kiangsi in 1915[25]. By the 1930s China had become the world's largest producer. Production between 1934 and 1944 varied between 5,000 and 18,000 ton of 60% oxide concentrates and represented between 30 and 60% of the world's production.

The ore appears in two main belts, the more northerly of which stretches through south Hunan, north Kwangtung and south Kwangsi. The southern belt runs from Fukien along the coast to Hainan. The most important deposits are at Tayu, south Kwangsi.

Tungsten has proved a valuable earner of foreign currency but, with the growth of national industry and the need for tungsten in the manufacture of all kinds of high grade steel, China's own market is likely to absorb an increasing proportion of its production.

ENGINEERING INDUSTRY

Probably the present engineering industry reflects more clearly than any other branch of industry its close links with the heritage of the past and also its break from it. Modern Chinese engineering is revealing so much of that inventiveness which was so fertile in earlier centuries—the knowledge of magnetism, astronomy, explosive chemistry and the use of many forms of power[28]. However, the Chinese in times past made comparatively little practical use of their inventions. Herein lies the difference between past and present, for today no effort is being spared to exploit to the full every new idea from whatever source.

The long period of quiescence and conservatism in China, during which the West underwent its industrial, commercial and technological revolutions, left the Chinese with a great leeway in all engineering departments, not least the shortage of engineering designers. One method of offsetting this shortage, used effectively since 1949, has been to secure the free interchange of technical and scientific information between factories, colleges and scientific institutes and 'to bring the wisdom of the masses into play', i.e. workers on the factory floor are invited to participate. All are urged 'to compare with, learn from and catch up with the advanced and help those who lag'. A national network co-ordinating research departments in all major factories throughout the country, has been set up.

In the early 1950s it was big national news when a Chinese-built factory started manufacturing so simple a tool as a pneumatic drill for drilling blast holes in mines. In 1967, the fact that China is making, in plant of her own designing and building, everything from pins to electronic computers is some indication of the advance and sophistication achieved in these years. The speed with which this has been accomplished has been fraught with dangers and mistakes, particularly in the heavy machine making and motor industries. Since 1960 much greater care is being given to trial testing before going into mass production.

The aim in industry is to achieve basic self-sufficiency. At the end of the First Five-year Plan it was claimed that 60 per cent of the nation's industrial needs were being met internally and that by 1963 this figure had risen to 80%. As standards of living and industrial needs rise, this percentage will require ever-increasing effort to maintain and increase.

Machine Making

China's first plant for producing machinery was erected in Peking in 1883, but it never functioned. Between that date and the inception of the First Five-year Plan, machine building throughout China Proper was confined almost entirely to the assembly of imported parts. During their occupation of Manchukuo, the Japanese developed some machine and tool making in Shenyang, but even this did not attain any great proportions.

Heavy Engineering—It was during the First and Second Five-year Plans that the most striking advances in heavy machine building were made. The work has continued since 1960 but at a slower rate and, as already seen, with the emphasis transferred to agricultural needs. Plant for building the heaviest machinery has naturally been erected either where the raw material is produced or in those places to which it can be transported easily. Thus the greatest centres have grown at Shenyang and Shanghai with Wuhan developing later. Both Shenyang and Shanghai deal with the construction of complete installations such as large hydro-electric power plants, oil refineries, blast furnaces, rolling machines, heavy cranes and steel presses, steam generating equipment and all kinds of mining equipment, including shafts, cutters, loaders, hoists and drills. The Shenyang Heavy Machinery Plant, founded in 1953, mass produces all grades of lathes and has built a big vertical lathe, capable of processing parts up to 1·25 m, and a horizontal 12 ton lathe, 8 m long[29]. It also specializes in turbine rotors. Up to 1965 its turbine rotor casting team, had produced nearly 100 rotors of different and increasing sizes: in 1953 a 10,000 kw rotor for Kwanting Reservoir Hydro-electric Station near Peking; in 1958 a 72,500 kw hydro-electric turbine for Hsinanching Station, Shekiang, and in 1964 it succeeded in casting a 100,000 kw water turbine of first-rate quality in exactness and smoothness[30]. Shanghai engages in similar heavy machine building. The Shanghai Hydraulic Machinery Plant recently built the biggest radial crane and much equipment for hydro-electric power stations. The Kiangnan Shipyard, Shanghai, which built the first 10,000 ton ocean-going freighter, successfully built a 12,000 ton hydraulic, free-forging press, 23 m high with a bed plate of 260 ton and capable of forging 200–300 ton ingots. The significance of this achievement lies not so much in the size of the press, although that is considerable, but in the engineering ingenuity required, since China had no factory equipped to handle such huge parts. Since 1959 Wuhan has rapidly developed its heavy machine building industry and recently produced a vertical boring and turning mill with a diameter of 6·3 m. Tatung is the main centre for building steam and diesel locomotives. Other iron and steel centres, notably Paotow, Harbin, Tientsin and Chungking are now entering the field of heavy machine building.

High Precision Machinery—At the other end of the engineering scale, China has developed her ability and capacity for making high precision machinery with startling rapidity. She is now making highly sophisticated instruments in virtually all fields. These include such items as capilliary spectroscopes, a large microscope with a resolution of X200,000, an electrostatic electronic accelerator with a voltage of several million electron volts, a microbalance accurate to one-millionth of a gram, automatic plasma-cutting equipment for refractory metals, and gear grinding machines for making ball bearing rings. Tientsin recently produced a hot rolling machine for rapid high precision production of fluted twist drills, using one of the very latest industrial techniques in the world[31]. While the main centres of this high precision work are at Shanghai, Tientsin, Nanking and Shenyang, its distribution is now becoming quite widespread.

MOTOR INDUSTRY

No motor vehicles were produced in China before 1949. In 1957 a few 'kaifang' or 'liberation' trucks were trial-produced at Loyang, but until 1958, reliance was placed on imports from U.S.S.R. In that year the Loyang Tractor Plant was opened and production began in earnest. The aim, as in the rest of industry, is to attain self-sufficiency and this, it is claimed, is nearly achieved in all fields of the motor industry, with the exception of saloon cars, a large proportion of which still come from eastern Europe. Attention has naturally been focused on the production of commercial vehicles and, since 1960, particularly on tractor building (see p. 80).

Loyang has developed into the greatest centre of the industry, but many other major plants, all of which are now geared for mass production to serve the 2,200 State tractor systems, have been built throughout the country. These are listed below giving their main specializations.

Loyang	Leading tractor plant, specializing in 75 h.p. 'Tungfanghung', 54 and 40 h.p. tractors and 160 h.p. bulldozers.
Changchun, Kirin	No. 1 Motor Vehicle Plant producing 'liberator' lorries and, recently, 6-seater saloons.
Tientsin	45 h.p. 'Tieh Niu', i.e. 'Iron Ox' tractor, light lorry and cross-country van—9-seater coaches.
Shenyang	Tractors and spare parts.
Nanchang	Tractors and spare parts.
Nanking	New cross-country truck for negotiating southern muddy roads.
Tsinan	8 ton heavy duty 'Yellow River' truck—10 ton two-way tip lorry.
Taiyuan	Taiyuan heavy machine plant—4 m^3 bucket excavator.
Anshan	100 h.p. 'Hung Chi', i.e. 'Red Flag' tractor.
Wuhan	7 h.p. 'Worker-Peasant' hand tractor.
Canton	10 h.p. hand tractor, 3·5 ton 'Red Guard' lorries.
Peking	Diesel-electric trucks and mounted cranes.
Huhehot	Diesel engines.
Chungking	25 ton dumping lorry, vans and 40-seater coaches.

Diesel engines, ranging from 50 to 300 h.p. are in mass production and are reported to be coming off the production line in sufficient numbers to meet current agricultural and industrial needs. Three types of high power, low super-charged diesel engines, ranging from 450 to 1,000 h.p. are being built[32].

CHEMICAL INDUSTRY

It is stated that in 1949 only 100 or so chemical products were being made in China. In 1952 the figure stood at 300; in 1957 at 2,000 and in 1962 at 8,000 and included products in every branch of the chemical industry. In October, 1965 an article in *Far East Trade* declared that 'the industry stood on the threshold of mass or experimental production of everything modern chemistry can make'. This is true, but what proportion is still experimental and what is in mass production is, at present, impossible to ascertain.

The emphasis that has been placed on the production of chemical fertilizer and its widespread manufacture in small plant has been shown on pp. 75–76. In 1949 ammonium sulphate alone and in small quantities was being produced. In 1963 chemical products included ammonium nitrate, ammonium bicarbonate, ammonium chloride, calcium cyanide (lime nitrogen), urea, calcium superphosphate, calcium magnesium phosphate and potassium sulphate.

On the pharmaceutical side there has been a very rapid growth. Chinese chemists are now not merely reproducing western drugs but are producing new ones flowing from their own research. In China, the production of penicillin, aureomycin and syntomycin was developed in the First Five-year Plan and streptomycin, chloromycin and neomycin during the Second Five-year Plan. Chinese chemists are claiming the production of streptomycin by a new technology that produces neither pain reaction nor post-injection fever. In the field of insecticides, antibiotics for the treatment of fruit and animal diseases, especially in relation to virus pneumonia in pigs, are being produced. Many of these pharmaceutical products are made in the chemistry laboratories by scientists and laboratory technicians and await mass production.

The manufacture of plastics has developed only since 1958, progressing very rapidly from celluloid and bakelite to a wide range of polythylene and cellulose products. In 1965, 26,000 ton of plastics for farming and industrial use were produced—five times the 1964 output. Of these 12,000 ton were for farm use, particularly polythene sheeting for the protection of rice seedlings. The use of plastics in this way claims to bring 10% increase in rice yield.

The largest chemical centres are at Kirin, Shanghai, Tientsin, Taiyuan and Lanchow.

BUILDING INDUSTRY

While China is justly famous for the beauty of its architecture, it is remarkable how comparatively little of its ancient buildings has survived the passing of the years. This low survival quotient is undoubtedly due, in part, to the ravages of war and internal unrest, but it is also due to the nature of the material used. Traditionally, the framework of buildings has been of timber, stone or brick being merely the infilling material. It is true that there are many stone monuments such as the beautiful Altar of Heaven in Peking and the An-chi Bridge at Chao-hsien, Hopei, but the greater proportion are timber structures as in the Imperial Palace and the Temple of Heaven. This is also true of humbler dwellings, which, in south and Central China are almost exclusively constructed of wood frame and baked or mud brick, *sha-mu* (Cunninghamia sinensis) which is resistant to white ant, generally being used for the wooden structure.

The amount of building construction which has taken place in China since 1949 is breath-taking, although not surprising since it is essential and complementary to the industrial and agricultural revolution. Writing of this, Kang Chao says, 'China in the first decade of the Communist rule had put out houses, buildings, roads, dams, reservoirs, etc. at a higher rate than industrial and agricultural goods'[33]. In the early years of this decade the question of style and quality of building was hotly debated—whether emphasis should be laid on high quality and beauty in the Chinese tradition or whether speed, cheapness and utilitarian needs should be the criterion. So far as dwellings and most industrial plant are concerned the latter has been the guide. Houses and workers' tenement blocks are usually built of drab grey brick. It is reported that over 90% of the walls in China at present are made of small, heavy solid clay bricks, which have poor heat and sound insulating properties[34]. Attention is now being given to this problem and new types of composition brick of cinder, coal ash, fly ash, oil shale or blast furnace slag mixed with aerated concrete are being used.

For the bigger industrial works, public buildings, sports arenas and halls reinforced concrete is used. In consequence there has been a vast expansion of the cement industry. In the 1920s demand for cement was small and was met largely by imports from Germany and Japan, and from the Green Island Cement Works in Hong Kong. In China only eight cement works existed and some of these were very small; the largest was the Chee Hsin Works at Tongshan, Hopei. After the Sino-Japanese War there was some development, and a large new cement works was built at Shihhweiyao, near Tayeh, Hupeh and opened in 1948. This was reputed at the time to be the biggest works in South-east Asia, having a capacity of 2,000 ton/day. It was well sited, being based on local coal and excellent local limestone.

Since 1949 cement production has leapt ahead, rising from less than 1 million ton p.a. to 7 million ton in 1963, and 9 million ton in 1964 and is still rising. In 1964 there were 12 plants, each producing between 700,000 and 200,000 ton p.a., and some 80 smaller works producing less than 100,000 ton p.a.[35]. In 1963 the first large cement works entirely designed and built by the Chinese was opened in Sitsun, Canton. This plant has an output of 400,000 ton p.a. and a rotary kiln of 125 m. Recently, however, the emphasis has been on building small shaft kilns of about 20,000 ton p.a. capacity on the grounds that these entail less capital outlay, are quick to build, are economical in fuel and transport, and serve local needs. The boast now is that every province, municipality and autonomous region has its own cement plants. Attention has turned to the grading of cement. There are now twenty varieties in production, including high grades for bridges, reservoirs, dams and the oil industry.

No figures are available showing the amount of timber cut since 1949 to meet constructional demands, but the increase must be very great indeed. Forestry authorities affirm that afforestation is taking place at an even greater rate than timber cutting.

LIGHT INDUSTRIES

Textile Manufacture

Silk—The beginnings of sericulture are sunk in the depths of Chinese mythology when, some 4,000 years ago, Hsu Lung-she is reputed to have discovered the art of reeling and weaving silk. Legend, which has the backing of Stein in his *Ancient Khotan*, has it that the Chinese guarded their secret of silk rearing and making until A.D. 419, when a Chinese princess, who was given in marriage to the King of Khotan, smuggled silkworm eggs and mulberry seeds in her baggage. Until then China has been the sole producer of silk and had enjoyed a lucrative trade with the West along the famous 'Silk Route' through Sinkiang[13]. Despite the loss of her monopoly and the development of sericulture in the West, China continued to be the main supplier to foreign countries and was still responsible for half the silk trade of the world at the turn of this century. In 1915 she exported 145,457 lb. of white, yellow, re-reeled and steam filature silk, 45,338 lb. of wild silk, 45,569 lb. cocoons and 156,592 lb. of waste silk. Wild silk at that time commanded a good market as it was considered the best material for aeroplane wings. From this date on until the middle of the 1950s, with the exception of a short prosperous period 1929–1932, the market rapidly declined[36]. This was due largely to Japanese competition and the development of synthetic fibres, but it was also due to poor organization, antiquated machinery, and carelessness and ignorance. Some effort was made to resuscitate the industry between 1932–36, but the Sino-Japanese War brought the industry to a very low ebb.[37]

The main silk reeling and weaving areas are sited in the cocoon-raising areas. White silk, the chief producing areas of which are in the Wusih district of Kiangsu and Shaohsing district of Chekiang, is processed mainly in Shanghai, which also carries out 90% of the printing and dyeing. Other centres are at Hangchow, Huchow and Hankow. A considerable amount of white silk is also produced in Kwangtung and is processed mainly in Canton. Yellow silk from Szechwan, Yunnan and Shantung, and wild silk, the product of silkworms fed on oak leaves, from the North-East and Shantung, is less well organized. The industry, although now under commune direction and somewhat better managed, is still largely a cottage industry. The machinery used is generally obsolete and the methods still primitive. Efforts are being made, especially in Chekiang, 'the home of silk', and Kiangsu to raise standards and to create new patterns, fabrics and motifs, but the silk industry everywhere faces severe competition, not only from new textiles, but also from the demand for land for food crops. It is a very uphill task.

Cotton—It comes as a surprise even to people familiar with China to learn that the ubiquitous indigo-blue cloth, worn by the masses of Chinese peasantry, is a comparatively recent innovation. Although the cotton seed was introduced into China as early as the eleventh century, its cultivation was little developed, possibly due to the opposition of the sericulturalists whose interests it would have challenged. The clothing of the common people was made from natural fibres, such as hemp and rami and from wild and waste silk. Cotton clothing remained a luxury of the rich until the latter part of the nineteenth century when foreign cotton cloth began to be imported in quantity and American varieties of cotton seed were introduced.

In the early 1920s cotton-growing was greatly extended in two belts, one along the Yangzte valley with main concentration in Kiangsu and Hupeh, and one in the Hwang-ho basin mainly in Honan and in the Wei-Fen valley. At this time all indigenous varieties were short staple of 0·7 in or less, but had the advantage of a high lint yield and relative freedom from pests to which the longer staple, imported American varieties were prone. By the 1930s Chinese production of cotton lint was averaging some 800,000 ton p.a. In spite of the development of modern textile mills in Shanghai, Tientsin and Wuhan, the demand for cotton cloth greatly exceeded national output and large amounts of cotton cloth and raw cotton were imported. A good deal of spinning and weaving of locally-grown cotton was done by the peasantry in their own homes.

Since 1949 a great deal has been done to extend the cultivation and the manufacture of cotton. Research into methods of cultivation and new varieties has not only increased output in the established and high-yielding areas of Kiangsu, Hupeh, Honan and Shensi, but has opened up new or previously little-developed regions. New varieties have enabled Liaoning, which has only 150–160 frostless days, to produce successfully long-staple cotton. Kunming, by means of new cultivation methods, is now also successfully growing long-staple cotton. Irrigation has greatly extended the growing area and output of Sinkiang and the north-west. As a result, production of raw cotton rose from a pre-war peak of 850,000 ton to 1·3 million ton in 1952, 1·65 million ton in 1957 and 2·4 million ton (planned) in 1962. Although no firm figures have been published since, reports from all districts since 1963 indicate that this upwards trend has been maintained.

The spinning and weaving industry, which was concentrated so much in the eastern provinces, most notably in Shanghai and Tientsin, has been greatly extended. New mills have been built in every cotton-producing area and many old mills have been renovated. The output of cotton yarn rose from 1,800,000 bales in 1949 to 6,100,000 bales in 1958 and cotton cloth from 1,890 million metres in 1949 to 5,700 million metres in 1958. Since 1963 it is claimed that production has increased by 15 to 17% p.a. In 1965, 46 new textile mills (37 cotton, 6 printing and dyeing and 3 silk weaving) were opened in provinces as far apart as Sinkiang and Kwangsi, adding in all 1·4 million spindles, capable of producing enough yarn for 1,230 million metres of cloth. The cotton mills built in 1965 included one of 150,000 spindles and 2,400 looms[38] in Wuhan (the largest in the city) and one of 50,000 spindles and 2,000 looms at Lanchow, the latter having an annual capacity of 46,500 bales of yarn and 56 million metres of cloth. This Lanchow mill, designed and built entirely in China, serves the newly-developed Kansu cotton fields, which are growing good, long-staple cotton[39]. The new cotton-growing areas in the north-west in the Turfan, Urumchi, Manass and south Sinkiang regions have each developed their own cotton industries. Recently there has been a big development in the Wei valley at Sian where the 4th State Cotton Combine of Shensi has built a mill having 100,000 spindles and 4,000 automatic looms with an annual capacity of 66 million metres of cloth.

In the last two years cotton manufacturers have been directed to give more attention to and cater more directly for peasant needs, in consequence of which it is reported that 1,200 million metres of coarse cloth, drills, corduroys, cotton serge and venetians were produced in the first 6 months of 1966. In spite of the very great increase in production which has been achieved in the last 16 to 17 years, cotton cloth is still in very short supply and is still tightly rationed.

Natural Fibres—As mentioned above, the common people of China in times past have relied largely on natural fibres for their clothing. Of these fibres hemp (*ma*) is the most important. It is grown in all provinces, but more intensely in the north and north-east than in the south. In addition to its use as a coarse summer cloth, it is used for all kinds of cordage. Ramie (*ssu-ma* or silk hemp) is, as its name implies, a finer fibre than hemp and weaves into a cloth very similar to linen, which is very acceptable in the hot summer months because its ventilation properties are superior to those of cotton. It differs from hemp in that it is a perennial plant, producing three or four crops a year over a period of about 20 years. Its main production area is in the middle Yangtze basin in the provinces of Szechwan, Hunan, Hupeh, and Kiangsi. It makes fine cordage and canvas. On account of its resistance to water it has been much used for fishing nets, but is now being supplanted by synthetic fibres for this purpose. Hemp and ramie are retted and sun dried to extract the fibre from the stems. Manufacture of both fibres is, for the most part, confined to the regions of production and is carried out in small local mills.

Since 1949 there has been a considerable increase of jute-growing in the Yangtze delta region of Kiangsu and Chekiang and around the shores of the Tungting and Poyang lakes, in the lake-studded lands of Hupeh and also in the delta flats of the Pearl river. Yields of between 3·75 and 5·0 ton/hectare are being achieved[40]. The main jute mills are

222

in Shanghai, Hangchow and Canton. The new mill, on the Soochow Canal near Hangchow has 10,596 spindles and 630 looms, making yarn, gunny bags and jute cloth.

Synthetic Fibres—This is an entirely new industry in China and of very recent and very rapid development. In November, 1964, it was reported that there were already more than 60 textile, knitwear, dyeing and printing mills producing chemical fibre products in polyester, vinylon and chinlon[41]. The main centres are in Shanghai, Peking and Shenyang, but many provinces are now producing significant quantities of polyvinyl chloride fibres, woven in mixtures and made into filter cloth, fishing nets and ropes. These new fibres are more resistant to abrasion, acid and alkalis than natural fibres and are steadily replacing them. A new mill has been opened in Sining, Tsinghai, an area rich in coal, salt and limestone, the raw materials for the manufacture of polyvinyl chloride fibre[42]. By 1965 China's synthetic fibre mills had an annual capacity of between 300–400 million metres, said to be equivalent to the production of 6 million *mow* devoted to cotton and mulberry[43].

Woollens—Apart from the spinning and weaving of local wool in cottages or small works in the north and west, modern manufacture of woollen goods was concentrated in Shanghai, the raw material coming mainly from Australia. With the recent development of new breeds of sheep, producing much finer wool in the Inner Mongolian and Sinkiang steppe-lands, there has been a rapid growth of the woollen industry in the north-west. By 1957 new factories had been built at T'ienshui, Sian, Yulin, Yinchwan, Sining and Urumchi. More recently, a large mill has been opened at Huhehot, employing 100 technicians and 2,000 workers, partly recruited from local herdsmen.

Footwear

In the early decades of this century the usual footwear of the common people was similar to that which had been worn for many previous centuries. There was rarely a household without its board onto which every piece of scrap cloth and rag was pasted until it attained a thickness of between one-quarter and one-eighth of an inch. This was then cut into the shape of shoe soles, industriously sewn through and through to give added strength and stiffness and then attached to a cloth upper. This was essentially women's work and, at least in the countryside, done within each household. Amongst the peasantry this still remains one of the most important forms of footwear. For work in the fields straw sandals or clogs were, and still are, worn, otherwise the peasant goes barefoot. The more wealthy wore cloth or felt shoes or boots with a thick felt sole.

As the century has advanced rubber-soled shoes with canvas or felt uppers have become increasingly popular, until today they are almost universally worn by the younger generations and are regular wear for the army. Hundreds of millions of pairs are being manufactured annually. These shoes and boots have the virtue of being cheap and fairly durable. In the cities, leather footwear is also quite common, the leather coming increasingly from the grasslands of the north and north-west. Black cloth shoes with felt soles are still often used for formal indoor wear.

Production of Rubber Footwear
(1,000 pairs)

1949	28,900
1953	76,360
1958	182,360

223

Food Processing

Apart from specialties, such as Peking Duck, special teas, ginger and dried fruits, which were sent to all parts of the country, food processing formerly was done locally for local consumption. It has been only in the last 60–70 years that it has been carried out on anything approaching a large scale in modern factories.

The modern flour milling industry was started by the Russians in Harbin and spread rapidly in the North-East and along the east coast provinces. In 1925 there were 123 modern flour mills, situated as follows[36]:

Manchuria	50	Shansi	1
Kiangsu	44	Honan	1
Hupeh	9	Anhwei	1
Shantung	6	Hunan	1
Chihli (Hopei)	5	Kiangsi	1
Szechwan	3	Yunnan	1

Tientsin and Shanghai mills relied to some extent on Canadian and U.S. wheat and all mills were handicapped by the irregular supplies of native wheat caused by unsettled conditions and interruption in transport. During succeeding years the milling industry developed, but continued to be handicapped for the same reasons. With the more settled political state of the country since 1949, modern flour mills have sprung up everywhere, particularly in the inland provinces of the north.

The egg products industry before 1949 was organized mainly for export. It was centred mainly in Hankow, which processed (froze, preserved or dried) over 2 million eggs a day at the peak of its production in the late 1920s. There has been no report of the progress of this industry since 1949.

The fact that land used for arable farming is much more productive of food calories per acre than if used for cattle-raising or dairy farming is the main reason why so little milk has been produced in China Proper. Whether a distaste for milk and milk products, particularly in south and central China, has also been a cause of this lack of dairy farming, or whether it has been simply an effect due to unfamiliarity, is an open question. Soyabean milk (*tu chiang*) is used as a substitute, especially for weaning babies. There has, however, been a marked change in habit and taste during the past 20 to 30 years and the demand for milk has risen rapidly. More dairy farming is being done in south China and many milk processing factories have been built in the grasslands of the north and north-west where irrigation is resulting in much better pasture. Inner Mongolia alone had 17 major milk processing factories producing powdered milk, condensed milk, butter, lactose and cheese[44].

The development of fruit and meat canning has also made great progress in recent years. The temperate fruits of the north—pears, plums and peaches—and the sub-tropical and tropical fruits of the south—lichee, tangerine, pineapple, mangoes and peanuts—are now being tinned for both the home and export markets. Beef and mutton are now being canned in increasing quantities in the northern and north-western provinces. Pigs are ubiquitous in China and little canning is done. However, special dried pork from Szechwan is distributed to other provinces.

Cigarettes

Tobacco is said to have been introduced into China from the Philippines during the early part of the sixteenth century and to have spread gradually over the country. By the beginning of the twentieth century nearly every province was growing the tobacco plant. It was used at first mainly medicinally and for snuff, and later for smoking in long thin-stemmed pipes or water pipes which had very small bowls and used only a pinch of tobacco at each filling. This filling occupied almost as much time as the actual smoking. On social occasions, when the men were gathered together, the pipe would be passed round the circle. Thus comparatively little tobacco was used and home supplies were sufficient to meet demand.

In 1913 the British-American Tobacco Co. started a factory in Shantung and began to promote the growing of American leaf. Cigarette smoking quickly became popular and there was a very rapid development of the trade. In the 1930s there were many large factories in Shanghai, Tientsin, Harbin, Mukden, Hankow and Canton. The cigarette-smoking habit has continued to grow and today is widespread—one of the few vices in this puritanical land. Some idea of the recent growth of cigarette manufacture can be gained from the following figures:

Cigarettes (thousand crates)*		Cured tobacco (thousand *tan*)	
1949	1,600	1949	860
1953	3,552	1952	4,430
1958	4,750	1958	7,600

* 1 crate=50,000 cigarettes.

Consumer Goods

Throughout the last 16 to 17 years emphasis has been consistently on the production of capital goods. Propaganda has continually appealed to the people's patriotism and social conscience to work hard, live sparingly and eschew waste. Nevertheless, incentive to effort in the form of increased consumer goods has not been entirely ignored. For the great mass of people there undoubtedly has been some rise in living standards. Evidence of this rise is seen in the continually increasing number of bank deposit accounts of the masses. It is reported that there were 160,000 new fixed deposit accounts opened in Peking in the first 6 months of 1965[45]. More concrete evidence of this rise in living standards is seen in the increasing quantity and variety of goods in the stores and shops—goods almost entirely of Chinese manufacture, such as sewing machines, wrist watches, clocks, vacuum flasks, electric torches, cameras, glass ware, transistor radios and cosmetics. Soaps and detergents are in greater supply. Matches, which formerly were of very poor quality have vastly improved. It used to be said, facetiously, that when one match from a boxful would ignite, then one might as well throw the rest of the box away. Bicycles are now more plentiful and are an important means of transport in the cities and country. In 1949 the annual production of bicycles was only 14,000. It had risen to 165,000 in 1953 and to 1,174,000 in 1958. No later figures are available. Big as these increased figures may appear, they must always be measured in relation to the needs of the 700 million people, who have to be served.

During the Cultural Revolution of 1966–67, Red Guards in various cities conducted campaigns against the possessors of 'luxury articles', such as cosmetics, wrist watches and transistors, highlighting the conflict in approach to life of the 'revolutionist' and the

225

'revisionist'. It remains to be seen what effect this campaign will have on the production of consumer goods in the next few years.

Porcelain

The former world-famous Chinese porcelain fell on evil days after the fall of the Ching dynasty (1911). Even the celebrated kilns at Kingtechen, Kiangsi were turning out very little porcelain of even medium quality. Liling, 20 miles west of Pingsiang, was reduced to one factory, and by 1925 Canton had ceased production. Most of the old glazing secrets were lost in this decline.

Since 1949 there has been a very considerable revival. Some 30 new kinds of glaze have been introduced. Kingtechen has again sprung into activity and new kilns cover a large area. Although some high-quality porcelain for presentation purposes is being turned out, production is being concentrated on meeting the needs of the masses. It is reported that 85 million pieces of glazed ware were produced in 1965[46]. While some of the ware is taken by road, the bulk is transported by river and canal. The kilns at Liling have also been revived and once again are producing under-glazed blue and white porcelain of good quality, which is much in evidence in public utilities such as the railway service. Canton's old-established large works are also in full production, as also are many others scattered through the provinces.

HANDICRAFTS

Handicrafts, which have been the basis of industrial production through the centuries in China, have posed a problem for the planners of a socialist society. Blacksmiths, carpenters, bamboo and coir artisans, stone cutters, embroidery workers and a host of others have worked mainly as independent individualistic units. The economy has been based on the family or household, generally of low productivity and standing low in the social scale.

With the development of the co-operatives and then the communes, attempts have been made to draw these handicraftsmen into the new organization, recognizing that the 'rural handicraft industry is an important component of the collective economy of the people's commune and that it is also "the vanguard" of the handicrafts that give direct aid and support to agriculture'. In 1965 it was estimated that there were about 10 million of these workers in the whole country. That this movement of incorporation has not been easy is evidenced by the following quotation from the *People's Daily*:

'The production teams find it rather difficult to control them. The handicraftsmen themselves are small producers and are spontaneously inclined toward capitalism. They always look for work which pays higher wages and, as a result, the farm implements of some production teams cannot be prepared in good time.'[47]

It has been thought necessary to go slowly and carefully in persuading them to adopt collective ownership and factory organization.

'Handicraftsmen in our country have rich experience in production. They are nimble minded and clever and dexterous in using their hands and are both resourceful and full of inventive spirit. Since the handicraft industry deals mostly with small products, the scale of handicraft enterprise should not be too large and the degree of centralization should not be too high. Attention should therefore be paid to preserving its small and flexible features.'[48]

226

Some success has been achieved in developing training centres for apprentices as in Soochow, the home of art and embroidery work, where a part-work part-study handicraft art centre has been established to teach designing, decoration, restoration and copying of old paintings. More than 1,000 apprentices have passed through the school since 1958[49].

FISHING INDUSTRY

China's shallow coastal waters and many great rivers have proved for many centuries fine fishing grounds. Fish have figured as an important item in the diet of the rich and middle class Chinese. Like pork, however, fish appeared on the table of the peasant only at infrequent intervals, in spite of the fact that most hamlets and villages in central and south China had their ponds in which some fish were bred. Since 1949 it is claimed that fish appears much oftener on the table of the masses. There can be no doubt that there has been a very big increase in the amount of fish taken since that date although some reserve must be placed on the last published figures for 1958, the year of the Great Leap[50].

		Million tons
1949	about	0·5
1952		1·66
1957		3·12
1958		6·03

Sea Fishing

China has a coastline of some 14,000 km, the greater part of which looks out on a wide continental shelf over which the warm Kuro-Siwo current from the south mingles with the cold Kamchatka current flowing southward along the Siberian and Korean coasts. These shallow seas, like the Grand Banks of Newfoundland, are fine fish breeding grounds. Although these grounds have been fished for many centuries, it is only with the introduction of mechanization within the twentieth century that they have begun seriously to be exploited. The Japanese for some decades have fished the region intensively with trawlers and drifters. Only since 1949 has China entered into competition. Most of China's fishing until then was concentrated on in-shore or fairly close off-shore work.

The kinds of fish caught vary somewhat from south to north. The croaker, in one form or another, and the cuttlefish, are found all along the coast. Between the Gulf of Tongking and the mouth of the Yangtze the most typical is the large yellow croaker, a fish of a foot or more in length and having few small bones. Farther north the small yellow croaker is found in large shoals in the Pohai, Yellow and East China Seas. It is the staple food of the fisher folk along the coast. Horsetails, rich in protein and fat, are deep sea fish, which in late summer swim into the shallow seas to spawn. Prawns abound in the Pohai and Yellow Seas. A great deal of these catches is preserved. Most of the large yellow croaker is either sun-dried or canned, although some is frozen. The small yellow croaker is usually salted.

In recent years there has been a big increase in shellfish breeding. In Liaoning the area of in-shore shoals for this purpose has been extended to 13,000 hectares; 50 species are reared, including oyster, corbicula, hard clam ark shell for which the region is famous, abalone and sea scallop[51]. Large amounts of shellfish are also raised in the sheltered bays of the south-east coast. Fukien rears razor clam, surf clam, oysters and ark shell. 10,000 ton of oysters are harvested in Santu Bay alone[52]. The artificial culture of kelp (*laminaria japonica*) together with red laver and agar is also being energetically pursued. This edible seaweed, which is the source of iodine and other industrial materials, was formerly raised only in the colder waters of the north.

Since 1949 mechanization has gone on apace. The main fishing all along the coast is now done by motorized junks. Although China now has shipyards specializing in the construction of trawlers, drifters and seine fishing boats, the main concentration during these years has been on the conversion of junks. A trawler costs 500,000 *yuan* to build and requires a highly skilled crew to work it, whereas a junk can be mechanized for 50,000 *yuan* and, apart from the need of a trained mechanic, already has its trained crew. These mechanized junks can fish over a wider range and for a longer season than the sailing junk. Nevertheless, quite recently modern trawler and drifter fleets have been built up, having Shanghai, Talien and Tsingtao as their bases, which ports also have processing plants and ice-making and cold storage facilities. In 1963 Shanghai shipyards built China's first whaler, which has been operating in the Yellow and East China Seas[53].

Fishermen, operating individually or in small groups as they generally do, and dealing in a very perishable commodity, are especially vulnerable to exploitation by the middleman and need protection. As in Hong Kong, where the Government has initiated and built up a strong fishing co-operative, so in China the well-being of the fishing community has been fostered. Sea-fishing co-operatives and communes have been established all along the coast, giving a security formerly lacking and resulting in a correspondingly increased output. They have been encouraged to make their homes on land rather than on their boats and to develop subsidiary occupations in agriculture and animal husbandry. Fishing communes in the Chusan Islands, one of China's leading fishing grounds, is reported to have sold 87,000 ton of fish to the State in May, 1967[54].

The only notable fish import into China is shark's fin, the necessary ingredient for the famous soup, which appears on the menu of most Chinese feasts.

Fresh Water Fishing

Fresh water fishing in China can be divided into two categories, the fish taken from its many rivers and natural lakes and those taken from artificial ponds.

All China's great rivers, notably the Yangtze, the Sikiang and the Sungari, abound in fish, but not to the same extent as the middle Yangtze, its lakes, the Tungting and Poyang and the lakes in the plain of Hupeh. Here the main catches are grass carp, snail carp, silver carp, big head (the delicious mandarin fish), anchovy, anadromous reeves and also the famous small ice fish, which is only a few centimetres long.

Of the inland lakes, Ulyungur Nor, North Dzungaria, is famous for its fish, which, with the development of communications, are beginning to find an easier market. Koko Nor (Lake Tsinghai), China's largest lake, has a unique scaleless species of edible carp. Neither the Mongolians nor the Tibetans living along its shores have been fish eaters and only recently has fishing been developed.

All the big new reservoirs resulting from dam building are being stocked. Sinankiang reservoir, Chekiang, China's biggest man-made lake, has been stocked with 35 million fish fry of 60 different species. There are now eight breeding grounds around the reservoir, three fishing fleets, a tool and repair factory, a fishing research centre and cold storage with a capacity of 20,000 ton.

The main fishing methods are with net, using lights at night, with trap, sometimes using otters to drive the fish, and with cormorants.

Fish breeding in artificial ponds has been practised for very many years. Most Chinese villages, particularly those in the centre and south, follow a common pattern of lay-out. Those in the plains are usually built on slightly higher ground above their fields, often with a small grove of trees above them, thus ensuring the proper *feng shui*. Immediately below the village is the pond, which receives garbage and sewage. This pond is generally stocked with fish, which are given the most rudimentary care.

Distinct from this rough fish breeding, the output from which is not very great, is the pisciculture in ponds made exclusively for the purpose and carried out carefully and intensively. This manner of fish culture, although practised before 1949, has grown with considerable rapidity everywhere since the formation of co-operatives and communes, especially in the Yangtze and Sikiang basins. In some communes in Kwangtung the ponds cover several hundred hectares. The ponds must be well constructed and at least 4 ft deep to guard against loss during the summer heat. Usually they are dug deeper at one end; this assists in harvesting and also provides a haven for the fish in the event of drought. The strips of land between the ponds are often planted with mulberry in the southern provinces.

One of the difficulties facing this pond form of pisciculture has been the securing of adequate supplies of fish fry. Until 1958 it has not been possible to rear fish fry in captivity. Supplies have come exclusively from the middle Yangtze and the Pearl river; this fish fry has been exported in recent years by air to all parts of South-east Asia. Experiments have been going on since 1921, but it was not until 1958 that the Aquatic Research Unit claimed success in breeding fish fry in captivity. This has been achieved by injecting hormones into female fish. The experiments claim that 70% of the females spawn and that 80% of the eggs hatch[55]. The cost is only a fraction of that for fish fry caught in the Pearl river or the Yangtze. The results are being popularized in other provinces.

The feed for the pond fish varies from province to province. Pig, cow and poultry dung, together with some night soil and bean cake is general. In Kwangtung silkworm pupae and sugar cane leaves are used. The fertile silt from the pond bottom makes top grade manure for rice, sugar cane and mulberry growing.

Income from pond fisheries, when properly managed, is high. In the wheat-kaoliang lands of Shantung the income from each *mow* of water surface is roughly five times greater than from cropland[56]. In the double-cropping rice region of Kwangtung the proportion is not as high, but even in the New Territories of Hong Kong it is reckoned that one *mow* of pond is worth two of paddy. The output from Kwangtung's ponds was reported as 72,000 ton in 1964, a 40% rise over 1962.

Increase in the Output of Major Products

	Steel (thousand ton)	Pig iron (thousand ton)	Coal (thousand ton)	Electric power (million kWh)	Crude Petroleum (thousand ton)
1949	158	252	32,430	4,310	121
1950	606	978	42,920	4,550	200
1951	896	1,448	53,090	5,750	305
1952	1,349	1,929	66,490	7,260	436
1953	1,774	2,234	69,680	9,200	622
1954	2,225	3,114	83,660	11,000	789
1955	2,853	3,872	98,300	12,280	966
1956	4,465	4,826	110,360	16,590	1,163
1957	5,350	5,936	130,000	19,340	1,458
1958	11,080 (8,000)	13,690 (9,530)	270,000	27,530	2,264

Note. The figures for the output of steel and pig iron in 1958 include steel and iron produced by indigenous methods. The figures within parentheses do not include steel and iron produced by indigenous methods.

	Cement (thousand ton)	Timber (thousand m³)	Sulphuric acid (thousand ton)	Soda-ash (thousand ton)	Caustic soda (thousand ton)
1949	660	5,670	40	88	15
1950	1,410	6,640	49	160	23
1951	2,490	7,640	149	185	48
1952	2,860	11,200	190	192	79
1953	3,880	17,530	260	223	88
1954	4,600	22,210	344	309	115
1955	4,500	20,930	375	405	137
1956	6,390	30,840	517	476	156
1957	6,860	27,870	632	506	198
1958	9,300	35,000	740	640	270

	Chemical fertilizers (thousand ton)	Penicillin (kg)	Metal-cutting machine tools (number)	Power machinery (thousand h.p.)	Electric motors (thousand kW)
1949	27	—	1,582	10	61
1950	70	—	3,312	11	199
1951	129	—	5,853	26	225
1952	181	46	13,734	35	639
1953	226	593	20,502	144	918
1954	298	2,189	15,901	172	957
1955	332	7,829	13,708	247	607
1956	523	14,037	25,928	657	1,069
1957	631	18,266	28,000	690	1,455
1958	811	72,607	50,000	2,000	6,052

	Power generating equipment (thousand kW)	Locomotives	Motor vehicles	Merchant Vessels (thousand dwt. ton)	Tractors	Combine harvesters
1952	—	20	—	16	—	—
1953	—	10	—	35	—	—
1954	—	52	—	62	—	—
1955	—	98	—	120	—	3
1956	—	184	1,654	104	—	22
1957	198	167	7,500	54	—	124
1958	800	350	16,000	90	957	545

	Cotton yarn (thousand bales)	Cotton cloth (million m)	Paper (thousand ton)	Rubber footwear (thousand pairs)	Bicycles (thousand units)
1949	1,800	1,890	228	28,900	14
1950	2,410	2,520	380	45,670	21
1951	2,680	3,060	492	65,060	44
1952	3,620	3,830	539	61,690	80
1953	4,100	4,690	667	76,360	165
1954	4,600	5,230	842	85,840	298
1955	3,970	4,360	839	97,450	335
1956	5,250	5,770	998	103,480	640
1957	4,650	5,050	1,221	128,850	806
1958	6,100	5,700	1,630	182,360	1,174

	Cigarettes (thousand crates)*	Edible vegetable oil (thousand ton)	Sugar (thousand ton)	Salt (thousand ton)	Aquatic products (thousand ton)
1949	1,600	444	199	2,985	448
1950	1,848	607	242	2,464	912
1951	2,002	731	300	4,346	1,332
1952	2,650	983	451	4,945	1,666
1953	3,552	1,009	638	3,569	1,900
1954	3,728	1,066	693	4,886	2,293
1955	3,567	1,165	717	7,535	2,518
1956	3,907	1,076	807	4,940	2,648
1957	4,456	1,100	864	8,277	3,120
1958	4,750	1,250	900	10,400	4,060

* One crate contains 50,000 cigarettes

Ten Great Years, compiled by the State Statistical Bureau, Foreign Language Press, Peking, 1960

REFERENCES

REFERENCES

[1] FEUERWERKER, A. 'China's Nineteenth Century Industrialization', *The Economic Development of China* (Cowan, C. D. Ed.), Allen, London, 1964
[2] HUGHES, T. J. and LUARD, D. E. T. *The Economic Development of Communist China*, 1949–1958, Oxford University Press, London, 1959
[3] PERKINS, D. H. *Market Control and Planning in Communist China*, Harvard University Press, Cambridge, Mass., 1966
[4] *Communique on Fulfilment of the National Economic Plan in 1956*, Peking, 1 Aug. 1957
[5] DONNITHORNE, A. 'China's Economic Planning and Industry', *China Quart.*, 17 (1964)
[6] WALKER, K. R. 'A Chinese Discussion on Planning for Balanced Growth, A Summary of the Views of Ma Yin-ch'u and His Critics', *The Economic Development of China and Japan* (Cowan, C. D. Ed.), Allen London, 1964
[7] FANG CHUNG. 'An Economic Policy that Wins', *Peking Review*, 11 (1964)
[8] MAO TSE-TUNG. *On Contradiction*, Foreign Language Press, Peking, 1960
[9] WU, Y. L. *The Steel Industry in Communist China*, Hoover Institute, Stanford, California, 1965
[10] LU, J. S. *Geology of China*, Murby, London 1939
[11] CRESSEY, G. B. *Land of the 500 million*, McGraw-Hill, New York, 1955
[12] CROZIER, B. 'China and Her Race for Steel Production', *B.I.S.F. Quart. Steel Rev.*, July 1959
[13] TREGEAR, T. R. *A Geography of China*, University of London Press, London, 1965
[14] ROGERS, A. 'Manchurian Iron and Steel Industry', *Geogrl Rev.*, (1948) 41
[15] HSIA, R. 'Changes in Location of China's Steel Industry', *China Quart.*, 17 (1964)
[16] MACDOUGALL, COLINA. 'City of Steel', *Far Eastern Economic Review*, 11 Nov. 1965
[17] SUN CHING-CHIH (Ed.). *Economic Geography of East China Region*, U.S. Joint Publications Research Service, 1961
[18] SUN CHING-CHIH (Ed.). *Economic Geography of South-west China*, U.S. Joint Publications Research Service 1960
[19] SUN CHING-CHIH (Ed.). *Economic Geography of South China*, U.S. Joint Publications Research Service, 1959
[20] *Far Eastern Trade*, Apr. 1958
[21] *N.C.N.A.*, Nanking, 2 Aug. 1965
[22] BALAZS, E. *Chinese Civilization and Bureaucracy*, Yale University Press, New Haven, Conn., 1964
[23] ERSELCUK, M. 'Iron and Steel Industry in China', *Econ. G.*, XXXII (1956)
[24] *People's Daily*, 5 Mar. 1958
[25] WANG, K. P. 'Mineral Resources of China with Special Reference to the Non-ferrous Metals', *Geogrl Rev.*, XXXIV (1944)
[26] CHANG, K. S. 'Geographical Bases for Industrial Development in North-west China', *Econ. G.*, XXXIX (1963)
[27] *N.C.N.A.*, Peking, 4 June 1965
[28] NEEDHAM, J. 'Science and China's Influence on the World', *The Legacy of China* (Dawson, R. Ed.), Clarendon Press, Oxford, 1964
[29] AN SHIH. 'Catch up with the World's Advanced Technical Level', *Sheh-Sheh Shou-ts'e (Current Events)*, 6 March 1965
[30] *China Reconstructs*, Nov. 1965
[31] MACDOUGALL, COLINA. 'Production Reports', *Far Eastern Economic Review*, 29 Sept. 1966
[32] *N.C.N.A.*, Peking, 19 Feb. 1966
[33] KANG CHAO. 'Growth of the Construction Industry in Communist China', *China Quart.*, 22 (1965)
[34] *N.C.N.A.*, 21 Feb. 1966
[35] *N.C.N.A.*, Peking, 31 Mar. 1964
[36] *China Yearbook*, 1925
[37] FEI HSIAO-TUNG. *Peasant Life in China*, Routledge & Kegan Paul, London, 1947
[38] *N.C.N.A.*, Wuham, 27 Sept. 1965
[39] *N.C.N.A.*, Lanchow, 4 July 1965
[40] *N.C.N.A.*, Peking, 24 May 1966
[41] *N.C.N.A.*, Shanghai, 21 Nov. 1964
[42] *N.C.N.A.*, Sining, 7 Oct. 1965
[43] *Peking Review*, 25 (1965)
[44] *N.C.N.A.*, Huhehot, 8 Sept. 1965
[45] *N.C.N.A.*, Peking, 22nd July 1965
[46] *N.C.N.A.*, Nanchang, 4 Dec. 1965
[47] *Ta-kung Pao*, Peking, 15 Feb. 1965
[48] T'ien Ping. 'Tremendous Changes in the Handicraft Industry in the Past 15 years'. *Ta-kung Pao*, Peking, 9 Oct. 1964
[49] *N.C.N.A.*, Nanking, 5 June 1965
[50] *Peking Review*, 17 Mar. 1959
[51] *N.C.N.A.*, Shenyang, 22 May 1966
[52] *N.C.N.A.*, Foochao, 13 Feb. 1966
[53] *China Reconstructs*, Mar. 1965
[54] *N.C.N.A.* Hangchow, 7 June 1967
[55] TU HSUEH-HAO 'Breeding Fresh-Water Fish', *China Reconstructs*, June 1966
[56] *Peking Review*, 46 (1965)

231

9

FOREIGN TRADE

WITH the exception of the period from 1840 to 1930, during which the Western Powers imposed an 'open door' policy on China, the Chinese Government has consistently had a controlling voice in its country's foreign trade.

Earliest trade was by caravan over the landward routes of the steppe, semi-desert and desert through the Jade Gate at Yumen. Goods carried by pack animal (camel, mule, horse, sheep and ass) were, of necessity, small in bulk and high in value. Exports from China during the Han dynasty (206 B.C.–A.D. 220) were almost entirely silk, destined for Roman consumption, while imports were mainly gold, silver, glass, amber and precious stones[1]. During the T'ang dynasty (A.D. 618–907) there was considerable expansion of overseas trade with Japan, Korea and the Near East, centred at Yangchow on the lower Yangtze. Much of this trade was carried by Arab and Persian traders, who must have been quite numerous since it is recorded that several thousand Arab and Persian traders were killed in a riot in Yangchow in A.D. 760[2]. By the eleventh century the commodities handled were much more varied. Exports included textiles (mainly silk), porcelain, tea, copper and precious metals; imports included incense, perfumes, spices, pearls, ivory, coral, amber, agates and crystals[3].

Western interest in China was aroused during the thirteenth and fourteenth centuries by the reports of returning travellers from the Far East, notable among whom were Marco Polo and Ibn Battuta. This interest was further stimulated by the voyages of discovery of Diaz and Vasco da Gama, opening a new route to India and the Far East. The Portuguese were the first westerners to establish any kind of a trade footing in China. In 1557, they were allowed by the Chinese emperor to erect 'factories' on the peninsula of Macau. These 'factories' were actually small enclosures or compounds in which they built living quarters and warehouses. Close on the heels of the Portuguese came British, Dutch and French traders all eager to start business.

At much the same time, i.e. from the fall of Kazan (1552) until the death of Peter the Great (1725), the Russians carried through a vast colonial expansion in Siberia, bringing Russia into trading communication with China on its northern borders. By the Treaties of Nerchinsk (1689) and Kiakhta (1727) strict rules of trade between the two countries were laid down, permitting 200 Russian traders to enter Chinese territory at Kiakhta once eveiy three years for a period of 80 days. The main commodities exchanged were furs and later woollen broadcloth from Russia, and silk, porcelain and brick tea from China.

A similar strict governmental control was exercised over trade with westerners in the south. Trade here was conducted from Canton and Canton alone. Here, in 1702, a foreign trade monopoly was set up, supervised by a Chinese minister, called the Hoppo, through whose hands all foreign trade had to pass. This organization was superseded in 1720 by a guild of thirteen Chinese merchants, the 'co-hong' appointed by the Chinese Government. Each foreign merchant was assigned to one of the Chinese merchants through whom he had to conduct all his business. Most of the trade was in British hands, conducted by the East India Company. The main goods handled were opium, woollen broadcloth and some furs in exchange for Chinese silk, porcelain and tea, which, unlike the brick tea supplied to the Russians, was of high quality[4].

Western merchants, full of energy and initiative, found this method of trading was restricting and frustrating, but the Chinese Court and Government was really not interested in foreign trade. Some idea of its attitude to traders and its condescending attitude to all barbarians can be gained from the following extract from Emperor Ch'ien Lung's edict in dismissing the British Government's mission under Lord Macartney in 1793[5]:

'The Celestial Empire, ruling all within the four seas, simply concentrates on carrying out the affairs of Government properly, and does not value rare and precious things. Now you, O King, have presented various objects to the throne, and mindful of your loyalty in presenting offerings from afar, we have specially ordered the Yamen to receive them. In fact, the virtue and power of the Celestial Dynasty has penetrated afar to the myriad kingdoms, which have come to render homage, and so all kinds of precious things from "over mountain and sea" have been collected here, things which your chief envoy and others have seen for themselves. Nevertheless we have never valued ingenious articles, nor do we have the slightest need of your country's manufactures.'

This attitude and the restrictions led to much ill-feeling and a great deal of corruption and smuggling. In the early decades of the nineteenth century the opium trade grew to vast proportions, so much so that it was causing a drain of silver from China. When, in 1840, Chinese officials, on orders from Peking, clamped down on the opium trade and confiscated and destroyed 20,000 chests of opium in Canton, war broke out between China and Great Britain. In this war, known as 'The Opium War', China was defeated. Peace was concluded by the Treaty of Nanking in 1842 and marks the beginning of the breakdown of Chinese isolationism and a revolutionary change in foreign trade organization.

The terms of this treaty, although concluded with Great Britain, basically affected all foreign countries. It forced China to open five of her ports, Shanghai, Amoy, Canton, Foochow and Ningpo to foreign trade. 'Most favoured nation' treatment on the basis of the 'open door', was accorded to all. Under the so-called Tientsin Treaties of 1858, after the 'Arrow' war, China was forced to open the Yangtze to steam navigation of ships flying foreign flags, and 'concessions', i.e. areas of land leased to foreign nations in which their own government and laws were administered, were granted. Along the Yangtze these concessions were at Hankow, Changsha, Chungkiang, Kiukiang, Wuhu, Nanking and Chinkiang and along the east coast at Soochow, Hangchow, Newchwang, Tientsin, Tsinan and Weihsien. Michie, writing in 1864, comments on the contrasting ways by which trade with China was furthered[4] between the north and south:

'The Russians have won their way into China by quiet and peaceful means, while we have always been running our head against a stone wall and never could get over it without breaking it down. The Russian meets the Chinese as Greek meets Greek; craft is encountered with craft; politeness with politeness and patience with patience. They understand each other's character thoroughly because they are so closely alike.'

With the opening of the treaty ports foreign trade increased very rapidly in volume and in variety. The Yangtze ports fed Shanghai with the vast resources of raw material of the basin and contributed to Shanghai's rise from an insignificant town in 1840 to the sixth port of the world in the early twentieth century. The main items in China's overseas trade in 1923 were:

Foreign Trade 1923

Main imports				HK Taels* (thousands)
Cotton goods (excl. yarn)			..	131,886
Rice	..	..	.. ..	98,199
Kerosene oil	..	..	..	58,292
Raw cotton	..	..	..	53,816
Sugar	..	..	..	51,998
Metal and minerals		..	..	44,938
Cotton yarn	..	..	..	41,634
Cigarettes	..	..	..	28,273
Flour	..	..	..	27,233
Machinery ..	..	..	..	26,678

* The Haikwan or Customs Tael equalled 583·3 grains of silver 1000 fine. It was entirely a money of account and had no coin representing it. In 1923 it was the equivalent of Mex. $1·50 or about 3s. 6d.

Main exports				HK Taels (thousands)
Raw silk cocoons, etc.		..	..	154,351
Beans and products		..	..	127,338
Raw cotton	..	..	..	32,605
Skins, hides, furs	..	..	..	25,982
Silk piece goods	..	..	..	24,542
Tea ..	..	..	..	22,905
Timber	..	..	..	21,301
Coal	..	..	..	20,545
Ground nuts	..	..	..	18,617
Wood oil	..	..	..	17,477

Although opium does not appear in the above figures, its use was considerable and its cultivation widespread at this time, when the country was divided and war-lords were dominant. Poppy growing was often made compulsory by the local war-lord, it being a profitable taxable commodity. Large quantities were also imported from Japan and Indo-China. Much of Yunnan's opium production was exported to Tongking and re-entered the country at ports along the east coast.

Foreign Trade Distribution, 1923
HK Taels (millions)

	Imports into China	Exports from China	Total
Hong Kong	248	176	424
Japan	211	198	409
U.S.A.	154	127	281
Gt. Britain	120	43	163
India	55	12	67
France	7	40	47
Germany	32	12	44
Russia	10	33	43
Korea	12	30	42

While the volume of foreign trade fluctuated violently during the first half of the twentieth century, its composition remained fairly constant. Exports were almost entirely raw or semi-raw materials, and imports were largely manufactured articles. After the establishment of the Kuomintang regime in 1927 there was a marked rise in the number of Chinese commercial firms engaged in foreign trade at the expense of foreign business houses, a trend which continued until 1949.

The establishment of the People's Government in 1949 brought with it radical changes in the organization, direction and composition of China's foreign trade. Steps were taken immediately to eradicate the 'semi-colonial' and private capitalist bases of the trade. Both Chinese and foreign private traders were quickly eliminated, although foreign firms were compelled to keep their doors open and maintain their staffs for several unhappy years. All overseas commercial dealings were placed in the hands of the Minister of Foreign Trade under whom fourteen corporations now operate*. All these corporations have their head-quarters in Peking, branches at the main ports and representatives abroad. In western Europe only two trade centres have been established, one in London and the other in Berne. China maintains a big trading organization in Hong Kong. As a consequence of this method of administering trade there is little or no contact between the ultimate buyer and seller. Contracts give inadequate security to the foreign exporter. The present terms give maximum protection to the Chinese side. 'There is a striking difference between the wording of their (the Chinese) contracts of purchase and of sale. The former binds the foreign seller very tightly, whilst the latter is in effect little more than a statement of intent.'[6] Nevertheless, because of the Chinese reputation of trading integrity and because the Chinese market holds such great potentials, trading with western capitalist nations persists and increases.

The direction of China's foreign trade changed very rapidly between 1949 and 1951. Ever since Great Britain forced open the Chinese doors in 1840, Chinese trade had been orientated seaward and was mainly with Japan, U.S.A. and western Europe. After 1949 China once again turned her eyes landward through the Jade Gate. Her reasons for doing this were political and economic. She naturally turned to countries of like communist ideology from whom she could obtain long-term credit if necessary and who were willing and able to supply her with urgently-needed capital equipment and complete industrial plant. Although trade with capitalist countries continued until the outbreak of the Korean War, 1950, it virtually ceased when the United Nations embargo was placed on most goods going into China. Trade with U.S.A. stopped completely and has not since been resumed[7]. By October, 1951, 77·9% of China's exports were going to the U.S.S.R. and 70% of her imports were coming from that country. Sino-Soviet trade was assisted and enhanced by U.S.S.R. loans and credits which were forthcoming until 1957. It should be noted that these loans were quickly repaid after 1960 and that from 1956 on China has contrived a constant favourable balance of trade even with the U.S.S.R.

The development and content of China's foreign trade can best be seen in the statistics which follow but it is well to remember that foreign trade comprises only about 4% of the gross national product. The decline in trade with countries of the Communist Bloc after the political rift with U.S.S.R. in 1960 is most marked, imports and exports falling to about one-third of their value between 1960 and 1965. Cuba alone among the members of this group showed any increase in trade. During the same period, trade with countries outside the Communist Bloc showed considerable increase. Agricultural raw materials continue to form the great bulk of Chinese exports, although the proportion is now less. This is due to the increase in made-up textiles and light industrial goods, such as enamel ware, leather goods, bicycles, sewing machines and light industrial plant.

* Trade Corporations: Animal By-products; Cereals, Oils and Fats; Silk; Tea; Foodstuffs; Imports and Exports; Machinery; Metals; Minerals; Native Produce; Sundries; Transport Machinery; Technical Projects; Transport (forwarding, insurance etc.).

Table 9.1. *China's Foreign Trade, 1960–1965[a] Imports.* (*From* F.E.E.R. Yearbooks)
(million U.S. $)

	1960	1961	1962	1963	1964	1965
Communist Bloc						
U.S.S.R.	817·0	367·4	230·0	187·04	135·33	189·00
Cuba	32·0*	95·6	—	72·74	81·40	97·30
E. Germany	87·4	49·6	19·6	10·03	—	—
Poland	50·1	26·6	15·0	19·32	14·37	—
Rumania	—	—	—	13·72	15·30	—
Hungary	—	—	—	—	4·15	—
Czechoslovakia	—	—	—	9·31	—	—
Total	954·6	442·6	264·6	313·28	250·55	286·3
Non-communist Bloc						
Japan	2·7	16·6	38·5	62·42	152·75	245·04
Australia	23·5	161·5	97·0	202·06	150·82	167·76
Canada	9·0	120·9	137·0	97·20	126·35	97·50
W. Germany	5·4	30·5	31·1	15·40	25·47	78·96
U.K.	89·8	36·5	24·1	37·40	49·96	72·34
France	52·8	36·4	43·3	58·39	49·61	60·09
Italy	39·7	29·7	19·0	9·31	18·49	56·42
Hong Kong	21·0	1·4	14·9	12·24	10·48	12·56
Argentina	1·4	4·2	22·7	3·09	91·74	83·73
Pakistan	14·8	10·0	1·6	12·90	14·83	43·35
Egypt (U.A.R.)	46·9	14·6	16·5	16·38	16·69	45·13
Ceylon	25·3	17·4	28·0	21·13	25·60	36·12
Indonesia	35·4	36·4	19·5	34·00	58·00	—
Malaya	—	3·8	0·7	5·40	0·34	—
Others	319·7	224·0	55·2	125·79	155·92	205·65
Total	687·4	741·9	549·1	723·11	947·05	1,204·65

* 7 months

Table 9.2. *China's Foreign Trade, 1960–1965: Exports*
(million U.S. $)

	1960	1961	1962	1963	1964	1965
Communist Bloc						
U.S.S.R.	848·4	551·6	510·0	412·59	314·22	225·4
Cuba	—	—	—	90·80	109·30	128·90
E. Germany	90·2	36·1	28·7	23·68	—	—
Poland	45·9	20·7	22·8	24·68	23·97	—
Rumania	—	—	—	10·36	17·25	—
Hungary	—	—	—	—	14·27	—
Czechoslovakia	—	—	—	29·03	—	—
Total	984·5	608·4	560·5	593·35	479·01	354·3
Non-communist Bloc						
Japan	20·7	30·9	46·0	74·61	157·76	224·7
Australia	10·6	6·9	11·0	14·78	22·85	26·84
Canada	5·8	3·2	4·3	4·77	8·69	13·39
W. Germany	69·4	39·7	39·3	40·80	51·74	72·70
U.K.	69·7	86·4	64·8	51·88	68·96	83·22
France	22·7	15·9	16·9	21·09	30·84	43·70
Italy	24·1	12·3	14·1	19·10	23·78	38·41
Hong Kong	207·5	180·0	212·3	260·21	344·75	406·31
Argentina	—	—	—	0·06	0·17	0·30
Pakistan	4·0	3·6	4·2	5·89	16·26	18·40
Egypt (U.A.R.)	20·8	18·9	19·7	19·90	17·84	26·74
Ceylon	27·8	7·3	8·6	29·01	42·90	23·91
Indonesia	51·9	35·1	—	31·00	34·00	—
Malaya	—	56·3	65·9	94·04	103·87	—
Others	216·5	152·4	142·1	157·89	204·11	314·07
Total	751·3	649·3	649·2	825·12	1,128·52	1,292·69

It is interesting to note that it is only with the big cereal exporting countries, Australia, Canada and Argentina, that any persistent unfavourable balance of trade is incurred. Although China has been diligent in extending trade transactions with developing countries in Africa and Latin America, these have not yet reached dimensions which warrant their inclusion in the trade of the first fourteen non-communist countries.

The course of Sino-Soviet trade and its general content are shown in the following tables. The big rise and fall of trade with U.S.S.R. between 1950 and 1964 should be noted; also the excess of Chinese exports from 1956, enabling China to complete the repayment of Russian loans by 1964. Petroleum products into China have fallen as internal production has increased. The large proportion which clothes, undergarments and fabrics occupy in Soviet imports from China is striking.

Table 9.3 (a). Sino-Soviet Trade
(million roubles)

Year	Imports from U.S.S.R.	Exports to U.S.S.R.	Excess of U.S.S.R. imports	Excess of Chinese exports	U.S.S.R. credits
1950	1,553	765	788	—	2,007
1951	1,914	1,325	589	—	—
1952	2,217	1,665	552	—	167
1953	2,790	1,899	891	—	440
1954	3,037	2,313	724	—	884
1955	2,993	2,574	420	—	1,655
1956	2,932	3,057	—	125	117
1957	2,176	2,952	—	776	23
1958	2,536	3,525	—	989	—
1959	3,818	4,401	—	583	—
1960*	735·4	763·3	—	27·9	—
1961	330·6	496·3	—	116·3	—
1962	210·10	464·70	—	254·6	—
1963	168·5	371·7	—	203·2	—
1964	121·8	282·8	—	161·0	—

* New rouble

Table 9.3 (b). Sino-Soviet Trade. (From Vreshniaya Toegovla)
(million roubles)

Soviet Exports to China

Major categories	1964	1963
Machinery and equipment	51·832	37·968
Petroleum products	19·422	54·666
Rolled steels	12·984	15·036
Lumber	8·442	8·026
Cultural and household articles	2·173	10·119
Others	26·947	42·685
Total	121·8	168·5

Soviet Imports from China

	1964	1963
Machinery and equipment	5·216	6·204
Ores and concentrates	11·909	23·299
Ferrous metals and alloys (tin, antimony and mercury)	2·748	11·236
Construction materials (incl. cement)	1·130	8·757
Fabrics	41·379	87·395
Clothes and undergarments	107·311	143·514
Leather shoes	4·773	6·484
Cultural and household articles	4·711	8·365
Vegetables, fruit and berries	16·874	13·002
Meat, milk foods, animal fats, eggs	2·289	3·328
Others	84·460	60·116
Total	282·8	371·7

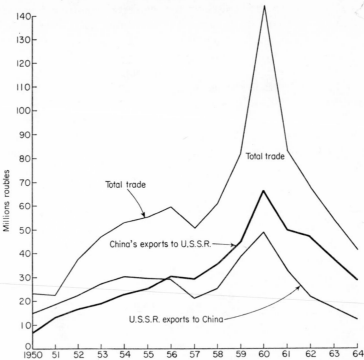

Figure 9.1. U.S.S.R. statistics, Moscow. (Statistics from 'Sino-Soviet Economic Relations', Alexander Eckstein *in* 'The Economic Development of China and Japan'. Ed. C. D. Cowan, *by courtesy of* Edgar Allen Ltd.)

Table 9.4. Sino-Japanese Trade, Jan.–Sept. 1965. (By courtesy of Current Scene)

Chinese Exports		U.S.$ million
Foodstuffs	99,358	
Rice		22,998
Soyabeans		36,457
Maize		14,964
Fibres and Textile material	6,706	
Animal and vegetable products	4,427	
Petroleum, oils, fats, waxes	7,652	
Animal and vegetable oils and fats		4,238
Chemicals	3,862	
Metals and minerals	26,161	
Iron ore		4,285
Pig iron		14,785
Non-metallic minerals and coal	9,942	
Salt		3,780
Chinese Imports		
Textiles	20,670	
Rayon products		19,562
Chemicals	79,422	
Fertilizer		53,375
Metal and metal products	33,597	
Galvanized steel sheets and plates		4,230
Other iron and steel mill products		25,612
Machinery	42,565	
Electrical machinery		5,416
Motor vehicles		5,330
Optical instruments		1,322

Japan's trade with China has risen very rapidly since 1960 and shows a more even balance between imports and exports than any other country. Now that trade between the two countries has been re-opened, Japan has resumed the importation of Chinese iron ore and pig iron. Foodstuffs, however, head the list of Japan's imports from China, rice figuring for the first time in 1965. China's main imports from Japan are chemical fertilizer, worked iron and steel and machinery.

The United Kingdom, in company with most west European countries, imports mainly raw materials and foodstuffs and sends machinery, manufactured articles and specialized iron and steel in exchange.

Table 9.5. U.K. Imports from China. (*By courtesy of* Sino-British Trade Review)
Approximate figures for 12 months, 1965; Imports from China £29·7 m
(£1,000 Sterling)

	Jan.–Oct. 1965	Jan.–Oct. 1964
Meat and preparations, dairy products	1,004	437
Fish and preparations	403	186
Rice	304	162
Tea, cocoa, butter and spices	1,001	394
Hides and skins	1,015	893
Oil seeds	1,017	1,782
Textile fibres	5,479	5,666
Raw and waste silk	574	308
Lambs' wool, camels' hair, cashmere	4,677	5,181
Metalliferous ores	1,034	238
Tungsten	930	226
Crude animal and vegetable materials	3,419	2,879
Bristles	3,005	2,450
Vegetable oils and fats	1,391	476
Tung oil, cotton seed oil	1,382	476
Chemical elements and compounds	449	380
Essential oils	361	260
Chemical materials, n.e.s.	626	273
Rosin	482	247
Fur skins, assembled	614	410
Plywood	156	197
Textile yarn, fabrics, etc.	2,678	3,811
Greys	1,432	2,649
Silk fabrics	262	261
Hatshapes, towels	104	155
Carpets	540	453
Non-ferrous metals	521	498
Tin	398	474
Clothing	189	106
Miscellaneous manufactures	670	499
Total	£36,117	£32,427

Hong Kong occupies a unique position in China's foreign trade. It constitutes China's shop window on the world. Imports into China from Hong Kong are virtually non-existent, while exports are higher than those of any country, not excluding U.S.S.R. Thus Hong Kong is the chief means through which China earns its sterling balance. China's main exports to Hong Kong in 1966 were:

Main Exports	HK$ (million)
Textiles, fabrics and made-up articles	615
Live animals, chiefly for food	419
Fruits and vegetables	223
Non-metallic mineral manufactures	136
Meat and meat preparations	127
Cereal and cereal preparations	125
Fish and fish preparations	124
Animal and vegetable crude materials, inedible	116
Dairy produce and eggs	106

Table 9.6. U.K. Exports to China

Approximate figures for 12 months, 1965: Exports to China £24·7m.

(£1,000 Sterling)

	Jan.–Oct. 1965	Jan.–Oct. 1964
Textile fibres	863	2,329
Wool tops	347	1,044
Man-made fibres	890	1,102
Chemicals	873	451
Textile yarn, fabrics, etc.	1,363	1,349
Man-made fibres	952	1,174
Iron and steel	1,494	2,468
Plates and sheets	1,456	2,330
Non-ferrous metals	4,013	236
Platinum	2,369	71
Copper, refined, unwrought	1,499	—
Machinery, non-electric	5,344	2,313
Machine tools	1,068	743
Textile machinery	224	323
Mining machinery	—	105
Pumps and centrifuges	282	240
Parts of machinery	2,739	44
Machinery, electric	1,970	1,336
Telecommunication apparatus	644	314
Measuring and scientific instruments	937	691
Transport equipment	918	1,740
Road vehicles and parts	778	319
Aircraft and parts	61	1,377
Measuring and controlling (non-electric)	1,089	607
Photo and optical supplies	215	118
Miscellaneous manufactures	87	59
Total	£32,175	£22,983

REFERENCES

[1] TREGEAR, T. R. *A Geography of China*, University of London Press, London, 1965
[2] REISCHAUER, E. O. 'Notes on T'ang Dynasty Trade Routes', *Harvard Journal of Asiatic Studies*, Vol. 4 (1940–41) 142–164
[3] BALAZS, E. *Chinese Civilization and Bureaucracy*, Yale University Press, New Haven, Conn., 1964
[4] MANCALL, M. 'The Kiakhta Trade', *The Economic Development of China and Japan*, C. D. Cowan (Ed.), Allen, London, 1964
[5] CRANMER-BYNG, J. L. (Ed.). *An Embassy in China, Being the Journal Kept by Lord Macartney, 1793–1794*, Longmans Green, London, 1962
[6] BOONE, A. 'The Foreign Trade of China', *China Quart.* No. 11 July–Sept. 1962
[7] HUGHES, T. J. and LUARD, D. E. T. *Economic Development of Communist China, 1949–1958*, Oxford University Press, London, 1959

10

TAIWAN

THE People's Government of the mainland and the Nationalist Government of the Republic of China are agreed on one thing, if on nothing else. Taiwan, they both claim, is an integral part of China. Neither physiography nor history come very strongly or readily to the support of this claim. Physiographically Taiwan is clearly one of the bases of the series of island arcs, which ring the western Pacific. Historically, it is only comparatively recently that the Chinese people, in appreciable numbers, have lived on the island*.

The existence of Taiwan was known to China in the seventh century A.D., but so little contact was maintained that, when Admiral Cheng Ho, returning from an expedition to Thailand in 1430, was driven off course and landed on the island he reported it as though he had made a discovery. His glowing accounts resulted in a few Chinese joining the Malayo-Polynesian aborigines, who inhabited the island. In 1624 the Dutch took possession of the southern part of the island, followed quickly in 1626 by the Spaniards in the north. The Dutch encouraged Chinese farmers to settle and work the land. However, Dutch and Spanish rule was shortlived, for in 1644 the Manchus conquered China and established the Ch'ing dynasty. In 1662, Cheng Ch'eng-Kung, better known to the West as Koxinga, a strong supporter of the fallen Ming dynasty, left the mainland with his army and drove the Dutch and Spaniards from Taiwan. The Cheng regime, in its turn, was conquered by the Manchu forces in 1683 and Taiwan became part of Fukien province; so it remained until 1887 when it was declared an independent province of China. From 1683 for the next 200 years there was a small but steady influx of Chinese farmers—an influx brought to an end by the annexation of Taiwan by the Japanese after the defeat of China in the 1893–94 war.

For the 50 years between 1895 and 1945 Taiwan, under Japanese Government, underwent great changes. Japan had three main objectives in its development of the island. It was to supply Japan itself with much-needed agricultural produce; it was to provide a market for Japan's fast-expanding industry, and it was to provide an overspill for its exploding population. It was eminently successful in the pursuit of its first two objectives, but in spite of attractive offers made to Japanese farmers and fishermen, few emigrants were forthcoming. On the other hand, although Chinese immigration was forbidden, the natural increase of the Chinese already settled was great and their numbers mounted rapidly. These are the Taiwanese of today.

The Japanese exercised a very strict police control over the whole country. They carried out the first population census and also a land survey and registration, which formed the bases of all their planning for modernization. Between 1920 and 1930 they carried through a big irrigation scheme, known as the Chianan Canal System, providing adequate water for the entire plain between Tainan in the south and the Choshui in the north. Another

* For a comprehensive treatment of the geography of Taiwan, the reader should turn to *Taiwan—ilha Formosa* by C. M. Hsieh, Butterworths, 1964.
China Quart., No. 15, July–Sept. 1963 is devoted to a survey of contemporary Formosa.

big irrigation scheme was developed by them on the Taoyuan plateau in the north by systematizing existing Chinese irrigation works. Improved techniques for rice-growing were introduced and its production greatly increased. Sugar and fruit cultivation, particularly pineapple-growing were also expanded.

It was never the intention of the Japanese to develop industry in Taiwan to the stage at which it would be in competition with home industry. However, in the later years of its colonial rule numbers of factories were started. These were mainly small concerns, usually employing less than 30 persons. One notable exception was the aluminium industry at Kaohsiung, based on electric power developed at the great hydro-electric plant built at Sun Moon lake in the central highlands. A number of small industries, such as tobacco, salt, opium and camphor, were made government monopolies in order to raise revenue.

The 50 years of Japanese rule in Taiwan ended abruptly in 1945 with the defeat of Japan in World War II and the island was returned to China. The Nationalist (K.M.T.) Government, which assumed control, was resented and resisted by the Taiwanese, i.e. by the descendants of the Chinese emigrants during the previous 200–300 years. The Taiwanese were bloodily suppressed in February, 1947 and since then Formosa has been ruled 'by what might properly be called a *party*-military dictatorship'[1]. After the defeat of Chiang Kai Shek and the withdrawal of the Nationalist forces to Taiwan the hold of the K.M.T. was greatly strengthened and was further reinforced in 1951 when the U.S.A. included Taiwan in its Pacific encirclement. American investment in Taiwan since the outbreak of the Korean war has been over U.S.$3,000 million[2].

Since the withdrawal of the Japanese in 1946 and the influx of fleeing mainlanders in 1949, there have been big changes in population composition. In 1945 the total population of 6,559,014 included 5,984,032 Taiwanese, 47,551 Chinese mainlanders, 167,561 aborigines and 355,596 Japanese. By 1950 the total had risen to 7,555,588 of whom 6,861,155 were Taiwanese and 168,304 aborigines. There were only 376 Japanese left and the number of mainlanders had risen to 524,940. Since then there has been a very rapid increase in numbers. In 1963 population totalled 11,883,523 of whom 10,349,254 were Taiwanese, 1,534,269 mainlanders and 210,701 aborigines. Taiwan today is a police state under the legal rule of the Republic of China, which is as dictatorial as that of the mainland of China and in which the Taiwanese have virtually no say. To whom then does Taiwan belong?

AGRICULTURE

Taiwan lies within the Lingnan Double-cropping Rice Region, the Tropic of Cancer cutting through the middle of the country. The greater part of the island is very mountainous, being over 3,000 m high in many parts and falling on the eastern side to abysmal ocean depths of over 4,000 m. With the exception of the narrow Taitung rift valley cutting through these mountains on the eastern side, it is only on the coastal plains of the more gently dipping west that agriculture is possible. Climate, on the whole, is favourable to agriculture. Temperatures are tropical or sub-tropical and rainfall is abundant. South and west regions have marked summer monsoon maxima. The north-east tip of the island has ample rainfall all the year with a slight winter maximum. As in south China, summers are long, hot and humid. The main climatic hazard to agriculture is the typhoon. Taiwan lies right in the path of the east Asian typhoons, which are most frequent in July, August and September and thus constitute a threat to the rice crop, particularly if they strike at the 'heading' period, i.e. when the rice kernel is beginning to form. As with the rest of south China, soils are subject to much leaching.

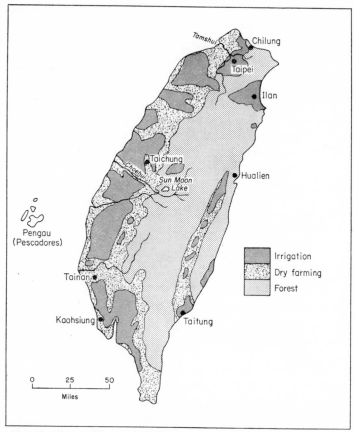

Map 68. Taiwan. (From C. M. Hsieh[3] *by courtesy of* Butterworths; London)

As mentioned above, agriculture was fostered and developed during Japanese rule. The cultivated area rose from 1·66 million acres in 1910 to 2·12 million acres in 1940. In 1959 it was 2·16 million acres, which constituted 24% of the total area. In 1949 the Government started to undertake land reform which it had signally failed to carry out during its rule on the mainland. Here in Taiwan, however, it was not inhibited by fear of offending its landlord supporters and was further aided by having ample U.S. financial assistance. Land reform was based on Sun Yat Sen's principles and his dictum of 'Land to the Tiller' and it was no less urgently needed here than on the mainland. Tenant farmers were paying 50–60% of their maincrop as rent and were responsible for all irrigation and fertilizer costs, which together swallowed 75% of their income. Private and Government-owned land was distributed to those actually working it. Landlords were allowed to retain 3 *chia*, i.e. 7·2 acres of paddy or 14 acres of dry farm land. They were compensated by receiving land values in 70% land bonds and 30% Government stock. Rents were then fixed at 37·5% of the main crop[2]. The result, as on the mainland initial land reform, has been the

243

fragmentation of the land. Only 1% of the land is in farms of over 25 acres; 85% is in less than 7·5 acres and 46% in less than 2·5 acres. The average size of farm is decreasing annually because of land inheritance customs. Apart from the facts that the landlords in Taiwan received compensation and that the redistribution of the land was carried through with comparatively little passion, this first stage in land reform was similar on mainland and island. However, there the similarity ceases since, on the mainland, it was merely a first step towards communal ownership, whereas in Taiwan private ownership was the objective.

To overcome the disadvantages of fragmentation and small individually-owned farms, big efforts were made in the 1950s to develop co-operation among the farmers. Good progress was made in the initial stages, but little has been heard of it recently. There is a severe lack of farm draught animals, there being only one head of cattle (water buffalo and yellow ox) to 5½ acres of arable land, a lower proportion than the mainland, yet mechanization has not made much headway owing to the handicaps of small farms, little capital and poor credit facilities[3].

Since 1949 new irrigation schemes have been undertaken. By far the biggest of these is known as Taiwan's T.V.A. In 1954 work was started on the island's most ambitious multi-purpose dam at Shihmen. The intention is eventually to provide irrigation water for the Taoyuan plateau, to regulate the flow of the Tamshui and thus facilitate drainage and prevent flooding on the Taipai plain and to provide hydro-electric plant of 120,000 kW. Unfortunately, the big Chianan system constructed by the Japanese has deteriorated

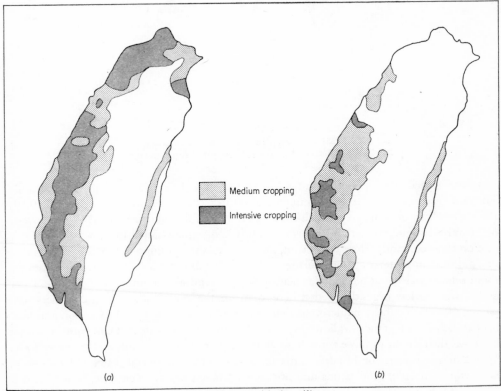

Medium cropping

Intensive cropping

(a)   (b)

Map 69. Taiwan: (a) rice; (b) sugar

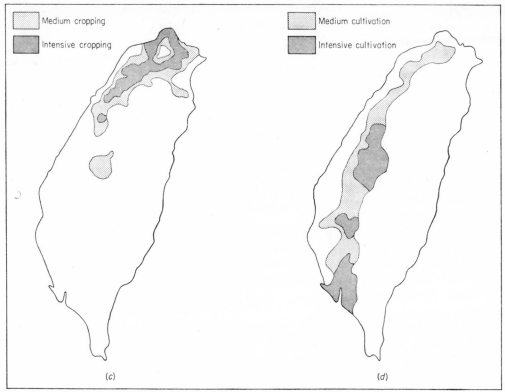

Map 69. Taiwan: (c) tea;   (d) banana

through silting and soil erosion and through failure to maintain the irrigation canals, so that what has been gained in the north has, to some extent, been lost in the south[3].

Rice is the most important crop and is grown throughout the whole length of the western coastal plain from Taipei to Kaohsiung; also intensively around Ilan and to some extent in the rift valley on the eastern side. Generally it is double-cropped with a winter catch crop as in Kwangtung. In exceptionally favourable circumstances a green summer catch crop is also taken. With improved irrigation and farming techniques output has been raised from 1·8 million ton in 1953 to 2·3 million ton in 1962. A high proportion of the crop was exported under the Japanese; today 90% is consumed at home. Sweet potato is widely grown and is a staple food of the peasant population.

Sugar ranks second in the crop list. It is the main cash crop and Taiwan's main dollar earner. Like rice, it is grown widely on the western lowlands, its main concentration being in the south-west on the Chianan irrigation area. Formerly sugar-growing occupied about half of the arable area, but recently rice has been a strong contender for more land. The long growing period of 18 months and the fluctuating market prices have led to a falling off of production from 9·2 million ton in 1953 to 6·7 million ton in 1962.

Tea-growing is confined almost entirely to the hilly regions in the northern end of the island; a small amount has also been developed in the centre in the Sun Moon lake region. The reason for this is the better annual distribution of rainfall in the north, giving a long

245

growing and picking period from April to November. The formerly popular semi-fermented oolong and paochung teas, which found a good market in U.S.A., have declined and their place has been taken by black tea. There has been a considerable extension of growing since the end of World War II. Production rose from 13,093 ton in 1953 to 21,728 ton in 1962.

The sudden demand for citronella oil after 1945 led to the rapid clearing of forests from the hill-sides to plant citronella grass. By 1951 nearly 45,000 acres were under this crop, but the demand was short-lived and most of the cultivation stopped. The formerly wooded mountain-sides have become prey to disastrous soil erosion. Many of the new, hurriedly-planted tea plantations have given insufficient attention to contouring and terracing and have added their quota to this menace of soil erosion.

Fruit has become one of the most promising agricultural products. Bananas, which in Taiwan's climate are quick growing, are easy to cultivate and easy to transport. They also find good overseas markets. Production has risen from 105,711 ton in 1953 to 148,786 ton in 1962. Pineapples, introduced from south China in the seventeenth century, are also of some importance. Peak production in 1939 was 160,000 ton. It slumped to 75,318 ton in 1953, but has since recovered and was 101,537 ton in 1962. Most of the pineapple growing is on very small plots. There are 16,000 growers on 17,300 acres[3]. The cultivation of citrus fruit (oranges, tangerines and pomelos) has more than doubled in the last decade from 32,292 ton in 1953 to 73,855 ton in 1962. Unfortunately much of Taiwan's citrus fruit is rather soft-skinned, which reduces its export value. Other fruits are papaya, mango, persimmon and peach. Most of the island's fruit- and tea-growing is in the hands of small farmers, whose knowledge and capital is limited. By failure to terrace and drain their hillsides properly they have contributed considerably to the recent serious soil erosion.

The eastern and central mountainous spine of the country is densely forested, much of which is hardwood. Under the Japanese the forests were carefully surveyed, registered and controlled. Much of the forest land is in private ownership, but today the best conifers (hemlock, cypress, pine, spruce and fir) are in national ownership. Although of great potential value, these forests have not yet been properly exploited because of transport difficulties. The Japanese built a narrow-gauge timber railroad into the heart of the Ali Shan area and tapped the vast timber resources, but this has not been developed to any extent since their withdrawal. Magnificent camphor trees provide the raw material for the manufacture of natural camphor, which was a state monopoly under the Japanese and is now in the hands of the Taiwan Provincial Government. Taiwan's fine forest cover provides essential natural protection against flood and drought on the plains below. Careless and unco-ordinated cutting of trees on the lower, more accessible western slopes is endangering irrigation works and cultivation.

Taiwan's main sea fishing grounds lie in the Taiwan Strait, especially around the Peng-hu islands. The catch is much the same as that of the southern mainland, i.e. large yellow croaker and shellfish. The western coast of Taiwan is bereft of the fine natural harbours of the rugged Fukien and Kwangtung coasts, and the industry is therefore centred mainly in ports at the northern and southern ends of the island in Chilung, Ilan and Kaohsiung and also in the Peng-hu islands themselves. Most of the fishing is in-shore or coastal, but some deep-sea trawling and long-lining is done by mechanized vessels of 50–100 ton, stationed mainly at Chilung. Although the sale of catches is now through wholesale fish markets, co-operation among the fishermen is not very advanced and they are inadequately protected against fluctuating prices. Fish culture is developed mainly along the coastal plain, particularly in the south-west. It is practised in the large irrigation reservoirs and in the farm ponds. During the two four-year plan periods (1953–1960) the estimated output of the fisheries industry increased by 10% p.a.[4]

INDUSTRY

Unlike on the mainland, recent surveys have revealed little of those mineral resources necessary for the development of heavy industry. Estimated reserves of coal, which is mainly Tertiary in formation, amount to only 737 million ton of which 236·5 million ton are considered workable in the present state of technical knowledge. The main coalfield lies in the north in a belt running south-west from Chilung (Keelung). Seams are thin, being only 1 ft to 2 ft 6 in thick and are badly folded and faulted. Most of the coal can be satisfactorily coked. The present average annual production is 2·7 million ton, which is adequate for current domestic consumption. The chief mining district is in the region south of Chilung.

The possibility of oil production in appreciable quantities is remote. Severe fracturing of the anticlinal folds in the sedimentary Tertiary rocks, running nearly the length of the western foothills, has rendered successful prospecting unlikely. 'In Taiwan nearly 260 wells have been drilled. More than 100 seepages are distributed throughout western Taiwan and the eastern range. Forty or more proved anticlinal folds with oil potentialities have been discovered on the island, but only six fields are producing oil or gas at present.'[3] Total production between 1904 and 1951 amounted to only 50 million gal.

If Taiwan's power resources are poorly served by coal and oil, the balance is redressed by its hydro-electric potential and actual. At the end of World War I, only 10,000 kW had been developed. In 1931 the Japanese began work on a big hydro-electric station. Utilizing the fine natural reservoir of the Sun Moon lake high up in the central highlands, they built a first and then a second station with a total capacity of 180,000 kW. By the early 1940s Taiwan was generating 267,000 kW of which 203,000 kW was hydro-electric. Toward the end of World War II all the power plant on the island suffered severe damage by U.S.A. bombing and it was not until 1950 that it was restored. Since that date there has been a great deal of development. The great dam at Shihmen alone has added plant of 120,000 kW capacity. By 1963 the total electrical capacity of Taiwan was 923,400 kW, three-quarters of which was generated by hydro-electric power. In all, there were 36 power stations, 10 of which were thermal (5 powered by coal and 5 by diesel oil). It is on this power that any development of industry has to rely.

Under Japanese rule, industry in Taiwan was geared strictly to the industrial needs of Japan itself. As stated previously, it was never the Japanese intention that it should in any way compete with home industry. Consequently Taiwan's production was confined largely to the provision and preliminary processing of raw and semi-raw materials. Had Taiwan possessed iron ore in exploitable quantities this would doubtless have been exported in that state to serve Japan's iron and steel industry. The dearth of iron ore has meant that there has been a meagre development of an iron and steel industry. Taiwan possesses only one blast furnace and only a few mills of moderate size.[3] Nevertheless there has been a marked increase in the output of steel from 18,000 ton in 1952 to 200,000 ton in 1960 due largely to the growth in demand from the fruit canning industry[4]. The non-ferrous minerals are in little better case. Gold and copper are the only two found in any appreciable

247

quantity. They are both located in the central and eastern highlands. There are three gold mines near Chilung, which work the gold-bearing quartz veins and which together produce 95% of the island's gold output[3]. The only significant metal industry is aluminium which was founded by the Japanese at Kaohsiung in 1935 and is based on the ample and cheap hydro-electric power. Bauxite was imported from the Chinese mainland until 1949 and now comes mainly from Malaysia. These works were the target of U.S.A. bombers in World War II and were very badly damaged, but they have been reconditioned and are again in production.

The textile industry, involving cotton, silk, wool and ramie, is new to Taiwan and has been fostered by U.S.A. aid. It is still in its early stages of development. Very little cotton is grown in Taiwan, the raw material coming from the U.S.A. At present there are, in all, 200,000 spindles and 1,200 looms, producing 85 million yards[2] of cloth; enough, it is claimed, for the island's needs.

The real mainstay of industry, however, is sugar manufacture. It is the most mechanized and the best organized, making good use of such by-products as yeast, which goes mainly to hog feeding, and bagasse or sugar waste, which is good raw material for paper making. Sugar export goes mainly to Japan. Closely associated with the sugar industry is jute production and the making of gunny bags. The growing of jute in Taiwan was initiated by the Japanese. Peak production under their rule in 1943 was approximately 6,700 ton. By 1955 it had risen to 18,300 ton and is now sufficient to meet the present demands of the sugar manufacturers.

There is no doubt that Taiwan has made very considerable economic progress under Nationalist rule. Assessing the agricultural and industrial development since 1949 Professor Frank King says: 'Over the past five years, the increase in GNP has averaged some 8% p.a., including a 4% increase in agriculture. Savings in 1964 were 24% of GNP and in the following year the U.S. aid programme, which had financed some 35% of Taiwan's investment over a 10 year period, ceased. Prospects for the future continue bright; Taiwan has become the case of a successful aid recipient.'[4]

REFERENCES

[1] GLASS, SHEPPARD. 'Some Aspects of Formosa's Economic Growth', *China Quart.*, No. 15, 1963
[2] *Joint Commission on Rural Reconstruction*, Taipai, Dec. 1956
[3] HSIEH, C. M. *Taiwan—ilha Formosa*, Butterworths, London, 1964
[4] KING, FRANK A. A. *A Concise Economic History of Modern China, 1840–1961*, Vora, Bombay (in press)

11

HONG KONG

THE island of Hong Kong came into British possession in 1841 by the Treaty of Nanking at the end of the 'Opium War'. It was then a barren, mountainous island of 29 sq. miles, virtually unoccupied except for a few fishing villages. Apart from the excellent anchorage which Victoria harbour afforded, it seemed to have little to commend it. Captain Elliot, the negotiating officer, who agreed with the Chinese to accept this island as a trading station instead of Chusan, was summarily dismissed by Palmerston, the then Foreign Secretary, who had the full support of the East India and China Associations in so doing, for it was regarded as a very poor bargain. Yet this barren island, which at first was regarded merely as a station from which trade with China could be carried on without restrictions and annoyances, has proved to be the base for the development of a most striking and unique colony[1].

In 1861 the peninsula of Kowloon was ceded to Britain thus adding nearly 4 sq. miles to British territory. In 1898, China agreed to lease for 99 years an additional 360 sq. miles of land to the north of Kowloon. This land, which includes some 230 islands, is known as the New Territories and will revert to China in 30 years time unless forcibly seized before then.

When the British took possession in January, 1841 there were probably not more than 2,500 inhabitants. By the end of the year there were 19,000. Since that date population has grown continuously and with increasing rapidity, with the exception of a dramatic fall between 1941 and 1945 during the Japanese occupation. The main reason for this rise until 1951 was the growth of Hong Kong as a commercial centre and entrepôt. Population has tended to fluctuate with boom and slump in trade, Chinese from Kwangtung moving in during times of prosperity and returning to their homes when employment fell. Hong Kong has also been a political refuge, a very present help to many mainlanders, high and low, in times of war and revolution. Not least among these was Sun Yat Sen himself. These movements in numbers, however, have been merely fluctuations within a steadily ascending trend.

The last great influx was occasioned by the defeat of the K.M.T. by the Communist forces in 1949. This has proved different in character from previous movements since refugees entering the Colony on this occasion have shown little inclination to return home when unrest has subsided and stable government on the mainland become established. Thus there has been a phenomenal increase in population during the last 15 years, particularly between 1950 and 1956.

A further reason for rapidly increasing numbers has been the great improvement in public hygiene and preventative medicine, resulting in a big fall in the death rate and a high natural increase. In its early decades the Colony bore a reputation for very bad health, the civilian death rate being as high as 10% p.a. and even higher in the army. There was a current expression in England 'Go to Hong Kong' which was synonymous with consignment to the nether regions. An active family planning organization is having some effect in

249

curbing this growth, which has imposed almost insuperable social problems of housing, education and water supplies. For example, in a community of some 3·5 millions, it is necessary to find 30,000 new places annually in primary schools alone. The population is essentially urban and is crowded in the extreme, 82% living in 13 sq. miles or $3\frac{1}{2}$% of the total area. The average urban density is 380 per acre, but in some parts, e.g. Wan Chai, it is as much as 3,000 per acre. Nowhere else in the world are housing problems as intense. Some idea of the recent population explosion can be gained from the following approximate figures:

1941	1,600,000	
1941–45	600,000	Japanese occupation
1946	1,600,000	
1950–56	increasing by 100,000 to 150,000 to an estimated total of 2,500,000	
1961	3,133,131	census
1965	3,722,600	
1966	3,785,300*	

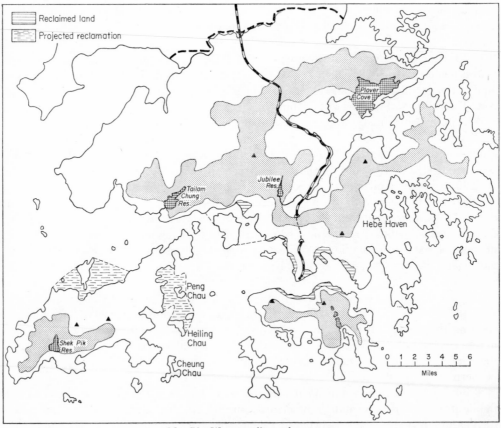

Map 70. Water supplies catchment areas

* Hong Kong: Report for the Year 1966, p. 243, Government Printer. The annual reports provide a valuable source of information on the Colony. Also 'Land Utilization in Hong Kong', Government Printer, 1967.

Almost from the moment of acquisition of the Colony in 1841 the provision of an adequate water supply has been a constant problem and one which has not yet been satisfactorily solved. Increasing population and ever-rising standards have always outstripped the latest provision. In spite of the fact that practically the whole area now forms a catchment for its two large and many small reservoirs, reliance also has to be placed on water supplies from the mainland. Under agreement with the People's Government, Hong Kong receives up to 15,000 million gallons annually from the Tung river. Even so, a poor summer monsoon rain or its retarded onset has, on more than one occasion recently, placed the cities on a ration of 4h water once every third day. This has been especially true since Hong Kong's rapid industrialization. The supplies from the two great reservoirs of Tai Lam Chung and Shek Pik have been augmented by the enclosure of Plover Cove, a work completed in 1967. It is estimated that this will almost treble the water storage of the Colony, adding 30,500 million gallons to the present 16,816 million.

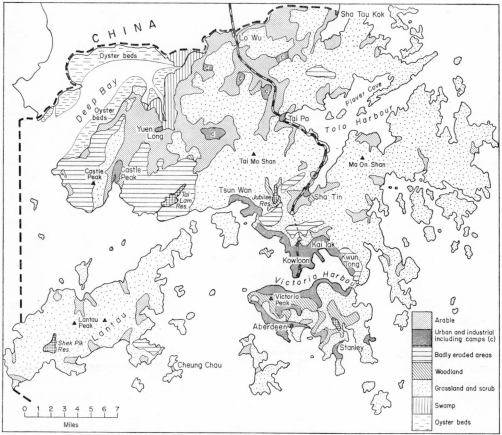

Map 71. Land use of Hong Kong and the New Territories. (Simplified from T. R. Tregear, 'Land Use Map of Hong Kong and the New Territories, 1957')

Both Hong Kong island and the New Territories are mountainous, the highest spots being Tai Mo Shan (3,144 ft) north of Kowloon and Lantau Peak (3,064 ft) on the island of that name. Of the total area 111 sq. miles are so steep and precipitous that the slopes are incapable of good plant establishment, while a further 20 sq. miles of disintegrating granite are very badly eroded. These heavily gullied regions lie mainly in the west, largely within the catchment area of the Tai Lam Chung reservoir and consequently present a constant menace through silting. To meet this danger the Forestry Department over the last 10 years has worked strenuously but not altogether successfully to afforest this inhospitable area. In company with the rest of south China the hillsides have suffered through the centuries from systematic deforestation by the peasantry[2]. The only part which carries an appreciable woodland cover is Hong Kong island itself. Here it has been possible to provide adequate protection to the young tree growth against the ravages of fuel hunters. Woodlands now cover 23 sq. miles or nearly 6% of the total.

About 155 sq. miles or 39% of the total area are covered by coarse grass or scrub, large patches of which are subjected almost annually to either intentional or accidental 'burning off' during the long dry winter, thereby adding to the dangers of erosion. This vegetation is put to very little economic use.

The only considerable area of lowland lies in the north-west, bordering Deep Bay and extending along the Chinese border region. Most of this plain is alluvial soil and it is here that three-quarters of the arable farming is concentrated. The remainder of the arable land is in scattered pockets in the innumerable small valleys. In all there are about 50 sq. miles of farm land or about one-eighth of the total land surface. The farming population numbers about 250,000. Some 23,000 acres or more than two-thirds of the farm acreage is devoted to rice, more than 20,000 acres of which is double-cropping paddy land. About 3,000 acres of the land bordering the swamps in the north-west grow a one-crop brackish paddy crop[2]. A catch crop, often of sweet potatoes, is taken from about one-third of the double-cropping paddy. Rice-growing is decreasing in favour of vegetables, the demand for which is constantly rising with the increasing urban population. Vegetable growing is assisted by a very efficient Government-sponsored collecting and marketing system. Until recently fruit-growing has received scant attention which is surprising in view of the nearby urban market. Fruit-growing is now expanding quickly. Production includes lychees, papaya, guava, Chinese lime, Japanese apricot and pineapple.

Poultry and hog raising has increased, assisted by such help as the Kadoorie Agricultural Aid Loan Fund. The value of the 250,000 to 300,000 pigs slaughtered annually is in the region of H.K.$30 million or nearly £2 million. Even so, the supply is only a fraction of the Colony's demand, the greater part coming in from the mainland daily.

At the mouths of the rivers that empty into Deep Bay in the north-west, there is an area of about 5 sq. miles of swamp and mangrove. This is gradually being reclaimed for arable purposes. At first it forms brackish paddy before being fit for double-cropping. Considerable oyster beds lie on the seaward side of this swampland around Deep Bay. This is an old-established industry of over 700 years standing. The extraordinary boundaries of the New Territories in this area should be noted. No attempt has been made by New Territories fishermen to harvest the oyster beds on the northern side of the bay since 1949.

Hong Kong has one of the largest single sea-fishing communities in the world. More than 60,000 live on boats and are engaged in the industry, while 150,000 depend on the industry in various ways. The main fishing ports are Aberdeen, Cheung Chau and Tai Po. During the last 15 years considerable effort has been made to assist the fishing community, which, in company with so many such groups, is subject to easy exploitation. About three-quarters of the fishing fleet of junks is now mechanized and the Fish Marketing Organization takes efficient care of marketing, cheap credit, education and welfare. With mechanization and larger craft, the fleets are going farther afield, thus relieving over-worked in-shore fishing grounds. Good work is also being done by the Fisheries Research Division.

During the last 10 years there has been a big expansion of pond fisheries, during which time their acreage has grown from 498 to 1,720 acres. These are mainly situated in the north-west around Yuen Long. Pond pisciculture in the New Territories is very similar to that practised in Kwangtung. It works under the disadvantage that it has not Kwangtung's ample and cheap food from the pupae of the silkworm to rely on, nor is the water supply as reliable. Nevertheless, a *mow* of pond, properly managed, gives an annual return of twice that of paddy. The main species stocked are carp of many kinds, and mullet; the fry is imported from the Pearl river estuary.

Hong Kong has comparatively little mineral wealth[3]. There are small deposits of feldspar, graphite, kaolin, quartz, wolfram and iron, but none of these is worked to any appreciable extent except the iron ore of Ma On Shan. The exploitation of this iron ore is in the hands of a Japanese company, the entire output being exported to Japan for processing. Kaolin forms the basis of a small local ceramics industry. There is no coal or oil and hydro-electric power has not been developed in conjunction with water conservancy.

The attention of the Colony, from its inception until 1950 or thereabouts, has been concentrated almost exclusively on commerce. Its prosperity throughout that time has rested on its value as an entrepôt. An assessment of its function and value was made in 1846 in these words: 'Hong Kong is a possible naval depot . . . as a market Hong Kong is valueless . . . . as a port of transhipment, it is of importance.' Its natural advantages are clear. It stands in the line of great oceanic routes at a point which also serves as an outlet for south China produce. It has a fine natural harbour of deep water, giving 17 sq. miles of safe anchorage and is sheltered by high surrounding hills. It was probably this asset of deep, sheltered water that enabled Hong Kong quickly to wrest trade from Macau at a time when ships were increasing rapidly in size and draught. Added to these advantages is the fact that it has been maintained as a free port—free of practically all import and export duties—throughout its history. Thus it became one of the greatest entrepôts of the world, handling the outgoing raw materials of China and the incoming manufactures of the West, and thus it continued, its trade and commerce increasing steadily, save only for the cyclic fluctuations of slump and boom, until its progress was shattered in 1941 by the Japanese occupation. From 1941 to 1945 Hong Kong's activities were attuned solely to Japanese requirements. Peace brought with it a trade boom, which was short-lived, for the Communist victory in 1949 and the subsequent Korean War brought about a 35% decline in Hong Kong's income[4]. The United Nations placed an embargo on the export of strategic commodities to China, which was strictly enforced. This and a U.S.A. ban on the importation of all goods of Chinese origin produced a violent shock and forced Hong Kong to look elsewhere than to entrepôt trade for a livelihood. The Hong Kong business world reacted with commendable energy and speed. Reinforced by an influx of capital and managerial skill of industrialists withdrawing from the mainland, Hong Kong has turned to industry. The shape and scope of this change can best be seen in the following statistics of industrial undertakings taken from Hong Kong Annual Reports:

Main Industrial Undertakings and Persons Employed

	1948	1956		1961		1966	
	(b)	(a)	(b)	(a)	(b)	(a)	(b)
Cotton spinning	1,755	19	14,271	35	20,759	33	20,101
Cotton weaving	6,488	146	9,838	259	27,276	237	31,277
Knitting	—	325	14,046	299	11,092	581	33,028
Wearing apparel (except footwear) ..	1,196	195	8,413	730	42,517	1,254	71,845
Metal products	9,914	476	26,062	679	28,026	1,394	34,265
Electrical apparatus	—	50	2,134	135	6,480	278	31,153
Shipbuilding and repairs ..	9,729	23	8,245	29	10,716	22	10,307
Misc. manufacturing industries ..	—	221	6,955	959	32,741	1,837	65,598
incl. plastic ware	33	113	2,987	500	13,488	1,099	33,773
incl. plastic flowers	—	—	—	263	12,566	341	17,963

(a) Undertakings   (b) Numbers employed

It will be seen that there has been a phenomenal growth in the textile industry, particularly in cotton spinning, weaving and knitting and also in wearing apparel. In all branches of textiles over 172,000 people were employed in 1966. The fact that these are engaged in 2,637 undertakings indicates that most factories are small. Only in cotton spinning are large mills to be found. The Chinese have been quick to learn the required techniques and skills, labour costs are low in comparison with the West and new machinery is being used. Consequently Hong Kong competition in the world textile market has been keenly felt.

Hong Kong had, already in 1948, a fair sized metal industry producing all kinds of small, light products such as enamel ware, vacuum flasks, hand torches and electro-plating. By 1966 it had grown to more than three times the size as also had the electrical apparatus industry, which is now very important. Amongst the large number of miscellaneous industries, the plastic wares are outstanding. Hong Kong's plastic toys, dolls, flowers and all manner of domestic articles are exported to Europe and North America. Shipbuilding and ship repairs have long been established and have served the Far East; although they have increased in efficiency, they have not grown appreciably in size.

By far the greatest single industry in Hong Kong today is the building industry, which has been responsible for radically changing the profile of Victoria and Kowloon, in fact, of all areas where urban building has occurred. 20 to 30 storeyed, ferro-concrete blocks, built in the last 15 years, dwarf the venerable business houses of earlier decades[4].

The very steep hills on the north side of Hong Kong island left early Victoria with virtually no flat land on which to build warehouses and offices. Early works of land reclamation have been steadily expanded throughout the years and have changed the shape of the water fronts of Victoria and Kowloon[1]. The pressures of population and the demands of sites for new industry have recently accelerated reclamation activities, notably at Tsun Wan where a village with a population of less than 5,000 in 1952 now houses an industrial city of 150,000 and is planned to expand to half a million in 1980. Another area of reclamation is at Kwun Tong to the east of the Kai Tak Airport runway. Here 1 sq. mile of the harbour has been reclaimed and is destined to house another industrial centre of 150,000. Further grandiose reclamation schemes for industrial development are envisaged for the north and north-east of Lantau Island[5].

Largely as a consequence of political changes in China and of U.N. and U.S.A. restrictions, the shape of Hong Kong's international trade has changed. The changes are brought out clearly in the following figures of imports and exports.

Table 11.1. *Imports into Hong Kong* (million HK$)

	1951	1956	1961	1966
China	863	1,038	1,028	2,769
U.K.	619	513	757	1,011
Malaya	394	152	140	—
Japan	392	810	864	1,839
U.S.A.	373	423	729	1,090
Thailand	156	185	256	267
Fed. Rep. of Germany	—	—	186	269
Total Imports	4,870	4,566	5,970	10,097

Table 11.2. *Exports from Hong Kong* (million HK$)

	1951	1956	1961	1966
China	1,604	136	—	—
U.K.	215	298	589	987
Malaya	741	373	267	224*
Japan	193	318	107	162
U.S.A.	162	117	679	2,036
Indonesia	245	501	173	102
Macau	228	58	15	—
Fed. Rep. of Germany	214	—	106	420
Total Exports	4,433	3,209	2,939	5,730

* Includes Singapore 152, excludes Sabah 46

It will be noted that total imports have risen far more than exports. China has more than trebled the value of goods sent out through Hong Kong and has virtually ceased all imports through that centre. U.S.A. has become the main recipient of Hong Kong's goods. Care has to be taken by Hong Kong producers that raw materials used in produce destined for U.S.A. do not emanate from China mainland. U.K. is the only country that trades with Hong Kong and has a balanced trade of imports and exports.

REFERENCES

[1] TREGEAR, T. R. and BERRY, L. *The Development of Hong Kong and Kowloon as Told in Maps*, Hong Kong University Press, Hong Kong, 1959
[2] TREGEAR, T. R. *Land Use in Hong Kong and the New Territories*, Geographical Publications and Hong Kong University Press, Hong Kong, 1958
[3] DAVIS, S. G. (Ed.). *Symposium on Land Use and Mineral Deposits in Hong Kong, Southern China and South-east Asia*, Pt. II, Hong Kong University Press, Hong Kong, 1964
[4] SZCZEPANIK, E. *The Economic Growth of Hong Kong*, Oxford University Press, London, 1958
[5] DAVIS, S. G. (Ed.). *Symposium on Land Use and Mineral Deposits in Hong Kong, Southern China and South-east Asia*, Pt. I, Hong Kong University Press, Hong Kong, 1964

APPENDIX

1,425 families; population 5,855. 976 families are agricultural, cultivating 8,500 *mow*.
Main products: Maize, Rice, Wheat, Cotton, Potatoes.
Before Liberation poor peasants held av. 4·76 *mow*.

Land Reform, 1949.

    2,260 *mow* confiscated
      260 rooms confiscated. N.B. rooms rather than houses
        6 carts
        7 draught animals

Before Liberation all fields were dry; produced 150–180 *catties/mow*.

Since Liberation, 260–400 *catties/mow* is maximum.

Increase of tools; draught animals (84–186); carts (49–150); also ploughs and harrows; 24 sprayers.

1954 started two Producer Co-ops. of semi-socialistic character, consisting of 2,530 *mow*, 313 families; 1,437 population of which 450 were men.

    Whole system voluntary; pooled land and divided income: 30% according to land pooled; tools, carts etc. taken over at fixed price and paid in three years.

Administration

    Managing Committee
    Supervision Committee   } all elected annually.
    Chairman
    Vice-Chairman

    4 Sub-committees concerned with production; Public safety; Finance; Culture and health.

    5 Production teams, each with its own production area and garden team, fishing and house building.

Cultivation

    Before Liberation only one fertilization per annum; now 2 to 3; this, plus deep ploughing have given bumper harvests.

    2 Kinds of maize, white and yellow:

        430 *catties/mow* from white
        328 *catties/mow* from yellow

No. 1 Producers Co-op. consists of 210 families; 80% have increased their income in the year; many are applying for entry; at mass meeting 10/12/55 475 additional families joined; 62 rich landlord families not eligible—may be admitted later.

No. 2 Producer Co-op. 887 families have joined; only 18 left out and 9 of these have applied. Living and cultural standards have gone up.

Education	Pre-Liberation	Now
Primary	234	918
Middle	—	830

No school fees but 4 *yuan/mow* term for heating, etc. 25 teachers.

People's Clinic and Health Centre.

Cultural House

Supply and Marketing Co-op.

Government Tax. Average of 20 *catties/mow*:
Land—3 grades fixed.

    (*a*) 150 *catties* and less exempt from tax,
    (*b*) 210 *catties/mow*,
    (*c*) 255 *catties/mow*.

Wages according to working points, plus 30% according to land contribution.
    Average earnings for one man: 300 *yuan* p.a.
    Family of two men and one woman (with four children): 700 *yuan* plus.

Spare Time School for Adults.

SOCIAL EXPENSES OF FARMERS IN THE NEW TERRITORIES, HONG KONG[1]

Funeral expenses of a farmer cultivating 4·7 acres:

Item	Amount H.K.$	Remarks
Coffin	400	
Labourers	20	
White cloth	180	
White towels	50	
Rough fibre cloth	5	
Reporting	10	Sending messengers to friends and relatives
Good-luck presents	100	
Firecrackers	40	
Funeral feasts	675	27 tables @ H.K.$25·00 each
Miscellaneous	20	
	1,500	

Wedding expenses of a tenant farmer cultivating 2·68 acres, five in family.

Item	Amount H.K.$	Remarks
Ceremony money to bride's family	600	Part used as bride's dowry
Feasts	800	20 tables @ H.K.$40·000 each

[1] D. Y. Lin, 'Report of 60 Families' 1955

Item	Amount	Remarks
Chinese band	50	
Sedan chair	10	
Firecrackers	30	
Raw meat for bride's family	80	Chicken, duck and pork
Gifts to bride's relatives	20	Generally to sisters and female relatives of bride
Incense and paper money (ancestral worship)	20	
Red paper scrolls	4	
Miscellaneous	40	
	1,654	

The family received $300 as gifts from friends and relatives, so that the actual cost is H.K.$1,354 (H.K.$16·00 = £1)

EPILOGUE

THROUGHOUT this book we have been looking at the economic bases and the economic and social achievements and failures of China, mainly from a geographical point of view. China's area is so great, the population is so huge, and the stages of development in many regions so diverse as inevitably to raise the question whether unitary government of the country is viable and whether some form of federal government or decentralization and devolution of power is not essential.

China Proper during the last 2,000 years has been knit by clear unifying factors of which common race is the most outstanding. Even today only some 35 to 40 millions out of its 700 million people belong to minorities not of Chinese origin. The remaining 94 per cent are either Han (Northern Chinese) or T'ang (Southern Chinese), who, although their many spoken dialects are vastly different, use the same written language. True, the written language has been the prerogative of the literati, a mere 10%, who throughout have formed the governing class. The third great unifying factor has been the common Confucian philosophy and code of behaviour, which regulated conduct and imposed standards of values in all walks of life. This code held strict sway for nearly 3,000 years and broke down only under the onslaught of Western intrusion in the nineteenth century. It collapsed finally in 1911 with the fall of the Ch'ing (Manchu) dynasty since when China looked first to Western democratic ideas for a new philosophy and finally, in 1949, embraced Communism, as interpreted by Mao Tse-tung, as its unifying faith.

Central to Mao's philosophy is the concept of 'contradiction', that within all things there are opposites, which struggle for mastery and which constitute the cause of all development. He thus repudiates any truth in determinism. Struggle, for him, is the very essence of life; its absence is synonymous with death[1]. Antagonism is essential. Writing in the midst of the Sino-Japanese war, 1936–45, when confronted by a military foe, he says: 'It is a good thing, not a bad thing, to be opposed by an enemy'. Also 'There is infinite joy in struggling against Heaven; there is infinite joy in struggling against Earth and there is infinite joy in struggling against man. Happiness is struggle.' Unhappily this concept of struggle against an enemy has carried with it a compulsion to and a cultivation of bitter and uncompromising hatred of the 'enemy' within and without China's borders. In so far as this negative principle of hatred has been deliberately cultivated, it carries with it the seeds of its own destruction.

In this belief in struggle lies the key to so many of the events and movements since 1949. The Great Leap Forward of 1958–59 was an outstanding example of the rousing and stirring of the nation to prodigious efforts to overcome production difficulties but, more deeply, the first real attempt to break with the old motivation of effort based on individual material incentives and self-interest. By Western standards the casualties of the Great Leap were so great as to be regarded as a disaster, but by Chinese revolutionaries, it is reckoned, on balance, as a success since they contend that it achieved great gains in the establishment of the communes and in the growth of social consciousness and a sense of unity.

During the two years in which this book has been written, China has undergone yet another revolution, the Cultural Revolution, which bids to be more profound and far reaching in its effects than any of its predecessors.* This movement has reproduced, in its initial stages, much the same fanatical and frightening hysterical enthusiasm and over-reaction of the Great Leap and much the same disruption of production. It has also been attended by many excesses. It has remained very much of an enigma to Western interpreters, who variously have seen it as a struggle for succession to Mao Tse-tung's leadership, as 'court' intrigue, as a disruption of the C.C.P. in a struggle for supremacy between 'revisionist' and 'revolutionary' factions. There will be an element of truth in each of these interpretations but, in the author's opinion, the Cultural Revolution must be regarded basically as a new ideological leap forward in an endeavour to 'secure the revolution'. It has been initiated by Mao Tse-tung expressly for this purpose and reveals his hopes and his fears.

His aim, which he has declared on countless occasions, is nothing less than the conversion of the whole Chinese people from their old clan and family loyalties and profit seeking motivation to one in which the good of the whole shall be the driving force. The incentive to all effort is to be the satisfaction of service to the masses rather than individual material reward. In other words, the driving force shall be spiritual rather than material, although Mao would hardly use this term. His belief is that with this change of motivation comes the power to move mountains and that failure to achieve this change in men's minds will mean the failure of the revolution. This, he contends, is the *sine qua non* of all true material advancement. To this end 'The Thoughts of Mao Tse-tung' are inculcated in-season and out-of-season, before, during and after work, to old and young and particularly to the lower-middle and poor peasantry, who comprise the vast majority, the 'masses', in whom Mao has placed his faith ever since 1927[2]. It is this faith in the peasantry rather than in the industrial proletariat which constitutes the deep difference between Chinese and Russian Communism.

Mao's fears spring from the dangers he sees in opulence and ease and the fact that the rising generations have not undergone the hardships or experienced the involvement and the inspiration of the pioneers of the revolution. Hence his belief in and initiation of repeated 'leaps' or constant revolutions, which are appeals to the spirit and are intended to keep alive the element of struggle which he considers so essential. This, it would appear, is the main reason for the Red Guard movement—an endeavour to involve the entire younger generation, which is in danger of sloth and loss of revolutionary fervour. Rising standards of living and of comfort, unless accompanied by socialist indoctrination of service and the 'good of the masses', tend to feed the bourgeois appetite for self-advancement and promote the reversion to capitalism. This is the fate, Mao contends, that has overtaken Russia, which has grown rich, lost its Marxist faith, become 'revisionist' and so betrayed its leadership of Communism. This distrust of ease is further reflected in Mao's dislike of large cities and may well have been an element in the development of the communes, which, in addition to their productive and devolutionary values, have tended to stem the tide of urbanization.

The Cultural Revolution appears as foolishness to Western eyes and to the sophisticated a stumbling block. However, the author is of the opinion that it is wiser to fix attention on its aims and aspirations rather than on present extravagances, excesses and mistakes. If

* See HAN SUYIN. *China in the Year 2001*, New Thinkers Library, Watts, 1967 for a Chinese interpretation of the Cultural Revolution.

EPILOGUE

Mao Tse-tung and those who follow him succeed in creating in one quarter of mankind this basic change of heart from Benthamite self-interest to socialist 'service before reward' and can also slough off this cult of hatred, it will indeed be a revolution of early Christian and early Islamic proportions. The next decade alone will be able to give the answer.

REFERENCES

[1a] MAO TSE-TUNG. 'On Contradiction', *Selected Works of Mao Tse-tung*, Vol. I, Peking, 1952
[1b] *On the Correct Handling of Contradiction among the People*, Foreign Languages Press, Peking, 1957
[2] MAO TSE-TUNG. *Report of an Investigation into the Peasant Movement in Hunan*, 1927

SELECTED BIBLIOGRAPHY

ADLER, S. *The Chinese Economy*, Routledge & Kegan Paul, London, 1957

AFANAS'YESKIY, Y. A. *Szechwan*, Moscow, 1962

ANDERSSON, J. G. *Children of the Yellow Earth*, Routledge & Kegan Paul, London, 1934

BALAZS, E. *Chinese Civilization and Bureaucracy*, Yale University Press, New Haven, Conn., 1964

BARNETT, A. D. *China on the Eve of Communist Takeover*, Thames & Hudson, London, 1963

BLACK, SIR R. *Immigration and Social Planning in Hong Kong*, The China Society, London, 1965

BOONE, A. 'The Foreign Trade of China', *China Quart.*, No. 11 (1962)

BOORMAN, H. L. 'Mao Tse-tung: the Lacquered Image', *China Quart.*, No. 16 (1963)

BUCHANAN, K. *The Chinese People and the Chinese Earth*, Bell, London, 1966

BUCK, J. L. *Land Utilization in China*, Commercial Press, Shanghai, 1937

BUCK, J. L., DAWSON, O. L. and WU, Y. L. *Food and Agriculture in Communist China*, Hoover Institute, Praeger, London and New York, 1964

CHANDRASEKHAR, S. *China's Population*, Hong Kong University Press, Hong Kong, 1959

CHANDRASEKHAR, S. *Communist China Today*, Asia Publishing House, Bombay, 1962

CHANG, H. W. 'Grapes in the "Land of Fire" ', *China Reconstructs*, Peking, June 1963

CHANG, K. S. 'Geographical Bases for Industrial Development in North-west China', *Econ. G.*, Vol. XXXIX (1963)

DE CHARDIN, P. T. *Letters from a Traveller*, Collins, London, 1957

CHAVANNES, E. *Les Memoires Historiques de Ssu Ma Chien*, Leroux, Paris, 1898

CHEN CHENG. *Land Reform in Taiwan*, China Publishing Co., Taiwan, 1961

CH'EN, J. *Mao and the Chinese Revolution*, Oxford University Press, London, 1965

CHENG, C. Y. *Communist China's Economy, 1949–1962*, Seton Hall University Press, 1963

CHI, C. J. 'Opening a Vast Coalfield', *China Reconstructs*, Oct. 1964

CHI, H. T. and CHANG, Y. F. 'Carving out Rivers in the Hills', *China Reconstructs*, Peking, July 1965

CHI, W. S. 'Water Conservancy in Communist China', *China Quart.*, No. 23, July/Sept. 1965

CHUN WEN. 'China's Farm Machine-building Industry', *Peking Review*, No. 26, July 1963

COMBER, E. See HAN SU-YIN

COTRELL, L. *The Tiger of China*, Evans, London, 1962; Pan Books 1964

Communist China 1955–1959. Policy Documents with Analysis. Harvard University Press, Cambridge, Mass., 1962

COWAN, C. D. (Ed.). *The Economic Development of China and Japan*, Allen, London, 1964

CRANMER-BYNG, J. L. (Ed.). *An Embassy in China, being the Journal Kept by Lord Macartney, 1793–1794*, Longmans Green, London, 1962

CREEL, G. H. *The Birth of China*, Waverley, Baltimore, 1937

CRESSEY, G. B. *Land of the 500 Million*, McGraw-Hill, New York, 1955

CROOK, D. and CROOK, I. *Revolution in a Chinese Village*, Routledge & Kegan Paul, London, 1959

DAVIS, S. G. *The Geology of Hong Kong*, Government Printer, Hong Kong, 1952

DAVIS, S. G. (Ed.). *Symposium on Land Use and Mineral Deposits in Hong Kong, Southern China and South-East Asia*, Hong Kong University Press, Hong Kong, 1964

DONNITHORNE, A. 'China's Economic Planning and Industry', *China Quart.*, No. 17 (1964)

DONNITHORNE, A. 'Economic Development in China', *The World Today*, Vol. 17, No. 4 (1961)

DONNITHORNE, A. *China's Economic System*, Allen and Unwin, London, 1967

DUTT, G. 'Some Problems of China's Rural Communes', *China Quart.*, No. 16 (1963)

EBERHARD, W. *A History of China*, Routledge & Kegan Paul, London, 1952

ENDACOTT, G. B. *A History of Hong Kong*, Oxford University Press, London, 1958

ERSELCUK, M. 'Iron and Steel Industry in China', *Econ. G.*, Vol. XXXII (1956)

FANG CHUNG. 'An Economic Policy that Wins', *Peking Review*, No. 11 (1964)

FEI, H. T. *Peasant Life in China*, Routledge & Kegan Paul, London, 1947

FEI, H. T. and CHANG, C. I. *Earthbound China: A Study of Rural Economy in Yunnan*, University of Chicago Press, Chicago, 1945

FENZEL, G. 'On the Natural Conditions Affecting the Introduction of Forestry in the Province of Kwangtung', *Lingnan Sci. J.*, No. 7 (1929)

FEUERWERKER, A. *China's early Industrialization: Sheng Hsuan-huai and Mandarin Enterprise*, Harvard East Asian Studies, 1958

FITZGERALD, C. P. *The Birth of Communist China*, Penguin, Harmondsworth, London 1964

FITZGERALD, C. P. *Revolution of China*, Cresset Press, London, 1952

FITZGERALD, C. P. *Flood Tide in China*, Cresset Press, London, 1958

FITZGERALD, C. P. *The Chinese View of their Place in the World*, Oxford University Press, London, 1964

FREEBERNE, M. 'Birth Control in China', *Population Studies*, Vol. XVIII, No. 1 (1964)

FREEBERNE, M. 'Demographic and Economic Changes in the Sinkiang Uighur Autonomous Region', *Population Studies*, Vol. XX, No. 1 (1966)

GLASS, S. 'Some Aspects of Formosa's Economic Growth', *China Quart.*, No. 15 (1963)

263

SELECTED BIBLIOGRAPHY

GORBUNOVA, M. N. 'Natural Conditions and Agricultural Development of the Province of Szechwan', *The Geography of Agriculture in Communist China*, V. T. Zaychikov (Ed.) (U.S. Joint Publications Research Service)

GREENE, F. *The Wall has Two Sides*, Cape, London, 1961

GREENE, F. *A Curtain of Ignorance*, Cape, London, 1962

HAN SU-YIN. *The Crippled Tree*, Cape, London, 1965

HAN SU-YIN. *A Mortal Flower*, Cape, London, 1966

HAN SU-YIN. *China in Year 2001*, Watts, London, 1967

HEENAN, B. 'Chinese Petroleum Industry', *Far Eastern Economic Review*, Nos. 5, 13 and 16 (1965)

HERRMANN, A. *An Historical Atlas of China*, Edinburgh University Press, Edinburgh, 1966

Hong Kong: Report for the Year, Government Printer, Hong Kong

HSIA, R. 'Changes in Location of China's Steel Industry', *China Quart.*, No. 17 (1964)

HSIA, R. *Economic Planning in Communist China*, 1955

HSIEH, C. M. *Taiwan—ilha Formosa*. Butterworths, London, 1964

HU, H. Y. 'Vegetation of China with Special Reference to the Main Soil Types', *Rep. 6th Int. Congr. Soil. Sci.*, 1956

HUGHES, R. *The Chinese Commune*, Bodley Head, London, 1960

HUGHES, T. J. and LUARD, D. E. T. *The Economic Development of Communist China, 1949-1958*, Oxford University Press, London, 1959

KAO, K. C. 'Great Strides Forward in Fertilizers', *China Review*, Feb., 1965

KANG CHAO. 'Growth of the Construction Industry in Communist China', *China Quart.*, No. 22 (1965)

KANG CHAO. 'Pitfalls in the Use of China's Trade Statistics', *China Quart.*, No. 19 (1964)

KING, F. A. A. *A Concise Economic History of Modern China, 1840-1961*, Vora, Bombay (in press)

KIRBY, E. S. *Introduction to the Economic History of China*, Allen, London, 1954

KUO, P. C. *China; New Age and New Outlook*, Penguin, London, 1960

KUO, L. T. C. 'Agricultural Mechanisation in China', *China Quart.*, No. 17, Jan./Mar. 1964

LAI, D. C. Y. and DWYER, D. J. 'Kwun Tong, Hong Kong—a Study in Industrial Planning', *Town Planning Review*, Vol. XXXV, No. 4 (1965)

LAI, D. C. Y. and DWYER, D. J. 'Tsuen Wan: A New Industrial Town in Hong Kong', *Geogrl Rev.*, LIV, No. 2 (1964)

LATOURETTE, K. S. *The Chinese, Their History and Culture*, Macmillan, New York, 1956

LATTIMORE, O. 'Inner Asian Approach to the Historical Geography of China', *Geogrl J.*, 1947

LATTIMORE, O. 'Chinese Colonization in Manchuria', *Geogrl Rev.* (1932)

LATTIMORE, O. *Collected Papers*, 1928-1958, London, 1962

LEE, J. S. *Geology of China*, Murby, London, 1939

LI, C. M. *The Economic Development of Communist China*, University of California Press, 1959

LI, C. M. *The Statistical System of Communist China*, University of California Press, 1962

LIN, N. J. 'Population Problems in China', *Contemporary China*, Vol. 1, 1956-7, Hong Kong University Press, Hong Kong, 1958

LINDSAY, T. J. 'Water Conservancy in China', *Contemporary China*, Vol. 1, 1956-7, Hong Kong University Press, Hong Kong, 1958

LING SHENG. 'Rapid Development of Civil Aviation', *Shih-shih Shou-tse (Current Events)* No. 9 (1964)

LIPPIT, V. 'Development of Transportation in Communist China', *China Quart.*, No. 27 (1966)

LITTLE, A. *The Far East*, Oxford University Press, London, 1905

LIU, J. C. 'Fertilizer Application in Communist China', *China Quart.*, No. 24, Oct./Dec. 1965

MA, Y. C. General Principles of Geographical Distribution of Chinese Soils', *Rep. 6th Int. Congr. Soil Sci.*, 1956

MACDOUGALL. C. 'City of Steel', *Far Eastern Economic Review*, 11 Nov. 1965

MACDOUGALL, C. 'Industrial Upsurge', *Far Eastern Economic Review*, 30 Sept. 1965

MACDOUGALL, C. 'Production Reports', *Far Eastern Economic Review*, 29 Sept. 1966

MALLORY, W. H. *China, Land of Famine*, American Geographical Society, New York, 1926

MANCALL, M. 'The Kiakhta Trade', *The Economic Development of China and Japan*, C. D. Cowan (Ed.), Allen, London, 1964

MAO TSE-TUNG. *Selected Works*, 4 Vol. (English and Chinese) Peking, 1962

MAO TSE-TUNG. *The Question of Agricultural Co-operation*, Foreign Language Press, Peking, 1959

MAO TSE-TUNG. *On Contradiction*, Foreign Language Press, Peking, 1960

MAO TSE-TUNG. *On Practice*, Foreign Language Press, Peking, 1964

MUZAFFER ER SELCUK, 'Iron and Steel Industry in China', *Econ. G.* (1956)

MYRDAL, J. *Report from a Chinese Village*, Heinemann, London, 1965

NEEDHAM, J. *Science and Civilization in China*, Vol. I–IV, Cambridge University Press, London, 1954

NEEDHAM, J. 'Science and China's Influence on the World', *The Legacy of China*, R. Dawson (Ed.), Clarendon Press, Oxford, 1964

OVDIYENKO, I. K. and KALMYKOVA, V. G. *Geographical Survey of North-west China*, (U.S. Joint Publications Research Service), Moscow, 1957

PAO, K. P. 'The Role of Electric Power in the National Economy', *Hsin Chien-she (New Construction)*, No. 4, 20 Apr. 1965

PAYNE, R. *Portrait of a Revolutionary: Mao Tse-tung*, Abelard-Schumann, New York, 1961

PERKINS, D. H. *Market Control and Planning in Communist China*, Harvard University Press, Cambridge, Mass., 1966

PHILIPS, R. W. and KUO, L. T. C. 'Agricultural Science and its Applications', *China Quart.*, No. 6, April/June 1961

REGIS, G. 'Developments in Chinese Agriculture', *Far Eastern Trade*, Jan. 1962

ROGERS, A. 'Manchurian Iron and Steel Industry', *Geogrl. Rev.*, 1948

ROSE, J. 'Sinjao, a Chinese Commune', *Geography*, Vol. 51, No. 233, Part 4, 1966

ROSE, J. 'Hong Kong's Water Supply Problem and China's Contribution to its Solution', *Geogrl. Rev.* Vol. 56, No. 3 (1966)

SCHRAM, S. *Mao Tse-tung*, Penguin, London, 1966

SCHWARTZ, B. 'The Legend of Maoism', *China Quart.*, Nos. 1 and 2 (1960)

SHABAD, T. *China's Changing Map*, Methuen, London, 1956

SHANG, C. L. and MU, C. P. 'Fifteen Years of Agricultural Mechanisation of State Farms', *Technology of Agricultural Machinery*, No. 11, Peking, 1964

SHEN, T. H. *Agricultural Resources of China*, Cornell University Press, Ithaca, New York, 1951

SHINKICHI ETO. 'Hai-lu-feng—the first Chinese Soviet Government', *China Quart.*, No. 8 (1961)

SHU, T. H. 'The Function and Power of Production Teams in Production Administration'. *Kung-jen Jih-pao*, Peking, July 1961

SMITH, W. *Iron and Coal in China*, Liverpool University Press, Liverpool, 1926

SNOW, E. *Red Star over China*, Random House, New York, 1938

SNOW, E. *The Other Side of the River*, Gollancz, London, 1962

State Statistical Bureau, *Ten Great Years*, Foreign Language Press, Peking, 1960

SU MING. 'Forestry in New China', *Jen-min Tsung-pao*, 16 Nov. 1950

SU, T. S. 'Irrigation Renews the Land', *China Reconstructs*, Nov. 1964

SUN CHING-CHIH (Ed.). *Economic Geography of East China Region*, Peking, 1961 (U.S. Joint Publications Research Service)

SUN CHING-CHIH (Ed.). *Economic Geography of Kwangtung*, Peking, 1958 (U.S. Joint Publications Research Service)

SUN CHING-CHIH (Ed.). *Economic Geography Central China*, Peking, 1960 (U.S. Joint Publications Research Service)

SUN CHING-CHIH (Ed.). *Economic Geography of South-west China*, Peking, 1960 (U.S. Joint Publications Research Service)

SUN CHING-CHIH (Ed.). *Economic Geography of Inner Mongolia*, Peking, 1957 (U.S. Joint Publications Research Service)

SUN CHING-CHIH (Ed.). *Economic Geography of North-east China*, Peking, 1959 (U.S. Joint Publications Research Service)

SZCZEPANIK, E. *The Economic Growth of Hong Kong*, Oxford University Press, London, 1958

TANG, H. S. 'Highlights of Land Reform in Taiwan', *Joint Commission on Rural Reconstruction*, Taipei, 1957

T'ANG, Y. J. 'Animal Husbandry's Place in the National Economy', *Hsin Chien-she (New Construction)*, No. 12, Dec. 1964

TAWNEY, R. H. *Land and Labour in China*, Allen, London, 1932

TEILLARD DE CHARDIN, P. *Letters from a Traveller*, Collins, London, 1957

Ten Great Years. See State Statistical Bureau

TENG, T. H. 'Report on the Multi-purpose Plan for Permanently Controlling the Yellow River and Exploiting its Water Resources', *People's China*, 1 Sept. 1955

TREGEAR, T. R. *A Geography of China*, University of London Press, London, 1965

TREGEAR, T. R. *Land Use in Hong Kong and the New Territories*, Hong Kong University Press, Hong Kong, 1958

TREGEAR, T. R. and BERRY, L. *The Development of Hong Kong and Kowloon as Told in Maps*, Hong Kong University Press, Hong Kong, 1959

TSAI, S. L. 'The Long March', *China Reconstructs*, XIV, No. 10

TSUI, Y. W. *Problems of Soil-Preserving Vegetation in the Middle Reaches of the Hwang-ho*, Academia Sinica 1957

TU, H. H. 'Breeding Fresh Water Fish', *China Reconstructs*, June 1966

U.S. Congress Joint Economic Committee, *An Economic Profile of Mainland China*, Washington, 1967

U.S. State Department, *United States' Relations with China*, Washington, 1949

VALKENBURG, S. 'Agricultural Regions of Asia: China', *Econ. G.* (1934)

WALKER, K. R. 'Collectivisation in Retrospect', *China Quart.*, No. 26, April–June 1966

WALKER, K. R. 'A Chinese Discussion on Planning for Balanced Growth—A Summary of the Views of Ma Yin-Ch'u and his Critics', *The Economic Development of China and Japan*, C. D. Cowan (Ed.), Allen, London, 1964

WANG, C. 'China State Farms—Production Bases of Farm and Animal Products', *Peking Rev.*, 28 April 1961

WANG, K. P. 'Mineral Resources of China with Special Reference to the Nonferrous Metals', *Geogrl. Rev.*, XXXIV (1944)

WARING, H. W. A. *Steel Review*, British Iron and Steel Federation, 1961

WILSON, D. *A Quarter of Mankind*, Weidenfeld and Nicolson, London, 1966

WINT, G. *Dragon and Sickle*, Pall Mall, 1958

WITTFOGEL, K. A. and SCHWARTZ, B. 'The Legend of Maoism', *China Quart.*, Nos. 1 and 2 (1960)

WU, C. C. *et al. Economic Geography of the Western Region of the Middle Yellow River*, Peking, 1956 (U.S. Joint Publications Research Service)

WU, Y. L. 'Principal Industrial Cities in Communist China', *Contemporary China*, Vol. V, Hong Kong University Press, Hong Kong, 1961–62

WU, Y. L. *The Steel Industry in Communist China*, Hoover Inst., Stanford, California, 1965

SELECTED BIBLIOGRAPHY

Wu, Y. L. *Economic Development and Use of Energy Resources in Communist China*, Hoover Inst., 1963
Wu, Y. L. *The Economy of Communist China, an Introduction*, London, 1965
Yang Min. 'Mechanizing Rice Planting', *Peking Rev.*, 5 July 1963
Yang, M. C. *A Chinese Village—Taitou, Shantung*, Routledge & Kegan Paul, London, 1946
Yang, P. H. 'How China Conquered Inflation', *People's China*, June 1960
Yao, S. Y. 'Geographical Distribution of Floods and Droughts in Chinese History, 206 B.C.–A.D. 1911', *Far Eastern Quart.*, Aug. 1934
Zaychikov, V.T. (Ed.). *Geography of Agriculture in Communist China*, U.S. Joint Publications Research Service, Peking, 1959

PERIODICALS

The China Quarterly
Contemporary China, Hong Kong University Press
Journal of Asian Studies (formerly *Far Eastern Quarterly*)
Far East Trade
Far Eastern Economic Review
Pacific Affairs
Pacific Viewpoint
Current Scene
Translations from China Mainland Press, Selections from China Mainland Magazines and Current Background, American Consulate General, Hong Kong

PEKING PUBLICATIONS

Peking Review
China Reconstructs

INDEX

Page numbers in bold type denote most important references. Page numbers in italic type refer to maps, diagrams and sketches.